SCHOOL, SOCIETY, AND THE PROFESSIONAL EDUCATOR

A Book of Readings

SCHOOL, SOCIETY, AND THE PROFESSIONAL EDUCATOR

A Book of Readings

Frank H. Blackington III
Michigan State University

Robert S. Patterson
University of Alberta

HOLT, RINEHART and WINSTON, INC.
New York • Chicago • San Francisco • Atlanta • Dallas
Montreal • Toronto • London

Copyright © 1968 by Holt, Rinehart and Winston, Inc.

All rights reserved

Library of Congress Catalog Card Number: 68–25814

2685956

Printed in the United States of America

1 2 3 4 5 6 7 8 9

PREFACE

This is an age in which we are told that words have uses rather than "real" meanings. It is claimed that words such as profession, professional, democracy, democratic, education, and educator are merely symbols, the uses of which are varied and largely honorific. This may be so. Nevertheless, we often must choose among contending usages. These choices can be made best when distinctions are clear and implications explicit. This suggests a host of value judgments. Judgments of this sort get to the heart of the educational enterprise, for few activities are as clearly value-laden and obviously tied to the social order as is education.

Young men and women preparing to, or already involved in, teaching must either act upon their own choices or upon the choices of others. In either case, they are commonly referred to tradition—pedagogical and political. Fortunately, or unfortunately, as the case may be, many traditions are available. Thus, a call to act in behalf of tradition raises more questions than it answers.

This volume is directed to teachers as they search for fundamental questions with regard to education as a means and as an end. As such, it inevitably leads to questions about what kind of a society is worth living in and for. What does or can or should the professional educator profess in a democratic society? Do different conceptions of democracy place different constraints on the professions of professionals and on the grounds upon which these professions are made? The authors assume that a search for questions and answers at this level of analysis will be most helpful to the teacher who must somehow find his way through a universe of conflicting claims to his loyalty.

The authors are indebted to a large number of people who have made significant contributions to this volume in its present formulation. While we are willing to be held accountable, it is only just that we acknowledge the value of the comments and conversations with several thousand students who have used these materials in one form or another. Heading the list of colleagues and constituting part of an environment of continuing intellectual stimulation, is George Barnett. We hope that this book can stand as part payment of our enduring indebtedness to him. Extended conversations over the years with colleagues Carl Gross, Milosh Muntyan, Stanley Wronski, John Hanson, George Ferree, Marvin Grandstaff, Thomas Green, Nathan Kroman, Keith Anderson, Geoffrey Moore, Wilbur Brookover, Ann Olmsted, Hermione Schantz, Stanton Teal, Ivan Barrientos, Gerald Raegan, Franklin Cordell, Philip VanderVelde, William Lauderdale, Richard Biship, Francis Silvernale, George Murr, Frank Krejewski, Frank McBride, David Roat, Donald Gerdy, Leta Reed, Edward Twedt, John Meeder, James Shute, Edward Rutkowski, Hugo List, Frank Nelson, and Patricia Baker have constituted a precious opportunity to refine our ideas. Since these colleagues have no place to defend themselves here, we will charge them only with our insights and take unto ourselves our insensitivities.

In addition, Elaine Spierling, has endured deadlines and drafts with unsurpassed cheerfulness. This quality she has shared with our families, who patiently have watched the present effort take shape. All of us have been one in the hope that this volume would be a genuine aid to those seriously interested in examining the more pressing questions confronting teachers in a democratic society.

It will come as no surprise to any of the above that this volume is not dedicated in their names. It is dedicated to their activity—their search for an understanding of what a better society might be and how it might be brought about. This has been the basis of our community. We invite the reader to join it.

East Lansing, Mich.   **F. H. B.**
Edmonton, Alberta, Canada   **R. S. P.**
June 1968

CONTENTS

SCHOOL, SOCIETY, AND THE PROFESSIONAL EDUCATOR

A Book of Readings

INTRODUCTION

Programs and textbooks are legion that claim to prepare teachers for their eventual responsibilities. Unfortunately, too many people participate in these programs or utilize these textbooks without giving adequate consideration to the probable outcome of such involvement. Socrates was concerned with this kind of unthinking participation when he questioned Hippocrates, who was on his way to be taught by a sophist. He asked: "Tell me, Hippocrates . . . as you are going to Protagorus, and will be paying him a fee for teaching you, what is he to whom you are going? And what will he make you into?"[1] How many have asked themselves such questions as they entered a professional school or as they began reading a textbook such as this? The redirecting of these Socratic questions to a prospective teacher entering a college or a university would undoubtedly bring forth the following replies: "I'm going to a college of education." "It will prepare me to be a teacher." The neophyte generally gives little thought to the vari-

[1]Benjamin Jowett (trans.), *The Dialogues of Plato,* "Protagorus," vol. 1 (4th edition; Oxford: Clarendon Press, 1953), p. 135. By permission of the Clarendon Press, Oxford.

1

ations among certification programs or conceptions of teaching. While these many variations could be singled out for detailed study, the nature and purpose of this book requires a broader classification, one that encompasses many of the variations.

Teacher Training versus Teacher Education

Nearly forty years ago, shortly after joining the faculty of Teachers College of Columbia University, George S. Counts raised a question the answer to which demonstrates the possible extent of differences in teacher preparation. He asked, "What is a School of Education?"[2] In reply to his own question he formulated on paper an institution that would include such areas of concern as parenthood, religion, journalism, recreation, libraries, exhibits, and adult education. In singling these out as aspects of teacher preparation he was indirectly focusing attention on the need for the preparation of teachers to be conceived in a broad light. Rather than restrict attention to training for a trade or craft, he was eager to introduce an emphasis on examining the relationships between the traditional concerns of the school and the broader aspects of society. He believed that this change in emphasis in his proposed institution ". . . would force even the least astute observer to see the magnitude of the educational enterprise carried on by modern society and even the most narrow-minded specialist to view his own particular province in perspective."[3] The matter of teacher effectiveness was to Counts a matter that went beyond the typical concerns of content mastery. Concerns of the "craft" that facilitated learning of content were important too, but they had to be seen in a broader perspective relating to other institutions and the total society. The evolution of teacher preparation from the "old normal school days" to inclusion within the rubric of university offerings also suggests the same shift in emphasis. No longer is the concern solely or even predominantly upon the technical or pedagogical devices that serve as prescriptions for successful practice in the classroom.

This broader conception of teacher preparation, which will be called "teacher education," can be better understood by further contrasting it with "teacher training." Teacher training was and is basically of an apprentice nature. Two fundamentals in apprentice training programs are the acceptance of the goals as "given" and a narrow job specification with a limited number of candidate responses available. The goals are assumed

[2]George S. Counts, "What Is a School of Education?" *Teachers College Record,* vol. 30 (1928–29), pp. 647–655.

[3]Counts, pp. 654–655.

to be worthwhile and endure examination largely in terms of whether they are being reached. The methodology is relatively standardized or repetitive and is itself examined in terms of the task to be completed. There is a limited concern with the theoretical underpinnings of the methodology itself. The tradesman, for example, often knows that a particular strategy works; often he can not explain why this is so. Moreover, such a question would be likely to generate irritation rather than interest.

Those concerned with teacher training see the teaching task and responsibility much more narrowly than those interested in teacher education. One can sympathize with this view as it makes the teaching task, upon shallow examination, much easier. One can, for example, pretend that social policy is not an educational concern. However, the shifting and often novel situations confronting the teacher demand something more than standard responses built to manage a basically repetitive task. Moreover, many of these shifts are a result of conditions external to the school and intimately connected to social and economic policy.

Teacher education, on the other hand, would put an emphasis on the same matter that Socrates was discussing with Hippocrates and that Counts was stressing in another way. Essentially, this involves a serious questioning of the worth or adequacy of the outcomes sought. In addition, "teacher education" would emphasize a basic understanding of the theoretical aspects underlying their methodology. Not only will such understanding aid them in standard situations, but it will be invaluable in the novel situations in which one can use such understanding for creative resolution of problems in contrast to relatively blind trial and error. These situations tend to throw the technician, the tradesman, and the apprentice for a loss. Lawrence Cremin voiced his concern about such people in classrooms when he said:

> . . . Education is too significant and dynamic an enterprise to be left to mere technicians; and we might as well begin now the prodigious task of preparing men and women who understand not only the substance of what they are teaching but also the theories behind the particular strategies they employ to convey that substance.[4]

It is important to note at this point that the distinction between training and education does not for a moment suggest that teacher education precludes or neglects the essential aspects of training: it is quite the contrary. Teacher training is included and placed within the broader context of the considerations already enumerated.

[4]Lawrence A. Cremin, *The Genius of American Education* (Pittsburgh: University of Pittsburgh Press, 1965) p. 59.

<table>
<tr><td>

Comparative Education
- By examining the variety of alternatives, insight can be gained into the matter of *what can be* and also explores *what is* in particular societies.
- Implicitly asks *what ought to be.*

</td><td>

History of Education
- Provides, through examination of the past, an understanding of *what is.*
- Provides various alternatives in historical context (that is, *what could be*).
- Implicitly asks *what ought to be.*

</td></tr>
</table>

Relationship between School and Society
- *What is*
- *What can be*
- *What ought to be*

<table>
<tr><td>

Social Sciences and Education
Sociology, Anthropology,
Political Science, Economics
- Examines the current relationship between school and society— *what is.*
- Working from consideration of the present, it affords some basis for predicting *what can be.*
- Implicitly asks *what ought to be.*

</td><td>

Philosophy of Education
- Explicitly offers alternative recommendations of *what ought to be.*
- Studied historically or comparatively, it offers explanation for *what is* and gives insight into *what could be.*

</td></tr>
</table>

Figure I

In teacher education programs this broader framework is most frequently provided through the content of the social-philosophical foundations. This content usually includes history, sociology, and philosophy of education, as well as comparative education. While these subjects offer the chance to examine the question of what ought to be, they also provide a basis for more clearly understanding the present situation (see Fig. 1). Those schools and educators stressing teacher training draw heavily upon those aspects of history, sociology, and history of education that orient students to the present. They tend to neglect or bypass those aspects that would require prospective teachers to examine their commitments about what ought to be the relationship between the schools and society. In short, teacher training neglects this whole foundational area. Our contention is that unless the philosophical questions are explored and developed, the program of preparation is none other than training. In stressing exploration of the philosophical questions, we would not want to exclude the need to understand the present situation through a study of the social sciences. This brings us back to the initial question posed by Socrates. Students, like Hippocrates, must recognize that not all teacher preparation programs are alike. They are not all directed toward the same goal or toward the same conception of teaching. The prospective candidate and the educator must ask themselves what a school of education should provide, what kind of teacher one should strive to be, and, why this should be so.

In B. F. Skinner's book, *Walden II*, Frazier raised this question in yet another way. Walden II is portrayed as a utopian community based upon principles of "behavioral engineering." So effective was the mastery and use of this science that Frazier and his managers were able to produce a society devoid of the undesirable elements of life. They were able to provide for the most human society. Those who visited Walden II reacted in vastly different ways. Some were enamored with what they found. Others, like the philosopher Castle, were extremely upset. Frazier, the initiator of this community, was the one to whom the challenges against the system were directed. In retaliation and frustration he directed to Castle, his most persistent attacker, a question requiring Castle to tell him what he would do if he found himself in possession of a science of behavior. Castle, somewhat frightened and taken back by the suggestion, indicated that he would throw it into the ocean. Frazier pointed out to Castle that such action would leave to others the control of and power to change people. Rather than guarantee the use of the power for good, Castle would by default turn over to "the charlatan, the demagogue, the salesman, the ward heeler, the bully, the cheat, the educator, and the priest" the right to direct people as their knowledge of the science would let them. While we may question the total effectiveness of the science possessed by Frazier, we cannot deny that our goal as educators is to be more effective in getting people to learn. We seek a mastery of a science of behavior. The task envisioned as the teacher's responsibility is that of changing people. Courses taken in teacher preparation (such as social science, methodology, student teaching, and subject matter specialities) are included in such programs to develop the ability to change people's behavior. Given that as the goal of preparation, does it not seem imperative that we go further and prepare teachers so that they are capable of asking the questions raised by Socrates? Does not a conception of a good teacher require that part of the educational experience guarantee that questions about purpose, theory, and relationship of school and society be raised?

The program we are suggesting can be represented diagrammatically by a series of concentric circles, with the outermost one representing the fully prepared teacher. At the core is the prospective teacher moving outward in no set order through a series of experiences. Some of these, such as the so-

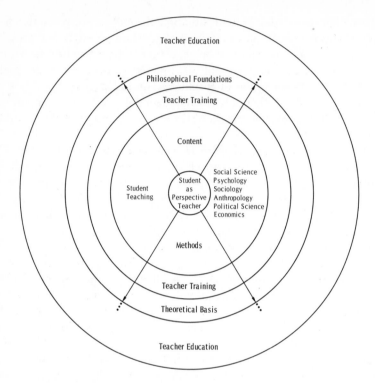

Figure 2

cial sciences, student teaching, content pertaining to teaching area, and methodology are immediate concerns of the technician. These concerns plus the theoretical framework and the philosophical considerations provide for teacher education or for the development of professionals in a field of education (see Fig. 2).

Professionalism in Education

The theme of professionalism pervades the total structure and content of this book. Such a theme is certainly in keeping with the current trend of society, which is pointing to ever more increased specialization and areas of *expertise. In using professionalism as synonymous with the outcome of our recommended teacher education program we are asking our readers to consider whether they feel professionalism is a desirable goal for educators to seek.* Actually, the examination process we encourage involves a dual investigation. First, it offers an opportunity to examine the present scene.

In raising the question as to whether or not teaching is a profession, there is a need to know what the current status of that occupational group is. This can be of great significance to the neophyte in obtaining an orientation to conditions as they are. The second thread and advantage to this type of examination is that it offers the chance to consider what could and ought to be. Each individual and group in society is in need of certain ideals or standards by which to gauge the desirability of various courses of action. It is only when such ideals are clearly understood that one can begin to appropriately make judgments on actions to be taken at the mundane, everyday level of "practicality." In this respect the examination of professionalism as an ideal becomes a matter of supreme practical importance.

Format of the Book

The theme of professionalism permeates the structure and the content of this book. Each of the parts of the book deals with a certain aspect that is essential to professionalism. Part One introduces these criteria in order to provide the reader with a model of professional behavior and a framework for discussion. Following this, it provides both an ancient and a modern example of the problem of using professionalism as an ordering principle for society. Even though Socrates lived some 2000 years ago, we can possibly gain some useful insights from his life if we consider how his behavior could be directed to conditions and problems in contemporary experience. Part Two examines the first of the criteria, the idea of purpose or service in education. It also points to an important distinction that we choose to make between "root" and "derived" questions. Many definitions provide an extensive list of criteria for determining professionalism, but in so doing they fail to note that certain characteristics are more central to the definition and that certain others are dependent upon the central characteristics. With this in mind we designate the matter of purpose as a basic or "root" question and then go on to study the complexity of the value choice through examination of both historical and current positions. Part Three is concerned with the specific preparation of teachers. Because the nature of the preparation is dependent upon the purposes that are set down for education, we classify this as a derived question. The distinctions made between teacher training and teacher education are explored in detail. There is also a limited opportunity to consider social science conceptualizations as a vital part of teacher preparation. Part Four is directed primarily toward the matter of professional autonomy. This immediately requires a consideration of the democratic framework and the question of whether professionalism is compatible with the basic tenets of democracy. Three alternative models for conceiving democracy and the place of professionalism are examined. The three models are: classical liberalism, modern liberalism, and functionalism. To facilitate comparison and application to education each of these models is examined under headings of authority, freedom and equality, and property and contract. Further comparison and application is made possible by reviewing the conditions under which each of these models would be in a position to attain responsibility and morality. The final section, Part Five, offers the conclusions of the authors concerning teaching with respect to the ideal of professionalism. It also considers the appropriateness of that ideal given the current conditions and values of our society.

Each part and chapter of the book is prefaced by a series of comments from the authors that serve to provide some direction to the selections that follow. Following the selections, a set of questions affords the student an opportunity to investigate the relevance of some of the concerns of the selection for particular and varied situations in education. Hopefully, these questions will point out value and need for a second reading of each selection. Much will be left to the student and to the instructor as far as filling in extensively on the details of many applications to education. Assistance may be derived from the suggested readings as one undertakes to extend the applications.

Conclusions

Although in introduction we must sketch outlines, part of the message of the book is already apparent. Pointedly, our concern is to clearly demonstrate:

1. The ultimate practicality of the social-philosophical concerns—this being the basis of the decisions and the method of deciding employed by educators;
2. the crucial importance of the concepts of profession and democracy for all educators;
3. the emasculating effect of certain aspects of the social and educational milieu upon professionals, as we define the term; and
4. the need for a continuing and forceful quest for those societal conditions that will facilitate the realization of ethical behavior on the part of professionals within the society.

This kind of demonstration we believe to be both possible and urgently needed. Though granting high priority to this task, we are more impressed with an even higher priority task. Convinced that we are right, we must guard against the easy answer. To be wrong, without helping our readers to recognize this fact, would be miseducative in the extreme. Thus, in addition to guiding the reader to an examination of education as social policy through an examination of professions, professionals, and their various relations, and in addition to acquainting the reader with a selection of literature relevant to the topic, we attempt to aid him in developing some analytical skills. Only with this as a safeguard can anyone attempt to join others in a true spirit of inquiry.

It is most important that the chosen selections be useful in developing a vision of what *is*, as well as a vision of the alternatives. The capacity to weigh and evaluate these alternatives implies the development of conceptual "scales" and the ability to see relationships. Hopefully the book is organized to facilitate such development.

PART ONE

PROFESSIONALISM

its dimensions and its values

In our introduction we suggested that education is a matter of social policy. In so doing, it was our intent to include both "formal" and "informal" education. Formal education or schooling has both social origins and consequences. So, too, does the learning (informal education) that is the result of simply living in a particular social order. Although the exact nature of the interrelationship between formal and informal education is obscure, the existence of an intimate relationship is a fundamental assumption underlying most discussions concerning social policy.

However important these relationships may be, education is more than learning. Some learnings are trivial and others are significant; some things learned are true and others are false. The trivial and the false are miseducative, if left unattended, because they either run directly counter to what is known or get in the way of things that are more important. The suggestion here is that education and educators must be at least as concerned with knowing as with learning. A crucial concern for educators, students, and society is the assessment of the various claims or "professions" in the name of knowledge.

Mankind has always been confronted with the problem of making decisions. There have always been those who could not or who would not master the available "knowledge." One decision that has to be made is what to do with and for those who would make decisions in ignorance or in challenge to the accepted knowledge of the day. Should men be compelled to make decisions according to the best available information? Each society has to answer this question and, in turn, give answer to what constitutes the best information and the way that information can be obtained.

We may convince ourselves that in simpler times this educational problem was rather straightforward in the ordinary affairs of men. Modern man, however, is beset with a remarkable extension of knowledge along with a similar extension of institutions that both generate and employ such knowledge. It is increasingly difficult to expect the average man to have a sufficiently sophisticated grasp of the "best information" by which he may regulate his ordinary affairs. Such an expectation seems totally unreasonable with regard to more momentous issues (such as national policy).

Gradually many aspects of our lives have been and are being turned over to others judged more capable of making the appropriate decision. Few people, for example, would attempt to defend themselves in court. The intricacies of procedure and the demand for precedent in this domain make amateur defenses inadequate and, indeed, pointless in the quest for justice. Similarly, few are able to prescribe medicine for themselves. In fact, so accepted has the superiority of medical judgment become on matters of drug prescription and treatment that legal provision exists in order to prevent the possibility of individual selection of other than patent medicine. These provisions have been extended to the point at which individual choices concerning the treatment of illnesses have been overruled. Parents and guardians may be required to follow expert advice if their own choice denies current medical knowledge. We recognize and accept such action in some areas of life. There remains, however, the question of treating other areas of life in the same way. Of particular concern, for purposes of our discussion, is the current state of teachers and of formal education. Is there the possibility of developing a body of specialized knowledge and skills in this area? If such could be found to exist would it be a realm that would warrant the obedience of individuals to certain demands even though they did not feel so inclined? Moreover, could there be legitimate demands placed by educators upon other institutions in terms of their informal educative effect?

Consider the role of the teacher in the classroom. He is continually confronted with decisions about the best way to utilize the student's time and talents. The teacher is also involved in making some decisions about what these talents are. There is need to consider the subjects to be studied, the materials to be utilized, the length of time to be spent, and the organizational pattern to be followed. In addition, the teacher must consider the adjustments that have to be made in the overall plan for the particular differences noted in the students. Any of these decisions is subject to examination and criticism by the student or the parent who may question, "Why do that?" The experiences demanded may well be frustrating or unpleasant. Who can best ascertain whether such an experience is needed and appropriate?

Without even attempting to answer such questions at this point, it is valuable to recognize that such considerations give rise to other concerns. What protection is there to ensure one that the usage of power implied in such questions will not be misdirected to the disadvantage of the unknowing? For example, when dentists recommend the addition of fluorine to the water supply what assurance does the public have that such a recommendation is not designed to provide additional business? Can the partially ignorant accurately determine when the knowledge is being misused—in education, in medicine, in affairs of state, or anywhere?

To indicate that there are cases in which people are benefited by the decisions of experts does not mean that the trend toward such decision patterns should be conceived as necessarily desirable. The extension of such decision patterns to larger and larger areas of life is often vigorously opposed. Safeguards are sought before there is any acceptance of an extension of decision-making power. *First* and foremost among these safeguards is the assurance that the knowledge in the domain of decision making is sufficiently advanced to be beyond the mastery or comprehension of the average citizen. *Second,* if the first condition is seen to exist there is the need for some security that the power associated with specialized knowledge will be used on behalf of, rather than against, the uninformed citizenry. Failure to provide the necessary assurance is frequently the excuse used for opposing the conditions under which full benefit could be gained from available knowledge.

Quite understandably, the search for safeguards affects the teacher and his relationships to society. It may be the case that teachers as a group do not presently possess the qualities essential to "expert" decision making. There would still be the question of whether this should be their goal. If this is a legitimate goal there is a need to examine the changes that must take place in order to prepare teachers and society for this realization. Perhaps one of the greatest transformations would have to take place within the ranks of the teachers themselves. For many, the present attraction of teaching does not reside in the bearing of significant responsibility for decisions that shape the lives of youth. This is especially true when the idea of education is extended to the informal realm. It is seen by many with a teacher training or apprentice orientation as an occupation devoid

of the demands and responsibilities characteristic of other so-called professions. This is not to deny that other professions such as medicine have their
share of doctors who are concerned with private health, remaining
oblivious to problems of public health and the institutional situations that
create or contribute to the lack of private and public health.

The appropriateness of applying the label "professional" to teachers is a
matter of considerable debate. Such a debate can only be validly undertaken if the participants have in mind some common understanding of
the criteria of professionalism. For this reason the selection in Chapter 1
deals directly with the question of the criteria of a profession and does so
in such a way as to make explicit its social policy aspects. As such it is one
illustration of the broader problem of standard setting. Chapter 2 contains
the selections "The Death of Socrates" and "A Design for Questioning."
They have been selected to demonstrate the range of questions that arise
concerning broader social policy when one considers the possible fulfillment of professional standards. These selections are aimed at encouraging
the reader to ask whether professionalism is a desirable goal and bringing
into focus the dilemma faced by individuals striving for professionalism
within particular social frameworks.

CHAPTER I

A Concept of Profession

As more and more groups in our society clamor for professional standing and recognition there remains a constant and continuing problem before the public. The easily stated but difficult to answer problem is "How do I identify a professional?" There are those who in reply would suggest the simplicity of the matter. Examine the characteristics of those currently called "professional." This will provide the basic material from which a common denominator of essential criteria can be selected. Such an approach presents an interesting problem (often not recognized, but very aptly demonstrated) with regard to the matter of going on "strike." Prior to the time when doctors in Saskatchewan and Italy went on strike, those examining the characteristic behavior of professionals were able to say that professionals did not strike. Following the action of these doctors the advocates of the "survey approach" to establishing criteria were confronted with one of two choices: (1) doctors were not professional, or (2) striking was now a professional act. Inasmuch as it was generally difficult to obtain acceptance to the first of these claims, the tendency was to accept the second of the alternatives. Given such a selection the problem of defining professionalism in this manner becomes apparent. A survey of the groups claiming to be professional can result in anything and everything being included under that name. More important, however, is the fact that it denies the very task it is assigned. Unless there is a standard whereby to check those claiming to be professional, there is no way to identify the charlatan.

Another factor of significance with regard to this question is related to

those individuals or groups that would seek professional recognition
through the display of some of the symbols of professionalism. The acquisition of a calendar for appointments, the wearing of a white coat, the
development of a peculiar jargon—all point to the move in this direction.
These can be misinterpreted to a point at which they are seen as central
identifying characteristics of a profession. Such a trend is dangerous, and a
definition or a set of criteria is needed to ferret out the centrol or basic
characteristics.

We have indicated that the survey approach to establish criteria is a
common one. The following selection contains the results of a number of
such surveys. In addition to the presentation of several criteria, the selection offers an important alternative. In so doing, the problem of definition
is made apparent. The alternative definition places increased emphasis on
the intentions of people. With such a definition and emphasis in mind, we
have chosen the following selection to demonstrate the difficulties of a profession in modern society. Thus, the reader has an opportunity to explore
the value of this conception of professionalism as an ordering or regulating
principle for the relations of people in society. The dilemmas presented in
this selection will be considered throughout the book. There is a need to
consider the extent to which the issues under discussion are real and relevant in our present setting.

THE PROFESSION AS AN IDEA*

Professions are more than institutions on paper. They are groups of people
with common goals who have attempted to institutionalize or systematize
their patterns of behavior. All professions attempt to establish a standard
of behavior which is clearly evident to member and to non-member alike.
Inasmuch as there are many professions, there is likely to be a wide variety
of standards. The lawyer[1] attempts to win cases and the doctor attempts
to cure them; these objectives require rather different skills and
knowledges. They also imply quite different types of training. More important than their differences, however, are certain commonalities which all

---

*William Vernon Hicks and Frank H. Blackington III, *Introduction to
Education* (Columbus, Ohio: Charles E. Merrill Books, Inc., 1965), pp.
363–376. Dr. Blackington is also co-author of *Professional Growth Through
Student Teaching,* and is currently Associate Professor of Education at
Michigan State University.

[1]It may properly be argued that if a lawyer has as his primary objective the winning of cases, he is not really a professional, that his professional objective should be
justice.

the real professions share. It is to these that we now turn for some understanding of what a profession is and what it means to be a professional.

SAMPLE DEFINITIONS

A variety of definitions has been offered for the term "profession." Horton lists the following ten criteria:

1. A profession must satisfy an indispensable social need and be based upon well-established and socially acceptable scientific principles.
2. It must demand an adequate professional and cultural training.
3. It must demand the possession of a body of specialized and systematized knowledge.
4. It must give evidence of needed skills that the general public does not possess—that is, skills that are partly native and partly acquired.
5. It must have developed a scientific technique that is the result of tested experience.
6. It must require the exercise of discretion and judgment as to the time and manner of the performance of duty.
7. It must be a type of beneficial work, the result of which is not subject to standardization in terms of unit performance or time element.
8. It must have a group consciousness designed to extend scientific knowledge in technical language.
9. It must have sufficient self-impelling power to retain its members throughout life. It must not be used for a mere steppingstone to other occupations.
10. It must recognize its obligations to society by insisting that its members live up to an established and accepted code of ethics.[2]

There seems to be merit in Horton's attempt to construct a definitive list of criteria; certainly some sort of definition of "profession" is necessary. Nevertheless, there are some serious flaws in his formulation. Although his set of criteria does seem to indicate a primary concern for the competence of the profession's membership, Item 10 does not seem to insure ethical behavior; presumably any code, as long as it is established and accepted, will do. The doctors of Dachau were behaving as professional men according to Horton's code. Even the basic knowledge or competence upon which a profession rests (in part) is undercut by the phrase "and socially acceptable scientific principles" found in Item 1.[3] This would make it appear that practice of a profession depends upon the climate of public opinion—that social approval is a prior condition to scientific knowledge as

[2] Byrne J. Horton, "Ten Criteria of a Genuine Profession," *Scientific Monthly,* vol. 58 (February 1944), p. 164.
[3] Also undercut by this phrase are Items 3, 4, and 5.

the basis of professional behavior. Thus social acceptability rather than
knowledge becomes the authority for action. Item 5 is a monument of redundancy—"scientific technique that is the result of tested experience."
Item 6 would seem to apply to anyone who wishes to keep his job and certainly indicates nothing that is unique to professions as such. Item 9 could
apply to the Mafia or Murder Incorporated as well as to law or medicine. It
must be admitted that the dual application of one descriptive sentence to
the Mafia and to the professions is not fatal to the worth of that sentence as
a *part* of a longer definition of "profession." Shared qualities by radically
different groups are possible—even probable. Nevertheless, Item 9 does
fail, as a criterion, to distinguish one kind of group from the other.

Our brief remarks directed toward this set of criteria, should indicate
some of the problems and dangers involved in attempting to define
"profession." Nevertheless, the task is a crucial one for any society because
it involves the total structure and life style of that society.[4] The risks of
muddy or partial definition clearly must be taken.

Myron Lieberman, not one to be dismayed by tasks such as this, suggests the following as definitive characteristics of a profession:

1. A unique, definite, and essential social service
2. An emphasis upon intellectual techniques in performing its service
3. A long period of specialized training
4. A broad range of autonomy for both the individual practitioner and for
the occupational group as a whole
5. An acceptance by the practitioner of broad personal responsibility for
judgments made and acts performed within the scope of professional autonomy
6. An emphasis upon the service to be rendered, rather than upon the
economic gain to the practitioners, as a basis for the organization and performance of the social service delegated to the occupational group
7. A comprehensive self-governing organization of practitioners
8. A code of ethics which has been clarified and interpreted at ambiguous
and doubtful points by concrete cases[5]

There is a distinct difference in emphasis between Horton's and Lieberman's lists. Although he in no way dismisses the criterion of knowledge,
Lieberman emphasizes the ethical imperatives incumbent upon those who
do have such knowledge. A careful reader gets, however, the feeling that
Items 1 and 6 are the only ones in Lieberman's list that approach the real

[4]Among the questions involved are: What is the role of the expert in society?
What constitutes expertness? What constitutes knowledge? What constitutes evidence?
What is the relationship among knowledge, evidence, and authority for action?

[5]Myron Lieberman, *Education as a Profession* (Englewood Cliffs, N.J.: Prentice-
Hall, Inc., 1956), pp. 2–6.

meaning of profession. The items in this list do seem to describe *some* of the typical characteristics of the strong modern professions, but a group might achieve the conditions described in Items 2, 3, 4, 5, 7, and 8 and still not succeed in establishing a profession—that is, these characteristics are shared by nonprofessional groups. They may be necessary for a profession, but they are not sufficient. We must continue the search for a more clear-cut statement of the meaning of profession which has the virtue of separating some of the characteristics of a group aspiring to professional status from the identifying characteristics of a profession. At the very best Lieberman's list is uneconomic. At the worst it is confusing, for it fails to make clear which of the items describe the established profession and which describe means of achieving that status.

A significantly different set of criteria was established by Flexner, who said, ". . . professions involve essentially intellectual operations with large individual responsibility; they derive their raw material from science and learning; this material they work up to a practical and definite end; they possess an educationally communicable technique; they tend to self organization; they are becoming increasingly altruistic in motivation."[6] Flexner drew his criteria out of what was then the case. The emphasis on knowledge to the exclusion of ethics is quite obvious. Historically, his concern is understandable. The battle to establish a standard minimum technical competence in the field of medicine had been a rugged one, and Flexner was not unmarked by it. The reader may wish to note the similarities of strength and weakness between the Flexner and Lieberman formulations.

A Fundamental Error

There is a general tone of uncertainty surrounding the attempts to define "profession." Each authority suggests, in effect, that there is no total agreement concerning the meaning of the term; he then proceeds to offer his own meaning. The authority upon which each new list is established seems to be the author's perception of what is or has been true of groups called professions.

The dangers in drawing up such a definition or list of criteria from this source are threefold. In the first place, "what now is the case" is continually changing. Consequently, such criteria continually fail (by their own standard) to distinguish the professional from the nonprofessional and the profession from the nonprofession. This, in itself, is a devastating criticism of such a method in a complex and rapidly changing society like

[6]Abraham Flexner, "Is Social Work a Profession" (Paper presented at the Forty-second Annual Meeting of the National Conference of Charities and Correction, Baltimore, Md., May 1915).

ours—one, incidentally, which desperately needs to be able to make this type of distinction. Equally serious is the fact that such a view of professionalism gives the members of that occupational group no institutionalized standard toward which to strive or by which to evaluate the success of their striving. There is no reference point for progress. If one asks, "Are we making progress?" no answer can ever be given unless "progress toward *what*" is clear. If the present state of affairs is the standard, then no outside reference point is available. Some standard is needed that will allow the membership to distinguish progress from mere change. The final inadequacy of this approach is that definition of the term "profession" is simply not an empirical task. It will not do anyone any good to go out and look for the characteristics of professions in order to compile a definition, because he will have to have prior knowledge of what a profession is *before* he can tell whether the characteristics he sees belong to it or not. To assume otherwise is to make the fundamental intellectual error which pervades much standard-setting in all fields of human endeavor;[7] that error is *the failure to recognize a philosophical task when confronted by one.*

A Further Attempt

Perhaps a more useful definition of "profession" is supplied by Tawney: "A profession may be defined most simply as a trade which is organized, incompletely, no doubt, but genuinely, for the performance of function."[8] In seeking a "simple" definition Tawney has avoided the previously noted mistakes of confusing means and ends, although his definition encompasses both; his use of the term "function" implies a legitimate social purpose, and also implicit in the definition are means to achieve the purpose. At the explicit level the emphasis in his definition is essentially ethical; that is, the explicit concern is largely for universal welfare rather than for the means by which this is achieved—namely intellectual activity resulting in the responsible action necessary for universal welfare. Implicit in the definition, however, is just such a means.

Tawney's definition has, in our opinion, such merit that we would suggest only substituting "vocation" for "trade," thus: "A profession may be defined most simply as a [vocation] which is organized, incompletely, no doubt, but genuinely, for the performance of function." This change is made for an American audience for whom the term "trade" might have a more limited and less favorable meaning than it has for the British.

[7]A philosophical position is taken here. It is open to criticism. The problem of the relationship of the rational and the empirical is complex and beyond the scope of this text.

[8]R. H. Tawney, *The Acquisitive Society* (New York: Harcourt, Brace & World, Inc., 1920), p. 92.

THE BASIC DIMENSIONS
OF A PROFESSION

The word "profession" clearly implies that members *profess* something. What do they profess? They profess just what they ought to—namely that they are different from the larger society in at least two basic ways:
1. That social function is the primary reference point for guiding their activity (work).
2. They possess, at this point in time, a specialized knowledge and means of verifying claims to knowledge that enable them to perform this function with an economy unique to that individual or group.[9]

Here, when all is said and done, are the two basic, definitive dimensions of a real profession. They stand as criteria by which any claim to professionalism must be judged. For an individual or a group to claim professional status without being able to demonstrate the achievement of both dimensions would be fraudulent. Perhaps it is here that we might find a basic reason for the fact that medical doctors are reluctant to advertise and are equally reluctant to make public claims concerning guaranteed outcomes. Note also, the open assertion by this profession that individuals are licensed to *practice* medicine. This indicates a healthy respect for the limitations of their present knowledge. All professionals, including educators, might do well to keep a close eye on the claims they make lest they be liable to the charge of fraud. To our knowledge, no education case has ever reached court on the basis of this kind of charge. Nevertheless, such a situation is conceivable.

One of the ways of determining the value of a set of criteria is to examine what cannot exist—that is, what kinds of things are eliminated—if the criteria hold. For example, it is common for critics of education to complain that Einstein or Rickover could not teach mathematics or physics in the public schools and that any number of other notables could not teach their specialties in the public schools because state certification codes contain requirements that they have not fulfilled. Such a complaint, however, misses the purpose of certification—*to insure that no incompetent is allowed to practice.* Thus, education may, at times, lose the services of eminently qualified people[10] who are making significant contributions elsewhere. This is the high price of standard setting; much more often, cer-

---

[9]It might be argued that the total society should be organized on these principles. Tawney does just this in *The Acquisitive Society.* If this were done, society would be entirely a group of professions distinguished from one another only by the division of labor.

[10]Medicine, among other professions, lost the services of the "Great Imposter." To the extent that such is true, there is a need to examine the criteria for possible and important modifications.

tification requirements prevent inadequately prepared persons from teaching. *Therefore, although the price is sometimes high, failure to set standards exacts a price which is exorbitant by comparison.* We would suggest that the two criteria mentioned above are useful in this screening task. Both are skewers with which we may puncture the claims of the quack—be he a "medicine man" pretending to be a man of medicine or an advertising agent pretending that public service is his reason for being. The quack can be exposed by applying the second criterion—". . . means of verifying claims to knowledge. . . ." Does he or does he not proceed on the basis of legitimate evidence? The "altruistic" advertising man can be exposed by applying the first criterion—social function as the primary reference point for action. When evaluating this agent's claim the student would be well advised to remember the age-old adage of *caveat emptor* (let the buyer beware). To put the point clearly, the business of the advertiser as businessman is to make money. If the public is well served by his action—wonderful; if not—it is a great pity, and he must make sure that he is not discovered.

PROFESSIONS AS A SOURCE
OF STRENGTH AND CONFLICT

The two basic professional dimensions discussed above are a source of great strength; without them we could not begin to associate the idea of integrity with the idea of profession. We are not here suggesting that all people who are *called* professionals have integrity; the lack of it, however, is the basis for the charge of unprofessional conduct.

The professions are valuable; and they are often valued by the larger society. The community or some portion thereof finds professional direction or advice "inconvenient" at times, and the professionals are rarely strong enough to act in the face of this kind of opposition.[11] Thus, the average professional frequently vacillates between conditions of mild and extreme frustration. This, we would hasten to point out, is not inherent in the nature of professionalism per se; it may, however, be an inherent condition of professionalism in modern industrialized societies. This condition may exist because the professional feels a continuing pressure to insist that certain actions be taken or not taken regardless of the popularity of the actions within the power structure of the community. Performing this duty, of course, might keep the true professional at odds with significant segments of the larger community as it is presently constituted. To the extent that our analysis is correct, then, the true professional must have a great deal of psychological strength. He must be able to find nobility in *engag-*

---

[11]Floyd Hunter, *Community Power Structure* (Chapel Hill, N. C.: University of North Carolina Press, 1953).

ing in controversy rather than retreating from it. He cannot, by definition, be "above the battle."

The factors discussed above constitute major motivating forces for the establishment of strong professional organizations to act as vehicles for the advancement of knowledge and ethical behavior and for the protection of its members from the larger society. In short, the professional must protect the larger society from itself and himself from the larger society.

PROFESSION AS ETHICAL BEHAVIOR

We have demonstrated that there are two points of reference one can use when talking about the notion of profession. One point involves a knowledge of means and the other a commitment to ethical ends (objectives). The fact that ethical goals are held as desirable and capable of achievement indicates an assumption that self-interest is not the only or even the most important motivating force for human behavior. Tawney's definition also implies that the standard of "function" (social purpose) could be the chief human motivating force.[12] Such an idea is not new; it has a long history in the Western tradition—certainly older than, even though a part of, the Christian tradition. Simply stated, it is the idea of ethical individualism—that one's identity is realized in giving rather than in taking; that one finds himself by losing himself, by, in effect, being his brother's keeper. This is one of the glorious paradoxes of human experience. Yet, the paradox is apparent only, for one loses the old self in order to find another. The self one finds as a result of losing himself is not the self of egocentric individualism; this other self is the *ethical self*. Only in this process does the egocentric person transcend his bounds and take upon himself one of the absolutely crucial characteristics of a professional.

Such behavior is not rare. We need only to look around our world to see countless conscious instances of it. A quick glance will show a Dr. Schweitzer in Africa, a mother risking or giving her life for her child, the behavior of a statesman heedless of the coming election as opposed to that of the politician ever-looking over his shoulder at the electorate—all of these behaviors allowing us some grasp of the outline of ethical individualism.[13] Yet, one further example—perhaps, if consciously done, the behavior of your father's planting a tree, in the shade of which he knows he shall never sit, is as good an illustration of ethical behavior as we are likely to see.

The individual, as well as the group, is professional only insofar as this

---

[12]Again, it could be held that other sources of motivation—such as self-interest (ego)—are those which lead to inhuman outcomes—that real brotherhood of man (social), as opposed to the biological, requires precisely this kind of motivating force.

[13]This does not mean that such a person will not make demands. Indeed, he will and he must, but the point of such demands will be to enable public (social) purposes rather than private (personal) purposes to be served.

attitude is reflected in his behavior. The professional commonly bands together with others and enacts codes of ethics which are designed to enforce standards for better service to the public and protection to other professionals. By such action, the group assumes responsibility for both collective and individual morality, and the individual assumes responsibility for group morality.

THE "LEARNED" PROFESSIONS

In the light of what has been said above, many alert readers may raise the question of whether the phrase "learned profession" is not a redundancy. This question certainly can be raised because "nonlearned profession" seems to be a contradiction in terms. We would suggest that a contradiction is not really the case. Historically, of course, the professions of law, medicine, and theology were called "learned" because of the kind of knowledge they possessed.[14] More broadly considered, it would appear that the usage of "learned" is really a recognition that the real key to professional behavior is "ethical" in nature, that is, that "learned" is a modifier indicating a very special type of ethically guided behavior.

If we hold to Tawney's definition of profession, all men can be considered professionals if they know enough to fulfill their social function and are committed to doing so. From the point of view of the "learned" professions, the "plain" professional is at best a man of "good opinion."[15] His lack of real knowledge is a severe limitation. In this connection, it must be pointed out that a member of the "learned" professions has his limits too. His knowledge gives him a greater, but not infinite, range of behavior patterns. Each of these people—the "learned" professional and the "plain" professional—gains his authority (rights) from his social function. This idea—that one's rights are derived from functions to be performed—is an extraordinarily important one for the professional. It is exceedingly useful in delimiting the legitimacy of a claim to authority on a wide variety of subjects. Certainly a person should normally lose his aura of authority as he progressively moves away from his particular function—an area in which he should have some particular competence. An awareness of this fact may be helpful in making sure that one is not influenced by the "halo effect"—that the good impression a man makes as a superintendent of schools, for example, does not spill over onto the claims he makes about, say, the proper construction of atomic-powered naval vessels, even if he has spent a number of years in the armed service.

---

[14]The term "learned person," as opposed to "craftsman," means at least that the former has theoretical knowledge of fairly comprehensive scope.

[15]In the Platonic sense, a man of good opinion is one who acts rightly because his aesthetic education has made certain good behavior virtually habitual. The same man could neither explain nor justify his behavior—having no knowledge of the theory upon which it is based.

Similarly, this man's views on the care, feeding, and general deportment of college presidents of the Ivy League, or any other variety, should be subject to the most careful scrutiny in spite of the number of institutions he has visited while recruiting teachers. All this may seem quite obvious; but apparently it is not obvious to many people, for we have seen one example after another of this kind of "thinking" in recent times.

Of equal importance to the delimiting power of the idea that one gains his authority from his social function is the fact that a clear notion of the functions to be performed does allow us to expect certain kinds of competencies of those employed to perform them. The specialization that comes with the creation of learned professions does much to identify areas of legitimate authority in human activity as well as the people who may have that authority.

AUTHORITY FOR ACTION

The problem of defining legitimate authority for action is a difficult one. This is an intellectual fact; it becomes a political fact as well in a society which tends, as we have said before, to equate democracy with the notions that one man's opinion is as good as another's or that the undifferentiated majority is always right. If all standards are to be relative to the individual, there can be no objective criteria for any effort by or measure of man. In this kind of "democracy" there is obviously no place for professionalism or the establishment of social institutions of any kind—particularly education. In the absence of objective principle, power becomes king; justice is defined to the benefit of the strong and to a calculated perpetuation of the lowly condition of those who are not strong; and society functions at the moral level of the jungle.

If we are to reject subjectivism (individual perception as standard) as the basis of professional authority, what shall we put in its place? Quite simply, we suggest that professionals, individually and collectively, have no absolute rights (authority) as such. Whatever authority the professional has is dependent upon the social functions he serves. It is derived from that function alone and is not independent of it. *Thus, authority is not found in persons but in principle.* A specific example of this kind of authority is that on which is based the claim to academic freedom as a right. The justification of a demand for academic freedom can most simply and honestly be made by referring to the social function performed by those making the demand. Let us assume that a historian makes such a demand. Presumably his function is to record and interpret events, past and present, in such a way as to contribute to the understanding of our culture. This is his contribution to the social welfare. In order to provide for (1) his ethical obligations (general welfare) he must have (2) all possible means—that is, he must be allowed absolute freedom of inquiry in order to maintain and continually develop the means (knowledge)—to fulfill this particular social function. If No. 1, the social function, is granted, it follows that No. 2, the means, must be provided. One can demand the means legitimately only if one has the obligation and capacity to fulfill a particular function. Consequently, the historian's demand for academic freedom is nothing more than a demand that society allow him the means necessary to fulfill his social functions. Neither ethical intent nor skill, taken in isolation, is sufficient for professionalism. Both are needed, and both are indispensable for the establishment and maintenance of professions.

A more concrete example of these relationships is seen in the case of the doctor who is a public health official. Let us assume that the doctor recognizes that restaurants must be inspected as part of a general campaign to maintain a decent level of public health. During his inspection, our doctor finds several of these business establishments operating kitchens and equipment that can conservatively be described as unclean. He would have, we assume, the power to close them down until they could assure sanitary conditions to the public. Let us now assume that it is the height of the tourist season and that this community is in the heart of the tourist region. Political conflict develops, and the doctor is denied the right to act.[16] At that particular moment, unless the doctor resigns, he is merely pretending to protect public health and is committing an unprofessional act; he is not a *real* doctor. Now, it may be argued that he ought to stay on to do his best under bad conditions, and any number of other reasons may be advanced that tend to legitimize a decision not to resign. The wisdom of such a decision can only be assessed when the particular local conditions are known. Ours, however, is quite a different order of question. It is logical and unqualified; and the answer to it clearly is that, in staying in the position under these conditions, the man is no longer entitled to be called a professional. Clearly, this case indicates the possibility that society may structure itself in such a way that it is impossible to institutionalize or "norm"-alize professional behavior for *any* part of its population.[17] When this condition is reached, society is operating according to the "fiddler theory"[18] and professional behavior becomes an accidental or incidental rather than a "norm"-al characteristic of that society.

THE UNASKED QUESTION

A significant but seldom-asked question is whether our society can permit the existence of institutionalized professional behavior (individually or

[16]We know that he has the *authority* as a competent medical practitioner to make a valid judgment. He simply does not have the power.

[17]It may develop value priorities and accompanying power blocks that make individual gain the primary criterion for decision-making.

[18]This notion means that money not only talks, but also should command, for example, "he, who pays the fiddler, should call the tunes."

collectively). (When we use "institutionalized" here, we simply mean systematized or "norm"-alized behavior.) It would seem that such a question is in order, for professionals presently being trained and those already trained are almost daily exhorted to be more professional. Yet such a question is seldom asked because an affirmative answer is assumed. Can we, however, safely assume a positive answer to this question in this day and age? If we can, then we may proceed in one manner—our present manner, by and large. If we cannot, then we must either stop the pretense or seek means by which reform can occur so that professionalism can exist.

We would strongly suggest that if the ethical and intellectual basis of professionalism is to be established, the larger society must operate by value systems the same as or similar to those by which the professions operate. In short, the professions must be supported by a people of "good opinion" if not "good knowledge." When, however, "worth" is measured by the individual[19] ledger book and the bank balance rather than by the social service performed, we have a situation in which the demands of the market place are supreme; in other words, decisions are made primarily with reference to immediate cost (in money). Individuals and institutions that behave in this manner are clearly in opposition to the professions in *principle*—however often their efforts may in practice coincide. Any such agreement is mutually *coincidental;* that is to say, the two groups agree for different reasons. Thus the demands of the market place must first be met by the doctor, lawyer, journalist, and so on, in order that each may pursue his own legitimate activities. Each must first make money in order to continue his practice. All too often each has to sacrifice his professional integrity in order to maintain the kind of public relations necessary for continuing in his chosen field. In short, each may have to behave unprofessionally in order to become a professional.

To the extent that the demands of the market place are supreme in our society (and this is a subject of current debate) the institutionalized professions are nonexistent within it. This is a matter of concern for the total society. Consequently, we have raised a question that our society has too long avoided. We suggest that, in itself, such avoidance raises suspicion about the innocence or intelligence of those who continue to duck the question.

WHAT IS THE ROLE OF THE EXPERT
IN A DEMOCRATIC SOCIETY?

If the foregoing analysis is essentially correct, there are several possibilities confronting the "civilized" world. On the one hand, it can regard the

[19] A corporation is a legal individual in our society.

present condition of men as good and/or as essentially beyond hope of change and seek to continue it. On the other hand, it can regard the present condition of man as bad or as susceptible of fundamental change and attempt to so reorder society that professions are securely established as a way of life. A further possibility is to propose another alternative that is at this moment unknown. More likely than not there will be attempts to improve things by attacking some of the symptoms of the fundamental problem described above. No amount of tinkering, however well intentioned, will be sufficient for significant change. This problem is too deep for such remedial efforts; it centers on the question of legitimate authority for action and right relations among men.

Because the question of whether true professionalism can exist in our society is crucial for all professions and for the society as a whole, we have felt that it should be raised in a book designed to introduce students to the profession of education. We hope that your future study in social foundations of education will lead you to some attempt to resolve the issues developed here.

FOR FURTHER THOUGHT

1. *If teaching is seen as being predominantly an art, does such a stance preclude the possibility of teaching being a profession? Why or why not?*
2. Even though the remainder of the book is concerned with exploring the place of teaching with regard to some of these criteria there is some value at this point in attempting to judge how teaching rates in relation to each criterion. For each criterion ask yourself two questions:
a. *Does teaching to any degree meet the demands of the criterion?*
b. *If your answer to the first question is affirmative, consider whether it meets the demands of the criterion to a sufficient degree to be labelled professional.*
3. *What are the major difficulties now confronting teachers in the struggle for professional recognition and acceptance? Are teachers justified in grasping for power to act as they see fit, even if society does not currently see them as worthy of such powers?*
4. *What justification, if any, would the teacher have for requesting a broad range of autonomy? Would Lieberman's suggestion in "The Future of Public Education," concerning public decisions on ends and teacher decision on means, place a false dichotomy between means and ends that would defeat the possibility of professionalism in education?*
5. *Does the current proliferation of teacher responsibilities work an additional hardship on those attempting to ascertain the degree of professionalism in teaching? Why or why not? What criteria are most seriously*

affected by such a trend? Do they in any way confuse the purpose of the school?

SUGGESTIONS FOR FURTHER READING

1. Innumerable sources exist providing definitions of professionalism. Morris L. Cogan offers a cross section of the attempts at definition in an article entitled "Toward a Definition of Profession," *Harvard Educational Review,* vol. 23 (Winter 1953). Other valuable sources in the analysis of the concept of professionalism include Ernest Greenwood, "Attributes of a Profession," *Social Work,* vol. 2, no. 3 (July 1957), and George Strauss, "Professionalism and Occupational Associations," *Industrial Relations,* vol. 2, no. 3 (May 1963).

2. Among the sources relating the concept of professionalism to education, some of the more comprehensive and worthwhile are A. J. Huggett and T. M. Stinnett, *Professional Problem of Teachers* (New York: The Macmillan Company, 1963); Myron Lieberman, *Education as a Profession* (Englewood Cliffs, N. J.: Prentice-Hall, 1956); and a yearbook publication of the National Society for the Study of Education entitled, *Education for the Professions* (Chicago: University of Chicago Press, 1962).

3. An approach contrasting that of this book is found in a book of readings edited by H. M. Vollmer and D. Mills entitled, *Professionalization* (Englewood Cliffs, N. J.: Prentice-Hall, 1966). Instead of pursuing the question of whether particular groups are "really professional" they have chosen what in their view is a more fundamental question. In the words of Everett C. Hughes the question is "What are the circumstances in which people in an occupation attempt to turn it into a profession, and themselves into professional people?" Despite this claim of being the most fundamental question, we feel it important for our readers to recognize that such a question or approach bypasses a most essential consideration. Until one explores the meaning of professionalism and until one determines its worthiness as a goal for the ordering of society, there is little value in ascertaining the means of becoming professionalized.

4. For those interested in the application of Tawney's definition of professionalism a careful reading of his book, *The Acquisitive Society* (New York: Harcourt, Brace & World, Inc., 1948), is recommended. Tawney uses his concept of professionalism as an ordering principle for society. Through such an ordering he hopes to eliminate the inequities which he saw as harmful in our present society.

5. There are those who advocate the need to examine teacher personality or characteristics to determine professional worthiness. For those

so inclined, we recommend Chapter 2 of the American Educational Research Association publication entitled, *Handbook of Research on Teaching* (Chicago: Rand-McNally, 1963). The authors of this chapter, Getzels and Jackson, deal with various instruments used for gaining information about teacher characteristics and provide findings and bibliographic materials relating to teacher attitudes, values, personality, and cognitive abilities.

CHAPTER 2

Professionalism: A Life
and Death Matter

As indicated in the last chapter, the problem of decision making is neither new nor unique to the teacher. The educator must develop and act on criteria. These criteria must include considerations relating to available knowledge about the child, subject matter, methodology, and the relationships of the school and society.

Questions about the possibility of knowing and ordering society on knowledge received early and exhaustive treatment in the work of Socrates. He saw the educative and miseducative potential of the social order as well as the school. He clearly recognized this as a life and death matter. Some lives, to him, were not worth living. Life is more than mere existence; it is identified with certain norms. Consequently, Socrates' conception of life went beyond the conception offered to us by the biologist. He was anxious to point out that if certain principles prevailed in society the contribution of the professional would not be generally appreciated.

We, like the ancient Greeks, live in a threatened age. "Ways of life" are continually threatened and today it is a commonplace recognition that life, in the sense of the physical survival of the species, is by no means assured. In this atmosphere men profess beliefs and act upon them as claims to knowledge about the right, the good, the effective and the ineffective. At bottom, these valuations are educational claims. As such they occupy the same status as the selection presented in Chapter 1.

If Socrates was correct, the teacher is continually involved in a life and death struggle. To teach is to advocate a standard. Thus to teach is either to give and to allow life or to withdraw and to discourage life. It is a serious affair not to be taken lightly. Presumably, this is why it should be a closely examined activity.

In the present chapter the reading entitled "The Death of Socrates" deals with some of these problems. It focuses, in part, on the problems of "knowing," as Socrates ends a life characterized by his antagonizing the politically powerful who professed to know more than they knew. It was clearly a life devoted to education in the sense of an abiding interest in the moral imperative of intellectual honesty—interested in learning, but focusing more forcefully and fruitfully on the problem of knowing as it affects man in his attempts to order himself and his kind.

THE SOCRATIC EXAMPLE

The life of Socrates has been subject to examination for a variety of reasons. The purpose of reconsidering his life and teachings here is that we feel he, better than any other, represents what we choose to label the *dilemma of the professional* in historical perspective. In the representation of that dilemma he also provides a possible model or ideal for professional behavior. He clearly stood out in his day and, by transfer and application, he stands out in ours as one confronted with the struggle of attempting to prove his competence and his concern for society. Today the same two qualities remain as central to professionalism: specialized knowledge and a predominant motivation to serve society. This demonstration of competence is difficult in light of the nature of professional competence. The superiority of the professional rests, in part, in his awareness of what he does not know. People, in general, do not see the strength and value of such a claim and find the uncertainty of the experimenting realm hard to live with. Socrates stood out as an individual attempting to gain acceptance while today numerous groups are struggling for the same recognition and the power that flows from such recognition.

In the following selection the reader will find that the rationale employed by Socrates in deciding to take the hemlock was essentially normative. Socrates indicated that his ideas constituted his very being. Inasmuch as these ideas would be denied him in the offer of exile, it appeared to Socrates that he was not being offered a chance to live. His action stands as a suggestion to us that professionalism depends upon a normative conception of being. Socrates was accused by his close associates of shirking his responsibility and even turning to cowardice in his choice to take the poison. They felt that he was neglecting his obligations and his previously affirmed intention to serve society. His response forces the thoughtful person to recognize the problem of defining service and locating the means to its accomplishment.

The concluding remarks of the commentator suggest that whoever attempts to live by high principles and to concern himself with other than the strivings for wealth, power, and luxury is doomed to taste the bitter brew as did Socrates. This raises the question of what place there might be for the professional in any society, ancient or modern.

THE DEATH OF SOCRATES*

COMMENTATOR #1 Today, we will take you back to 399 B.C. in Athens, Greece, where the Hellenistic world is waiting the climax of the trial and condemnation of the philosopher Socrates. Today Socrates must, according to Athenian law, perform his own execution and drink the poison hemlock. Charged with corruption of the minds of the youth and teaching them not to recognize the legally accepted Gods of the state, the barefooted sage denied these accusations at the public trial and artfully turned the arguments against his accusers. He was scornful of their ignorance and contemptuous of their motives and when judged guilty on an almost evenly divided vote, he refused to propose a reasonable fine as his punishment. He thus made a compromise impossible and all but invited the death sentence. And now as the moment of doom is rapidly approaching, the strange fact is that no one in Athens wants Socrates to die. His enemies, led by the democratic politician, Anytus, indeed sought to silence him but not to martyr him. And his friends, we are told, are still desperately trying to find some way out of this tragic entanglement and save Socrates from the fatal cup. We take you now to Athens, outside the prison where Socrates is being held.

COMMENTATOR #2 We are watching the sinking sun here and counting the minutes in the waning light. Just behind that wall is the cell in which Socrates is awaiting the end. This morning a group of philosophers, close friends, among them Crito and Apollodorus, were permitted inside and we were informed by the authorities that they have been conversing with Socrates all day.

An hour ago Xanthippe, the philosopher's wife, entered the prison and this was taken as a fearful sign that all preparations have been irrevocably made to carry out the death sentence. There are still those

*The Death of Socrates reprinted by permission of CBS Films Inc., New York.

who cannot believe that Anytus will be so foolish and stubborn as to allow Socrates to die against the will of the great majority of Athenians of all factions. Thus there is still a desperate hope here that somehow before the sun goes down the proud philosopher will emerge alive and tomorrow they will see him, as usual, in the market place, or the theater, the Lyceum, or on the steps of the Acropolis, debating the nature of truth, honor, courage, and justice.

(WE SEE A MAN OF ABOUT FIFTY, SENSITIVE, SOPHISTICATED, AND CYNICAL MOVE INTO THE SCENE AND JOIN A GROUP.)

There is Aristophanes, the famous playwright of satirical comedies. He has no doubt just come from the theatre of Dionysius where his play "Lysistrata" is in rehearsal. It was Aristophanes' play "The Clouds" which Socrates mentioned at the trial as an example of the work of some of his enemies to discredit him. Citizen Aristophanes—one moment—do you believe that Socrates should die for his crimes?

ARISTOPHANES   What crimes? He committed no crimes. Socrates has strong beliefs and opinions. But so have I and so has any man of intellect. Anytus and his ignorant mob cannot silence criticism of themselves by silencing Socrates. Only stupid men would get Athens into such a monstrous situation of condemning to death one of its most prominent thinkers—and being stupid men they don't know now how to get out of it. In his fumbling sodden greed for rule and power Anytus will yet kill us all, I'm sure.

COMMENTATOR #2   But Socrates himself said that you, Aristophanes, gave credence to the accusations against him in your play "The Clouds."

ARISTOPHANES   In my play "The Clouds" I lampooned Socrates as mercilessly as I knew how. I disagreed with his philosophy and I still do. But that was in a play and not at a public trial. And Socrates or anyone else had the privilege of doing the same to me.

COMMENTATOR #2   Didn't Melitus say that he and others were inflamed against Socrates as a result of "The Clouds"?

ARISTOPHANES   Oh Melitus. Poor poet. Poor in rhyme and still poorer in reason. Yes in the play I portrayed a man like Socrates who ran a THINKING SHOP. And I showed him in one of my better scenes walking along looking up into the sky and falling down a hole in his path. But that was comedy. And not my best comedy.

COMMENTATOR #2   I understand you also showed how Socrates taught young men to cheat payment of their debts and to beat their own fathers and if I am not mistaken, also to deny the existence of the Gods.

ARISTOPHANES   That is true. And what Socrates taught did result in such instances. I witnessed them myself.

COMMENTATOR #2   Aren't these also the nature of the charges that Melitus made against Socrates?

ARISTOPHANES   I knew they would blame me. Melitus is covering up his own guilt. He is preparing for the day when he himself will be brought before the judges. I am a playwright. I am not an executioner. Melitus was directly ordered to accuse Socrates by Anytus.

COMMENTATOR #2   Why does Anytus hate Socrates?

ARISTOPHANES   Socrates has always made a mockery of this democracy by alphabetical rotation as it is now being practised here in Athens. But under these democratic rules our most difficult and important decisions of government are given over to barbers, shoemakers, farmers, potters, and, with equal solemnity, to sweepers and trash collectors.

COMMENTATOR #2   Did Socrates corrupt Anytus' son?

ARISTOPHANES   No one can very well corrupt an honest man.

COMMENTATOR #2   Do you think there is any chance that Socrates might yet be saved?

ARISTOPHANES   I hope that he will. I think that he will not. But valuing what is most dear to me my greatest concern at this moment is to protect myself.

(HE GOES OFF OUT OF THE SCENE.)

COMMENTATOR #2   Someone has just come out of the prison—it is Crito, close friend of Socrates. He is going to speak to us.

CRITO   Socrates is well and calm. Xanthippe is with him now for their last meeting. He has been discoursing with us all day on the meaning of the soul's immortality.

(CRITO IS SILENT NOW AND SO IS THE CROWD. A MAN'S VOICE IS HEARD SPEAKING AND WE SEE MELITUS PUSHING HIS WAY THROUGH TO THE CENTER.)

MELITUS   I must be heard, citizens—I am owed a hearing—

COMMENTATOR #2   That is Melitus speaking now. He was the main accuser at the trial.

MELITUS   In the market place there are people who are howling for my life. The same people who urged me to accuse Socrates. Is this justice? Is this reason?

I did not want Socrates to be condemned to death. I thought he would be fined as I would have been, and gladly paid it, had the jury found my accusations false. Where are you now those of you who voted against Socrates? Why don't you defend me? I did my duty as a citizen. I spoke for Athens, for democracy. Socrates would not accept the verdict. He forced the death penalty. He offered no other way out.

He twisted my words and he twisted our intentions, and brought this end upon himself. Anytus this very morning offered to look aside and allow Socrates to escape. Crito knows this. He spoke to Anytus. Let Crito say now if I lie.

CRITO It is true. Escape was arranged and offered to Socrates. He refused.

MELITUS Why did he refuse? Tell us, Crito.

CRITO He is an old man. Athens is his city and his home. He will not accept banishment and exile at the hands of Anytus. He prefers to die.

MELITUS He *prefers* to die! *Socrates* prefers it! Not Melitus! Not Anytus! Thank you, Crito—thank you for revealing the truth.

(MELITUS LOOKS AROUND FOR SUPPORT. THE CROWD IS SILENT, COLD. DEFEATED, HE PUSHES OFF THROUGH THE CROWD AND OUT OF THE SCENE.)

CRITO Socrates always said that Melitus was of little consequence in the whole matter—an earnest but unhappy, misled young man.

SPECTATOR Crito—is there any hope at all that Anytus will still act to save Socrates?

CRITO Socrates will not accept anything less than the declaration of his innocence and complete freedom. Anytus would not agree to this.

SPECTATOR Who has spoken to Anytus?

CRITO I have—others—Plato and Xenophon, I believe are still with him —excuse me—

(HE HAS SEEN THE PRISON DOOR OPENING. XANTHIPPE IS COMING OUT. CRITO EXCHANGES A WHISPERED WORD WITH HER. THEN INDICATING TO HER ESCORTS TO STAY WITH HER, HE GOES INSIDE.)

MAN Socrates is not going to die! Anytus has agreed to free him! One of Anytus' own slaves overheard the agreement. He brought the news to the market-place!

(THE CROWD STIRS HOPEFULLY. THEY GATHER AROUND HIM.)

MAN He swore he heard it. Anytus told it to Plato and Xenophon. Five minutes ago! It could be true—it could be true!

(THERE IS CONFUSION, EXCITEMENT. SOME OF THE CROWD BREAK AWAY TO SPREAD THE RUMOR. THE MAN NOW MOVES UNDER THE WINDOW OF THE CELL.)

MAN   Socrates! Socrates, hear me! Anytus has agreed to free you!

COMMENTATOR #2   There have been rumors like this one all day. And they were found to be false. But in these last minutes it is not unreasonable to believe that Anytus might finally take a decisive action in his own interests. Could Plato and Xenophon have succeeded in persuading him?

(AT THE INNER COURTYARD OF ANYTUS' HOME. PLATO AND XENOPHON ARE SEEN TOGETHER TENSELY AND ANXIOUSLY PACING THE STONES. WE SEE ANYTUS EMERGE FROM THE HOUSE. POLYCRATES, AN ADVISER, IS WITH HIM. ANYTUS IS CLEARLY DISTURBED, BUT NOT AT ALL IN PANIC. HE IS EVEN SMILING A LITTLE. HE WALKS DIRECTLY UP TO PLATO AND XENOPHON.)

COMMENTATOR #3   Here we are in the courtyard of Anytus' home. There is no sign here of any such event. As you can see there are Plato and Xenophon still waiting for Anytus to hear them the last time. I would think that if Anytus had acted in some manner to free Socrates now he would certainly so inform the two young men, if only to relieve them of their anxiety and himself of their annoying presence. Here comes Anytus now—and that is Polycrates, one of his main advisers.

ANYTUS (TO POLYCRATES)   Observe, Polycrates, our two young philosophers so nobly devoted to the cause of spreading truth.

PLATO   The sun is sinking fast, Anytus—and so with it, perhaps, your regime.

ANYTUS (STUDYING THE YOUNG MEN BUT STILL TALKING TO POLYCRATES)   What shall I think of such truth-seekers who in my own home and behind my back bribe one of my slaves to incite all Athens with a cruel lie that Socrates was freed.

XENOPHON   You would not debate with us. You kept us waiting until we could bear it no longer. We had to act to prove to you the true will and desire of Athens.

POLYCRATES   And to put on Anytus the blame for Socrates' death.

XENOPHON   If there is no death—there will be no blame.

ANYTUS   Socrates was offered his life. If he now chooses to die it is his will, not mine.

PLATO   He chooses to live but not as a man adjudged guilty, not as a prisoner, and not in exile. For any such punishment does dishonor to the rightness of his beliefs and these he will not allow to perish even if his body must.

POLYCRATES   You are urging us then to subscribe not only to his complete pardon, but also to the rightness of his beliefs.

PLATO   I could not expect so much sudden intelligence. I am urging you only to look after your own beliefs—for if Socrates dies now—it is yours which will be judged and condemned. And more than your beliefs your property and your lives will go on trial.

POLYCRATES (WITH SARCASM) But if by dying Socrates can accomplish this grand overthrow, why do you want him saved, Plato? Men die in battle for much smaller gains. Wouldn't you be willing to die now if by so doing you could destroy us and our rule of democracy?

PLATO I would prefer to live and see the same accomplished by reason and generosity.

ANYTUS Alcibiades and Critias were pupils of your master. Did they rule with reason and kindness?

(PLATO IS SILENT FOR A MOMENT.)

POLYCRATES Answer, Plato. Answer for the fifteen hundred Athenian lives they wantonly butchered to suppress the democracy.

XENOPHON (INDIGNANTLY) Is Socrates to blame for two pupils who misused his teachings for their personal profit and power? Are *all* who Socrates taught Critias and Alcibiades? If you do not approve of his teachings—argue, debate against it if you can. But to ascribe all the world's evil to Socrates is not an argument. It is a declaration of absolute and divine knowledge. Are you now claiming to be Gods?

POLYCRATES Divine wisdom is Socrates' claim, not ours.

PLATO Socrates' wisdom lies in the humblest of pretensions. He claims no advance knowledge of truth, only a method of finding it.

ANYTUS Time is running out. I do not want Socrates to die. You say you do not want Socrates to die. At every step of the trial your master was offered the mildest of punishments. Even the demand for death was proposed as a way out for him legally to claim another jurisdiction. He insisted on testing his beliefs with his life. What do you propose I should do?

PLATO Free him. Free him without conditions.

ANYTUS I have no power to free him. No one man has that power in Athens. He was condemned by a majority of 500 jurymen.

PLATO At your request, Anytus.

ANYTUS At his own insistence. We are back to fruitless debate.

XENOPHON Assume the power and free him.

ANYTUS I cannot break the laws which I cherish beyond mine or Socrates' private welfare.

PLATO The will of the majority is now that Socrates must not die. As a true believer in the principles of majority rule you should carry out that belief in the intention of your laws and not bind yourself by their stupid inadequacies.

ANYTUS You are very clever young men. You know how to twist arguments to your own advantage almost as skillfully as does Socrates. But when all is said there remain two opposing principles of a way of life and a way of government. I have risked death before and I will risk it again for my beliefs. And if Socrates chooses to die for *his* beliefs and this is his manner of warring on mine—then I cannot blame him or save him—I can only accept the fact of such a battle.

PLATO   Are these your last words, Anytus?

ANYTUS   They are.

(PLATO BOWS. AND WITH BITTER HATRED SILENTLY EXPRESSED THE TWO YOUNG MEN LEAVE. ANYTUS AND POLYCRATES REMAIN STANDING THERE.)

I feel no remorse in this old man's desire for death, Polycrates. But what a sorrow that so penetrating a thinker and a patriot and gentle lover of his city is to be lost to the cause of *our* enemies and his.

(HE LOOKS TOWARD THE DYING SUN.)

So be it, Socrates, and may the Gods and the future find proper honors for you.

COMMENTATOR #3   We have word that all preparations for the execution have been completed. We take you back inside the prison where the authorities have permitted us to witness the end.

(A LARGE BARE CHAMBER IN WHICH THERE IS ONE WOODEN BENCH FOR SITTING AND ANOTHER FOR RECLINING. A GROUP OF EIGHT TO TEN FRIENDS OF SOCRATES ARE GATHERED. THEY WHISPER OCCASIONAL WORDS OF STUNNED SORROW.)

COMMENTATOR #2   We are in the cell now. Socrates has requested that he be allowed to bathe himself and he is still in the bath-chamber with Crito. At the wall to the left is Apollodorus. The young man with him is Critobulous, the son of Crito. And there in the corner are Simias and Cebes and Phaedo. To their right Euclid and Terpsion who came from Megara. Before he went to bathe Socrates engaged in a long discourse on the meaning of the soul's immortality. It was as if he were speaking out in the market place and there was nothing in his behavior to suggest that this was a man who was about to die. Here he comes now—here is Socrates.

(ALL TURN SUDDENLY AS THE HEAVY DOOR IS OPENED BY THE JAILOR AND SOCRATES ENTERS FOLLOWED BY CRITO.)

SOCRATES (NOTING THE EMBARRASSED WATCHFUL SILENCE OF THE ASSEM-
BLAGE) I was just saying to Crito that the women will be happily relieved now of the trouble of washing me after my death. But Crito
sees no humor in this. Do you, Crito?

CRITO (TRIES TO SMILE) I was not thinking of the problems of the women.

SOCRATES How shall we bury you, Socrates, he sadly asks me in the
bath chamber. We have spoken here for an hour or more and we have
all agreed that upon drinking the poison my body will remain and my
soul shall go to the joys of the blessed—yet there is still no effect of
these words on Crito. I cannot make him believe that I will be the
same Socrates who has been conducting this argument.

He fancies another Socrates, a dead body, and he would still sorrow
at my hard lot. "Apollodorus," he says, "has brought a fine garment
for you, Socrates." Is this true, Apollodorus?

APOLLODORUS I have it here. I thought you might desire to wear it for
such—an occasion.

SOCRATES (SOCRATES EXAMINES THE GARMENT.) What is my own? Good
enough to live in—but not to die in?

APOLLODORUS The thought seemed proper. I do not mean to offend you,
Socrates.

SOCRATES If I were to be offended, my dear friend, it would not be for
this—but for your belief that you must bury me in splendor and grief.
You know that I am a man who has cast away the pleasure and orna-
ments of the body and has sought after the pleasure of knowledge.
Is it not your wish to honor me for *that*?

APOLLODORUS It is my most profound wish.

SOCRATES I think I am well adorned. I have arrayed myself not in some
foreign attire—but I hope in the proper jewels of temperance, justice,
courage, and truth. Thus, if you wish to lay me out in finery, lay me
out in those and be of good cheer in doing so. As for the manner of
burying my body, do with that whatever is usual and what you think
best.

(HE LOOKS UP AT THE WINDOW.) The sun is almost gone. Of what else
shall we talk? (THERE IS SILENCE.) Is there nothing left? Have you
already buried me? Is this the funeral?

PHAEDO (A CRY OF DESPAIR) Why did you refuse the chance to escape?

SOCRATES (SLOWLY—TROUBLED) I thought I had answered that ques-
ton, Phaedo. Do you remember what I said at the trial?

PHAEDO You said that if Athens could not endure your discourses and
cross-examinations that it would be irrational to expect that in a foreign city you would be more welcome.

SOCRATES I said more.

(SOCRATES IS NOT UNKIND BUT SHARP NOW, AND FIRM IN HIS TONE.)

PHAEDO You said that to discourse daily about virtue and the greatest good of man is your life's purpose and if not allowed that right you have no more reason to live.

SOCRATES And do you agree with that, Phaedo?

PHAEDO I do. But I am still troubled. No one in Athens wants you to die. Not even Anytus.

SOCRATES Are they anxious so for my body or my beliefs?

PHAEDO I would say your name, your being.

SOCRATES Did they condemn my name or my being or my beliefs?

PHAEDO Your beliefs.

SOCRATES And what are my beliefs; my body, my name, or my being?

PHAEDO They are your being.

SOCRATES Then are they anxious for my being to live?

PHAEDO No.

SOCRATES Then what are they offering me?

PHAEDO To live bodily without your being.

SOCRATES Is that a manner of life, Phaedo, or death?

PHAEDO A manner of death.

SOCRATES Then what am I being offered, Phaedo?

PHAEDO Death.

SOCRATES Thank you, Phaedo. A few more questions. If I choose for my body to die, do my beliefs continue?

PHAEDO They do.

SOCRATES And my beliefs are my being?

PHAEDO Our beliefs are all our beings.

SOCRATES Then what am I choosing?

PHAEDO I would say you are choosing to live.

SOCRATES This is what Anytus knows as well and that is why he would permit me to escape to exile for in so doing I would truly renounce my life. I am choosing to live thereby and not to die. (THE GROUP IS TRYING TO BELIEVE THIS—BUT THEY FIND IT HARD.) You still seem puzzled, Apollodorus?

APOLLODORUS I know that death is a matter that must befall each of us. And I know in dying one can do with it good or do evil.

But I ask if a man does not have responsibility to his friends and to his children and if in refusing to go on living this will not be seen as an act of desertion of responsibility—or even cowardice.

SOCRATES A good question. I will try to answer it. But you must help me, Apollodorus. What is the principle upon which my responsibility to my friends is based?

APOLLODORUS   To receive their friendship and to return it.

SOCRATES   And of what does friendship consist?

APOLLODORUS   To be good in all things toward each other.

SOCRATES   You are repeating yourself.

APOLLODORUS   Yes I am—to—to give the best of oneself to the other.

SOCRATES (LAUGHING)   A little better. And what is the best of me? My
money, my property?

APOLLODORUS   Your teachings, Socrates.

SOCRATES   And how did I come upon these teachings?

APOLLODORUS   By your purpose to search for truth.

SOCRATES   You admit I must give up this purpose in escaping. Will I
then be serving my friends with the best of me?

APOLLODORUS   No.

SOCRATES   With what then would I be serving you?

APOLLODORUS   With our desire to see you live.

SOCRATES   Is it your desire to see me live without purpose? (APOLLO-
DORUS IS SILENT, CONFUSED. HE BREAKS INTO TEARS.) Don't weep here,
dear friend. And if you must—leave now, I beg you. As for my children, I did not agree upon bringing them into the world that for their
material comfort I would at some time dishonor my principles. When
my sons are grown I would ask you, oh my friends, to trouble them
as I have troubled you. If they seem to care more about riches or
anything more than about virtue—reprove them as I have reproved
you. And if you do this, both I and my sons will have received true
friendship at your hands.

CRITO   I must speak too, Socrates. I would not be your friend otherwise—I—

(THE DOOR OPENS. THE JAILER COMES IN.)

JAILER   The sun is near the rim. I must proceed now by the orders
given me.

SOCRATES   You have brought the poison?

(THE JAILER MOTIONS FOR THE ATTENDANT TO ENTER. HE COMES IN.
HE CARRIES THE CUP ON A SMALL WOODEN PLATTER.)

SOCRATES (TO CRITO)   I know what you want to ask me, Crito. You asked
it this morning and I didn't answer you. I have been thinking of how
to answer, for the question troubles me deeply as well. (TO JAILER)
Can you wait? Is the sun all but down?

JAILER   I have waited much beyond the time allowed for I too do not wish to see you die, Socrates. Do not be angry with me now if I tell you that the sun is indeed gone beyond the hilltop and I have been holding it back only in my mind.

SOCRATES   How then am I to proceed now? Will I have any senses left between the drinking and the effect?

JAILER   It is usual that it take some moments for the numbness to start.

SOCRATES   Describe it to me.

JAILER   You walk about until there is a heaviness in your legs. Then it will be best to lie down. The poison will then act from your legs upward.

SOCRATES   Would you give the cup to my friend Crito?

JAILER   Fare you well, Socrates—you know I must do my errand.

SOCRATES   I return your good wishes and know you are generous in your sorrow. Crito, I will try to answer your question. Since I have never claimed to know the truth itself but only better than any man how to search for it—how do I now know that I have done right in all this—in the manner of living and the manner of dying?

CRITO   I ask no answer—

(HE FALTERS.)

You were and are the wisest, the most honorable of men—I wish it were that I could take this poison and spare you.

SOCRATES   Thank you, Crito. You would spare me nothing and I would suffer *then* greatly for you. What is the answer? The answer is that in doubting the truth as others saw it I had to search for my own. It is not what I have discovered as truth that may be so right. It is that I taught *how to discover what is false,* and only in so doing can the truth be known. For this principle of so teaching I feel secure in my purpose and choice of my life and death. Have I answered you satisfactorily, Crito?

CRITO   You have.

SOCRATES   You deceive me, Crito. But I have answered myself satisfactorily and I'm sure you will think more about it tomorrow. My dear friends—I pray that my journey may prosper now from this to that other world. Gods of our great earth and of my beloved city of Athens, grant me this prayer—

(HE DRINKS THE POISON.)

No numbness—nothing yet.

(HE RISES AGAIN AND WALKS TO THE SMALL WINDOW AND LOOKS OUT.)

Look how the sun goes down with majestic peace and order and beauty. If each man's soul could find such a shape and movement as this—the reason and joy of heaven would indeed be on this earth.

(HE FEELS A STIFFNESS BEGINNING IN HIS LEGS. HE LOOKS DOWN AT THEM, THEN HE NODS TO CRITO AS IF TO SAY IT HAS BEGUN.)

The numbness gathers upward like a cold night.

(CRITO GENTLY UNFOLDS THE GRAY CLOTH COVER OVER THE DYING MAN'S BODY AND BRINGS IT UP TO THE NECK. SOCRATES CLOSES HIS EYES.)

Crito—I owe a debt to Asclepius. Will you remember to pay it?
CRITO   I will, Socrates. Is there anything else?

(SOCRATES SMILES. HE TRIES TO OPEN HIS EYES. THE SURGE OF SOME WARM THOUGHT IS IN HIM BUT HE CAN NO LONGER EXPRESS IT. A SUDDEN SPASM GRIPS HIM. HE TREMBLES.)

COMMENTATOR #1   Thus was the tragic end of Socrates, the barefoot philosopher of Athens, the first master of the method of dialectic in the search for truth. And this knowledge became the property of his friends as well as his enemies as man's quest continued through the ages for the meaning of freedom and justice and virtue and truth. Indeed Socrates did not know all the answers. No one man can know them all.

Among his distinguished pupils, including Plato and Xenophon, there were those who in his name later did much evil and those who did much good. But in Athens that night, and the days following, in the homes and in the streets, on the steps of the Acropolis, and in the palaestra, there was a great sorrow. They could not but grieve for the loss of this stubborn old man, simple and gentle of soul and sharp and clear of mind, who would never let them rest in their comfort and vanity and ignorance.

And they were forced to think better and deeper of the true dignity and noble aspirations of man beyond his strivings for luxury, wealth, and power. The cup of poison then became in their minds a test and symbol of high principles and purity. And all who would live by such goals were bound for centuries after to taste again in some way this bitter brew.

FOR FURTHER THOUGHT

1. Consider a case in which a book was recommended by teachers as a most valuable source in helping students to gain a realistic picture of a particular period of history. Shortly thereafter there was a public outcry requesting the removal of the source. Assuming that the teachers have valid grounds for claiming the usefulness and essential nature of the book with regard to accepted goals of education, *can they withdraw the source upon public demand and be classified as professional? Would such an approach be comparable to Socrates' complaint about turning certain decisions over to those unqualified to make such important decisions? Should the preparation of teachers be such that they are the best able to make judgments regarding methodology and curriculum in the classroom?*

2. As long as local control of education continues, there remains the likelihood of significant differences in goals or purposes of education. It remains a possibility that a goal pursued in one community could be at complete odds with those of another community. *Given such varying conceptions of purpose is there any possibility of a profession of teachers being established?*

3. The actions of teachers who claim that there is a need to bring certain matters into focus through strikes and sanctions are seen by some to be indicative of a shirking of responsibility or a failure to meet obligations. *Are there some conditions under which teachers might be expected to remain in the classroom that would suggest a real disservice? Could the teacher striking be seen as doing the greatest service or performing the most professional act as Socrates viewed his own taking of the hemlock?*

4. Socrates remained convinced of the worth of his goal or service despite the public outcry against it. He had other ways for checking the validity or the worth of his objectives. *Is service necessarily providing the public with what they want? Should professional educators see their service to society as offering skills and encouragement to examine the current ends of society?*

5. *What assurance does the professional have that he is right? Does the fact that he does not have final answers make his position less tenable? Untenable? Does the tentative knowledge base of professionalism make such a position incompatible with those groups in our society laying claim to a more absolute knowledge base? Can professional educators loyally operate, for example, in a parochial school system?*

6. *Why might the professional today expect to taste the bitter brew as did Socrates? What actions can analogously be related to the actual*

taking of the hemlock? Are teachers who leave a school system because of deplorable conditions tasting the bitter brew? Are those teachers who apply sanctions to bring redress of grievances tasting the bitter brew? (Note that such behavior suggests, on the part of the educators, the possession of knowledge of those conditions that are essential to the performance of their service.)

THE ACT OF QUESTIONING

Because things are commonplace we often assume that they are answers to unasked questions. Everything cannot be held in doubt at once. Nevertheless, education involves, among other things, the questioning of the commonplace conclusions and the assumptions that suppport them. Involved in the act of questioning is the desire to make a good choice, the assumption that there are better and worse choices, and an assumption of the possibility of knowing.

These assumptions bring with them certain basic questions. One of the first to be raised is "Who can make the best decision?" Such a question presupposes some criterion for the selection of the decision maker. In other words, it raises the prior question of *what* is to be the principle for the selection of the *who?* The answers are familiar. Among them we find "the individual," "the parent," "the owner," "the community," and "the expert." Behind each candidate lurks the guiding principle that each would employ in making decisions. In some cases there is the belief that there is no knowledge in the realm of values. Thus it is argued that each man has a right to his own decision or opinion. The same point of view is often advanced in support of majority rule. Others assume that ownership validates any decision. (They may say, for example: "This child is mine and no one can tell me what to do with him!") One final possibility to be mentioned here is the claim that specialized knowledge is possible, thus making some decisions and some decision makers more legitimate than others. The worth of any of these candidates is dependent in large measure upon (1) the accepted conception of knowledge in the domain in which the decision is being made, and (2) a clear understanding and acceptance of the purpose to be achieved. Without a clear cut agreement on these matters, nothing but confusion and conflict can exist with regard to the manner in which decisions should be made.

The following selection deals with a realm generally thought to be free of the above concerns. A variety of claims are introduced as possible legitimate considerations for making decisions in behalf of an injured person. The reader will find a pattern of questions raised within the reading itself as a vehicle for focusing on the issues at hand. Internally, the reading presents a fascinating set of problems of social policy. The issue external to the selection itself resides in the possibility of comparable situations in education (formal and informal), the possibility of comparable principles for determining action, and its relationship as a whole to considerations raised in prior selections. It should be noted that this selection suggests many of the Socratic issues studied earlier in a modern setting.

------◀◆▶------

AN ANALOGY TO RAISE QUESTIONS*

As a result of a most unpleasant car accident a crowd congregated around a smashed vehicle and a number of injured occupants. Not long after the first car had arrived on the scene of the accident a man pulled his car over to the side of the road and hurried to where the bystanders and the injured were gathered. After having perused the situation he focused attention on the person who appeared to be most seriously injured.

As the new arrival on the scene hastily began to perform labor on behalf of the patient someone from the crowd, fearing the possible extension of damage to the injured, queried the self-appointed samaritan as follows: "Who do you think you are to be able to treat the person in this way?" Once the questioning mood had been established others joined in asking, "By what right do you move him?" *To what extent were the questions of the crowd legitimate? What right and responsibility, if any, did they have to interfere?* Assuming that the questions of the crowd were legitimate, *what answer could the man have provided that would have given him the right to handle the injured party?*

Somewhat impatient with the interfering questions the man quickly and pointedly replied, "I am a doctor."

Many had anticipated such a reply from their observance of the way in which he handled the injuries. Others, not as observant, had weighed the possibility of his being a friend, a relative, a minister, or even a concerned bystander. A whole host of alternatives had entered their minds, all carrying with them the question as to the right to touch and treat the injured party. *Of the many replies that could have been given, would any one of them have offered a more legitimate claim to touch the injured? What is the basis for that claim to legitimacy?—ownership? concern? knowledge?* Note the outcomes of applying that principle in other situations.

*From an unpublished paper by Robert S. Patterson entitled, "An Analogy To Raise Questions." Dr. Patterson is currently Associate Professor of Education at the University of Alberta.

Each of the possible alternatives implied an ordering principle suggesting a basis for legitimate action. The most commonly thought of reply was, "I am a doctor." Implicit in this statement is the claim or the profession of an individual that he is competent or qualified to deal with the problem at hand. Those accepting this claim are acknowledging that given his perception of the problem, the knowledge and skill possessed by a doctor would be most useful to the injured person. Those who would defend the right of a relative to administer to the ills of the person are saying that either they do not perceive the ailment to be sufficiently serious to warrant application of specialized knowledge and skill, or that the family tie justifies whatever treatment or care the relative chooses to administer regardless of the seriousness of the case. This is much like a principle of ownership. Still others would be prepared to accept action by concerned or interested parties. Like the relatives, these concerned persons might not possess any knowledge relevant to the situation. Interest and concern are the basis for their action. However noble the intention in this instance, there is no guarantee that the efforts will not be quite harmful. Which of these principles for action—knowledge, ownership, or concern—offers the most legitimate claim for touching the injured party? Interestingly enough the succinct retort, "I am a doctor," led to another line of thought and question. Some of the injured and some of the interested bystanders began to raise questions as to the right of the doctor to treat one person and not another. What right did he have to deny them his services? *As the status of the doctor was acknowledged, what right did he have to concentrate his attention on the one injured party? Did he possess anything that provided him with a better basis for judging such matters? Was the doctor treating the people equally or fairly?*

Those who challenged the decision of the doctor to treat the prone patient rather than any of the others who were injured were in fact suggesting that the doctor was being unfair. They were supporting the claims of those who felt that they were the more seriously hurt. In so doing, either the knowledge and decision-making ability of the doctor or his motives were being challenged. He was being told that either he did not know true medical need when he saw it or that he was ignoring more serious injury to favor one person on the basis of some unknown motive. Does the knowledge possessed by the doctor qualify him above anyone else to judge the medical needs of various people? Does the failure to treat everyone at once indicate that the injured were being unfairly treated? Fairness or justice conceived as sameness of treatment ignores the individual differences that exist in the variety of injured persons.

The condition of the patient and the order of treating the various ailments interested some of the spectators: it clearly challenged the doctor. The injured party had the following readily observable difficulties: a broken arm and fingers, lacerations, profuse bleeding, and badly damaged teeth. In addition to the above listed problems the doctor was able to discern symptoms that indicated the presence of shock and internal hemorrhaging. The question for the doctor was, "What order of service should I follow?" There were at least three levels of injury for the doctor to consider:

(1) Those injuries that did not require immediate attention in order for the patient to live;
(2) those injuries requiring immediate consideration and remedy if the patient was to live; and
(3) those injuries, not of a serious nature, but of such a nature that they had to be dealt with prior to the most serious of the ailments being handled.

Given the varying disorders of the patient there was a need to decide where to begin treatment. *To what extent was the doctor best able to decide upon the order of treatment? Why? Would his ability to decide such matters depend upon the definition of health operative in the case? How would a distinction between long range and immediate goals help the doctor explain his course of action?*

Some of the injuries were much more apparent than others. The doctor's knowledge and experience provided him with a basis for determining where to begin. Among the group present his judgment would be the most reliable because of this knowledge. There were many opinions about more appropriate actions, but these were all based on a less complete awareness of the ills. By chance they might have suggested the identical course of action taken by the doctor. *But to take that action for the wrong reasons or without as complete an awareness as that of a doctor is not to agree with him at all.*

As those watching saw the doctor concern himself first with the clearing of the patient's mouth, then with the provision of warmth through a blanket, and then with a tourniquet to quell the bleeding, questions again arose as to his ability to make such decisions. When he departed even further from their anticipated plan of treatment to consider the internal problems, which he knew to be most vital and of which the spectators were ignorant, an even greater rumbling took place. There was real doubt as to the priority of treatment that he was offering. One outspoken soul who had had training in first aid raised the question, "Why don't you swab the wounds to cleanse them or set the broken arm or fingers?" The crowd, somewhat amazed at his display of "competence," quickly agreed with him and pressed the issues further with the harried doctor. He was too busy to even bother acknowledging their questions. He had heard the questions, but had felt the need to dismiss them at that particular time. His only obligation was to the injured person before him. *Inasmuch as the members of the crowd were unable to intelligently raise questions is there any reason to preserve their right to question? Did the spectator with limited first aid training have more right to question than any of the others? If we accept the right of the crowd to question, is there the possibility that such questioning might interfere with the doctor's effectiveness? Who is best able to determine whether answering the questions will interfere with the doctor's performance? To what extent should the doctor's right to treat the patient be determined by his ability to provide pleasing and acceptable answers to questions directed to him?*

The questions from the crowd made the doctor's task more difficult. To silence these questions completely might have been justified if the questions in some way were endangering the injured party. The doctor had to decide whether they were a threat. He did decide that to answer the questions would threaten the well-being of his patient. If knowledgeable persons such as the doctor could not act until they had satisfied the whimsical concerns of the crowd, political strategy and salesmanship would have to become standard equipment for professionals. To silence the crowd would be to deny the possibility of useful considerations coming from the masses. At the same time, satisfactory answers for the ignorant could well hinder service. Only the doctor could determine whether the task of answering would defeat his purpose of serving the patient.

By this time it had become quite apparent to the doctor that the injuries were of such a nature as to require a blood transfusion. Having made all preparation for this possibility in the ambulance that had been hurriedly called to the scene, the doctor and others were somewhat taken aback when one of the other injured persons struggled forward in an attempt to destroy the equipment provided for the transfusion. Before being able to achieve his purpose the apparently dazed and stunned man fell to the ground near the ambulance. *Given the fact that the person bent on destroying the transfusion equipment was temporarily speechless could there be any valid reason for his behavior? Is destruction of a doctor's equipment permissible on any basis? How do a doctor's definitions of life and health affect the remedy he prescribes? In what way could life and health be defined to make his prescription inappropriate?*

The dazed and temporarily speechless passenger knew something that he felt would alter the doctor's course of action. He had only one way to effect the end that he sought. To permit destruction of the equipment would require a life or death reason. The doctor had decided that physical death would result without the transfusion. Nothing appeared to be sufficiently more serious than that. Perhaps a different type of death was possible if he completed the transfusion. Like Socrates, the doctor came to recognize the normative conceptions of death. Spiritual death was perhaps feared more than physical death by the injured parties, thus service had to be measured in relation to one of these conceptions. Those witnessing this action quickly attributed it to injuries and shock, but the doctor uncovered what he felt might have been another reason for such bewildering conduct. In searching the patient's belongings for a card denoting blood type he found a membership card identifying the patient with a religious group that would have been averse to his actions on behalf of the patient.

Now it was his turn to ask some important questions: "Do I have the responsibility or the right to pursue this action further? Did I have the right in the first place?" *Does the information concerning the religion of the injured party constitute an acceptable basis for the doctor to alter his treatment? Does the information in any way affect the initial judgment made as to who has the right to treat the injured party? Would you have drawn back from the case? Would you have torn up the card?* The doctor was concerned with preserving life. His right to act had been established because his knowledge and skill were the most reliable tools for the assurance of the desired end. Another variable, heretofore only implicitly apparent, becomes a vital concern. Does an individual possess rights that transcend the right of the doctor? Here, professionalism as a principle is a matter of social policy. When people live together there must be a basis for resolving their counter claims to rights. To say that the doctor no longer has the right to treat the patient with a transfusion is to claim that freedom of the individual legitimizes choices not based on the accepted knowledge of the profession. Religion and medicine in this case offer countering claims as to what is good for the patient. In such cases involving children, the state often takes the child from the parent to make the transfusion possible. At that level society chooses between the countering claims to knowledge.

Can the doctor be classified as a professional if he cannot apply his knowledge to realize the desired end? Is professionalism possible in a society in which public knowledge is not the ordering principle? This last question had been a particularly vital one to the doctor throughout the experience. Only he knew that he lacked a medical certificate. He was on his way to take his final medical exams. When he had arrived at the scene he saw a need and realized that he would be empowered by his claim that he was a doctor. This claim would allow him to accomplish things on behalf of the injured that he might otherwise have been denied. At the time there appeared to be no doubt as to the validity of the action; later he began to question it. *Was the man less than a doctor because he lacked the certificate? Inasmuch as he did not possess the certificate did he still have the right to treat the patient? Were his strategy and his actions immoral? If so, are they any more immoral than the behavior of the professional who is properly certified, and who has to cajole the public into letting him do what he thinks is right? Is it immoral for society to have laws making the certified doctor libel for treating involuntary patients, thus encouraging doctors to drive by the scene of an accident?*

The doctor did not expect the possession of the certificate to make him any more capable of coping with the needs of the injured person. He also realized the limitations the crowd might place on him if he did not respond that he was a doctor. Perhaps society had driven him to his immoral behavior. Inasmuch as there was no available and commonly agreed upon absolute truth, each regarded his opinion to be of equal worth. If the doctor believed this he could have withdrawn from the case and left the individual to suffer the fate of his previously made choices. On the other hand, if he believed that knowledge was not absolute and that there were knowledgeable and ignorant choices, he faced a serious dilemma. Society was unable to judge possession of appropriate knowledge. Should he allow people to suffer from their ignorance, or should he distort the truth in order to act? He wondered if he could ever be professional in such a society—even with his certificate.

FOR FURTHER THOUGHT

1. *Wherein does the right reside for deciding matters pertaining to the education of members of our society? Is your answer consistent with the one given with regard to the right of the doctor to prescribe treatment? With whom should the final decision rest? Why?*
2. Just as the behavior of the doctor was subject to criticism by the spectators, so each teacher is subject to examination and criticism. *Who is best able to decide upon the value of the criticism? When a patient tells a doctor that he has had drowsy spells since taking a certain medicine who can best say whether there is cause for alarm? Similarly, if a parent claims that his child is experiencing frustration over a subject, who can best judge what action should be taken?* (Note that neither example discourages the reaction of the participants, but instead examines who can make the best decision given the available information.)
3. Our present educational scene is marked by concerns of teachers for programs, material, and so forth, that will assist in reaching the so-called "deprived" child. As schools are caught up in providing food, health,

and family services there are those who would criticize the priority of concern by saying: "*Who can best decide whether such activities are essential as preparatory acts to the major concern of the school?*" "*How are priorities of action to be determined?*" "*Is it useful to distinguish between immediate and long range goals?*"

4. There are those in our society operating under the "halo" of success in fields apart from education who pose as knowledgeable critics of education. *How is one to know whether the criticism is valid?*

5. *Is there an obligation to answer the critics of education to their satisfaction before one has the right to teach? Does the professional have a responsibility to educate the public so they will readily accept his actions? If this latter role interferes with the service to the client, which role takes precedence? In education, for example, if the public reacts adversely to modern mathematics, does the teacher have the responsibility to continue to teach it in spite of opposition, or should treatment under such means cease until the public approves?*

6. *How does the definition of education or the purpose of education affect the possible "treatments" prescribed and conducted by teachers in relation to their students? Inasmuch as religious groups ascribe different purposes to education, does that provide a valid basis for questioning procedures or regulations for the school? Is a disagreement over inclusion of religious activities in the schools attributable to disagreement over purpose?*

7. *How important is certification to the granting of autonomy to teaching? Who can best decide the necessary standards for certification—the public, those within the professional community?*

Summary of Part One

The basic questions of this part have centered upon the definition of a professional, the range of appropriate actions for the professional, and the problems likely to be faced by the professional in society. The life and decisions of Socrates have been presented as most adequately representing the dilemmas associated with considerations of professionalism. In his day, Socrates' claim to service was denied by his society. Whatever the period in history, however, the professional is one who claims that he is able to render the best service to society in a particular domain of human endeavor. Society can ill afford to ignore the possible gains and enrichments to be derived from the acts of professional people.

The study of professionalism offers a framework for exploring what might be the most desirable relationship between individuals, groups, and the total society. For our purposes we must ascertain whether the demands of professionalism on the individual teacher, the total group of educators, and the society are consistent with our basic value commitments and are acceptable as the principle for action. If professionalism can be seen as a worthy ideal, and if we have clearly delineated those actions and relationships that are essential to the attainment of that ideal, we have provided an important directive force to teaching and to teacher preparation. An important dimension of this, which will be explored later in the book, is the compatibility of the ideal of profession with the ideal of democracy. These two goals are harmoniously related, thus strengthening the value of their attainment.

Essential to professionalism is the definition that we use. While we encourage the reader to examine his own understanding of this term, we are anxious to have some thought given to our own recommendation. We feel that professionalism is characterized by *a claim and a dedication to service of society in and through a specialized competence or range of knowledge and skills not generally available to the public.* The possession of these qualities without the requisite powers for action in accordance with these convictions and knowledge is the basis for denying the existence of professionalism. Socrates performed the only truly "professional" act by refusing to alter his claim to service without good reason, even though the public demanded it. He took the course of action which he felt he must.

The consideration of the issues involved in the readings and questions of Part One provide a framework for studying the rest of this book. There are two basic questions that need to be considered: (1) Is there a unique social service or purpose that is to be rendered by teachers? and (2) On what authority or justification does one answer such a question? These are what we choose to call the "root" or crucial questions in education. A closely related but derived issue is, what are the necessary conditions for achieving such a service? To raise this latter issue is to presuppose a clear answer to the "root" question. Without such a clear answer the instrumental or methodological question is at best premature. An examination of the ideal of profession is an examination of the question of its ordering principle. Similarly, because education tends to be deeply embedded in its supporting social system, education must examine the question of the ordering principle for the whole society—all its institutions and individuals.

SUGGESTIONS FOR FURTHER READING

1. Students interested in a more thorough and a more traditional account of the events leading up to and including the death of Socrates should consider the following Platonic dialogues: *Euthyphro, Apology, Crito* and *The Phaedo* (Indianapolis: The Bobbs-Merrill Co., Inc., 1956).
2. This chapter challenges the reader to make applications of the models to teaching. Readings that focus on the question of teaching and pro-

fessionalism and those that would be helpful in thinking through the application to teaching are Harry S. Broudy, "Teaching: Craft or Profession?" *The Educational Forum*, vol. 20 (January 1956); G. Homer Durham, "Advancement of Teaching as a Profession," *Journal of Teacher Education* (September 1957); and Richard A. Smith, "Maturity of Education as a Profession," *Journal of Teacher Education* (September 1957).

3. A number of the questions raised by the material of this chapter are focal points for subsequent chapters of this book. Because of this, readings pertaining to such matters as teacher preparation, certification, power, authority and freedom will be found at the end of the respective chapters dealing with these topics.

PART TWO

PURPOSE OR SERVICE IN EDUCATION

a root question

We have tried to raise a number of questions in the minds of our readers. In particular, we introduced questions about (1) the life style of Socrates, (2) a modern parallel, and (3) a contemporary response that reiterates the dilemma of the professional. It is entirely possible to read and think about this material with understanding and still fail to see its import or significance. Such a magnification of understanding is absolutely essential to teacher education. Support for such a claim is found in the writings of Alexander Meiklejohn. He said:

> One of the greatest failures of our contemporary training of teachers is that they become mere technicians. They learn the tricks and devices of the classroom. But they do not learn the beliefs and motives and values of the human fellowship for the sake of which the classroom exists. The primary question of teaching theory and practice is one of purpose. Why do we teach? What should we teach? For whom do we teach? What is our goal, and what is the source of its authority over us? Those are the questions which must be an-

swered if our teachers are to be themselves members of the fraternity
into which they seek to initiate their pupils.[1]

Such a statement not only lends support to our immediate concerns about
purpose; it also offers an excellent framework for the total considerations
of our book.

All the readings to this point have dealt with conceptions of service. The
behavior of the professional is guided by his concept of service. Such a
conception is not always clear. Clear or unclear, it serves as his guide to
making all sorts of decisions. Clarity is obviously an immense aid to the
educator who must always answer the question of "why?" Why don't you
offer more science? Why isn't there a three year course in French? Why do
you allow such books in the library? Why waste time with frill subjects?
Comprehensive answers to such questions can be expected only when
there is a clear conception of the service to be rendered.

In the same way, a clear knowledge of the purpose and rules of baseball
gives us an understanding of what orders the selection of players and
managers and what determines the relationships of owners to managers
and players. It also orders the relationships of all to the umpires. All the interactions of those involved are principled by the purpose of the activity.
Moreover, our judgments about what constitutes unskilled, unethical, and
irrelevant behavior are similarly principled.

Presumably little league baseball has a different purpose and therefore
has modified rules. Behavior appropriate to major league competition
would often be considered out of place in this context. For example, the
ideal of making the game an enjoyable experience and giving everyone a
chance to play is not that of a manager hoping to win the pennant. On the
other hand, playing the best nine boys for the total game would be un-
forgivable behavior on the part of a little league coach.

Another example from the larger social scene might be useful here.
Much has been said about the quality of television programs presented in
this country. Critics claim that the producers, writers, and sponsors have
collaborated to reach the lowest common denominator of intellect and interest in order to achieve the largest audience possible. The large audience
is seen as desirable because it allows the sponsor a larger group of potential buyers for the particular product in question. Some writers have com-
plained that their scripts have been altered because it was felt that the presentation would in one way or another fail to maximize sales. To the extent
that these charges are true (and that is *not* the issue here), the behavior of
the sponsor is perfectly reasonable. If the principle is one of maximizing

[1]Alexander Meiklejohn, *Education between Two Worlds* (New York: Harper &
Row, Publishers, Incorporated, 1942), p. 278.

profit these decisions are understandable. To criticize the sponsor's decisions is to do one of two things: (1) To criticize profit as a legitimate principle for ordering activities, or (2) to criticize the sponsor's judgment concerning the fact that a particular program will or will not maximize that profit.

A writer may feel that a script should be judged solely upon certain aesthetic qualities, on the significance of its message, or on its dramatic appeal. In that case, his behavior is principled or ordered by that particular conception of service. Many times both sponsor and writer could agree that a particular show was a "good" one, *but for quite different reasons.* If, however, the writer argues that a script should stand as written because it will either help or not hurt sales his behavior is then principled in the same manner as that of the sponsor. This becomes a tacit acceptance of the profit motive as an ordering principle.

What is most useful and most interesting is the fact that once one finds the ordering principle one finds an explanation for much of the behavior of those associated with the activity—be it baseball, business, or education. In this sense such behavior is reasonable to the extent that it is consistent with its intent or purpose. It is important to note the fact that because a set of behaviors is reasonable or understandable is no reason to say that such behavior is good. We might wish to question the goals toward which they were directed.

This is the root question—what shall order our behavior? The two different teacher preparation patterns discussed in the introduction to this text are ordered by different concepts of education. Those who believe that education should meet the demands of the community find their ordering principle in the community, whatever its demands might be. Teacher training has tended to follow this route, regarding "service" to be giving the community whatever it wanted.

Those who question this principle assume the possibility of unrealistic or unethical demands coming from the community and must assume that there is some standard external to the wishes of the community that must reign. Consequently, they are involved in a search for an ordering principle around which community activities can be organized. This behavior is professional and is the route to and the root of what we call teacher education. This is the crucial ethical distinction between an apprentice and professional preparation program.

Many people think that a "practical" education teaches one how to do something. This is, in a sense, practical. The highest form of practicality rests, however, in deciding whether a certain thing is worth doing and what principle shall order that judgment. This is the distinction between "teacher training" and "teacher education" in another form.

Chapters 3 and 4 are designed to introduce some of the concepts of service that could order one's behavior. Chapter 4 focuses particularly on this problem in the context of a rapidly changing society. Two fundamental questions should guide one's reading of these chapters: (1) What concepts of service are being offered? and (2) How is each concept defended?

CHAPTER 3

The Continuing Quarrel

Criticisms of education are legion. Such discontent is generally directed toward the method and content of schooling. A variety of spokesmen encourage the inclusion of many different experiences in the school program. These suggestions range from driver education to sex education. Each of these pressures for change constitutes an implicit recommendation for the schools. However, before any appropriate discussion of such matters can be undertaken there is the need to resolve a conflict of an even more basic nature; that is, the question of purpose.

There are those who suggest that the ends of education are agreed upon. Such a point of view leads to the claim that there is a need to get on to a consideration of content and methods or the means essential to the attainment of these purposes. The problem with such a suggestion is that it does not go beyond the level of "nominal" agreement on which it precariously rests. There is little question that many would endorse a goal such as "developing social, civic, and economic competence." The difficulty arises when one attempts to find out what is really meant by such a term. We offer this as a warning to the reading of the following selections because there might well be a tendency to think that the four authors are talking about the same goal. They are, for example, all in favor of education. Hopefully, a closer examination will disclose the opposing focuses of their positions.

Boyd Bode has stated that it gives him little comfort to be told that he is on the way and moving fast *unless* he knows and agrees with the goal to be realized. Many discussions in education are at the level of movement and speed rather than purpose. The attempt is made to win people to programs whether they be matters of method, curriculum, text, and so forth, without making explicit the ends that are sought. It is possible that people endorse the same programs, but that they do so for entirely different reasons. Such a programmatic agreement again demonstrates the unexamined nature of the question as to what is the purpose of the school.

Recognition of these two types of agreement should provide a more adequate basis for exploring the increasing amount of criticism concerning our schools. Have people assumed that we have "real" agreement on the purpose of the school? Have others bypassed the question in their quest for action and accepted a programmatic agreement? Whatever the case, there remains the fact that each criticism leveled at our schools at least implicitly questions what the school is proposing to do. Each stands as a recommendation for a change of direction.

Any attempt to evaluate the worth of a criticism rests upon the understanding of the purpose to be accomplished. Attacks aimed at our schools for failing to keep up with the Russians scientifically, for being too "progressive," or for lacking a discipline orientation can only be profitably discussed if one has some clear-cut conception of what the school is supposed to do.

A most vital aspect of this concern over purpose resides in the manner of determining the most desirable purpose. Robert M. Hutchins suggests that "the purpose of education is to improve men." Along with his explanation of this end he offers liberal education as the most valid program for its realization. William K. Frankena examines an often voiced end of education when he looks at moral and spiritual values. As he clarifies the meaning of this purpose he offers a program designed to cope with the problems associated with religion in the schools. John L. Childs points out the deliberate or purposeful nature of formal schooling. Each statement of purposes, according to Childs, is an indication of a certain group's "conception of basic life interest and meanings." Sidney Hook discusses the nature and the place of liberal and vocational education. In so doing he too is providing a recommendation as to the ends or purposes of education. As the readings demonstrate, there are numerous contenders. Are all of equal worth? Should the professional educator endorse any and all that he might encounter? Are there some that are more becoming to the acts of a professional? Such a line of questioning readily transfers us to the other "root" question found in our text, that is, the question of authority. At this point we will delay the authority question and emphasize the consideration of what is service?

Some would argue that service is providing the people with what they want. Such a conception sees a professional as one skilled in the means of accomplishment but having no particular advantage in deciding on the appropriate ends to be accomplished. This suggests that one could be expected to accomplish certain goals in education in one community that are totally in opposition to expectations in other areas. Do you serve people or society by providing them with whatever they want? Is there any responsibility to provide direction and leadership in regard to determination of the purposes of the school?

There must be a very clear specification of the purpose of the school in order to answer Spencer's question, "What knowledge is of most worth?" Whatever conception of service or purpose is determined, there is no way of avoiding this question. The readings that follow offer suggestions either as criticisms with implicit suggestions or as direct recommendations. *The reader should note that while the approaches differ, each author is raising a question about purpose.* While our concern at this point is to examine the nature of purpose it would be useful for the reader to keep in mind the related concern of a later section, that is, what justifies that particular purpose or conception of service? Only through careful and thoughtful examination of alternatives can the teacher or prospective teacher hope to play a useful part in the current and seemingly continuous debate in education.

The readings in this section also make reference to the problem of determining purposes in an era of change in society. This particular problem will be examined in the next chapter.

EDUCATION FOR THE IMPROVEMENT OF MAN

In the following selection Robert Maynard Hutchins, an outstanding proponent of the liberal tradition in education, provides a goal for educators that would undoubtedly gain the acceptance of the multitudes. He claims that the purpose of education is to improve men. As other writers in this section are reviewed, the reader can profit from a consideration as to whether they too would endorse such a goal. The recognition that they would immediately brings us to a consideration of the relationship between the means and the ends in education. How is the teacher to select the content for the curriculum? What textbooks should be utilized in mastering that content? What pedagogical devices are essential to successful presentation of the material? These questions are concerned with the means necessary for the attainment of specific ends. They cannot be answered satisfactorily unless there is a clear understanding of the end or ends to be obtained. There is a need to clarify the meanings attached to that goal. Through such a clarification process men can determine whether their directions are identical, as the words used to describe them would suggest.

Hutchins represents a conservative force in educational circles seeking to improve men through examination of those aspects of our tradition that emphasize the intellectual and rational growth of man. The course of study he recommends, labeled as "liberal" education, consists of the great works of our heritage. Implicit in his position are assumptions about the nature of man and the "elements of our common nature." These assumptions center on man as a rational animal and thus tend to render schemes of specific vocational education "miseducative." Such vocational endeavors are judged to be poor preparation for life. Such a position stands as a criticism of much current practice in American education. Not only are modern concerns for vocational education challenged, but so-called "progressive" methods and subject matter are contemptuously regarded by this conservative element.

Whether acceptable or not to the reader as a valid position the article serves as a useful introduction to the controversy over purpose. It represents a strong force that is not numerically large, but nevertheless potent as a result of its able spokesman, its popularity among the socio-economically powerful, and its prominent part in our historical development. Are the results achieved through liberal education desirable and available for the large numbers to be educated in a democratic society?

--------◄◆►--------

THE CONFLICT IN EDUCATION IN A DEMOCRATIC SOCIETY*

The obvious failures of the doctrines of adaptation, immediate needs, social reform, and of the doctrine that we need no doctrine at all may suggest to us that we require a better definition of education. Let us concede that every society must have some system that attempts to adapt the young to their social and political environment. If the society is bad, in the sense, for example, in which the Nazi state was bad, the system will aim at the same bad ends. To the extent that it makes men bad in order that they may be tractable subjects of a bad state, the system may help to achieve the social ideals of the society. It may be what the society wants; it may even be what the society needs, if it is to perpetuate its form and accomplish its aims. In pragmatic terms, in terms of success in the society, it may be a "good" system.

But it seems to me clearer to say that, though it may be a system of

*From pp. 67–85, 88–90, 91–92, 92–93 *The Conflict in Education in a Democratic Society* by Robert M. Hutchins. Copyright 1953 by Harper & Row, Publishers, Incorporated. Reprinted by permission of the publishers. Dr. Hutchins is currently the President of the Center for the Study of Democratic Institutions and was formerly the President of the University of Chicago. He is a noted author and a firm proponent of "liberal" education.

training, or instruction, or adaptation, or meeting immediate needs, it is not a system of education. It seems clearer to say that the purpose of education is to improve men. Any system that tries to make them bad is not education, but something else. If, for example, democracy is the best form of society, a system that adapts the young to it will be an educational system. If despotism is a bad form of society, a system that adapts the young to it will not be an educational system, and the better it succeeds in adapting them the less educational it will be.

Every man has a function as a man. The function of a citizen or a subject may vary from society to society, and the system of training, or adaptation, or instruction, or meeting immediate needs may vary with it. But the function of a man as man is the same in every age and in every society, since it results from his nature as a man. The aim of an educational system is the same in every age and in every society where such a system can exist: it is to improve man as man.

If we are going to talk about improving men and societies, we have to believe that there is some difference between good and bad. This difference must not be, as the positivists think it is, merely conventional. We cannot tell this difference by any examination of the effectiveness of a given program as the pragmatists propose; the time required to estimate these effects is usually too long and the complexity of society is always too great for us to say that the consequences of a given program are altogether clear. We cannot discover the difference between good and bad by going to the laboratory, for men and societies are not laboratory animals. If we believe that there is no truth, there is no knowledge, and there are no values except those which are validated by laboratory experiment, we cannot talk about the improvement of men and societies, for we can have no standard of judging anything that takes place among men or in societies.

Society is to be improved, not by forcing a program of social reform down its throat, through the schools or otherwise, but by the improvement of the individuals who compose it. As Plato said, "Governments reflect human nature. States are not made out of stone or wood, but out of the characters of their citizens: these turn the scale and draw everything after them." The individual is the heart of society.

To talk about making men better we must have some idea of what men are, because if we have none, we can have no idea of what is good or bad for them. If men are brutes like other animals, then there is no reason why they should not be treated like brutes by anybody who can gain power over them. And there is no reason why they should not be trained as brutes are trained. A sound philosophy in general suggests that men are rational, moral, and spiritual beings and that the improvement of men means the fullest development of their rational, moral, and spiritual powers. All men have these powers, and all men should develop them to the fullest extent.

Man is by nature free, and he is by nature social. To use his freedom rightly he needs discipline. To live in society he needs the moral virtues. Good moral and intellectual habits are required for the fullest development of the nature of man.

To develop fully as a social, political animal man needs participation in his own government. A benevolent despotism will not do. You cannot expect the slave to show the virtues of the free man unless you first set him free. Only democracy, in which all men rule and are ruled in turn for the good life of the whole community, can be an absolutely good form of government.

The community rests on the social nature of men. It requires communication among its members. They do not have to agree with one another; but they must be able to understand one another. And their philosophy in general must supply them with a common purpose and a common concept of man and society adequate to hold the community together. Civilization is the deliberate pursuit of a common ideal. The good society is not just a society we happen to like or to be used to. It is a community of good men.

Education deals with the development of the intellectual powers of men. Their moral and spiritual powers are the sphere of the family and the church. All three agencies must work in harmony; for, though a man has three aspects, he is still one man. But the schools cannot take over the role of the family and the church without promoting the atrophy of those institutions and failing in the task that is proper to the schools.

We cannot talk about the intellectual powers of men, though we can talk about training them, or amusing them, or adapting them, and meeting their immediate needs, unless our philosophy in general tells us that there is knowledge and that there is a difference between true and false. We must believe, too, that there are other means of obtaining knowledge than scientific experimentation. If knowledge can be sought only in the laboratory, many fields in which we thought we had knowledge will offer us nothing but opinion or superstition, and we shall be forced to conclude that we cannot know anything about the most important aspects of man and society. If we are to set about developing the intellectual powers of men through having them acquire knowledge of the most important subjects, we have to begin with the proposition that experimentation and empirical data will be of only limited use to us, contrary to the convictions of many American social scientists, and that philosophy, history, literature, and art give us knowledge, and significant knowledge, on the most significant issues.

If the object of education is the improvement of men, then any system of education that is without values is a contradiction in terms. A system that seeks bad values is bad. A system that denies the existence of values denies the possibility of education. Relativism, scientism, skepticism, and anti-intellectualism, the four horsemen of the philosophical apocalypse, have produced that chaos in education which will end in the disintegration of the West.

The prime object of education is to know what is good for man. It is to know the goods in their order. There is a hierarchy of values. The task of education is to help us understand it, establish it, and live by it. This Aristotle had in mind when he said: "It is not the possessions but the desires of men that must be equalized, and this is impossible unless they have a sufficient education according to the nature of things."

Such an education is far removed from the triviality of that produced by the doctrines of adaptation, of immediate needs, of social reform, or of the doctrine of no doctrine at all. Such an education will not adapt the young to a bad environment, but it will encourage them to make it good. It will not overlook immediate needs, but it will place these needs in their proper relationship to more distant, less tangible, and more important goods. It will be the only effective means of reforming society.

This is the education appropriate to free men. It is liberal education. If all men are to be free, all men must have this education. It makes no difference how they are to earn their living or what their special interests or aptitudes may be. They can learn to make a living, and they can develop their special interests and aptitudes, after they have laid the foundation of free and responsible manhood through liberal education. It will not do to say that they are incapable of such education. This claim is made by those who are too indolent or unconvinced to make the effort to give such education to the masses.

Nor will it do to say that there is not enough time to give everybody a liberal education before he becomes a specialist. In America, at least, the waste and frivolity of the educational system are so great that it would be possible through getting rid of them to give every citizen a liberal education and make him a qualified specialist, too, in less time than is now consumed in turning out uneducated specialists.

A liberal education aims to develop the powers of understanding and judgment. It is impossible that too many people can be educated in this sense, because there cannot be too many people with understanding and judgment. We hear a great deal today about the dangers that will come upon us through the frustration of educated people who have got educated in the expectation that education will get them a better job, and who then fail to get it. But surely this depends on the representations that are made to the young about what education is. If we allow them to believe that education will get them better jobs and encourage them to get educated with this end in view, they are entitled to a sense of frustration if, when they have got the education, they do not get the jobs. But, if we say that they should be educated in order to be men, and that everybody, whether he is a ditch-digger or a bank president, should have this education because he is a man, then the ditch-digger may still feel frustrated, but not because of his education.

Nor is it possible for a person to have too much liberal education, because it is impossible to have too much understanding and judgment. But it is possible to undertake too much in the name of liberal education in youth. The object of liberal education in youth is not to teach the young all they will ever need to know. It is to give them the habits, ideas, and techniques that they need to continue to educate themselves. Thus the object of formal institutional liberal education in youth is to prepare the young to educate themselves throughout their lives.

I would remind you of the impossibility of learning to understand and judge many of the most important things in youth. The judgment and understanding of practical affairs can amount to little in the absence of experience with practical affairs. Subjects that cannot be understood without experience should not be taught to those who are without experience. Or, if these subjects are taught to those who are without experience, it should be clear that these subjects can be taught only by way of introduction and that their value to the student depends on his continuing to study them as he acquires experience. The tragedy in America is that economics, ethics, politics, history, and literature are studied in youth, and seldom studied again. Therefore the graduates of American universities seldom understand them.

This pedagogical principle, that subjects requiring experience can be learned only by the experienced, leads to the conclusion that the most important branch of education is the education of adults. We sometimes seem to think of education as something like the mumps, measles, whooping-cough, or chicken-pox. If a person has had education in childhood, he need not, in fact he cannot, have it again. But the pedagogical principle that the most important things can be learned only in mature life is supported by a sound philosophy in general. Men are rational animals. They achieve their terrestrial felicity by the use of reason. And this means that they have to use it for their entire lives. To say that they should learn only in childhood would mean that they were human only in childhood.

And it would mean that they were unfit to be citizens of a republic.[1] A republic, a true *res publica*, can maintain justice, peace, freedom, and order only by the exercise of intelligence. When we speak of the consent of the governed, we mean, since men are not angels who seek the truth intuitively and do not have to learn it, that every act of assent on the part of the governed is a product of learning. A republic is really a common

---

[1] I owe this discussion to the suggestions of Scott Buchanan.

educational life in process. So Montesquieu said that, whereas the principle of a monarchy was honor, and the principle of a tyranny was fear, the principle of a republic was education.

Hence the ideal republic is the republic of learning. It is the utopia by which all actual political republics are measured. The goal toward which we started with the Athenians twenty-five centuries ago is an unlimited republic of learning and a world-wide political republic mutually supporting each other.

All men are capable of learning. Learning does not stop as long as a man lives, unless his learning power atrophies because he does not use it. Political freedom cannot endure unless it is accompanied by provision for the unlimited acquisition of knowledge. Truth is not long retained in human affairs without continual learning and relearning. Peace is unlikely unless there are continuous, unlimited opportunities for learning and unless men continuously avail themselves of them. The world of law and justice for which we yearn, the world-wide political republic, cannot be realized without the world-wide republic of learning. The civilization we seek will be achieved when all men are citizens of the world republic of law and justice and of the republic of learning all their lives long.

LIBERAL EDUCATION

As Aristotle remarked, politics is the architectonic science. This is one way of saying that the political philosophy accepted by a state will determine the kind of education it has. It is also a way of saying that the practical political situation in which a state finds itself has an overwhelming effect on its educational system. Plato arrived at his curriculum by asking what made a good man and a good soldier. A discipline was included only if it met both requirements. If, as it is sometimes argued, it is the destiny of the West to go to war with the East, then the educational system of the West will have to be designed with this end in view. Education is a secondary subject.

One difficulty is that we cannot answer any educational question of importance by appealing to the test of experience. The countries of the West appear determined to become industrial, scientific, and democratic. There have never been countries that were industrial, democratic, and scientific before. Entirely apart, therefore, from the usual difficulty of proving anything from history, and entirely apart from the difficulty of showing that any social experiment has succeeded or failed, which results from the inordinate number of variables that is always present, the experience of earlier societies would be of little use to us in solving the present problems of education. Even if we knew what their experience showed, it would be almost irrelevant now.

And yet there has always been an education that has been regarded as the best for the best. It has been regarded as the education for those who were to rule the state and for those who had leisure. Unless experimental science has made all the difference, it would seem that some light might be obtained by asking whether and to what degree the education that has always been regarded as the best for the best is still good for them or for anybody else.

How much difference can experimental science make? If it is true that the truth can be discovered only in the laboratory, then we can know very little indeed about education; for we cannot know even whether the statement is true that truth can be discovered only in the laboratory. The truth of that statement cannot be and has not been proved in the laboratory. The questions that science can answer are questions of fact about the physical world. They deal with the material conditions of existence. What is called social science cannot tell us what kind of society we ought to aim at. It is doubtful whether it can even tell us what the consequences of a given social policy will be. The reason, again, is the enormous number of variables that enter into any social situation. I do not deprecate the efforts of social scientists to understand society. I would merely indicate the limits of their disciplines. The great successes of physical science should not blind us to its limitations, either. We can learn from science and technology how to build a bridge. We may, perhaps, learn from social science what some of the social, political, and economic consequences of building the bridge will be. But whether those consequences are good or bad is not a question in either physical or social science.

And so it is of all the most important questions of human existence. What is a good life? What is a good society? What is the nature and destiny of man? These questions and others like them are not susceptible of scientific investigation. On some aspects of them science can shed some light, and such light should be welcomed. But these questions do not yield to scientific inquiry. Nor do they become nonsense, as the logical positivists would have us believe, because they are not scientific.

Here we see again that education is a secondary subject, depending in this case upon philosophy. If there is no knowledge except scientific knowledge, if one object of education is to communicate knowledge, then the object cannot be achieved except through education in science. Unfortunately, the question whether there is knowledge other than scientific knowledge is one that science can never answer. It is a philosophical question.

If the rise of experimental science does not change the educational situation beyond adding new and most important branches of knowledge, does the rise of industry and democracy change it? It certainly does change it in very significant respects. But does it change it in the respect in which we are now interested, in respect to content? Let us look at the education that has been regarded as the best for the best and ask ourselves whether this is still the education that states the ideal, to what extent it is the best today, and to what extent it may be usefully offered to those who were not regarded as the best when this education was developed.

In the West this education has gone by the name of liberal education. It has consisted of the liberal arts, the arts of reading, writing, listening, speaking, and figuring, and of the intellectual and artistic tradition that we inherit. It was designed for those who were to rule the commonwealth, and for those who had leisure. It has always been thought that those who could profit by it were a small fraction of the population. It has never been denied, as far as I know, that it was the best education for the best. The question I wish to raise is first, whether it actually was the best education, and second whether it is so today, and for whom.

For reasons I have already given, I cannot prove that this education was the best. I cannot prove it in any scientific way. It is dangerous to try to prove it by the quality of the men it produced. Who knows that it produced the men? So it is dangerous for a university president to boast about his distinguished alumni. If he is entitled to credit for them, he must also take the responsibility for those who go to the penitentiary. I can appeal to the common opinion of mankind; but mankind could have been wrong. I think it enough to show that this education was characteristically human and that it was characteristically western. When I say that it was characteristically human, I am saying once more that education is a dependent subject; for what I mean is, of course, that liberal education conformed to an idea of man that I regard as sound. This is the conception of man as a rational animal, an animal who seeks and attains his highest felicity through the exercise and perfection of his reason. It is impossible to avoid being a liberal artist; for a man cannot choose whether he will be human or not. He can make the choice only between being a good liberal artist or a poor one.

Liberal education was characteristically western, because it assumed that everything was to be discussed. Liberal education aimed at the continuation of the dialogue that was the heart of western civilization. Western civilization is the civilization of the dialogue. It is the civilization of the Logos. Liberal education made the student a participant in the Great Conversation that began with the dawn of history and continues at the present day. Great as other civilizations have been in other respects, no other civilization has been as great as this one in this respect.

Such an education can be called a good education, relative to the conditions under which it developed and flourished. But can it be called nothing more than that? Must we say that industrialism and democracy mean that some other education should now supplant it? We know that this education has already been supplanted in the United States.

By the end of the nineteenth century liberal education in the United States was largely in the hands of the teachers of Greek and Latin. A liberal education was a classical education. The teachers of the classics devoted themselves for the most part to instruction in the languages. It was possible to spend years in the study of the Greek and Latin writers without discovering that they had any ideas. The teachers of Greek and Latin were not interested in ideas. They were drillmasters. The languages in which they gave instruction were required for graduation from all respectable colleges, from all preparatory schools, and even from some public high schools.

In the first twenty-five years of this century the flood overwhelmed the high schools and colleges of the United States. Neither the students nor their parents were prepared to believe that what the classical drillmasters were doing was of any importance. And it must be admitted that the students and their parents were largely right. The classical drillmasters did not reform. They did not insist upon the importance of the classical heritage to modern western man. They were, as I have said, not much interested in that. Instead they insisted that their courses continue to be required. By 1925 the flood swept them away. It was characteristic that in the final battle at Yale, at which I was present, the issue was not about liberal education, or about the importance of the classical heritage, but only about whether one year of Latin should be required for the degree of Bachelor of Arts.

The Twentieth Century was right about the classical drillmasters. It was wrong about liberal education. And it was certainly wrong about what it substituted for liberal education. It substituted for it an infinite, incoherent proliferation of courses largely vocational in aim.

Liberal education consists of training in the liberal arts and of understanding the leading ideas that have animated mankind. It aims to help the human being learn to think for himself, to develop his highest human powers. As I have said, it has never been denied that this education was the best for the best. It must still be the best for the best unless modern times, industry, science, and democracy have made it irrelevant. The social, political, and economic changes that have occurred have not required that liberal education be abandoned. How could they? It is still necessary to try to be human; in fact it is more necessary, as well as more difficult, than ever.

Liberal education was the education of rulers. It was the education of those who had leisure. Democracy and industry, far from making liberal education irrelevant, make it indispensable and possible for all the people. Democracy makes every man a ruler, for the heart of democracy is universal suffrage. If liberal education is the education that rulers ought to have, and this I say has never been denied, then every ruler, that is every citizen, should have a liberal education. If industry is to give everybody leisure, and if leisure, as history suggests, tends to be degrading and dangerous unless it is intelligently used, then everybody should have the education that fits him to use his leisure intelligently, that is, liberal education. If leisure makes liberal education possible, and if industry is to give everybody leisure, then industry makes liberal education possible for everybody.

In most countries, even those in which the education of adults is most highly developed, such education is thought of as compensatory: it makes up for the deficiencies in the formal schooling of the individual. Where formal schooling is vocational, adult education is vocational, too. Where schooling is liberal, as it has largely been in the United Kingdom and Scandinavia, adult education is liberal; for it is thought unjust and undesirable that those who because of the accidents of youth could not complete the formal schooling that the average citizen obtained in childhood and youth should remain without it all their lives.

But this surely is too limited a view of the education of adults. That education should be liberal, and it should be interminable. We are led to this conclusion by looking at the nature of man and the nature of knowledge. The man who stops learning is as good as dead, and the conditions of modern industrial society, which put little strain on a man's intelligence in the conduct of his work, place a premium on the premature cessation of thought. It is impossible to say that a man can develop his highest powers once and for all in youth. He has to keep on using them. I am not suggesting that he must go to school all his life. But I am proposing that he should learn all his life; and I think he will find that informal association with others who have the same purpose in view will help him and them to achieve it. . . .

When I urge liberal education for all, I am not suggesting that all the people must become great philosophers, historians, scientists, or artists. I am saying that they should know how to read, write, and figure and that they should understand the great philosophers, historians, scientists, and artists. This does not seem to me an unattainable goal. If it is, unless some better kind of liberal education can be invented than the one that I have described, we shall be forced to abandon universal suffrage; for I do not believe that men can solve the problems raised by their own aggregation unless they can learn to think for themselves about the fundamental issues of human life and organized society. If anybody knows a better way of helping them learn to think for themselves about these issues, I hope he will present it. It seems to me that we must agree at least on this: the alternatives are democracy, with liberal education for all, and aristocracy, with liberal education for the few. If we choose the latter alternative, as Plato did, we may ignore, as Plato did, the education of the masses. All the educational system has to do with them is to find some innocuous way in which they can put in their time until we are ready to have them go to work.

Since education in the West is built very largely on the doctrine of individual differences, so that the study of the individual child and his individual interests is supposed to be the principal preoccupation of his teachers from his earliest days, and premature and excessive specialization is a common characteristic of both the American college and the British public school, it will be argued that a program of liberal education for all ignores the most important thing about men, and that is that they are different. I do not ingore it; I deny it. I do not deny the fact of individual differences; I deny that it is the most important fact about men or the one on which an educational system should be erected.

Men are different. They are also the same. And at least in the present state of civilization the respects in which they are the same are more important than those in which they are different. Politics, the architectonic science, teaches us that we are remorselessly headed toward the unification of the world. The only question is whether that unification will be achieved by conquest or consent. The most pressing task of men everywhere is to see to it that this consummation is achieved by consent. And this can be done only by the unremitting effort to move toward world community and world organization. The liberal arts are the arts of communication. The great productions of the human mind are the common heritage of all mankind. They supply the framework through which we understand one another and without which all factual data and area studies and exchanges of persons among countries are trivial and futile. They are the voices in the Great Conversation that constitutes the civilization of the dialogue.

Now, if ever, we need an education that is designed to bring out our common humanity rather than to indulge our individuality. Our individual differences mean that our individual development must vary. If we all struggle to make the most of our individual human powers, the results will be different, because our powers differ. But the difference is one of degree, and not of kind. In a modern, industrial, scientific democracy every man has the responsibility of a ruler and every man has the leisure to make the most of himself. What the modern, industrial, scientific democracy requires is wisdom. The aim of liberal education is wisdom. Every man has the duty and every man must have the chance to become as wise as he can. . . .

Since education is a secondary, dependent subject, as ideas change, the idea of education changes with them. No man can mourn the death of many ancient educational prejudices. The notion one encounters in the East that the aim of education is to raise the educated beyond the contamination of manual labor, or labor of any kind, is going and must go if the peoples of Asia are to struggle upward to the point where the masses can live human lives. It should not be supplanted by the notion that the aim of education is to learn a trade and get rich on the American plan.

Nor should the West deceive itself into thinking that the industrialization of the world and an increase in its productive capacity can alone set us on the path to peace. The desire for material goods is insatiable. If our educational effort is directed chiefly to increasing the supply of material goods, we shall awaken to discover that we do not know what to do with them. . . . Civilization is the deliberate pursuit of a common ideal. Education is the deliberate attempt to form men in terms of an ideal. A materialistic civilization cannot last. An education that attempts to form men in terms of a materialistic ideal cannot save them or their civilization.

The strand in the civilization of the West that has saved it from materialism and its consequences is the tradition of free inquiry. It is this that has made it possible to say that western civilization is the civilization of the Logos. Liberal education, up to the end of the twentieth century, carried forward the Great Conversation. The collapse of liberal education in the United States has taken us into the doctrines of immediate needs and adjustment to the environment, and has ended in the concept of the educational system as a gigantic play-pen in which the young are to amuse themselves until we are ready to have them do something serious. This concept deprives free inquiry of its justification, threatens academic freedom, and puts the educational system at the mercy of any individual or organization that confuses patriotism with conformity.

FOR FURTHER THOUGHT

1. Hutchins criticizes those proposed systems that emphasize adaptation, immediate needs, or social reform. *What is it about them that would be contrary to his established goals of education? Is it because Hutchins feels that education should not meet immediate needs or reform society that he opposes these alternative systems? Does this suggest that the only difference between Hutchins and others is the means of accomplishing their purposes, or does the similar wording of ends promote merely a nominal agreement?*
2. For Hutchins the only experiences worthy of the name "education" are liberal studies. Such activities must be covered by all and must precede any narrow specialist training. *What does Hutchins mean by liberal education? Is such a program feasible given the vast differences in pupils?*
3. Hutchins asserts the need for a community to possess a common purpose and a common concept of men and society. *Does such a unity exist*

*in our society either with regard to purpose or with regard to the nature
of man and society? If so, what is it? If not, does its nonexistence and
our position in the world refute Hutchins' claims?*
4. Inherent in Hutchins' philosophy is a certain outlook on truth, knowledge, and value. *Summarize briefly that position. Why is he opposed to
relativism, scientism, skepticism, and anti-intellectualism? If any or all of
the latter were prominent considerations in our society would their
prominence make Hutchins' position less tenable?*

EDUCATION FOR THE GOOD LIFE

The selection by W. K. Frankena offers a different approach to a basic
and timeless question in education. It examines possible ends of education,
such as the moral life and the good life, and it explores the worth of
religious content as a means purported to be essential to the attainment of
these goals. The apparently neutral stance taken by Frankena brings him
into conflict with a bevy of religious groups and authorities. An understanding of the basis of this conflict can be derived from a contrasting
statement such as the following from Pope Pius XI: "The true Christian
product of Christian education, is the supernatural man who thinks,
judges, and acts constantly and consistently in accordance with right reason illumined by the supernatural light of the example and teachings of
Christ." The Catholics are not the only religious group to challenge
Frankena's position. Regardless of the source of the challenge, there is the
claim that there is a need for a close relationship of church and school, and
an inclusion of religious content in the curriculum of the schools. Frankena
attempts to build an argument designed to disarm the proponents of such
a position. He does not, however, refute the basic assumptions about man
and about knowledge central to the position held by proponents of religion in the schools.

Essential to an understanding of the debate over the schools and religion
is the recognition that different assumptions underly each stance. The
differences on (a) the nature of man and (b) the methods of establishing
or ascertaining truth are at the core of the controversy. Any attempt to
resolve differences without exploring these areas will achieve nothing more
lasting or pervasive than programmatic agreement.

No position article is included to represent the opponents to Frankena.
Such can be readily found. From the article at hand we feel the reader can
develop an understanding of the essential points of conflict in the many
manifestations of the church-state controversy. Frankena's ideas of the
good life as opposed to the moral life provide useful distinctions for those
with similar assumptions. To the advocate of religion in the schools his

distinctions probably demonstrate that Frankena understands neither the good nor the moral life. When such a level of disagreement is reached, the centrality of purpose to curriculum or to other instrumental questions is seen. The reader is left with the quest set by Alexander Meiklejohn when he asked, "What is our goal, and what is its source of authority over us?"

PUBLIC EDUCATION
AND THE GOOD LIFE*

This paper is an attempt to say something about the subject which usually goes under the title of "moral and spiritual values in the public schools" and sometimes under the clearer but still less lovely label "character education in state-supported institutions." More specifically, it will address itself to one of the problems about public education for the good life, namely the problem which is raised by the doctrine of the separation of church and state. It seems to me that this is one of the topics in the philosophy of education on which a philosopher, and in particular a moral philosopher, may be able to shed some light.

To get the problem stated let us assume, as Plato and Aristotle do, that the end of the state and of education is the good life of the members of society. As C. M. Bowra writes, however, "The Greeks distinguished between the good man and the good life."[1] A recent television speaker made the same distinction in saying of someone that "he was too good for his own good." The point is that there are two kinds of good life. One kind of good life is much described in funeral orations, for funeral orators are (or at least used to be) prone to say, and to say it loudest when it is least true, that the deceased person led a good and virtuous life, and that no one surpassed him in benevolence and justice. When we say that a man has led a good life in this sense (and notice, we say "led" not "had" here), we mean that he has led a *morally* good life, a life of honesty and service, a "good and useful" life. But the phrase *a good life* has another meaning also. Dur-

*William K. Frankena, "Public Education and The Good Life," *Harvard Educational Review*, vol. 31, no. 4 (Fall 1961) pp. 413–426. Dr. Frankena, Professor of Philosophy at the University of Michigan, has served as Visiting Professor of Education and Philosophy at Harvard. Among his many publications are *Philosophy of Education, Ethics*, and *Three Historical Philosophies of Education*.

[1]C. H. Bowra, *The Greek Experience* (New York: Harcourt, Brace & World, 1957), p. 85.

ing the war Richard Tregaskis told in his *Guadalcanal Diary* of being in a
fox-hole watching the descent of a bomb which seemed certain to strike
just where he was crouching. It did not, of course, but in the brief moment
during which Tregaskis expected it to, his past flashed before him, and he
said to himself, "Well, it's been a good life; I would live it again." He did
not mean that he had lived a morally good life. No doubt he had, but for
him to say so would have been out of place. What he meant was that on the
whole his life had been an enjoyable or happy one, which he would choose
again if given a chance. It was good in the way Browning is lyrical about in
the lines:

> How good is man's life, the mere living! how fit to employ
> All the heart and the soul and the senses for ever in joy!

There is, then, the good life in the sense of the morally good or virtuous
life, and the good life in the sense of the happy or satisfying life. For convenience of reference in the rest of the paper, I shall call the former the
moral life and the latter the *good* life. Now, when I said above that the end
of education is the good life, I meant that education must promote both
the good life in this narrower sense and the moral life, or in more traditional terms, both the happy and the virtuous life. It must do what it can to
make men good, and it must do what it can to make their lives so satisfactory that they would be willing to live them again in preference to others
they might be offered.

Perhaps no one will dispute the view that public education, formal or informal, if it exists at all, must be concerned to promote the good life. Not
all would grant, however, that the public schools may properly seek to advance the moral life, though they give different reasons for their opinion.
Nevertheless, I shall assume here that public education is and should be
concerned to promote morality as well as happiness. But, while formal
public education, on this assumption, has the same ends as education in
general, it is in a special position. Just because it is supported by the state,
it has a limitation which private education does not have. This limitation is
not just a matter of constitutional law or of the intentions of our founding
fathers, as many seem to think; it is a matter of philosophical principle
which underlies, or at any rate should underlie, both the constitution and
the thinking of our founders. The limitation, as I understand it, is that, in
the interests of freedom of conscience, thought, and worship, the public
schools, being organs of the state, cannot teach religion. Like the state itself, they must be neutral with respect to the various churches and
religions; they must be neutral even as between religion and anti-religious
philosophies of life. They can and should teach informative courses *about*
religion—its history, beliefs, institutions, influences, and so forth—but they

may not seek to inculcate or propagate any particular kind of ultimate creed, religious or non-religious. What J. S. Mill says about universities applies to public education as a whole:

> . . . it is not the teacher's business to impose his own judgment, but to inform and discipline that of his students. . . . The proper business of a University is . . . not to tell us from authority what we ought to believe, and make us accept the belief as a duty, but to give us information and training, and help us form our own belief in a manner worthy of intelligent beings. . . .[2]

This neutralist, but not necessarily secularist, conception of the relation of state-supported institutions to religion has been subject to heavy attack during "the current upsurge of religiousness" which the events of our century have brought about. The spokesmen of religion are generally against it, and many public school teachers, themselves religious, are uncomfortable with it. In the rest of this paper, however, I shall take it for granted.[3]

At this point we come face to face with our problem. We have said both that public education should promote the good and the moral life, and that it should be neutral with respect to religion. But, from these two propositions taken together, it follows that public schools and colleges can promote the good life and the moral life only if and insofar as these do not require or rest on religion, that is, on religious belief and observance. We must therefore try to determine whether, how, and to what degree public education can be concerned to advance the good life and morality when they cannot be concerned to advance religious faith and worship. Robert M. Hutchins raises this problem when he says:

> . . . public institutions seem required by the Constitution to be secular. Yet it must be admitted that religion is of the greatest moral importance. . . . Men, simply because they are men, are unlikely to find within themselves the power that can bring the good life and the good state to pass. . . . If a college cannot make its students religious, it cannot, to that extent, make them good.[4]

But his subsequent discussion does not help us very much, because he is concerned with higher education in general, not with public education as

[2]J. S. Mill, *Inaugural Address* (London: Longmans, Green & Co., n.d.), pp. 39–40.
[3]For a statement of my position see "A Point of View for the Future," in *Religion and the State University*, E. A. Walter, ed. (Ann Arbor: University of Michigan Press, 1958), pp. 295–309.
[4]Robert M. Hutchins, *Freedom, Education, and the Fund* (New York: Meridian Books, 1956), pp. 91–92.

such, whether higher or lower. The drift of his thesis that religion is indispensable to the good and the moral life, however, must be noted, for one who accepts this thesis *without qualification* must conclude *either* that our public schools must teach religion, *or* that they cannot promote morality or the good life. Either way, as I see it, the upshot for him is that public education should go out of business. On the other hand, it need not go out of business, if there is any important extent or way in which the good and the moral lives are independent of specifically religious beliefs and experiences.

To deal with this problem we must now try to discern somewhat more clearly and fully just what the public schools, in their programs of education for the good and the moral life, are debarred from doing on the above view of their relation to religion. Let us look first at education for the good life, that is, non-moral education. What is it that the schools might possibly do here? (1) They might teach an individual, on the basis of human experience and reflection, what the ingredients of the good life—the values of human life—are. (2) They might provide him with an experience and an appreciation of some of these values, for example, the enjoyment of music or poetry. (3) They might furnish him with knowledge, which is at once one of the great goods of life and a necessary means to the realization of the others. (4) They might train his intellect, imagination, and sensibility so as to enable him to discover further knowledge, perhaps even to discover new values or forms of satisfaction. (5) They might help him to work out a philosophy of life, which seems to be one of the things human beings need to be happy.

Now we can see what the *public* schools, by the fact that they are debarred from teaching religion, are precluded from doing with respect to the good life. They cannot advocate any specifically religious values, that is, values whose realization is conditioned by religious belief or observance, as necessary for the good life. They cannot provide the student with any first-hand experience of such values, for example, of the values of worship or of "the peace that passeth understanding," though they can through the teaching of art and literature give him an imaginative realization of these values, along with others. Whatever knowledge they may pass on to him, they cannot pass on any of the "truths" of religion, natural or revealed. The fear of the Lord may be the beginning of wisdom, as the author of *Proverbs* asserts, but the public school cannot teach the "wisdom" of which this "fear" is the beginning, though it may and should inform its pupils about the history, beliefs, and institutions of the religions which are inspired by this "fear." As for teaching its pupils a philosophy of life—this it cannot do for the same reason that it cannot teach a religion. As Mill says, all it can do is to give them "information and training" so that they may form their own belief "in a manner worthy of intelligent beings."

Coming to education for the moral life, we find that the case is similar.[5] As non-moral education must teach *values* and provide the knowledge and intellectual training necessary to realize them, so moral education must teach *principles* of conduct, together with the knowledge and intelligence needed to apply them. For we must know what to do, and, as Aristotle pointed out, the process of determining what we should do takes the form of a "practical syllogism." There is (a) the rule, for example, that of keeping promises or of not harming anyone. There is (b) the factual knowledge that one has made a certain promise or that certain actions will cause harm to certain people. And there is (c) the conclusion that one should or should not do a certain deed. To begin with, at least, the principles and the factual knowledge which we use in such practical syllogisms must be taught us by our elders; we may revise or add to them later, but the ability to make such revisions and additions must also be a product of our education.

Here again there are some things that the public educator cannot do. Firstly, there are some principles which he cannot teach, even if they are valid, for example, that we ought to worship God. Such principles depend on the truth of certain corresponding theological beliefs, and so may not be inculcated by the state or its agencies. Secondly, at least in our culture, we normally expect a moral rule to be supported by a reason; recent moral philosophies even go so far as to claim that "morality" means "the intelligent following of rules the point of which is understood."[6] And reasons for a rule may be of two kinds. They may be such as to *justify* the rule, or they may be such as to *motivate* people to act according to it. If a child asks "Why should I keep my promises?" and I answer, "Because people won't like you if you break them," I give a motivating reason; but if I reply, "Because you are taking unfair advantage if you don't keep them," I give a justifying one. So the moral teacher must teach reasons along with his principles; to parody another *Proverb*, with all our getting we must get understanding. *But*, if he is a public school teacher he cannot teach, as a reason for doing anything, whether justifying or motivating, any belief about God or about a hereafter. Such theological justifications and "religious sanctions" he must avoid. Hamlet was taught that the Almighty had set his canon 'gainst self-slaughter, as a reason for not making one's quietus with a bare bodkin, but that was before the day of proper public schools. The proper public school teacher, while he need not (in fact may not) deny the validity of theological reasons, must in his official teaching

---

[5]For a discussion of some general problems of moral education see my "Toward a Philosophy of Moral Education," *Harvard Educational Review*, vol. 28 (1958), pp. 300–313.

[6]R. S. Peters, *The Concept of Motivation* (London: Routledge & Kegan Paul Ltd., 1958), p. 87.

limit himself to more humanistic and this-worldly ones. He may teach the tragedy of the Prince of Denmark, but cannot recommend his reasoning.

Moral education involves more than teaching *principles,* however; it also involves teaching *virtues,* that is, "right habits" or dispositions to act in accordance with moral principles. But just as there are certain widely accepted *values* and *principles,* so there are also certain highly regarded *virtues* which cannot be part of the content of public education, for example, what the ancients called piety or what the Christians call faith and hope (and at least part of what they call love). The public schools may seek to teach St. Thomas' human virtues but not his theological virtues—which indeed cannot be taught at all but only infused by divine operation.

Specifically religious values, principles, and virtues, then, as well as specifically religious reasons and sanctions, are not to be taught, inculcated, or employed in public schools, however concerned they may be to advance the good or the moral life. This may be disturbing to the proponents of religion, but the spokesmen of public education must insist on it, and its practitioners must remember it whenever they are acting in their official capacities. It may be remarked, however, that just as the public educator is debarred from teaching values, principles, or virtues which presuppose the acceptance of religious beliefs, so he is also debarred from teaching any values, principles, or virtues which presuppose the acceptance of anti-religious beliefs, for example such naturalistic ones as those of John Dewey. But it should be added at once that he may try to give his students an *understanding* of both the religious and the naturalistic ways of thinking, feeling, and living through a study of representative poems, paintings, and other works of art, as well as of representative religions and philosophies. He cannot seek to conduct them in either way, but he may and should try to show them what each way is like to one who follows it. In such imaginative realization of opposing ways of life, for which belief is not required but only a "willing suspension of disbelief," lies one of the chief contributions of the study of art and literature.

This seems a good place to speak of the vexed and vexing subject of "spiritual values." Is there a place for such values in the public schools? It is almost like asking if the public schools can be on the side of the angels or against sin? One cannot without qualification say *yes,* but one hesitates to say *no* even qualifiedly. For the phrase *spiritual values* is at once vague and emotionally charged. What does it mean? It is not only the term *spiritual* that is unclear. The word *values* is also used here in a confusing way. It is used not only to stand for what I have called *values* (that is, things which are good), but also for what I have called *principles, virtues,* and even for *beliefs.* Let us for the moment allow it to keep this wide meaning. Then what does *spiritual values* mean? It might mean (and, I am inclined to say, should mean) "specifically religious values." In this sense, as I see it, public education cannot be concerned to promote spiritual values. But *spiritual values* is often used to include also values which are not so specifically religious—namely, aesthetic, moral, and intellectual ones. In this sense of the phrase there definitely is a place for some "spiritual values" in the public school.

In saying, as we have, that certain so-called values, principles, and virtues (namely, religious ones) cannot be part of the concern of public education even though its aim is to promote the good and the moral life, we have been implying that there are still others which do not depend on the acceptance of any religious belief and which may therefore be a part of its concern. Here, however, we run up against the contention, referred to earlier, that religion is indispensable both to the good and to the moral life. If this contention is true without qualification, then, as we saw before, public education must disown the endeavor to advance either the good life or the moral one—in short, must go out of business. We cannot here discuss it as fully as we should for a definitive answer, but we can try to make some clarifications and come at least to some partial or tentative answers.

Like the phrase *spiritual values,* the thesis of the indispensability of religion is very unclear and emotionally charged. Those who maintain it rarely make clear just what they mean by *religion,* just what they mean by *indispensable,* or just what they think religion is indispensable to. Let us begin with a partial clarification of the term *religion.* In discussions of the treatment of religion in state-supported institutions *religion* is sometimes used to mean any kind of ultimate creed, and sometimes to mean only such ultimate creeds as are typified by Judaism, Christianity, or Islam. In the former sense, even atheism and naturalism are religions; in the latter, however, they are anti-religions. I propose that we use *religion* in the latter or narrower sense, and have so been using it. Then the thesis that religion is necessary to the good and the moral life does not mean merely that *some* kind of ultimate commitment is required. This, I think, may be admitted. The thesis means, rather, that a specifically theistic kind of ultimate commitment is required. And, in this sense, it is not obviously true.

It may, of course, be admitted that such a religious commitment *is* required for *some* widely-accepted values, principles, and virtues, namely, the specifically religious ones of which we were speaking earlier. But it cannot simply be taken for granted that these values, principles, and virtues, widely-honored as they may be, are in fact genuine, valid, or well-founded. They may be, but to assert that they are presupposes the truth of the religious beliefs on which they depend, and the truth of these religious beliefs cannot simply be assumed, particularly not in a debate about any public functions. For, if these beliefs are not true, then the religious values, principles, and virtues in question have no sound basis, and need not be taken seriously. Some may still try to argue that they will have a beneficent effect if they are taken as regulative ideals, but others will reply that they are a snare and a delusion, distracting mankind from its proper study. To this debate the state and its schools can hardly be a party. Nor can we be a party to it here.

Even if we grant, however, that such *religious* values, principles and virtues are valid and are an indispensable *part* of the good and the moral life, it may still be that there are *others* to which religion is *not* indispensable. And, if there are important values, rules, and virtues which do not necessarily rest on specifically religious beliefs and observances, then it may well be contended that these are properly a concern of the state and its schools, and that the peculiarly religious ones are more properly the care of the individual, his church, or some other private and voluntary association to which he belongs. It is an old and respected principle that we must distinguish the temporal and the eternal, the natural and the spiritual. The same authority who said, "He who is not with me is against me," also said, "Render unto Caesar the things which are Caesar's, and unto God the things that are God's."

With these general remarks out of the way, we may divide the doctrine of the indispensability of religion into two parts: first, the claim that religion is indispensable to the good life, and, second, the assertion that it is indispensable to the moral life. In connection with the former we at once encounter the historic thesis that the supreme good and the highest happiness consist in the contemplation of, or communion with, God. If this thesis is correct, then a life which knows not God is at best a very incomplete and truncated good; it may be worthless, dust and ashes, a broken cistern that can hold no water; it may even be a snare and a delusion whose apparent values only serve to distract man fatally from his true long run interests. We cannot here try to determine the validity of the thesis; but we may note, that, whether it is true or false, it need be taken seriously only if there is a God, and that, even if true, it does not prove there is a God. I do not mean to question that there is a God. I doubt, however, that his existence can be proved in any publicly available way, and, if this is true, then we certainly cannot take it for granted in such a discussion as the present one. Nor can we take for granted the claim that man's true interests lie, not in any values he can enjoy in this life, but in his finding an assurance that he will know God in another.

The crucial question for our purposes, as was indicated a moment ago, is whether there are any important values or ingredients in the good life which are not dependent on any religious belief. To many people it seems clear that there are such goods as knowledge, artistic creation and appreciation, friendship, love, freedom, sense of achievement, and so forth, which do not have any religious faith as a necessary condition of their attainment or enjoyment. Some may reply that these goods are illusory or even delusive, but to say this presupposes a certain religious conception of the universe and so begs the question. In any case, not all religious thinkers have taken this hard line. It may be that the values mentioned gain an additional dimension if they are woven into a religious life, but it is at any rate plausible to hold that they do or at least may bring a genuine worthwhileness into the life of an unbeliever as well. Even if they do not constitute a good which is self-sufficient in Aristotle's sense, they may still be desirable in themselves.

If this is so, then it is also plausible to maintain that religion is not so indispensable to the good life that only a religious institution can minister to such a life. For then it is possible that there is a part or aspect of the good life for which a neutral institution such as the state may be concerned, even if there is also another part or aspect of it which is beyond the care or competence of such an institution. That is, there may be good things which are Caesar's, as well as good things that are God's. St. Thomas implies as much when he finds a place for natural as well as supernatural happiness.

The question whether religion is necessary to morality is too large to deal with adequately in the space that remains. But perhaps we can accomplish something worthwhile if we make some distinctions. For those who answer the question in the affirmative usually neglect to make these distinctions, and so can be at least partly answered by making them. There are, in fact, several senses in which morality may be and has been said to be dependent on religion. (1) It is often held to be *causally* or *genetically* dependent on religion. This is asserted, for example, by those who argue that our democratic morality is a historical outgrowth of the Christian religion, coming into the world as a result of the advent of this religion. This contention is not unquestionable, but let us grant it for the sake of discussion. It does not follow that our morality is strictly dependent on religion. Even if historically our morality was a product of Christianity, it may still be that our morality could have arisen in some other way. History only happens once, and, as Hume pointed out, one instance does not prove a necessary connection or even a constant conjunction. In any event, even if part of our morality has religious faith as a necessary condition, it does not follow that all of it does.

(2) Morality may also be said to rest on religion in a *psychological* sense. That is, it may be held that the *motivation* to be moral presupposes certain religious or theological beliefs—in short, that morality requires religious sanctions or motivating reasons, as I called them earlier. This is what D. E. Trueblood means when he speaks of "the impotence of ethics" in *The Predicament of Modern Man*, and it seems to be what Hutchins has in mind in the passage quoted above. Now this contention is not in the least plausible if it is meant to say that *no one ever* has *any* motivation to

do what is right which is not the result of some specifically religious conviction on his part. Many people have often been moved to do what is right
by considerations which are not religious. Perhaps all who are moral have
sometimes been moved by such considerations as a desire for peace or for a
stable social order, even if St. Augustine talks in one place as if he would
have been an Epicurean of the worst sort if he had not believed in God
and a hereafter. For some moral persons religious considerations seem
never to play a part at all. Trueblood himself allows that atheists like
Dewey are often kind and good. So the contention must be modified to say
either (a) that *some* people will only be moral if they have certain
religious beliefs, or (b) that no one will be *completely* moral who does not
have these beliefs, or (c) that *most* people will be adequately moral only if
they have these beliefs.

Let us consider these three more qualified tenets. I should like to point
out that it is very difficult to get conclusive empirical evidence for or
against such assertions, and that those who make them seldom adduce
such evidence in a form which cannot be challenged. Still, it does look as if
(a) is true, that is, that *some* people will be moral only if they have certain
religious beliefs. But, notice, this fact does not prove that these religious
beliefs are true or even that they should be taught. It certainly does not
prove that there is no room in the schools for moral education which is
non-religious; the most it would show is that such education must be
supplemented, perhaps in the home or the church, by a religious one.

As for (b)—that only a religious person will be completely virtuous, or
at least as virtuous as mortal man may—this too may be true. But, once
more, it does not follow that all moral education must be pervaded by
religion; at most it follows only that public education needs to be supplemented by a religious one—and this follows only if there is independent
ground for believing that religion is true. For it will hardly do to offer
religious beliefs as reasons for being moral, if the only reason for believing
them is that they are necessary for being moral.

(c), which says that most people will perform their duties adequately
only if they hold religious beliefs, is much more doubtful. It would be very
difficult to find in history or to create in an experiment situations so controlled or so structured as to show it to be true. Trueblood and others have
averred that the events and experiences of the twentieth century constitute
"a great body of evidence . . . of the moral decay that follows a loss of
theistic conviction."[7] Presumably they are thinking either that the conduct
of Nazi Germany and of Communist Russia is a consequence of a loss

[7] D. E. Trueblood, *The Predicament of Modern Man* (New York: Harper & Row,
Publishers, 1944), pp. 56–57.

of theistic conviction in those countries, or that there is moral decay on our own side which is due to such a loss. Let us suppose that there has been, on whatever side, a widespread decline of religious faith and also a widespread moral decay. This would by no means establish that the former was the cause of the latter. There are other developments in our century which might have caused whatever change in conduct there has been besides a decline in religious faith, for example, nationalism, fear, and so forth. It may even be that something more basic is the cause of both the religious and the moral change. It can, in fact, be maintained with some plausibility that the present upsurge of religiosity is itself due to some pervasive economic, political, or social phenomenon of our time, and, if this is the case, it may be that some such phenomenon, and not the increase or decrease of religion as such, is what determines our moral behavior and thinking.

But suppose that (c) is true—that the average individual will be even adequately moral only if he has religious convictions. What follows? Even then all that follows is that a public or religiously neutral moral education must be supplemented, not that it should go out of business. And, once more, this need for religious supplementation follows only if religion is true on other grounds. For the only alternative would be to say that religion should be taught as a prop for morality even though it is not true. But to say this is to condone myth-making and propaganda; and, moreover, it hardly seems to comport with the spirit of religion itself.

(3) So far we have dealt, respectively, with the claims that morality is *historically* and *psychologically* dependent on religion. But the crucial issue is whether morality is *logically* dependent on religion, that is, whether theological premises are required to *justify* statements about our moral duties—not only about specifically religious duties but also about others, not only about so-called duties to God but also about duties to our fellow-man. I made this distinction between *justifying* a moral judgment and *motivating* people to act on it earlier when I was talking about teaching reasons as well as moral rules, but must say a little more about it here, for the distinction is often neglected by religious as well as non-religious moralists. Take, for instance, the religious rule which many regard as a moral duty, "We ought to worship God." Suppose A asserts it and B asks, "Why?" Then A may give an answer which is intended to *convince* B on intellectual grounds that he has a moral obligation to worship God, or he may give one which is calculated only to *motivate* B to worship God. He does the latter if he replies that the Lord is a jealous God and will not hold him guiltless who has other gods before Him, but shows mercy unto thousands that love Him and keep His commandments. But he does the former if he reasons as follows:

> We ought to be grateful to those who have been good to us.
> God has been good to us.
> Therefore we ought to be grateful to Him.
> But being grateful to Him entails worshipping Him.
> Therefore we ought to worship Him.

Here A is offering B a moral justification for his rule, not just a motive for obeying it.

Moreover, A's argument has at least one theological premise, namely, "God has been good to us," and so, in his reasoning, the duty to worship God is *logically* dependent on a religious proposition. I think we may say that the same thing is true of all specifically religious obligations—if they are duties at all, they logically presuppose at least one religious premise for their justification. Now I am not concerned to ask whether there are such duties, but whether the same thing is true of *all* of our moral obligations. Do they *all logically* presuppose some theological premise or other? Can one never *justify* a rule of duty without using such a premise? I see no reason for thinking so. It seems to me that I do give a moral justification of, say, the rule to keep promises, if I show that promise-keeping is necessary for the stability and well-being of society in the world. Of course, someone may still ask me why he should be concerned about the well-being of society, but then he seems to have switched the question from that of justification to that of motivation.

In fact, it cannot be true that *all* moral principles depend *logically* on a prior theological premise. Look at A's argument again. It does rest on a theological premise, as we saw. Its very first premise, however, is not a theological proposition, but a *moral* one, namely, "We ought to be grateful to those who have been good to us." And any argument to *justify* any moral rule must have a similar structure, that is, it must begin with a basic moral principle. Else one cannot draw a moral conclusion. It follows that justifying arguments rest ultimately, at least in part, on moral principles which do *not* depend *logically* on theological or other premises. One of these ultimate moral premises may even be the rule that we ought to do what God commands; but this is a moral principle and not a theological proposition, and it does not follow logically from any theological proposition.[8] One may, of course, ask even in the case of such an ultimate moral principle, "Why should I do what it enjoins?," but then one is asking, not for a moral argument, but for motivation or some kind of non-moral argument. And, as we saw before, the answer need not involve any religious considerations.

---

[8]Of course, one might claim that the ultimate moral premise is a definition or true by definition, but then one must establish the acceptability of one's definition and one cannot do this simply by deducing it logically from theology.

(4) At this point, it might be contended that the ultimate principles of morality must be matters of divine revelation, if what has just been said is true. Then it might be said that morality is at least *epistemologically* dependent on religion or rather on a faith that certain principles have been divinely revealed. But, if by this is meant that some such special revelation as Moses is supposed to have received on Mt. Sinai is required, the view can hardly be sustained. As St. Paul said, even "the Gentiles which have not the [revealed] law—are a law unto themselves," having "the [moral] law written in their hearts, their consciences also bearing witness."[9]

There is a different kind of "revelation" which is sometimes said to be necessary as a basis for morality, namely, the "realization" of other people as persons whose lives have the same "inner significance" that ours have. Josiah Royce describes this realization of our neighbor, which he calls "the moral insight," most vividly, and William James dramatizes it even more in the essay "On a Certain Blindness in Human Beings," where he speaks of this "higher vision" which pierces the "great cloudbank of ancestral blindness weighing down upon us" and "makes an epoch in [the] history" of the person to whom it comes. And he calls it a "religious insight." Now, I am inclined to agree that a morality without this insight is in some way truncated, as Henri Bergson holds.[10] But I find it misleading to call it a "religious" rather than a "moral" insight, for, while it may involve some kind of regeneration on the part of one who has it, it is not clear that it presupposes any belief of a specifically religious or theological nature, for example, the belief that there is a God or that human beings have immortal souls. In any case, however, there seem to be forms of morality like F. H. Bradley's morality of "my station and its duties" or Bergson's "closed morality" which do not rest on such a "higher vision of an inner significance," and even if these moralities are truncated, they may be an important part of our moral education.

Well, much more might be said about the thesis of the indispensability of religion to morality. I might have pointed out that if one rests morality on religion, one encourages moral scepticism in those who find religion uncertain or false, for example, the Sartrian existentialists. I might have shown that, if religious ideas have influenced moral ones, so have moral ideas influenced religious conceptions, as is illustrated by Plato's critique of Greek theology in the *Republic*. I might even have mentioned Matthew Arnold's view that religion is "morality touched by emotion," which John Dewey restated in *A Common Faith*. But it is not my intention to denigrate religion in any way, even if I have not been willing in this discus-

[9]Romans 2:14. See also Reinhold Niebuhr's criticism of Karl Barth in *The Nature and Destiny of Man* (New York: Charles Scribner's Sons, 1941), Part II, pp. 254–256.
[10]See the article referred to in Note 5.

sion to take its truth for granted. It may be that religion is necessary for certain reaches of both morality and the good life. This I have not been concerned to dispute. Nor have I been trying to justify the existence of public education. What I have been arguing is this: (1) that public education, if it exists at all, should be concerned to do what it can to promote the good and the moral life, (2) that, because it is publicly-supported, it cannot seek to inculcate any religious belief as part of its endeavor to advance the good or the moral life, and (3) that this fact does not mean that it must go out of business, since there are important values, principles, and virtues to which religion is not indispensable, logically, psychologically, or otherwise.

All this it is important to say now, when there is such strong pressure on the state-supported schools to do something more "positive" about religion. For one of the main grounds on which this pressure rests is the conviction that religious belief and experience are indispensable to both the good and the moral life whose promotion must be the concern of the state and its agencies—a conviction which is usually vaguely formulated and inadequately supported, but which many feel so deeply that they are ready to give up the neutrality of the public schools and to jeopardize the freedom of thought which it was designed to protect. The thought behind this paper is that this conviction is only partly true at best, that the public schools may remain nonmalevolently neutral and yet have an important sphere of operation relative to morality and the good life, and that, if and insofar as religion is required for certain dimensions of happiness and virtue, these schools should rather be supplemented than subverted.

FOR FURTHER THOUGHT

1. Various religious groups are concerned about the nature of a child's educational experience to the point that they establish their own schools to guarantee the proper schooling for their young people. *What does such behavior suggest regarding the adequacy or the appropriateness of public school offerings? What do they imply as far as the goals of the moral life and the good life are concerned?*
2. The Amish, due to their religious convictions, are opposed to formal schooling that takes their young people beyond the eighth grade. Also, during their eight years of schooling the Amish emphasize their religious ideals. They indicate in defense of their position that (a) they have lower divorce rates, less juvenile delinquency, and so forth, than a large percentage of society, and (b) those living by their standards lead a life that is good in the sense that it is worthy of reliving. *Would such*

a defense suggest to Frankena that there is a valid, evidential basis for including religion in the public schools?

3. Important to the defense of Frankena's position, with regard to religion in the public schools, is his reliance upon a particular epistemology. Such an approach demands a public test and something more than coincidence to establish necessary relationships. *Is such a test a fair expectation from the standpoint of the proponents of religion in the public schools? Why or why not?*

4. Frankena claims that the schools may "remain nonmalevolently neutral and yet have an important sphere of operation relative to morality and the good life." *Why might that very neutrality be seen as a negation of provision for morality and the good life? In what way would such a countercharge against Frankena's position point out the basic disagreement over purpose?*

EDUCATION FOR MORALITY

The excerpt taken from the book by John L. Childs entitled *Education and Morals* criticizes "formalism, utopianism, and traditionalism" in education. As such it stands as a criticism of many of the conservative forces in education partially represented by Hutchins and the religious respondents to the article by Frankena. Childs' philosophy can be categorized under that all-encompassing title of "progressive education." While such a category can offer some broad understanding of the position being expounded it offers little specific detail. So inclusive are some of these categories that contradictory or conflicting elements creep in under the same classification. Dewey, claimed by some to be the true voice of progressive education, recognized this danger. He found it necessary on various occasions (such as the one that prompted his writing of the book *Experience and Education*) to challenge many that were claiming to be "progressive" educators.

While it may be difficult to ascertain definitely what common positive aspects exist under this rubric it is possible to claim that the "progressives" were unified in what they were against. They disliked ideas of final truths, universal or absolute values, and the highly rationalistic emphasis of some schools of thought. In general, they opposed the "traditionalists." They wanted education to reach beyond a singular concentration on cultivating the intellect. In so doing they wanted to emphasize a broader curriculum and novel pedagogical devices and activities having a close connection to the life of the child. Such a position has come to dominate in pure or corrupted form the educational philosophy and practice of the day. It was challenged in its inception and continues to be attacked today as being responsible for the weaknesses and shortcomings of current educational practice.

————————◆————————

EDUCATION AND MORALS: AN EXPERIMENTALIST PHILOSOPHY OF EDUCATION*

EDUCATION AND CHOICE AMONG LIFE ALTERNATIVES

The moral nature of education stems from the fact that schools are organized and maintained by adults, not by the children who attend them. Adults engage in deliberate education because they are concerned to direct the processes by which their children mature and learn to become participating members of their society. A manifestation of preference for certain patterns of living as opposed to others is therefore inherent in every program of deliberate education. Schools always exhibit in their purposes and their programs of study that which the adults of a society have come to prize in their experience and most deeply desire to nurture in their own children. Hence the curriculum of a school is an index to the values of the particular human group that founds the school. It is because some conception of what is humanly significant and desirable is implicit in all nurture of the young that we may say without exaggeration that each program of deliberate education is, by nature, a moral undertaking.

Our thought about education will be confused at its very root if we do not perceive that a school can never be a morally indifferent institution. Each school operates within a definite historical-social situation. This situation is marked by genuine life alternatives. Amid these plural and competing patterns of living, the school seeks to emphasize and to foster certain types of growth, and to hinder and to avert other types of growth. Were one invariant line of development alone open to the young, there would be no need for adult guidance. Thus, both lay and professional educational leaders misconceive the essential meaning of a school whenever they pretend to be neutral or indifferent to what happens to the children under their jurisdiction. In the last analysis, the success or failure of a school is measured in *moral* terms, that is, by what it does with and for

*From *Education and Morals: An Experimentalist Philosophy of Education* by John L. Childs. Copyright, 1950. Reprinted by permission of Appleton-Century-Crofts, Division of Meredith Publishing Company. Dr. Childs, Professor Emeritus at Teachers College, Columbia University, and Adjunct Professor at Southern Illinois University, has among his major publications *American Pragmatism and Education, Education and Morals,* and *Education and the Philosophy of Experimentalism.*

the human beings entrusted to its care. All of the other functions of a
school are ancillary to this primary responsibility of directing the growth of
the immature members of its society.

Obviously, there can be important differences in judgment about what
kinds of human behavior are so fundamental and desirable that they
should be cultivated in the school. In view of our present limited
knowledge of the process of human maturation and learning, there can also be legitimate differences about the best means of nurturing cherished
attitudes, techniques, interests, tastes, outlooks and patterns of conduct in
the young. But the fact that we still have much to learn about both the
ends and the means of education provides no sound ground for the notion
that we can educate, and at the same time avoid responsibility for making
judgments about the kind of person, or persons, we want the immature to
become. This elemental moral responsibility is inherent in each program of
deliberate education, for the cultural selections and rejections inescapably
involved in the construction and direction of an educational program
necessarily have consequences in the lives of those who are nurtured in it.

This tendency to pattern the intellectual and emotional dispositions of
the young is present in every type of educational program—democratic as
well as authoritarian, secular as well as religious, scientific as well as humanist, liberal as well as vocational, individualist as well as collectivist. In
sum, the making of choices that have to do with the destinies of human
beings cannot be eliminated from that directing of experience and learning
which is the distinctive function of the school. It is choice among significant
life alternatives that is the essence of the *moral* act, and choice among
values necessarily pervades those human actions by which the program of
a school is organized and communicated. . . .

The more knowledge that we accumulate about human beings and the
process by which they develop, the more we are confident that the patterns
of human nature are neither uniquely given at birth nor do they automatically develop by a process of the unfolding of a pre-formed self.
Inherited factors set broad limits for the growth of the individual human
being, but evidence from a variety of sources—biological, psychological,
and anthropological—indicates that a wide range of possibilities lies within these native determinants. The manner in which these organic potentialities of the human infant will be synthesized into a mature human being
is always conditioned by factors of culture and experience. William James
did not exaggerate when he declared that many different selves are open to
each individual at the beginning of life, "but to make any *one* of them actual, the rest must more or less be suppressed."[1]

---

[1]William James, *Principles of Psychology* (New York: Holt, Rinehart and Winston,
Inc., 1890), vol. 1, pp. 309–310.

Learning continues throughout life, but the early years are the formative ones. It is then that the basic intellectual and emotional dispositions are developed. During the early years of their existence, individuals acquire their characteristic modes of feeling, appreciation, and perception, as well as their governing principles of response to their fellow human beings. All of their subsequent learning tends to be assimilated to the patterns of personality gradually articulated and more or less integrated during this plastic and formative period. Hence in directing and ordering the experience of the young, we are not merely selecting the fields of subject-matter and life-activity in which they shall gain knowledge and competence, we are also inescapably sharing in that foundational process that determines the very mode of their personhood.

Bernard Shaw has contended that "the vilest abortionist is he who attempts to mold the mind of a child."[2] In this striking phrase he has summarized a view held by some of those who have been identified with the "child-centered" educational movement. Shaw, however, both mistakes and mis-states the issue. The primary fact is that the life and the mind of the child is necessarily molded, for it is through the nurture provided by other human beings that each child achieves its most distinctive human traits. Apart from this group nurture, were the child fortunate enough to survive, he would not achieve a type of existence much above that of other animals. It is through this association with others that the infant acquires the characteristics that we designate as mind. The actual choice therefore is not between a process of unfolding from within and a process of molding from without; it is a choice between alternative ways of having the human surroundings effect this molding of the child. The real question is whether the development of the child is to come as a by-product of the accidents and pressures of his own unplanned and unguided interactions with his surroundings, or whether his growth is to come as the result of an experience in a special environment planned for this educational purpose. Schools are organized and supported because adults have faith that better results will be attained if the young grow to maturity in an environment that has been deliberately organized for the purpose of introducing them to the life and thought of their society. If we really oppose any and all molding of the life of the child, we should in consistency repudiate the whole enterprise of deliberate education because this patterning of the development of the individual is its basic purpose and justification. The actual moral problem therefore is not one of molding versus not molding; it is rather the problem of discovering the means by which the nurture of the

[2]George Bernard Shaw, Man and Superman, "The Revolutionist's Handbook" (New York: Dodd, Mead & Co., 1948).

child can be made a process of enrichment and liberation, not one of exploitation and enslavement. . . .

ENDS AND MEANS IN EDUCATION

It is also important for educators to recognize that a scientifically
grounded pedagogy is no substitute for clear ideas about the values and
purposes of education. The scientific study of both the nature of the child
and the process of human maturation and learning is making indispensable
contributions to the work of education. No teacher worthy of the name can
afford to ignore these tested findings. But knowledge of these scientific
findings does not in and of itself define our educational objectives. For example, knowledge of the fact of individual differences, and of the uniqueness of each child, does not relieve us of responsibility for making judgments about the way in which that inherited uniqueness is to find its appropriate expression within the context of our changing modes of life and
thought.

Studies in human learning show that learning is an active, dynamic
affair, and the leaders of progressive education have rendered an important service by developing an activity curriculum to provide more adequately for these dynamic aspects of the learning process. But "pupil initiative" and "wholehearted purposeful projects" are in no sense a
substitute for adult guidance; they should rather be viewed as improved
means of making that guidance more effectual. The more knowledge that
we can get about the process by which the powers of the child ripen, the
better we shall be able to plan the program of the school, but knowledge of
"the human maturation sequence" does not justify a "hands-off" policy in
education. As a matter of fact, such findings as we have about child
development show that "the human maturation sequence" is by no means
exclusively an affair of the biological organism; it is deeply influenced by
environmental factors, and after the first years, the rôle of a culturally conditioned experience becomes primary in determining the further lines of
personal growth. Confronted with plural and conflicting cultural patterns,
educators cannot escape responsibility for choosing main lines of human
development.

Those educators who have combined the psychological principles of
child growth with the moral principles of democracy and have developed
the conception that the supreme aim of education should be the nurture of
an individual who can take responsibility for his own continued growth
have made an ethical contribution of lasting worth. But acceptance of the
objective of developing a person who can eventually take over his own
education does not at all imply that the school should arrange its affairs so

that each child, unhindered by adult guidance, will be left "free to develop in his own way." To attempt to do this is to negate the very purpose of deliberate education. We establish schools because we recognize that the child does not know the principles and the means of his own development, and because we also realize that the kind of scientific and humane conduct we call "mature" and which is presupposed in the principle of responsible "self-education" is not an original endowment. It is a genuine ethical insight that distinguishes intellectual and emotional maturity from mere slavish conformity to custom, but we err whenever we assume that what is prized as "maturity" is the product of an unguided, spontaneous unfolding of an inborn pattern of human personality.

Although method is fundamental in the nurture of the young, method, in and of itself, cannot determine the objectives of our educational program. To define these educational objectives we must have a definite conception of the kind of person we are seeking to develop. If that conception is to be more than a formal abstraction, it must take account of the actual life conditions and relationships of the society in which the child is to live, along with those more general principles of human conduct which men of many different societies have come to honor because these principles have been confirmed by all that they have experienced.

Education is grounded in respect for the achievements of human beings. If man did not have regard for that which he has learned and created, he would not organize schools to communicate his culture to his young. But in a democratic society, education is also grounded in respect for each human personality. It seeks the growth, not the enslavement, of the immature members of its society. Fortunately, these two basic values are not in conflict; on the contrary, they mutually support one another. We can manifest respect for the child and contribute to his progressive liberation through the procedures of deliberate education only as we have respect for the knowledge and values that man has derived from that which he has suffered and undergone. No educational theory or method is to be trusted which opposes respect for the child to respect for human experience and knowledge.

In fine, education is a value-conditioned activity. The school seeks to cultivate selected values in the young by means of both the subject-matters and the methods that it employs in its program. In education, as in other human arts, our practice becomes intelligent as it grows, both in its awareness of the ends that it is seeking to attain and in its mastery of the means which it must use to attain these ends. The fact that these ends or outcomes involve the lives of the immature deepens—it does not diminish— our responsibility to know what we are trying to accomplish when we undertake to educate.

THE MORAL NATURE OF DELIBERATE EDUCATION

As we have emphasized in all the foregoing, deliberate education is never morally neutral. A definite expression of preference for certain human ends, or values, is inherent in all efforts to guide the experience of the young. No human group would ever bother to found and maintain a system of schools were it not concerned to make of its children something other than they would become if left to themselves and their surroundings. Moreover, in order to develop the preferred and chosen patterns of behavior, it is necessary to hinder other and incompatible kinds of growth. A school is ineffective as an educational agency whenever the emphases in certain aspects or departments of its work are denied or negated in other parts of its program. In education, as in other realms of human activity, the actual practices of a school are more potent than its verbal professions. Maximum results are achieved when both the declared aims and the actual deeds of a school are unified, and its children are reared in an environment that supports in its daily practices that which it affirms in its theory.

As we have already stated, the term *moral*, as used in this discussion, does not pertain to a restricted phase of the work of the school. The moral interest pervades the entire educational program. It is involved whenever a significant choice has to be made between a better and a worse in the nurture of the young. The moral factor appears whenever the school, or the individual teacher or supervisor, is *for* certain things and *against* other things. The moral element is preëminently involved in all of those selections and rejections that are inescapable in the construction of the purposes and the curriculum of the school. It appears, for example, in the affairs of the playground—in the kind of sports that are favored and opposed, and in the code of sportsmanship by which the young are taught to govern their behavior in the actual play of the various games. It appears in the social life of the school—in all of the behaviors that are approved or disapproved as the young are taught the manners—the conventional or minor morals—of their society. It appears in the school's definition of the delinquent and in its mode of dealing with him. It appears in the way children are taught to treat those of different racial, religious, occupational, economic or national backgrounds. It appears in the department of science: in the methods the young are expected to adopt in conducting their experiments, in their reports of what actually happened during the course of their experiments, as well as in the regard of the teachers of science for accuracy, for precision, and for conclusions that are based on objective data rather than on wishful thinking. It appears in the department of social studies: in the problems that are chosen to be discussed, in the manner in which they are discussed, in the historical documents and events that are emphasized, as well as in the leaders that are chosen to illustrate the important and the worthy and the unimportant and the unworthy in the affairs of man. It appears in the department of literature: in the novels, the poems, the dramas that are chosen for study, in what is considered good and what is considered bad in the various forms and styles of human conduct and expression. It appears in the organization and the government of the school: in the part that superintendent, supervisors, teachers, pupils are expected to play in the making and the maintenance of the regulations of the school. It appears in the methods of grading, promoting, and distributing honors among the children of the school. It appears in the celebration of national holidays: in the particular events that are celebrated as well as in the historical and contemporary personalities who are chosen to exemplify the qualities of citizenship and worthy community service. It appears in the programs for the general assemblies of the schools: in the various leaders from the community who are brought in to speak to the children. It appears in the way teachers are treated: the amount of freedom and initiative they enjoy, in the extent to which teachers are permitted to take part in the life of their community, and the degree to which the young believe that they are studying under leaders who are more than docile, routine drill-masters in assigned subjects. It appears in the way the community organizes to conduct its schools: in the provision it makes in its schoolgrounds, buildings, and equipment, in the kind of people it chooses to serve on the school board, and in the relation of the members of the board to the administrative and teaching staff. In sum, the moral factor enters whenever and wherever significant decisions have to be made about either the organization, the administration, or the instructional program of the school. All of these decisions, whether they relate to curriculum or to extra-curriculum affairs, exert an influence on the attitudes and the behaviors of the young.

Thus judgments about life values inescapably pervade and undergird the whole process of providing and guiding experience. More than many teachers recognize, a scheme of values—a structure of things considered significant, worthful and right—operates in their endless responses to the daily behavings of their pupils. Many of these educational values concern the very fundamentals of human existence. They have to do with such elemental things as the rights, the responsibilities, the beliefs, the tastes, the appreciations, the faiths and the allegiances of human beings. As we introduce the young to the various aspects of human experience—familial, economic, scientific, technological, political, religious, artistic—we inevitably encourage attitudes and habits of response in and to these affairs. In order to encourage, we must also discourage; in order to foster, we must also hinder; in order to emphasize the significant, we must identify the nonsignificant; and, finally, in order to select and focus attention on certain subject-matters of life, we have to reject and ignore other subject-matters. Were our values different, our selections and our rejections would also be different. The process of selecting and rejecting, of fostering and hindering, of distinguishing the lovely from the unlovely, and of discriminating the important from the unimportant, is unending in education. It is this process of choice and emphasis that defines what is meant by the term *moral* as it is used in this book.

As thus interpreted, the concept of the *moral* refers not primarily to the particular ethical quality of the life interests, outlooks, and practices involved in any given educational program, but rather to the more elemental fact that *choices* among genuine life-alternatives are inescapably involved in the construction and the actual conduct of each and every educational program. These choices necessarily have consequences in the lives of the young, and through them in the life of their society. Viewed from this perspective, education undoubtedly ranks as one of the outstanding moral undertakings of the human race.

SOCIETY AND EDUCATION

The purposes and the subject-matters of the school are not developed by a process of adult contemplation carried on in a social vacuum, nor do they arise spontaneously from the interests and activities of school children. They are invariably developed through the evaluative and selective response of adults to the traditions, the conventions, the life practices, and the changing conditions of their society. Thus a school is a very human institution. Its program is never formulated by "nature," by "history," by "the state," by "religion," by "science," or by any impersonal agency or process; it is always constructed by ordinary human beings whose value judgments and educational selections are necessarily influenced by factors of time, place, status, interest, belief, knowledge and custom. Both religious and secular programs of education bear the marks of the particular societies in which they have originated, as well as the definite cultural interests they have been designed to serve.

Search into the materials and the purposes of any school and you will come upon that which extends beyond the school. You will encounter the language, the literature, the practical and fine arts, the science, the institutions, the moral ideals, and the faiths of an historical, human group. You will find these things, however, not in the gross form in which they exist and function in the society that creates the school, but abstracted, sifted, classified, and graded into a curriculum for the nurture of the young. Considerations both of group welfare and of pedagogy play a part in this process by which the affairs of a human society are selected and transformed into a curriculum for the school. But no matter how drastically these life materials may be refined and rearranged in the subject-matters and activities of the school, they are always taken originally by somebody, for some definite purpose, from the totality of the ways of life and thought of a human society. As these group practices, interests, beliefs, and outlooks change, the program of the school also changes. In this basic sense education *is* a social affair. Educational choices are always, in the last analysis, social choices.

Human Interests and the Purposes of Education

The historical and the comparative study of man's educational activities shows that the actual ends for which different societies, and different groups within the same society have chosen to educate have been many and various. As we emphasized in the first chapter, adults tend to make central in their program for the nurture of the young whatever they consider of major importance and value in their ways of life and thought. Even the needs and the possibilities of the young are always defined in terms of the particular mode of life that the adults who organize the school desire and expect the young to lead. It is therefore natural that educational purposes, materials, and methods have differed as widely as have types of human association, systems of value, and patterns of authority and leadership.

Military castes, for example, have resorted to education in order to fashion the young into efficient "bayonets" for their armed forces. Social and political despots have used education for the purpose of breeding devoted and docile "subjects" of their autocratic regimes. Revolutionary communists have organized schools to train the young in the ideology of the class-struggle, and to fashion them into "militant warriors" in the world-struggle to overthrow the existing capitalist system. Supernaturalists have elaborated school rituals and programs in order to nurture "devout believers" in a revealed plan of life and education. Literary humanists have made a curriculum of the "great books" and have sought to develop the "gentlemen of culture"—the cultivated person who is possessed of "the conscience of truths valid for all and the will to undertake duties common to all." Experimental scientists have sought to develop the "man of the laboratory," equipped with the attitudes, faiths, and allegiances implicit in the objective experimental process of discovering and testing truth. Ardent nationalists have demanded a common system of schools devoted to the cultivation of the "patriot"—the obedient citizen whose final authority and supreme object of affection and loyalty is the fatherland. Absolute pacifists have founded schools dedicated to world brotherhood and the religion of humanity, and designed to create the "conscientious objector"—the person who instinctively believes that "all

war is sin" and who will have no part in its organized slaughter of fellow
human beings. Private enterprisers have propagandized for a school that
will make each child into a "rugged individualist," committed beyond
recall to the system of private ownership and the principle of "free" and
"unregulated" acquisition. Liberals have sought a school system that would
cultivate the "informed and critical mind," contending that the "enlightened citizen" is the only secure foundation for a humane mode of existence.

Diverse as the foregoing educational purposes and programs are, they
have certain common features. Each of these educational programs defines
some historical group's conception of basic life interests and meanings.
Each has a conception of the kind of person it wants the school to produce,
and its norm or standard for human personality is derived from its interpretation of fundamental group values and relationships. Each of these
groups is concerned to construct a definite program through which its preferred and predominant pattern of living will be bred into the dispositions
and the habits of the young. It has no thought of letting "the child develop
in his own way," whatever that may be held to mean. Each expects that its
teachers will be faithful in the work of communicating its chosen values to
the young. Although the "ethical" quality of these programs varies enormously, they are all "moral" undertakings in the elemental meaning of the
term *moral:* each has its governing principles of evaluation and choice in
matters of taste, faith, allegiance, and human conduct.

Life Imperatives and Educational Programs

Fortunately, the clash in purpose and program is not quite so sharp as
the foregoing list of life interests and educational objectives suggests. The
history of education shows that the predominant life-alternative, or value,
favored by any particular cultural group, or sub-group, has seldom been
the sole interest included in its total educational program. Militarists,
tyrants, revolutionists, supernaturalists, literary-humanists, scientists, nationalists, pacifists, capitalists, and liberals: all, alike, live under the com-
pulsions of the here and now. This means that each must take account of
the stubborn requirements of human existence—collective and personal.
In order to provide for these life-imperatives, adults have to do more than
train the young in a single cherished and selected aspect of life; their
educational programs must also provide some opportunity for the new-
born to learn about the varied human arts and institutionalized practices
that are essential to the maintenance of their society.

A militarist, for example, may be consumed by his interest in guns and
soldiers, but in his total political and educational program he courts
disaster if he ignores the need for bread, and that whole structure of
economic and social institutions and relationships by which bread is produced and distributed. As a militarist he may have no regard for letters

and science as such, but in the modern world an illiterate, and scientifically and technologically untrained army has little chance to survive in the ordeal of total war.

The supernaturalist educator may esteem salvation in the life beyond the grave above all other values, but he cannot afford to be indifferent to the mundane aspects of life. Most parents will not accept discipline in the life eternal as a substitute for competence in reading, writing and arithmetic. They also expect their children to learn geography, science, history and civics as well as the doctrines that comprise the catechism of the church. The curricula of church and public schools therefore have much more in common than one might suspect if he has heard only the strictly theological defense of the religious school. Supernaturalists are also children of their age; they are not wholly immune to the "climate of opinion" in which they live and think. Today, the tendency increases in their ranks to reject asceticism and all forms of withdrawal from society as modes of preparation for the life eternal, and to hold instead that the best preparation for the next world is the most adequate and meaningful living in the present.

So, also, for the literary-humanist: he may believe that the "unkillable classics" constitute the only significant source of human enlightenment, but when he designs his educational program, stubborn realities will demand that he give some attention to our scientific and technological ways of thinking and of making a living. When he builds his school plant, he will probably furnish it with the best of modern equipment. More than he is aware modern influences will also pervade the classrooms of his school —even the imperishable principles of the classics will be taught and studied by those whose minds have been conditioned by the affairs of their own age and society.

The utilitarian-vocationalist may be passionately devoted to narrow technical training in the interest of more efficient and more profitable production, but the imperatives of the life of an organized community—a community without which his whole system of technology and factory production could not survive—will require him to give place to many other life interests and subjects in the curriculum of his vocational school.

The experimentalist may accord the attitudes and methods of scientific inquiry the supreme place in his philosophy of life and education. But when he undertakes to organize a school for the nurture of the young, he will find that the important and distinctive demands of family, economy, vocation, government, religion, and art will compel him to make educational provision for many human interests other than the disinterested pursuit of truth. All of the subject-matters of life can and should be explored by the critical and objective method of experimental science, but the method of science is in no sense a substitute for a direct experience of these varied subject-matters. Important and fundamental as is the interest in

knowledge, it is by no means the only human interest, and it would be a
very inadequate school that restricted its attention to the method of experimental inquiry.

The shift from an agrarian to an industrial-urban civilization has greatly
strengthened this tendency to broaden the perspectives, the interests, the
purposes and the subject-matters of the school. For most of human history,
the young have learned the arts by which life is sustained, not primarily by
instruction given in the school, but by direct and responsible participation
in these productive activities under the supervision and direction of the
adults engaged in them. In our highly articulated, specialized, and
technological civilization, this ancient system of apprenticeship is rapidly
disappearing, and with it is going much of the opportunity of the young to
learn through direct sharing in the productive affairs of their community.
In order to adjust to this transformed social and economic situation, the
functions and the responsibilities of the school have been greatly expanded, and the period of schooling has been correspondingly extended.

It is only natural that this rich and diversified curriculum, open to all the
children of the community, should have greatly altered the educational situation. One consequence has been a decline in the emphasis on the
transmission of doctrines in the education of the young. In a school in
which increasing attention must, of necessity, be given to the preparation
of the young for the things that they have to do as citizens and as members
of particular occupational groups, concern with mundane affairs tends to
take much of the time that used to be centered on the study of doctrines
and the memorizing of moral maxims. In our complex, technological society the school has been compelled to give major attention to the introduction of the young to those basic life functions upon which the
general welfare depends.

The Democratic Conception
and the Aims of Education

The development of democracy has also eliminated certain historic
types of educational purpose and program. In any society that is really
governed by the democratic principle of the worth and dignity of each human personality exploitive systems of education are necessarily precluded.
The democratic community negates its own moral foundations whenever it
regards the child as a mere potential "bayonet" for its armed forces, as a
mere future "hand" in its system of factory production, or as a mere instrument of any kind to be fashioned for the perpetuation of an established
institution, or the interests of a special class. A society that is grounded in
the conception that governments are instituted among men to promote
"life, liberty and the pursuit of happiness," and which holds "that
whenever any form of government becomes destructive of these ends, it is
the right of the people to alter or to abolish it" cannot consistently support

an educational practice that is designed to fashion human beings into the mere instruments of the state. The supreme moral trait of the democratic community is that it has no good other than the good of individual human beings.

Moreover, in a democratic society authority and leadership in education, as in government, are not supposed to be lodged in the hands of any ruling group—hereditary, military, ecclesiastic, or economic. It is the very essence of democratic theory that authority and ultimate control in all public affairs should be transferred from all such limited groups to the people as a whole. In accordance with this principle we have sought to organize a system of public schools in the United States in which the responsibility for the determination of the educational program would rest with the local communities, and with the various state authorities, not with the Federal government—that is, with the parents and their own chosen representatives on local school boards, not primarily with national or church officials. It has been our conviction that a school system thus responsive to the interests and the preferences of parents would tend to make the needs and the welfare of the child its primary concern. We have also assumed that schools which are controlled by the very groups whose children are enrolled in them could not easily be manipulated to serve the special interests of privileged classes. On the whole, events have justified this faith; the American school has been disposed to make the growth, not the exploitation, of the child its controlling objective.

But even in a democratic society the needs of the immature do not define themselves, nor do they remain constant in a world in which change is real. As we have already emphasized, in order to define desirable patterns of growth for the individual child, we must take account of the kind of life that we expect and desire him to lead. This pattern of life is not an isolated and private thing. It involves, to be sure, the individual child with his distinctive native endowment, but it equally involves the community with its public modes of life and thought. The deeper the regard of the educator for the worth and dignity of the child, the deeper his interest in the community should become. Any program of education tends to become abstract, formal, and therefore a mechanical routine whenever its purposes and materials are considered to be the property of a self-sufficient school, for this means that dynamic continuity between the work of the school and the life that goes on outside the school has been disrupted. A school best provides for the growth of the child when it maintains living interaction with the community of which he is a part.

Names and Realities in Human Conduct

A theory of morals is of course implicit in the foregoing view of the relation of the program of the school to the ongoing affairs of its society. This moral theory holds, in the first place, that human rights and human responsibilities do not constitute a separate and fixed system, but that they are conditioned by the concrete ways in which a human group makes its living and carries on its whole schedule of interrelated life activities. This theory assumes, in the second place, that as knowledge grows and new means of control and modes of living develop, traditional patterns of human rights and duties may also have to be modified. In other words, this social conception of education is the correlative of a moral theory which holds that morals are related to human interests and evolving conditions of life, and hence are not absolute and transcendental, but empirical, institutional, and historical in nature.

It is easy to deceive ourselves and to conceal this empirical and social character of morals. All that is necessary to make morals appear to be unconditioned and immutable is to concentrate attention on moral terms or names, and to ignore the actual human relationships and behaviors that are denoted by these moral terms. Thus an educator may affirm that even revolutionary social changes are of no concern to him, for he knows that in each and every society a child should be taught to be unselfish, to be honest, to be chaste, to be loyal, and to make his behavior conform to all of the fundamentals of the moral code. There is, to be sure, a measure of truth in this educational affirmation, for in the course of its experience the human race has gained many ethical insights. But this emphasis on continuity and permanence in the moral life of man becomes harmful whenever it is taken to mean that new knowledge and powers of human control, and altered conditions of life, do not make necessary fresh appraisals of the behaviors that are to be considered authentic expressions of these traditional moral principles.

For example, changes in modes of production have in no way eliminated the importance of the distinction between the "selfish" and the "unselfish" in human conduct, but these economic changes are calling for a fundamental review of the rights of both the owner and the worker. Considerations of public welfare in our interdependent world are now demanding that the right of the owner to do as he pleases with that which he owns, and the right of the worker to leave his job when and as he desires, be altered. Now these are not superficial moral changes; they involve fundamentals in human relationships and behaviors in the economic sphere. The meaning of the concepts of "selfishness" and "unselfishness" must be revised to correspond to these new realities in our interdependent ways of making a living. So also in the realm of family relationships. The development of effectual contraceptive measures has aroused deep controversies about what should now be considered "moral" in this aspect of human behavior. The evidence indicates that a new standard is developing in this ancient sphere of the "moral," and already important church groups are strongly supporting on ethical grounds the principle of planned parent-hood. Nor does the concept of "loyalty" in the realm of political affairs au-tomatically define itself. World-wide totalitarian political movements have resulted in novel political affiliations and practices which have raised the most difficult kind of questions about the meaning of citizenship and the criteria by which "loyalty" is to be measured in contemporary political, educational and similar public undertakings.

In brief, unless education is to serve outmoded and reactionary ends, it must accept responsibility for defining the kind of behaviors which now should be associated with such traditional and basic moral categories as "honesty," "unselfishness," "chastity," "loyalty," "equality," "respon-sibility," and "freedom." The present has its deep continuities with the past, but it also has its significant discontinuities. The discontinuities, moreover, are as real as the continuities. Education, during this period of social transition and strain, will not promote democratic interests, if it seeks to make "moral absolutes" out of historic rights and forms of human conduct. To serve democratic purposes, education must play its part in the important task of moral discovery. It can do this only as it is willing to con-tinue to examine and test its educational values by whatever we gain of new knowledge and also by that structure of human relationships and ac-tivities which is ever developing in the society outside the school. An unex-amined morality is not fit to fashion the educational program of a democracy in this period of social transition. Apart from intelligent study of the changing affairs of its society, the school has no adequate means of determining the worth of its moral foundations. Recognition of the reality of change must be one of the fundamental principles in the philosophy of education of our period.

Basic Meanings in the Social Interpretation of Education

Measured by all the crucial scientific criteria, human beings constitute a common *biological* family. All members of this human family share a basic organic inheritance. But *culturally* they are members of many different hu-man societies. These societies, located in various parts of the world, are the products of a long development. They have their common features, but they also have their distinctive traits. Each of these societies, taken as a whole, is unique. The things which differentiate one human group from other territorial and cultural groups are no less real than those elements in its ways of life and thought that it shares with other human societies. It was this perception which led the Commission on the Social Studies of the American Historical Association to declare that:

Education always has a geographical and cultural location; it is therefore specific, local, and dynamic, not general, universal, and unchanging; it is a function of a particular society at a particular time and place in history; it is rooted in some actual culture and expresses the philosophy and the recognized needs of that culture. . . .

Although the basic biological equipment of man seems to be comparatively invariant and may therefore be expected to give certain common elements to education everywhere and at all times, human civilization has characteristics of neighborhood, region, nation, and more extended cultural areas, which lend unique qualities to every working educational program, however persistent and pervasive may be the universal elements entering into it[3]

It is significant that the eminent members of this Commission of the American Historical Association decided to emphasize in their concluding Report that deliberate education should be viewed not primarily as a function of humanity in general, but rather as a function of particular human societies, each with its own individualized past, its own language and literary heritage, its specialized skills and modes of making a living, its distinctive structure of customs, laws, and institutions, as well as with its own unique beliefs, sentiments, moral outlooks, and conceptions of human excellence and of human destiny. For the historian, accustomed to think in the categories of time and place, societies are many, not one; dynamic, not static; individualized and evolving, not fixed specimens of an immutable human pattern. Individual human beings, in their actual psychological natures, are creatures of these historical cultural groups. They think, evaluate, and respond out of an intellectual and moral consciousness that is saturated and hallowed by the history and the achievements of their people. It is not surprising then that when these culturally conditioned groups of human beings undertook the deliberate nurture of their young, they should have created systems of schools which in their subject-matters and their purposes reflected the societies into which they had been born, and which had shaped the very forms of their own being.

But this argument from history is not decisive. The fact that education down to the present has been an undertaking which has varied with factors of time and place, does not in and of itself warrant the conclusion that education in our shrinking and closely integrated world should continue to be that sort of an enterprise. It is wholly fair to ask those who adopt the so-

[3]American Historical Association, *Conclusions and Recommendations,* The Report of the Commission on Social Studies (New York: Charles Scribner's Sons, 1934), pp. 31–32.

cial interpretation of education to justify their position in terms not of historical origins, but rather in terms of present human values. Certainly a discussion of education and morals should be willing to meet this demand, for the deepest concern of morals is with what *should be,* not simply with the description of what *has been,* or *now is.* We shall therefore conclude this discussion of society and education by enumerating some of the considerations that make it desirable for us to continue to view education as a human undertaking in which factors of time and place are centrally important.

In the first place, this social theory of education is in harmony with the imperatives of educational practice. In spite of present cultural changes, no advocate of universalism in education has been bold enough to contend that the children of the United States should be nurtured in the Chinese language, or that the children of China should be nurtured in the English language, or that the children of these two countries should be educated in a new world-language. In other words, in the case of such basic interests as language and literature, it is generally recognized that stubborn historical factors make it both necessary and desirable that the program of the school be rooted in the cultural heritages of actual human groups. Even following the total military defeat of Japan and Germany, no one has recommended that the children of these two countries be educated in the language of one of the victorious Powers.

The situation is no less compelling when we come to the subject of history. Men in different parts of the world have had their own and distinctive experiences, and these diversified pasts are not dead; they constitute the very substance of the cultures in which men now live and through which they develop their objects of allegiance and devotion. History, moreover, is the past of the present, and to be significant must be explored from the perspective of some actual present. These perspectives are as many as are present human societies. Hence proposals for "objectivity" in the teaching of history have never assumed that the children of the world should be taught a colorless, universalized human history. These proposals for more impartial historical textbooks have recognized the necessity and the desirability of plural accounts of what human beings, organized in different societies, have done and undergone. The demand for objectivity in the preparation of school history books has therefore been the demand that these various cultural and national accounts strive to be more accurate and fair in their report of other cultures and other national groups, particularly in their interpretations of past transactions and conflicts with these groups. It has been accepted that it would mean impoverishment, not enrichment, were all of these individualized human records to be merged in one common, authoritative history of universal man.

The same considerations obviously hold for vocational education, for education in citizenship, for worthy home membership, and for the creative use of leisure time. Without taking into account the operating institutions and practices of its own society, the school would have no adequate means for the construction of its educational program in these vital dimensions of human experience.

Since the school, in one way or another, must make this reference to the affairs of its society, the adherents of the social interpretation of education hold that this evaluation of the life of a people should be made deliberately with public responsibility for whatever cultural selections and rejections are actually involved in the construction of its program. The ends of objectivity will be better served in education when choices among life-alternatives are recognized and avowed, not concealed or denied.

This social view of education, in the second place, can help us overcome the tendency to *formalism* in the work of deliberate education. The constant temptation of the school is to permit its materials and schedules of activities, once they have been selected, classified, graded, and organized into a curriculum, to become an autonomous program of self-perpetuating interests and subjects. The school begins to die both emotionally and intellectually whenever it thus becomes imprisoned in an inherited curriculum and begins to turn its back on the society that it was organized to serve. To make the communication of meaning a living thing, the teacher must grasp the connection of his "subject" or sphere of human interest and knowledge wih that which his people have suffered and enjoyed and with that which they now do and undergo. Education, moreover, is an affair of the young just as literally as it is an affair of the heritage of the group. These young are living as well as learning. They live by participating in the affairs of their family, neighborhood, community, and country. A primary aim of education should be to make this participation more meaningful by placing it in a wider historical and geographical and cultural context, and by helping the young to acquire the knowledge, the skills and the techniques which make this participation more effectual. Growth in meaning and growth in capacity for participation in the life of a human group are not effectually cultivated in a school which makes its own world a rival and a substitute for the world outside the school. An increasing number of educators perceive that both "subjects" and "children" become abstractions whenever they are dealt with as entities independent of the life of the community. They recognize that educators can become wise about the nurture of the immature members of their society only as they continue to grow in their understanding of that world *from* which the young come to school, *in* which they continue to live during the period they study as pupils in the school, and *to* which they must go to work out their own careers when their years at school have been completed.

The social conception of education, in the third place, can help save us from the evil of utopianism in education. By utopianism is meant any projection of social and educational ends which fails to take responsible account of actual cultural conditions, and hence evades responsibility for developing the concrete means by which its ideal ends are to be achieved. Whenever we view moral ideals as absolute and unconditioned things, we are apt to get involved in this kind of romanticism. Our country, for example, is committed by both religious and political ideology to the principle of the dignity and worth of "all men." To the extent that we believe in democracy we are necessarily opposed to all patterns of discrimination and enforced segregation based on factors of religion, race, color, sex, class, or national origin. But notwithstanding our official democratic affirmations, the plain fact is that the ideal of equality in the economic, political and cultural affairs of our country is at present most inadequately realized. Our historic system of property ownership often operates in present-day industrial society so as to favor a privileged few at the expense of the many; our political system in its actual operation in many states now denies Negroes elemental civil rights; and existing American attitudes and practices tend to subject the members of minority religious groups to a variety of discriminations. Education in and for democracy must share in the struggle to get rid of these inequalities. But educators can assist in this important task of democratic, social reconstruction only as they recognize that these discriminations are stubbornly grounded in the past experience of the American people. That experience still lives in characteristic mental habits. The pioneer and agrarian experience of the American people, for example, has disposed many of both farm and city to a firm faith in the system of economic individualism, even though their own interests would now be better served in a regime of coöperative planning. We misconstrue the nature of the present economic problem if we do not appreciate the strength of this faith in individualism, and discern the ways in which it is often manipulated by minority groups that have a vested economic interest in the maintenance of the *status quo*. Experience also demonstrates that racial attitudes and the group mores that underlie our segregated school system have deep roots in the past. It is apparent that education can serve as an agency for social progress only as it takes full account of these group attitudes and the factors in our cultural history which have produced them.

But to take account of existing attitudes and prejudices does not mean that we must weakly surrender to them; it rather means that our proposals for reconstruction should be so formulated that they will strengthen, not weaken, the forces that are striving to dissolve this legacy of discrimination. Democratic advance is undoubtedly a function of human courage as well as of intelligence, but no amount of courage will bring us nearer the goal of equality unless that courage is informed by the kind of understanding which comes from historical and social analysis.

Education frequently fails to enjoy the coöperation of many thoughtful people of genuine democratic interest because of its tendency to make vague moral slogans a substitute for analysis of the conditions with which it has to deal. Actually we know our moral ends only as we know something of the means by which these ends are to be attained. Because the social interpretation of education tends to focus attention on conditions and means it gives promise of developing a morality in education that will be free from the weakness of sentimental utopianism.

Finally, the social interpretation of education can help us discern the defects of traditionalism in education. By traditionalism is meant not sincere regard for the human past, but rather the social and educational view which assumes that we already have a completed system of truth concerning the essentials of human nature, moral values, and the patterns of human civilization, and which also assumes that this completed system contains the answers to whatever problems of human belief, human conduct, and social policy may beset us. On this basis, education becomes merely a process by which the young are indoctrinated with the truths of this closed, authoritarian system. Only those educators who are so immersed in a system of intellectual and moral abstractions that they are immune to the instructions of ordinary human experience, can thus convince themselves that change, and novelty, and moral uncertainty are not real factors in the experience of human beings.

In our period of profound social transformation and transition it is no contribution to the resolution of the problems of mankind to minimize the drastic nature of the adjustments which men must now make if they are to continue to survive. . . . Every resource in our intellectual and moral heritage will be needed to help us make satisfactory adjustments to these emerging modes of life, but we shall also do well to accept the fact that we are confronted with novel life conditions which call for real moral pioneering if we are to make our new powers of control over the physical environment serve the ends of a good life. Both the nature of our problems and the means for resolving them will be more adequately understood if old and young seek to educate and re-educate themselves in terms of the actual social situations in which they are now involved. A fundamental merit of the social interpretation of education is that it invites educators to view their task as a significant part of the total task of building a civilization that is in harmony with the deep moving forces in the modern world.

FOR FURTHER THOUGHT

1. Childs claims that the success or failure of a school is measured in moral terms. He is clearly not examining the pragmatic question, but instead is looking at the matter of ultimate ends to be attained. *What reasons does Childs have for claiming that each program of deliberate education is a moral understanding?*

2. In the chapter it is acknowledged that there are important differences in judgement concerning the ends of education to be pursued. Similarly, the claim that we have limited knowledge about the process of human learning and maturation is affirmed. *Are both problems capable of diminution in the same way? Does the recognition of the existence of these problems suggest that professional behavior is not possible in education?*

3. The claim is made that knowledge of the nature of the child and his developmental stages is a necessary but not sufficient basis for making educational decisions. *Why is such information a necessary ingredient of "good" educational decisions? What additional dimensions are essential to quality decisions? What is the relationship of the facts of human learning and maturation and the determination of educational objectives?*

4. *If Childs were to defend the position that education necessarily varies with factors of time and place on the grounds that historically such had always been the case, what line of argumentation might be established to question his judgement? What justification does Childs have for asserting a need to provide variable educational experiences? Does such a position deny the reality of a common human nature?*

5. Essential to the development of his position is Childs' acceptance of democracy as a fundamental tenet of our society and way of life. Essential to that acceptance, however, is the affirmation of certain behaviors and ideals as being more in keeping with the concept of democracy. While a later section of this book deals in much more detail with this matter, it is useful at this point to note how the definition attached to democracy affects one's stance on many educational issues. *What is essential to Childs' usage of the term "democracy"? Avoid the pitfalls of vague terminology. What conception is he opposing even though it has been a part of our tradition?*

EDUCATION FOR THE PRODUCTIVE LIFE

It is possible through a wider reading of Sidney Hook's works to place him in the "progressive" school of thought heretofore described. This selection, taken from his book entitled *Education for Modern Man*, is introduced to provide a basis for examining a question of instrumentality in education. It points us specifically to questions of purpose in education.

With the increasing demands for skilled labor and with the high rate of school drop-outs there is a marked tendency to advocate that the schools become centers for vocational preparation. Advocacy of such a purpose for the schools is not new. With this suggestion, however, usually goes the thought that vocational education is a specific job orientation program. It is here that the disagreements arise. There are those such as Hutchins who have traditionally criticized this narrow conception of education. He, and others like him, would want education to prepare one for a vocation, but they would hope to find a much different means of realizing that end. This disagreement should now lead the reader to question whether in fact there is an agreement on the end of education as vocational preparation. Hook, in analyzing the subject, distinguishes between vocational and liberal education. The program he recommends attempts to merge the offerings and emphases of the two programs.

In many controversies terms like vocational or liberal education function as slogans or "war cries." Such use does not afford an adequate basis for judging any means proposed for their attainment because the terms in such a context lack clarity. We are again reminded of the fact that the selection of content, materials, textbooks, and so forth, depends upon a clear specification of the ends to be attained. We must decide the nature of the vocational goal to be undertaken by the school. When such a decision is made we then will have a basis for formulating the school program to most adequately realize that goal. Until that time the debate will likely continue to no avail.

EDUCATION FOR MODERN MAN*

Nothing is more familiar than the contrast drawn by modern educators between liberal education and vocational education. But as soon as we try to track down the specific differences between them we discover that no hard and fast lines can be drawn. Usually a liberal education is so defined that if it has any other end beyond itself, if it involves more than the joys of consummatory experience, it is illiberal. It thus automatically excludes any activity connected with "earning one's living." . . .

In the modern world, liberal education has always been a serious enterprise despite the existence of some students who did not take it seriously, who regarded it as a personal adornment or a badge of social superiority. It was always connected with earning one's living, although the "livings" were of a highly selected sort. The notion that the opposite of the liberal arts were the useful arts, and that therefore the liberal arts could be designated as useless, would have been dismissed as preposterous even by the most traditional of educators. For the curriculum of the liberal arts col-

*From *Education for Modern Man*, by Sidney Hook. Copyright 1946, © Copyright 1963, by Sidney Hook. Reprinted by permission of Alfred A. Knopf, Inc. Dr. Hook is Chairman of the Department of Philosophy at New York University. Among his many publications are *Education for Modern Man, Political Power and Personal Freedom*, and *From Hegel to Marx*.

leges of the past few centuries trained for vocations, too. The teachers, ministers, lawyers, physicians, and better-paid public servants were largely drawn from the ranks of the college educated. A liberal arts education was in fact a sufficient preparation for many kinds of careers. Like the great medieval universities, but in lesser measure, they were really professional schools.

In the contemporary world this is still true. But it is often concealed by dubbing some careers "professions" and regarding the others as "vocations." Flatly to contrast the "professions," even when we prefix the adjective "liberal" to them, with "vocations" is to express an invidious distinction. It is derived from the scorn felt by those who imagine they use only their brain as an instrument in earning their living, toward those who seem to use only their hands. It is explained mainly by the fact that most "vocations"—in ordinary times—carry with them less power, less money, and less prestige in the eyes of the community than most professions. . . .

A liberal education should do something more than prepare the student to earn his own living. But it should at least prepare him for it. The crucial question is *how* he should be prepared. No conception of liberal education is worth a second glance which professes to be unconcerned with the quality of the life a student will lead after he is through with his formal schooling—a life in which the fruits of his schooling first become apparent. All the great educators of the modern world, despite their differences as to what constitutes the best education, agree that it should be complete in the sense that it should fit men to grapple with their duties as citizens of the community. But a citizen of the community is not only a "political" entity. He is a producer, a consumer, a potential warrior, a critic, a teacher in some respects, a learner in others. He is sometimes more of one or another. But in the life of the citizen they are all related. This thought was expressed long ago by John Milton whose conception of a "complete" education is a measure by which we may still judge what belongs to a desirable education, and how it belongs. "A complete and generous education," he said, "is one that fits a man to perform skillfully, justly and magnanimously, all the acts, both public and private, of peace and war." Vocational education is part of a complete and generous education.

The fundamental problem of vocational education today, to the extent that vocations are still available, is whether it should be considered as a form of vocational *training*, serving industry and government, or whether it should be considered as an aspect of liberal education in which preparation for careers in industry and government is justified by *both* the needs of a developing personality and the interests of the community. Here, as elsewhere, we can observe a meeting of extremes which in effect makes allies of the lily-pure academician and the tough-minded practical man. The first finds utterly distasteful the idea that vocational interests should obtrude on the course of study. In his heart he believes that students who study for any other reason save the sheer love of it degrade learning. They therewith prove themselves in his eyes to be no true students at all. The second regards liberal arts studies as irritating conventional preliminaries to useful subjects whose mastery has a cash value. Wherever possible, he seeks to give vocational courses a content that is directly relevant to the tasks that must be performed on the job. For all their opposition, both agree on sharply separating liberal from vocational study, although they differ in the grounds offered for the separation. Both are united in strong opposition to any plan to make vocational education integral to liberal education. . . .

Vocational education conceived as job-training represents the greatest threat to democratic education in our time. It is a threat to democracy because it tends to make the job-trained individual conscious only of his technological responsibilities, but not of his social and moral responsibilities. He becomes a specialist in "means" but indifferent to "ends" which are considered the province of another specialist. The main concern is with "getting a job" and after that with "doing a job" no matter what the political direction and moral implications of the job are. Social programs are judged simply by whether they promise to provide the jobs for which the technician is trained. If a democratic community can supply the opportunity for work, well and good; if it can't, and a totalitarian party or government offers the opportunity, why not? Observers have noted that the technically trained students in institutions of higher education in Germany and Italy have in the mass been much more susceptible to totalitarian propaganda than students whose education has primarily been in the pure sciences. An education that is narrowly vocational, without cultural perspective or social orientation, unillumined by knowledge of large scientific principles considered in a large way, undisciplined by a critical method that sets the range of relevance for methods of technical thinking, is even worse for democratic purposes than a narrow and pure scientific training which, as a special kind of professionalism, is bad in its own way. For the problems on the job are *applications* of scientific knowledge in contexts of social values and human relationships. And it is these which conventional vocational education persistently ignores.

The high incidence of interest in vocational training among youth today reflects the expectation that our economy will have a place for them. The underlying assumption is that the seller's market for the vocationally trained will indefinitely continue in peace as well as in war. This is far from being a sure thing.[1] The history of American capitalism does not provide grounds for great confidence. Vocationally trained talents rusted for al-

[1] For an interesting discussion of the factors bearing on the employability of vocationally trained youth, see Selden C. Menefee, *Vocational Training and Employment of Youth*, Research Monograph 25 (Washington, D. C.: U. S. Government Printing Office, 1942).

most a decade after the depression. Educators made desperate efforts to revamp curriculums so as to keep youth out of the labor market. We may witness the same thing again. Dearth of vocations may be the most powerful argument against vocational education of the present type. But it would be the weakest argument, and the wisdom it would enforce, besides being costly, would be limited. For, even if prosperity were to continue unabated in years of peace, there is no reason why a truncated vocational education should be substituted for an integrated liberal one. We could well forego the difference in national wealth that would result from keeping young people out of the labor market for a few years, if it added to the immeasurable but more genuine wealth of a well informed, critically minded youth.

Such a critically minded youth would think not only about jobs but about the economy as a whole which provided the jobs and sometimes took them away. Such a youth would not be educated to "adjust" themselves to an economic and social order as if it were as perennial as the course of the stars. They would be encouraged to view it in its historical development. They would be taught to recognize its present-day problems as *occasions for choices* which they, among others, have to make. They would adjust not to the present but to the future as if it were present. To adjust to the future as if it were present is never an automatic reaction. For it is the essence of reflection.

There is a paradox connected with vocational training. The more vocational it is, the narrower it is; the narrower it is, the less likely it is to serve usefully in earning a living. Techniques, know-hows, operative skills change so rapidly in industry that the student who has been trained to perform certain specific tasks runs the risk of suffering from what Veblen called "trained incapacity." This is particularly true for manual crafts. Those who are muscle-bound, either physically or intellectually, must unlearn and relearn, for all their previous vocational training, if they are to continue to earn their living. Proper vocational education stresses doing, of course. Its skills are largely practical, not abstract. But at the same time it must nourish and strengthen powers of flexibility which will enable students intelligently to breast the waves of vocational change. (To a certain extent, this is achieved in the kind of vocational education we call "professional." . . . The impact of automation may so restrict the market for vocations that in the future the entire problem will be transformed into one of creative use of leisure; but until that time comes the issues surrounding vocational education remain acute.

The indictment against vocational education summarized above would be signed with both hands by those who desire to keep liberal education uncontaminated by concern for earning a livelihood. They offer two distinct solutions to the problem. The first is a sharp separation between liberal arts education and vocational education. Liberal arts education above the elementary levels is to be open to anyone who can qualify for it. After it is completed, it may be followed by vocational education. The second solution is much more radical. It has the great merit of making the problem disappear from view. It proposes that vocational education be left to apprentice experience on the job, and that the schools abandon all vocational instruction. . . .

But it is this very *separation* between the two kinds of education which is pedagogically defective. Vocational education is simply overlaid on liberal education. The bearings of the general ideas and philosophy acquired through liberal education are not integrated with the vocational subject matter at the points where they are most important. Why a man works, the effects of his work, its relation to the tasks of the community are questions quite germane to his vocational activity. They are best studied in specific contexts. The worker remains a citizen while he is at his job. His knowledge of the fact will ofttimes make a difference even to what he does and how he does it. What is called a liberal education should be a continuous process, and there is no reason—except unfamiliarity with the idea—why vocational education should not be liberalized to include the study of social, economic, historical, and ethical questions wherever relevant instead of assuming, as in the existing practice, that education in these matters is something already gone through and forever done with. . . .

The greatest obstacle to this attempt to integrate vocational and liberal education flows from the suspicions of the specialist against introducing anything outside the narrow confines of his specialty. He regards cultural studies in professional schools as a kind of academic boondoggling. It wastes time which in his eyes is already insufficient for the technical matters students should know. The specialist has a natural tendency to view the whole curriculum from the standpoint of his own professional concern. Yet he recognizes how narrowing and educationally disastrous such a perspective is when it is drawn by *other* specialists. This recognition should serve as one of the checks upon his natural appetite. Even in liberal arts colleges, as we have already observed, many subjects, particularly the sciences, are taught from the specialist's point of view to the detriment of broader understanding and abiding interest on the part of students, most of whom, if they become specialists, will be specialists in something else.

Recent tendencies in our best vocational schools, viz., our professional schools, show a growing realization that vocational and liberal education cannot be sharply separated. A dawning perception is now manifest that the best specialist is not necessarily the man who has received the most vocational training. The work of the physician, the work of the lawyer, the work of the engineer in different ways demand a *continuing* familiarity with subjects that would seem to the specialist to be utterly irrelevant to his proper vocational tasks....

This is not confusing liberal and vocational education. It is relating them in such a way that no matter how a man earns his living he will not lose sight of the communal traditions to which he owes his knowledge and skills, the communal responsibilities he shares with his fellows, and the communal tasks to which he can make his distinctive contribution. Vocational education which fails to do this is illiberal and had best be abandoned.

The difficulties of giving organizational form to this integrated curriculum are tremendous. But they must be faced. There are certain healthy developments in existing practice which should be encouraged. In many courses in the liberal arts colleges today an attempt is made to provide either some work experience or firsthand contact with practical activities in which general principles are given application. Instead of being done in a haphazard and episodic way, this should be systematized.[2] During the third and fourth years of the typical liberal arts college, studies are concentrated around a vocational interest but in isolation from the vocation. Guidance by self or others is hardly likely to be sound unless the student is given an opportunity to savor for himself the quality of his prospective vocational career.

FOR FURTHER THOUGHT

1. Frequently, distinctions are made between liberal and vocational education. Hook employs these terms in the preceding selection. *What meaning do you attach to these terms? In defining them, is it possible to make them synonymous? What distinction, if any, would Hutchins make between the two terms?*

2. Hook asserts that vocational education, conceived as job training, represents the greatest threat to democratic education in our time. While it will be useful to explore this claim again when we look at the nature of a democracy, it is important to explore why he feels that job training is a threat to democracy. *Is there anything inherent in either the concept of democracy or job training that would put the two at odds? Is there any legitimate basis for claiming that vocational education is more democratic when accompanied by an understanding of culture and an appreciation for the critical method?*

3. According to Hook, the need for a job and life preparation, which includes both a consideration of means as well as ends, is essential. He

[2]The best example to date of systematization is the Antioch College co-operative work-study program.

claims that the dimension of ends *must* be added to preparation for work. *What does such a stance suggest for teacher preparation?* Relate your answer to the concepts of teacher training and teacher education found in the introduction and again in Part III.

4. The academician and the practical man agree that liberal studies should be sharply separated from vocational studies. *Why does this constitute an example of programatic agreement? What are the reasons each would use to divorce the two studies?*

SUGGESTIONS FOR FURTHER READING

1. There are numerous textbooks in the history of education that can readily serve as sources of information about historical periods and the dominant educational aims of the respective periods. R. Freeman Butts, *A Cultural History of Western Education* (New York: McGraw-Hill, Inc., 1955) and H. G. Good, *A History of Western Education* (New York: The Macmillan Co., 1960) are two reliable sources of this type. John Brubacher focuses the first chapter of his book, *A History of the Problems of Education* (New York: McGraw-Hill, Inc., 1966) on the topic of education aims. Some older, but worthwhile sources on the topic of aims are M. I. Emerson, *Evolution of the Educational Ideal* (Boston: Houghton Mifflin Co., 1914) and J. P. Monroe, *The Educational Ideal* (Boston: D. C. Heath & Co., 1906).

2. Comparative education studies also afford the student a basis for examining educational aims by looking at a number of modern alternatives. *Contemporary Education* (New York: Harcourt, Brace & World, Inc., 1965) by Cramer and Browne, as well as *Educational Patterns in Contemporary Societies* (New York: McGraw-Hill, Inc., 1964) by Thut and Adams provide such comparative analyses of educational aims.

3. For a broader view of more recent and contemporary expressions of the school's purpose students are encouraged to read, in addition to the sources from which the readings of this chapter are taken, such works as: Theodore Brameld, *Toward a Reconstructed Philosophy of Education* (New York: Holt, Rinehart and Winston, Inc., 1956); John Dewey, *Democracy and Education* (New York: The Macmillan Co., 1961); Jacques Maritain, *Education at the Crossroads* (New Haven: Yale University Press, 1960); A. S. Neill, *Summerhill* (New York: Hart Publishing Co., 1960); Alfred North Whitehead, *The Aims of Education* (New York: The Macmillan Co., 1929); and Arthur Bestor, *Educational Wastelands* (Urbana: University of Illinois Press, 1953). In addition to these major sources there are innumerable periodical articles offering variations of these same themes.

4. The analysis of aims in education can be fruitfully explored through

literature emphasizing valuing in relation to education. Worthwhile representatives of this nature include George Axtelle, "How Do We Know What Values Are Best," *Progressive Education* (April 1950); Otto Dahlke, *Values in Culture and Classroom* (New York: Harper, 1958); C. J. B. MacMillan and George Kneller, "Values and Education," *Review of Educational Research* (February 1964); and Bernard S. Miller, "The Quest for Values in a Changing World," *Social Education* (February 1965).

CHAPTER **4**

Changing Times, Changing Purpose?

The foregoing chapter has provided a basis for examining the nature and importance of purpose. Specifically avoided in Chapter 3 was the question of purpose in relation to changing societal conditions. It is generally recognized that we live in an age when new developments appear regularly. Can and should the purposes of the school be altered to more appropriately fit the changes?

In the early 1930s George Counts outlined in an article entitled *Dare the Schools Build a New Social Order?*, what he thought was the appropriate responsibility of the school. It was his contention that

> . . . if an educational movement, or any other movement, calls itself progressive, it must have orientation; it must possess direction. The word itself implies moving forward, and moving forward can have little meaning in the absence of clearly defined purposes. We cannot like Stephen Leacock's horseman, dash off in all directions at once. Nor should we, like our presidential candidates, evade every disturbing issue and be all things to all men. Also we must beware lest we become so devoted to motion that we neglect the question of direction and be entirely satisfied with movement in circles. Here, I think, we find the fundamental weakness . . . of American education generally. Like a baby shaking a rattle, we seem utterly content with action, provided it is sufficiently vigorous and noisy.[1]

Such insight is of particular value to us today. Our society is marked by a continuous and rapid change. Job descriptions are changing, technology is enlarging our opportunities for learning and entertainment, and great distances have been reduced in importance through growth in transportation

[1] George Counts, *Dare the Schools Build a New Social Order* (New York: The John Day Company, Inc., 1932), p. 6.

121

and communication facilities. Not only can we cover the earth rapidly, but we are successfully reaching out into space and on to the surface of the moon. Leisure, formerly a concern of the elite, is now becoming increasingly possible for larger portions of the population. These are representative of the many changes transpiring in modern society. They seem to demand comparable changes in man and his institutions. The school becomes a focal point for undertaking such change.

There is no shortage of advocates of change in the name of progress. We find numerous examples of individuals or groups applying pressure to alter existing conditions. As highway deaths and insurance rates go up, more and more concern develops over the need for properly qualified drivers. The school becomes the likely place for offering such instruction. As sex offenses or morality lapses increase, the school is seen as the bulwark against such undesirable developments. The responsibilities and activities that can be forced upon the school are extensive. Many of these may fall outside the purview of the school. If the schools are to protect the public, they need both a basis for limiting what is included and the power and determination to make certain that the school is performing its proper role.

The proliferation of activities suggested for the school requires that choices be made as to what is most central to its purpose. Limitations of time, space, and personnel make it impossible to cope with all that is suggested as worthy of attention in the formal education of the young. The attempt to select activities most central to the purpose of the school is recognition that change is not in itself a sufficient goal; it is recognition that we cannot ride off in all directions at once. Change does not necessarily mean progress. As Counts has pointed out, change can only be evaluated when clearly defined goals are established and understood. To recommend and to accept changes just because of a desire for something new is to be like a baby with a rattle. The child is totally satisfied with the action and noise, and never really explores the direction of the action or the worth of the noise. Perhaps sheer noise and random action are sufficient for babies. They are not, however, the mark of a civilization.

The demand for clarification of purpose is not a demand for neglect or lack of consideration of changing conditions in society. Such clarification is emphasized *in order that the school can more effectively relate to the changing conditions of the larger society.* In periods of flux there is always the question as to how institutions can most effectively relate to the change. Does it require that the purposes of the institution be changed? Can the purposes remain constant with only the means being subject to alteration? Should both be changed or both remain constant? These are questions we want the reader to focus attention upon in this chapter. The establishment of a clear-cut direction for the school in a period of flux is most difficult. The selections that follow point out the factors involved in complicating this choosing of direction and also offer some guidelines for consideration.

William O. Stanley's piece succinctly presents the dilemma of the teacher and the school in an era of change. When confusion, conflict, and uncertainty prevail what should serve as the direction for educators and education? In the selection following Stanley's, George Spindler offers a model for describing a society in a state of flux. Traditional and emergent values are his two major categories for describing society in transition. The satirical selection of the case history provided by Dr. Harold Benjamin (J. Abner Peddiwell) affords us a most enjoyable illustration of the problems of education in an era of change. The last selection, that of Robert M. Hutchins, raises questions about the continuation and expansion of a program that might well be obsolete following our modern "ice age."

THE EDUCATIONAL DILEMMA

The complexity, the rate of change, and the contradictions in the values of American society make the role of the school an especially difficult one. If the school is to obtain its direction from society, where in society are the major determinants or directions to be found? Stanley clearly portrays this dilemma of education in our society.

At no time in our history has there been such an apparent diversity in our society and in the demands upon the school. There is little wonder that criticisms of the school and its programs are extensive. Given the numerous directions in which the school is expected to go, there is ample reason to expect the disenchantment of many with the failure of the school to be all things to all people. To think of resolving the current conflicts or of removing the bases for debate is, as Stanley aptly states it, "to search for a consistent way of mediating a partially confused and chaotic culture in the process of transformation."

Stanley's analysis provides a valuable framework for the considerations of this chapter and is directly connected with the dilemma of the professional and the democrat.

———————◆◆———————

*EDUCATION AND SOCIAL INTEGRATION**

ORDER AND CLARITY A CRITICAL PROBLEM IN A TRANSITIONAL ERA

On the other hand, it is exceedingly difficult to establish or to maintain a consistent program of education in a society characterized by fundamental

*Reprinted with permission by the publisher from William O. Stanley, *Education and Social Integration* (New York: Teachers College Press, 1933), pp. 128–130. Copyright, 1953, by Teachers College, Columbia University. Dr. Stanley is currently Professor of Philosophy of Education at the University of Illinois. He is also co-author of *Social Foundations of Education*.

confusion and conflict. For, in such societies, there is no conclusive standard of the public welfare and, hence, no certain conception of the kind of character which the school should undertake to build. Consequently, the educator has no clear definition of the ends and purposes of education which is generally acknowledged or taken for granted by all parties to the educational enterprise. Moreover—and for the same reason—there is no common perception of the function and role of the school or of the nature and scope of pedagogical authority. In the absence of a common persuasion and outlook, drawn from the substantial core of a unified culture, the various individuals and groups, holding divergent conceptions and beliefs about such vital matters as the nature of man, the goals and standards of public welfare, and the role and function of the school, espouse different theories of education. Any one of these theories may embody a coherent program of instruction. But, to the precise degree that society is divided and confused with respect to its basic intellectual and moral postulates, no unified and consistent pattern of education is likely to win general assent, either in the profession or with the public at large. Under these conditions, the achievement of order and clarity in education, unless it is imposed by a ruthless and powerful minority, is a problem of extraordinary proportions. For its solution demands not simply the fabrication of an intelligible and consistent program of instruction—as a matter of fact, alternative programs meeting this specification already exist—but the re-establishment of the social consensus or else the negotiation of a viable agreement upon the ends and purposes of education (including the formation of character) in the midst of a profound confusion and conflict about the basic intellectual and moral postulates of society and the ultimate standards of the public welfare.

These paragraphs depict, in some measure the dilemma which now confronts American education. Order and clarity in the education offered by the American public school are imperative necessities, from the standpoint of both individual and public welfare. Yet the confusion and the conflict attendant upon a transitional era offer but little foundation for a comprehensive, coherent, and lucid educational program capable of commanding universal assent. Obviously in constructing a consistent program of study and instruction for the public schools, the educational profession cannot ignore the confusion and conflict in the contemporary culture nor can it arbitrarily impose either a common set of values or a unified way of life on the society which it serves.

If the educational profession undertakes to ignore the potent sources of confusion and conflict in society itself, the work of the school will inevitably be negated and hampered by the impact of the culture. To a limited extent, the school, with the aid of the home, can construct a sheltered and artificial environment for the nurture of children. But unless this environment somehow comes to grips with the major dislocations and disturbances of our time, any integrity of character and peace of mind which it may create will crumble and vanish at the first touch of reality. An ivory tower integration, granted that it is possible at all, does not meet the urgent need for order and clarity in education or for the development of sound and wholesome personalities.

If the educational profession attempts to impose on its students a set of values and a way of life not approved by society, it has far exceeded both the limits of its effective power and the bounds of its legitimate authority. Formal education is so small a part of the total nurture of the culture that it is absurd to suppose that the school, by its own unaided effort, can shape the character of the child to a form which has few, if any, roots in the ideals, customs, and institutions of his social group. Moreover, if the educator were to undertake any such venture, without regard to public opinion or to the balance of political forces operative in the community, he would very quickly discover that the ultimate control of the school has not been vested in the teaching profession. And, finally, as the vicar of society, charged with the important task of inducting the young into the culture, the educational profession has no authority or right, by the terms of its commission, to impose on its students either a way of life or a set of values which have no sanction or warrant other than the unilateral decision and choice of the teaching body.

Thus, the educational profession finds itself caught on the horns of a dilemma. The task of the school, in every society, is that of mediating between the child and his culture. Out of this process of mediation must grow integrated, wholesome personalities of a particular type enjoined by the fundamental aspirations and ideals of society. But, in a transitional era, the direct induction of the young into the culture just as it stands can result only in the development of disintegrated and disoriented personalities. Since society itself is no longer clear and certain (at many points) about either its fundamental postulates and goals or the kind of personality demanded by those standards and purposes, the educational profession, as the vicar of society, has no obvious and secure mandate to guide and direct its educational choices. Yet the profession cannot abjure coherence and symmetry in education, nor can it arbitrarily impose a pattern of its own selection. Hence, the search for order and clarity in education at the present juncture is essentially a search for a consistent way of mediating a partially confused and chaotic culture in the process of transformation: a way, moreover, which is, at the same time, compatible with the development of integrated personalities and acceptable to most, if not all, of the major social groups in our society.

FOR FURTHER THOUGHT

1. The relevance of Stanley's article rests upon his thesis (and our agreement with it) that American society is characterized by fundamental confusion and conflict. *Is such an assumption warranted? Whether or not one accepts his thesis that America is wrought by internal conflict does not void Stanley's judgment. What evidence might he have examined to lead him to his conclusion?*

2. Stanley claims that a profession has no legitimate authority to attempt to impose a set of values and way of life on its students not approved by society. Consider whether this makes a profession culturally relative. *If each society is to determine the nature of the service to be rendered is it possible to perform in one society actions that would be regarded as professional actions only to have these same actions seen as unprofessional elsewhere? Does this preclude the possibility of an international professional organization? Inasmuch as we emphasize local control of education, could we make the society the local community and thus see actions as professional in one community and not in another? Does the conclusion that professionals are only better than laymen with regard to means rather than ends fit into Stanley's position?*

3. If one accepts Stanley's claims with regard to the confused and conflicting nature of our societal values, the teacher is placed in a difficult position in attempting to educate the young of the society. As he points out, the task of the school is to mediate between the child and his culture and in this mediatory act create integrated, wholesome personalities. *How are those in the schools to ascertain what it is with which they should be concerned? Can they be sure that they have the true core of the culture or only that which is most vocally and powerfully represented? Until the search for clear direction is established is not the school doomed to failure in that if it follows the confusion of society the products turned out will also be confused?*

4. Stanley argues that the professional imposition of values is illegitimate. In addition he emphasizes another aspect of the same question to the point at which one begins to wonder whether it is the reason for imposition being illegitimate. This other dimension of the question can be tied to the word "power" (this is explored in Part III). Notice those instances in which Stanley claims that teachers cannot afford to go against the will of society if they expect to succeed. Few would agree that such action would be sound. Those who are truly powerful often are able to effect change without those who are being changed realizing it. *Is such use of power legitimate? Could educators, with a basic understanding of the principle of advertising, legitimately direct people to accept something that they would not originally have accepted? Would a programmatic or*

nominal agreement be acceptable and promote desirable action? If not, what is the standard for ascertaining legitimate action? (Relate this to Chapter 7.)

THE CHANGING CONTEXT OF AMERICAN EDUCATION

The selection from Spindler makes the claim that American society is fraught with divergent and conflicting values. In an attempt to enhance our understanding and appreciation of these incongruities in our values he categorizes them into traditional and emergent patterns and makes a judgment as to the place generally occupied by educational personnel.

According to Spindler, the existence of these major cultural shifts means that "people and institutions are left in a state of flux." Inasmuch as contradictory views of life are held, there is a continual basis for conflict and disagreement. Any institution (such as the school) or any person filling a role (such as a teacher) is left with a choice as to appropriate direction and action.

Standards of morality, success, and achievement are all subject to attack as new and more flexible patterns are accepted. A social scientist's documentation of these trends offers little solace to one concerned with lessening the present dilemma of education. It simply affirms, in an only too apparent manner, the difficulty of selecting the best goal for the school. It further offers useful insight into the values that appear to be on the ascendancy and those that appear to be going out of style. Even here, however, there is uncertainty as to the degree of adoption or rejection of these value patterns. It must be recognized that differences and contradictions exist, but such a recognition must sharpen the basic problem of determining from that information the direction in which the school should proceed.

————◄◆►————

EDUCATION IN A TRANSFORMING AMERICAN CULTURE*

The American public school system, and the professional educators who operate it, have been subjected to increasingly strident attacks from both the lay (non-educationist) public, and from within the ranks. My premise is that these attacks can best be understood as symptoms of an American

*George D. Spindler, "Education in a Transforming American Culture," *Harvard Educational Review*, vol. 25, no. 3 (Summer 1955), pp. 145–156. Dr. Spindler is Professor of Education and Anthropology at Stanford University. He is also the author of *Transmission of American Culture* and *Socio-Cultural and Psychological Processes in Menomini Acculturation*.

culture that is undergoing transformation—a transformation that produces serious conflict. I shall discuss this transformation as a problem in culture change that directly affects all of education, and everyone identified with it.

The notion of social and cultural change is used persuasively, if carelessly, by too many writers to explain too much. Generalized allusions to technological change, cultural lag, the atomic age, and mass society, are more suggestive than clarifying. We must strike to the core of the change. And my argument is that this core can best be conceived as a radical shift in values.

The anthropologist, and I speak as one but not for all, sees culture as a goal-oriented system.[1] These goals are expressed, patterned, lived out by people in their behaviors and aspirations in the form of values—objects or possessions, conditions of existence, personality of characterological features, and states of mind, that are conceived as desirable, and act as motivating determinants of behaviors. It is the shifts in what I believe are the core values in American culture, and the effect of these shifts on education today, that I wish to discuss. I will present these shifts in values as the conditions of life to which education and educators, whether progressives, experimentalists, conservatives, or in-betweens, must adapt—and to which they are adapting, albeit confusedly. My emphasis within the value framework will be upon shifts in the conception of the desirable character type, since education can never be freed from the obligation to support, if not produce, the kind of personality, or social character deemed desirable in society.

But first I must specify what sources are to be used as the factual baseline for generalization, even though there is no avoiding the necessity of going beyond these facts in the discussion to follow. There is a body of literature on American culture, as a culture, and the changes within it. I have drawn most heavily from the anthropologists, like Margaret Mead (4), Clyde and Florence Kluckhohn (2, 3), Gregory Bateson (6), Lloyd Warner (8), and Geoffrey Gorer (1), and a few sociologists, like David Reisman (5).[2] Their writings range from the highly intuitive to the relatively observation-based. Though there is concensus, and a surprising degree of it, on the part of these students of American culture, little they say can be or is intended by them to be taken as proven.

[1]The relationship between anthropology and education is a relatively new one. For further information on the connections and applications between the two see *Education and Anthropology*, G. D. Spindler, ed. (Stanford, Calif.: Stanford University Press, 1955).

[2]A more complete, and annotated bibliography will be supplied upon request to the author.

These writings are useful, but most emphasize static patterning in values more than change in values. To extend my factual baseline I have been collecting relevant data from college students for the past four years. The sample consists of several hundred students, ranging in age from 19 to 57 years, mainly graduates in professional education courses, and representing socio-economic strata describable as lower-middle to upper-middle class. The sample is as representative of this professional group and these economic strata as any regionally biased sample can be. I have used two simple value-projective techniques. The aim has been to find out what features of social character (the term I will use to designate those personality elements that are most relevant to social action) the students in the sample hold as being valuable and that presumably determine much of their behavior in classrooms. The first of these techniques is a series of 24 open-ended statements; such as "The individual is _____," "Intellectuals should _____," "All men are born _____." The second of these techniques is to require each student to write one brief paragraph describing his (or her) conception of the "Ideal American Boy."

The various qualifications, problems, and discrepancies in analysis appearing in the treatment of the results cannot be discussed here. Let it suffice to say that I have subjected the responses of the students in the sample to a straight-forward content analysis—counting numbers of responses that fall into certain categories appearing from the data themselves.[3] Perhaps some examples will illustrate both the techniques and the kinds of materials from which I am going to draw in the rest of this article.

From the open-ended sentence value-projective technique, results like these have been obtained: "All men are born _____," "equal" (70 percent of all responses), "wolves," "stupid," "dopes," "hot-blooded" (a miscellaneous negative category of 28 percent—provided mainly by females in the sample); "Artists are _____," "queer," "perverted," "nuts," "effeminate" (a negative-hostile category of 38 percent of all responses), "different," "people," "few" (a neutral category of 35 percent), "creative," "smart," "original," "interesting" (a positive category of 25 percent); "Intellectuals should _____," "be more sociable," "be more practical," "get down to earth" (a mildly derogative category of 36 percent), "keep it under cover," "drop dead," "shut up" (an openly hostile category of 20 percent), "apply their intellect," "study," "create," "think" (a neutral to positive category of 40 percent); "Nudity is _____," "vulgar," "obscene," "profane," "repulsive" (a negative-moralistic category of 43 percent), "pleasant," "self-expressive," "beautiful," "healthy" (an enthusiastic-positive category of 20 per-

[3]The analysis is still in process and will be subject to modifications in procedure. The statements in this article are based on a preliminary analysis of 328 individual protocols.

cent), "depends on how interpreted," "alright in some places," "depends on who is looking" (a relativistic category of 30 percent).[4]

The values are self-evident, and do not call for discussion, as such, for the moment. What is more important is that this fairly homogeneous sample of students provides a wide range of response to each of these statements, excepting for the purposefully stereotyped "All men are born _____." And not only is there a wide range of response evidenced, but many of the categories of response to a single statement can be considered as contradictions with respect to each other. This suggests that although there are clear modalities of values in this sample, there are also differences between people and groups of people in respect to what they believe is good.

The material gathered together as results from the "Ideal American Boy" technique are even more suggestive. A sentence-content analysis procedure reveals that the desirable features of character are ranked in the following order, from highest number of mentions, to lowest number: He should be *sociable*, like people, and get along well with them; he must be *popular*, be liked by others; he is to be *well-rounded*, he can do many things quite well, but is not an expert at anything in particular; he should be *athletic* (but not a star), and *healthy* (no qualifications); he should be *ambitious* to succeed, and have clear goals, but these must be acceptable within limited norms; he must be *considerate of others*, ever-sensitive to their feelings about him and about events; he should be a *clean-cut Christian*, moral and respectful of God and parents; he should be *patriotic;* and he should demonstrate *average academic ability*, and *average intellectual capacity*.

These are the characteristics of the ideal American boy seen as most important by the students in the sample. Leadership, independence, high intelligence, high academic ability, individuality, are mentioned relatively infrequently (in about 20 percent of the descriptive paragraphs). But individuals do vary in the pattern of characteristics that are combined in the paragraph. Some emphasize the high achievement and individualized characteristics just mentioned. Some include elements from the modal list and combine them with these latter items. But the majority emphasize the sociable, well-rounded, average characteristics ranked above.

The implications seem clear. The keynote to the character type regarded as most desirable, and therefore constituting a complex of values, is *balance, outward-orientedness, sociability,* and *conformity* for the sake of harmony. Individuality and creativity, or even mere originality, are not stressed in this conception of values. Introspective behavior is devaluated (even intellectuals are suspicioned by many). Deviancy, it seems, is to be tolerated only within the narrow limits of sociability, of general out-

---

[4]Where percentages do not total 100 it is because various miscellanea are omitted.

wardness, of conformity for harmony ("Artists are perverts"). The All-American boy is altogether average.

The materials just cited not only serve to illustrate the technique, but more important for present purposes, indicate rather clearly the fabric of the value pattern that I believe to be emerging as the dominant core of the social character values in American culture (providing one can assume, as I am here, that the middle-class culture is the core of our way of life—the pattern of norms against which lower and upper class cultures are seen as deviations). From this point on, I shall use the implications of this data, along with the content of anthropological and sociological writings on American culture, without further reference to the factual baseline itself. The purpose is to sketch in bold strokes the major dimensions of culture change in our American society and relate them in explanatory style to the contretemps of modern public education and educators.

In doing this, I cannot indicate all of the logical and analytic steps between data and generalization, since this is not a research report. The statements I will make now about American values, their shift, and the effect on education, are based upon the varying responses of different age groups in the sample, upon person-to-person variation in responses, and upon variations in response and particularly contradictions of response within single individual protocols (the total set of responses for a single individual).

On the basis of these kinds of data, and in the light of the perceptive works of the fore-mentioned writers on American Culture, I believe it is clear that a major shift in American values has, and is taking place.[5] I find it convenient to label this shift as being from *traditional* to *emergent*. The values thus dichotomized are listed under their respective headings below, with explanatory statements in parentheses.

I believe American Culture is undergoing a transformation, and a rapid one producing many disjunctions and conflicts, from the traditional to the emergent value systems outlined above. It is probable that both value systems have been present and operating in American Culture for some time, perhaps since the birth of the nation. But recently, and under the impetus of World Wars, atomic insecurities, and a past history of "boom and bust," the heretofore latent tendencies in the emergent direction have gathered strength and appear to be on the way towards becoming the dominant value system of American Culture.

Like all major shifts in culture, this one has consequences for people. Culturally transitional populations, as anthropologists know from their studies of acculturating Indian tribes, Hindu villages, and Samoan communities (among others), are characterized by conflict, and in most severe

---

[5] I have been particularly influenced by the writings of David Riesman and particularly by David Riesman, Nathan Glazer, and Reuel Denny, *The Lonely Crowd* (New York: Doubleday & Company, Inc., 1953).

TRADITIONAL VALUES	EMERGENT VALUES
Puritan morality (Respectability, thrift, self-denial, sexual constraint; a puritan is someone who can have anything he wants, as long as he doesn't enjoy it!)	*Sociability* (As described above. One should like people and get along well with them. Suspicion of solitary activities is characteristic.)
Work-Success ethic (Successful people worked hard to become so. Anyone can get to the top if he tries hard enough. So people who are not successful are lazy, or stupid, or both. People must work desperately and continuously to convince themselves of their worth.)	*Relativistic moral attitude* (Absolutes in right and wrong are questionable. Morality is what the group thinks is right. Shame, rather than guilt-oriented personality is appropriate.)
Individualism (The individual is sacred, and always more important than the group. In one extreme form, the value sanctions egocentricity, expediency, and disregard for other people's rights. In its healthier form the value sanctions independence and originality.)	*Consideration for others* (Everything one does should be done with regard for others and their feelings. The individual has a built-in radar that alerts him to other's feelings. Tolerance for the other person's point of view and behaviors is regarded as desirable, so long as the harmony of the group is not disrupted.)
Achievement orientation (Success is a constant goal. There is no resting on past glories. If one makes $9,000 this year he must make $10,000 next year. Coupled with the work-success ethic, this value keeps people moving, and tense.)	
Future-time orientation (the future, not the past, or even the present, is most important. There is a "pot of gold at the end of the rainbow." Time is valuable, and cannot be wasted. Present needs must be denied for satisfactions to be gained in the future.)	*Hedonistic, present-time orientation* (No one can tell what the future will hold, therefore one should enjoy the present—but within the limits of the well-rounded, balanced personality and group.)
	Conformity to the group (Implied in the other emergent values. Everything is relative to the group. Group harmony is the ultimate goal. Leadership consists of group-machinery lubrication.)

form—demoralization and disorganization. Institutions and people are in a state of flux. Contradictory views of life are held by different groups and persons within the society. Hostilities are displaced, attacks are made on one group by another. And this applies as well to the condition of American Culture—the context of American education.

The traditionalist views the emergentist as "socialistic," "communistic," "spineless and weak-headed," or downright "immoral." The emergentist regards the traditionalist as "hidebound," "reactionary," "selfish," or "neurotically compulsive." Most of what representatives of either viewpoint do may be regarded as insidious and destructive from the point of view of the other. The conflict goes beyond groups or institutions, because individuals in our transitional society are likely to hold elements of both value systems concomitantly. This is characteristic, as a matter of fact, of most students included in the sample described previously. There are few "pure" types. The social character of most is split, calling for different responses in different situations, and with respect to different symbols. So an ingredient of personal confusion is added that intensifies social and institutional conflict.

I hypothesize that the attacks upon education, which were our starting point, and the confusion and failure of nerve characterizing educators today, can be seen in clear and helpful perspective in the light of the conflict of traditional and emergent values that has been described. It is the heart of the matter. The task then becomes one of placing groups, institutions and persons on a continuum of transformation from the one value system to the other. Without prior explanation, I should like to provide a simple diagram that will aid at least the visual-minded to comprehension of what is meant. With this accomplished I will provide the rationale for such placement and discuss the implications of it in greater detail.

The diagram is meant to convey the information that different groups operating in the context of relations between school and community, educator and public, occupy different positions on the value continuum, with varying degrees and mixtures of traditional and emergent orientations. It should be understood that the placements indicate hypothecated tendencies, that no one group representing any particular institution ever consists of "pure" value types, but that there is probably a modal tendency for the groups indicated to place on the transformation, or continuum line, in the way expressed in the diagram. (See Figure 3.)

The rationale for the placement of the various groups on the value continuum is fairly complex, but let me try to explain some salient points. School boards are placed nearest the *traditional* end of the continuum because such boards are usually composed of persons representing the power, *status-quo*, elements of the community, and of persons in the

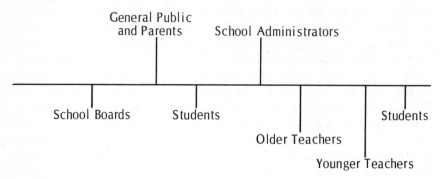

Figure 3

higher age ranges. They are therefore people who have a stake in keeping things as they are, who gained their successes within the framework of the traditional value system and consequently believe it to be good, and who, by virtue of their age, grew up and acquired their value sets during a period of time when American Culture was presumably more tradition-oriented than it is today.

The general public and parent group, of course, contains many elements of varying value predilection. It is therefore unrealistic to place this public at any particular point in the value continuum. But I hypothesize that the public *tends* to be more conservative in its social philosophy than the professional education set. The placement to the left of center of the continuum ("left" being "right" in the usual sense) takes on further validity if it is seen as a placement of that part of the public that is most vocal in its criticism of educators and education—since most of the criticisms made appear to spring out of value conflicts between traditionalist and emergentist positions. Parents complain that their children are not being taught the "three R's" (even when they are), that educators want to "socialize" the competitive system by eliminating report cards, that children are not taught the meaning of hard work. These all sound, irrespective of the question of their justification or lack of it, like traditionalist responses to change in an "emergent" direction.

Students are placed at two points on the transformation line because it is clear that those coming from traditionalist family environments will tend to hold traditionalistic values, but hold them less securely than will their parents (if our hypothesis for over-all change is valid), while other students who come from emergent-oriented families will tend to place even further, as a function of their age and peer groups, towards the emergent end of the line than their parents would. This is only partially true, indeed, for such a rationale does not account for the fact that offspring in revolt (and many American children from 6 to 16 are in a state of revolt against parental dictums) may go to extremes in either direction.

School administrators, older, and younger teachers, place at varying points on the emergent half of the transformation line. I have placed them there because I believe that the professional education culture (every institution has its own way of life, in this sense) that they have acquired in the schools and colleges of education has a clear bias towards an emergent-oriented ethos. Many of my educationist colleagues will reject this interpretation, and indeed, such interpretations are always guilty of over-generalization. Others of my colleagues will welcome such a characterization, but still question its validity. My case must rest on the basis of contemporary educational philosophy, theory, and practice. The emphasis is on the "social adjustment" of the individual, upon his role as a member of the group and community. Most of the values listed under the *emergent* heading are explicitly stated in educational literature as goals. Some of them, such as conformity to the group, are implicit. This value, in particular, grows out of the others, is more or less unintended, and constitutes a *covert* or *latent* value, by definition. This is, admittedly, a little like accusing a man of hating his mother, but not knowing it, and such accusations are usually rejected, or rationalized out of existence. But I believe that it is literally impossible to hold the other values in this system and avoid placing a strong emphasis on group harmony, and group control of the individual. My data, at least, gathered largely from graduate students in professional education courses, indicate that this is the case.

But educators and schools do not all come off the same shelf in the supermarket. Older teachers will tend, I hypothesize, to hold relatively traditionalist views by virtue of their age, and time of their childhood training (when they acquired their basic values)—a period in American culture when the traditionalist values were relatively more certain and supported than they are at present. Younger teachers were not only children and acquired their personal culture during a relatively more emergent-oriented period of American history, but they have been (I hypothesize) exposed to a professional education culture that has become rapidly more emergent-oriented in its value position. They are therefore placed near the extreme of the transformation line in the emergent direction.

School administrators come from a different shelf in the same section of the supermarket. They, to be sure, range in age from young to old, come from different family backgrounds, and have been exposed in varying degrees to the professional education culture. But sociological and anthropological studies of the influence of status and role on behavior and perception indicate that these factors tend to over-ride others, and produce certain uniformities of outlook. The school administrator's role is a precarious one—as any school principal or superintendent knows. He faces towards several different audiences, each with different sets of demands—school boards, parents, power groups, teachers, and students—as well as other administrators. He has to play his role appropriately in the light of all these demands. The fact that many cannot, accounts for the increasingly short tenure of personages like school superintendents. But to the extent that he plays *across the board* he will place somewhere towards the center of the line of transformation. Furthermore, his dependence upon the school board, and the power groups in the community, in many cases will tend to make his outlook relatively more conservative, and probably more traditionalistic, than that of his teachers—at least the younger ones. There are many exceptions, of course. I am only claiming *tendencies*.

My thesis, I hope, is clear by now. I am attempting to explain, or help explain, the increasingly bitter and strident attacks on schools and educators, and the conflict and confusion within the ranks. I have claimed that this situation can better be understood as a series of complex but very real conflicts in core values. And I have tried to show the direction of the values shift in American culture and place the various actors in the drama upon a transformation line within this shift.

In this perspective, many conflicts between parents and teachers, school boards and educators, parents and children, and between the various personages and groups within the school system (teachers against teachers, administrators against teachers, and so on) can be understood as conflicts that grow out of sharp differences in values that mirror social and cultural transformation of tremendous scope—and for which none of the actors in the situation can be held personally accountable. This is the real, and perhaps only contribution of this analysis. If these conflicts can be seen as emerging out of great socioculture shifts—out of a veritable transformation of a way of life—they will lose some of their sting. To understand, the psychiatrist says, is to forgive.

But now, though it seems indeed improper at this point, permit me to add another complication to an already complicated picture. I have tried to make it clear that not only are there variations in values held by groups and different parts of the social body and school institutions, but that there are also various values, some of them contradictory, held by single individuals as diverse streams of influence in their own systems. This is always true in rapid culture-change situations, as the anthropologist and philosopher know.

This means that the situation is not only confused by groups battling each other, but that individuals are fighting themselves. This has certain predictable results, if the anthropological studies of personal adaptation to culture change have any validity. And I believe that those results can be detected in the behaviors of most, if not all, of the actors in the scene. Let me try to clarify this.

I will deal only with teachers, as one of the most important sets of actors on this particular stage. I hypothesize that the child training of most of the people who become teachers has been more tradition than emergent value-oriented. They are drawn largely from middle to lower-middle social class groups in American society, and this segment of the class structure is the stronghold of the work-success ethic and moral respectability values in our culture (even in a culture that is shifting away from these values). Furthermore, it seems probable that a selective process is operating to draw a relatively puritanistic element into the public school teaching as an occupation. Self-denial, altruism, a moralistic self-concept, seem to be functional prerequisites for the historically-derived role of school teacher in American society (I might have said "school-marm.").

If this can be granted, then only one other ingredient needs to be added to explain several persistent types of personal adaptation to value conflicts observable among school teachers. That ingredient is one already spelled out—the relatively heavy emphasis, within the professional education culture, on the emergent-oriented value system. Teachers-to-be acquire their personal culture in a more tradition-oriented familiar environment, but they encounter a new kind of culture when in training to become school teachers—in the teacher-training institutions. There is, in this experience, what the anthropologist would call a discontinuity in the *enculturation* of the individual.[6] This is a particular kind of culture-conflict situation that anthropologists have recently begun to study, but mostly in non-western societies undergoing rapid change towards a western way of life.

On the basis of observations of a fair sample of teachers in coastal communities and in the middle west, I hypothesize that three types of adaptation to this personal culture-conflict situation and experience are characteristic.

> *Ambivalent:* This type is characterized by contradictory and vascillating behavior, particularly with respect to the exercise of discipline and authority. The type tends to be *laissez-faire* in some classroom situations, and authoritarian in others, depending upon which behavior is called into being as a defense against threat of loss of control.
>
> *Compensatory:* This type is characterized by one of two modes of behavior. The teacher overcompensates consistently either in the direction of the emergent or the tradition-centered values. In the first mode he (or she) tends to become a member of a *group-thinkism* cult—a perversion of progressive educational philosophy in action. The total stress is placed on social adjustment. Individuality

---

[6] *Enculturation* is a new, but useful term being used by social scientists. It stands for the process through which the individual acquires the culture of his group or society.

is not sanctioned to any significant degree. Conformity to the
group becomes the key to success. The type, in its extreme form,
is a caricature of the better features of the emergent-centered
value set. The second type compensates for internal culture-conflict
in the opposite direction, and becomes an outright authoritarian.
Tight dominance is maintained over children. All relationships
with them are formalized and rigid. No deviation is allowed, so
curiously enough, there is a convergence in the end-results of both
types. This type is a caricature of the better features of the tradi-
tion-centered values set.

Adapted: This type can be either traditional or emergent
value-oriented. But the compensatory and ambivalent mechanisms
operating in the first two types are much less intense, or absent.
The teacher of this type has come to terms with the value conflict
situation and experience, and has chosen (consciously or unconsciously) to act within the framework of one or the other value
set. There is consequently a consistency of behavior, and the mode
of classroom management and teacher-student relationship is not
a caricature of either value system.

No one is in a position to say which of these types is represented in
greatest numbers among American public school teachers today, and there
are few "pure" types. Certainly there are many traditional and emergent-
oriented teachers who have adapted successfully to the personal culture-
conflict situation and discontinuity of enculturative experience described.
But equally certainly there are many school teachers who fall more clearly
into one or the other typologies. It would be asking too much to suppose
that a cultural values-conflict situation as intense as the one transforming
American culture could be handled without strain by the key agent of the
culture-transmission process—the school teacher. But again, to understand
is to forgive.

In any event, it seems clear that if conditions are even partially of the
nature described, the group culture-conflict situation resulting in attacks by
representatives of those groups upon each other is intensified and at the
same time confused by the personal culture-conflict problem. Both processes must be seen, and understood, as resultants of a larger culture-
transformation process.

In conclusion to this by-far unfinished analysis (the next 20 years may
tell the more complete story), let me make it clear that I am not castigat-
ing either the emergentists, or the traditionalists. Value systems must always be functional in terms of the demands of the social and economic
structure of a people. The traditional mode has much that is good about it.
There is a staunchness, and a virility in it that many of us may view with
considerable nostalgia in some future time. But rugged individualism (in
its expedient, ego-centered form), and rigid moralism (with its capacity

for displaced hate) become non-functional in a society where people are rubbing shoulders in polyglot masses, and playing with a technology that may destroy, or save, with a pushing of buttons. The emergentist position seems to be growing in strength. Social adaptability, relativistic outlooks, sensitivity to the needs and opinions of others, and of the group, seem functional in this new age. But perhaps we need, as people, educators, anthropologists, and parents, to examine our premises more closely. The emergentist can become a group conformist—an average man proud of his well-rounded averageness—without really meaning to at all.

And lastly I would like to reiterate the basic theme of this article. Conflicts between groups centering on issues of educational relevance, and confusions within the rank and file of educators, can be understood best, I believe, in the perspective of the transformation of American culture that proceeds without regard for personal fortune or institutional survival. This transformation, it is true, can be guided and shaped to a considerable degree by the human actors on the scene. But they cannot guide and shape their destiny within this transformation if their energies are expended in knifing attacks on each other in such a central arena as education, or if their energies are dissipated in personal confusions. I am arguing, therefore, for the functional utility of understanding, and of insight into the all-encompassing transformation of American culture and its educational-social resultants.

FOR FURTHER THOUGHT

1. The classification of personnel associated with instruction in the school by Spindler puts them all on the "emergent" side of the continuum. Such a classification would suggest a commonality in the teaching and administrative forces. Further analysis of the place of these groups on the continuum suggests differences between the administration and the teachers and differences between older and younger personnel. *Would this suggest, in order to obtain a common conception of service necessary for professional standing, that professional groupings would not be possible if teachers of all ages were included or if teachers and administrators were included? If teachers disagree on both means and ends, as this classification suggests, what remains as the unifying principle to suggest the existence of a profession?*

2. The basis for classifying all teachers is "emergent" oriented rather than traditional. Spindler's judgement is that the dominant philosophy is one of emphasizing "social adjustment" of the individual and his role as a member of the group and community. *How would the traditionalist differ with the emergentist on this philosophy? Review the purposes*

*stated in Chapter 4 to find statements that would substantiate the claim
made by Spindler. Is it possible to find among the traditionalists, statements suggesting that the philosophy described by Spindler is capable
of acceptance by both groups, thus suggesting a nominal agreement?*

3. In describing the purpose of his article, Spindler notes that the important concern he feels is the need to understand differences in values
as the result of social and cultural transformations for which individuals
are not personally responsible. Not only do groups differ, but individuals
are torn internally by these conflicting values. *Given these conflicts, are
there ways of ascertaining the more desirable from the less desirable?
Is there implicit in Spindler's description a recognition that "might
makes right"?*

4. The subtlety of Spindler's appeal for developing understanding is an
appeal for emergent values of social adaptability, relativism, and sensitivity to the needs of others. The defense for such a position rests on the
assumptions that value systems *must be functional* with regard to the
demands of the social and economic structure and that these values *are
functional* in our society. *Are both of these assumptions valid? What challenge would the traditionalists offer this position?*

CHANGE: A CASE STUDY

The excerpt taken from Dr. Harold Benjamin's *Saber-Tooth Curriculum*
deals satirically with the problems of education in an era of change. It is
possible, in his presentation of paleolithic education, to find ideas and proponents that can be identified with such historical figures as Spencer,
Hutchins, Dewey, and many others. Most valuable for purposes of our
examination here, however, is the position taken by Benjamin in relation
to the place of the school in a changing society. At a time prior to the ice
age, "saber-tooth-tiger-scaring-with-fire" was a legitimate school subject.
The school was aimed at mastering the skill of scaring with fire. Such an
aim was only an intermediate step to the more encompassing problem of
general security. When the ice age came and change was wrought the
saber-tooth tigers disappeared from the scene. No longer was there a direct
tie between tiger-scaring as a school subject and the affairs of life. Little
security could be derived from the possession of these skills when a new
threat was imminent.

The legitimacy of the subject and others like it was questioned in the
new ice age. It is valuable to know whether the subject was questioned because it no longer met the old aim or whether a new aim was seen. Some
saw the aim of the school as being the development of a specific skill (that
is, saber-tooth-tiger-scaring). Others saw this as only a means to the aim of
providing security. Did the goal remain constant in the new ice age period
with only the means requiring adjustment? Were both the ends and the

means subject to change in light of the new conditions? The equilibrium of New-Fist's society and educational system was destroyed by the coming of the ice age. With the coming of the ice age came a whole host of new conditions for which the members of his society were unprepared. Apply the analogy of the ice age to our society today and ascertain which forces or factors might be having the same influence on us and on our "ice age." In either situation, paleolithic or modern, does the significant change in conditions warrant a change in the purposes, or the means of education, or both?

———————————◄◆►———————————

THE SABER-TOOTH CURRICULUM*

The first great educational theorist and practitioner of whom my imagination has any record (began Dr. Peddiwell in his best professorial tone) was a man of Chellean times whose full name was *New-Fist-Hammer-Maker* but whom, for convenience, I shall hereafter call *New-Fist.*

New-Fist was a doer, in spite of the fact that there was little in his environment with which to do anything very complex. You have undoubtedly heard of the pear-shaped, chipped-stone tool which archeologists call the *coup-de-poing* or fist hammer. New-Fist gained his name and a considerable local prestige by producing one of these artifacts in a less rough and more useful form than any previously known to his tribe. His hunting clubs were generally superior weapons, moreover, and his fire-using techniques were patterns of simplicity and precision. He knew how to do things his community needed to have done, and he had the energy and will to go ahead and do them. By virtue of these characteristics he was an educated man.

New-Fist was also a thinker. Then, as now, there were few lengths to which men would not go to avoid the labor and pain of thought. More readily than his fellows, New-Fist pushed himself beyond those lengths to the point where cerebration was inevitable. The same quality of intelligence which led him into the socially approved activity of producing a superior artifact also led him to engage in the socially disapproved practice of thinking. When other men gorged themselves on the proceeds of a successful hunt and vegetated in dull stupor for many hours thereafter, New-Fist ate a little less heartily, slept a little less stupidly, and arose a little

*From *The Saber-Tooth Curriculum* by J. Abner Peddiwell. Copyright 1939 by McGraw-Hill, Inc. Used with permission of McGraw-Hill Book Company. Dr. Harold Benjamin, former Dean of the College of Education of the University of Colorado and the University of Maryland, and Emeritus Professor of Education at George Peabody College for Teachers, is a noted author and editor. He is, of course, J. Abner Peddiwell.

earlier than his comrades to sit by the fire and think. He would stare moodily at the flickering flames and wonder about various parts of his environment until he finally got to the point where he became strongly dissatisfied with the accustomed ways of his tribe. He began to catch glimpses of ways in which life might be made better for himself, his family, and his group. By virtue of this development, he became a dangerous man.

This was the background that made this doer and thinker hit upon the concept of a conscious, systematic education. The immediate stimulus which put him directly into the practice of education came from watching his children at play. He saw these children at the cave entrance before the fire engaged in activity with bones and sticks and brightly colored pebbles. He noted that they seemed to have no purpose in their play beyond immediate pleasure in the activity itself. He compared their activity with that of the grown-up members of the tribe. The children played for fun; the adults worked for security and enrichment of their lives. The children dealt with bones, sticks, and pebbles; the adults dealt with food, shelter, and clothing. The children protected themselves from boredom; the adults protected themselves from danger.

"If I could only get these children to do the things that will give more and better food, shelter, clothing, and security," thought New-Fist, "I would be helping this tribe to have a better life. When the children became grown, they would have more meat to eat, more skins to keep them warm, better caves in which to sleep, and less danger from the striped death with the curving teeth that walks these trails by night."

Having set up an educational goal, New-Fist proceeded to construct a curriculum for reaching that goal. "What things must we tribesmen know how to do in order to live with full bellies, warm backs, and minds free from fear?" he asked himself.

To answer this question, he ran various activities over in his mind. "We have to catch fish with our bare hands in the pool far up the creek beyond that big bend," he said to himself. "We have to catch fish with our bare hands in the pool right at the bend. We have to catch them in the same way in the pool just this side of the bend. And so we catch them in the next pool and the next and the next. Always we catch them with our bare hands."

Thus New-Fist discovered the first subject of the first curriculum—fish-grabbing-with-the-bare-hands.

"Also we club the little woolly horses," he continued with his analysis. "We club them along the bank of the creek where they come down to drink. We club them in the thickets where they lie down to sleep. We club them in the upland meadow where they graze. Wherever we find them we club them."

So woolly-horse-clubbing was seen to be the second main subject in the curriculum.

"And finally, we drive away the saber-tooth tigers with fire," New-Fist went on in his thinking. "We drive them from the mouth of our caves with fire. We drive them from our trail with burning branches. We wave fire-brands to drive them from our drinking hole. Always we have to drive them away, and always we drive them with fire."

Thus was discovered the third subject—saber-tooth-tiger-scaring-with-fire.

Having developed a curriculum, New-Fist took his children with him as he went about his activities. He gave them an opportunity to practice these three subjects. The children liked to learn. It was more fun for them to engage in these purposeful activities than to play with colored stones just for the fun of it. They learned the new activities well, and so the educational system was a success.

As New-Fist's children grew older, it was plain to see that they had an advantage in good and safe living over other children who had never been educated systematically. Some of the more intelligent members of the tribe began to do as New-Fist had done, and the teaching of fish-grabbing, horse-clubbing, and tiger-scaring came more and more to be accepted as the heart of real education.

For a long time, however, there were certain more conservative members of the tribe who resisted the new, formal educational system on religious grounds. "The Great Mystery who speaks in thunder and moves in lightning," they announced impressively, "the Great Mystery who gives men life and takes it from them as he wills—if that Great Mystery had wanted children to practice fish-grabbing, horse-clubbing, and tiger-scaring before they were grown up, he would have taught them these activities himself by implanting in their natures instincts for fish-grabbing, horse-clubbing, and tiger-scaring. New-Fist is not only impious to attempt something the Great Mystery never intended to have done; he is also a damned fool for trying to change human nature."

Whereupon approximately half of these critics took up the solemn chant, "If you oppose the will of the Great Mystery, you must die," and the remainder sang derisively in unison, "You can't change human nature."

Being an educational statesman as well as an educational administrator and theorist, New-Fist replied politely to both arguments. To the more theologically minded, he said that, as a matter of fact, the Great Mystery had ordered this new work done, that he even did the work himself by causing children to want to learn, that children could not learn by themselves without divine aid, that they could not learn at all except through the power of the Great Mystery, and that nobody could really understand the will of the Great Mystery concerning fish, horses, and saber-tooth tigers unless he had been well grounded in the three fundamental subjects of the New-Fist school. To the human-nature-cannot-be-changed shouters, New-Fist pointed out the fact that paleolithic culture had attained its high level by changes in human nature and that it seemed almost unpatriotic to deny the very process which had made the community great.

"I know you, my fellow tribesmen," the pioneer educator ended his argument gravely, "I know you as humble and devoted servants of the Great Mystery. I know that you would not for one moment consciously oppose yourselves to his will. I know you as intelligent and loyal citizens of this great cave-realm, and I know that your pure and noble patriotism will not permit you to do anything which will block the development of that most cave-realmish of all our institutions—the paleolithic educational system. Now that you understand the true nature and purpose of this institution, I am serenely confident that there are no reasonable lengths to which you will not go in its defense and its support."

By this appeal the forces of conservatism were won over to the side of the new school, and in due time everybody who was anybody in the community knew that the heart of good education lay in the three subjects of fish-grabbing, horse-clubbing, and tiger-scaring. New-Fist and his contemporaries grew old and were gathered by the Great Mystery to the Land of the Sunset far down the creek. Other men followed their educational ways more and more, until at last all the children of the tribe were practiced systematically in the three fundamentals. Thus the tribe prospered and was happy in the possession of adequate meat, skins, and security.

It is to be supposed that all would have gone well forever with this good educational system if conditions of life in that community had remained forever the same. But conditions changed, and life which had once been so safe and happy in the cave-realm valley became insecure and disturbing.

A new ice age was approaching in that part of the world. A great glacier came down from the neighboring mountain range to the north. Year after year it crept closer and closer to the headwaters of the creek which ran through the tribe's valley, until at length it reached the stream and began to melt into the water. Dirt and gravel which the glacier had collected on its long journey were dropped into the creek. The water grew muddy. What had once been a crystal-clear stream in which one could see easily to the bottom was now a milky stream into which one could not see at all.

At once the life of the community was changed in one very important respect. It was no longer possible to catch fish with the bare hands. The fish could not be seen in the muddy water. For some years, moreover, the fish in this creek had been getting more timid, agile, and intelligent. The stupid, clumsy, brave fish, of which originally there had been a great many, had been caught with the bare hands for fish generation after fish generation, until only fish of superior intelligence and agility were left.

These smart fish, hiding in the muddy water under the newly deposited glacial boulders, eluded the hands of the most expertly trained fish-grabbers. Those tribesmen who had studied advanced fish-grabbing in the secondary school could do no better than their less well-educated fellows who had taken only an elementary course in the subject, and even the university graduates with majors in ichthyology were baffled by the problem. No matter how good a man's fish-grabbing education had been, he could not grab fish when he could not find fish to grab.

The melting waters of the approaching ice sheet also made the country wetter. The ground became marshy far back from the banks of the creek. The stupid woolly horses, standing only five or six hands high and running on four-toed front feet and three-toed hind feet, although admirable objects for clubbing, had one dangerous characteristic. They were ambitious. They all wanted to learn to run on their middle toes. They all had visions of becoming powerful and aggressive animals instead of little and timid ones. They dreamed of a far-distant day when some of their descendants would be sixteen hands high, weigh more than half a ton, and be able to pitch their would-be riders into the dirt. They knew they could never attain these goals in a wet, marshy country, so they all went east to the dry, open plains, far from the paleolithic hunting grounds. Their places were taken by little antelopes who came down with the ice sheet and were so shy and speedy and had so keen a scent for danger that no one could approach them closely enough to club them.

The best trained horse-clubbers of the tribe went out day after day and employed the most efficient techniques taught in the schools, but day after day they returned empty-handed. A horse-clubbing education of the highest type could get no results when there were no horses to club.

Finally, to complete the disruption of paleolithic life and education, the new dampness in the air gave the saber-tooth tigers pneumonia, a disease to which these animals were peculiarly susceptible and to which most of them succumbed. A few moth-eaten specimens crept south to the desert, it is true, but they were pitifully few and weak representatives of a once numerous and powerful race.

So there were no more tigers to scare in the paleolithic community, and the best tiger-scaring techniques became only academic exercises, good in themselves, perhaps, but not necessary for tribal security. Yet this danger to the people was lost only to be replaced by another and even greater danger, for with the advancing ice sheet came ferocious glacial bears which were not afraid of fire, which walked the trails by day as well as by night, and which could not be driven away by the most advanced methods developed in the tiger-scaring courses of the schools.

The community was now in a very difficult situation. There was no fish or meat for food, no hides for clothing, and no security from the hairy death that walked the trails day and night. Adjustment to this difficulty had to be made at once if the tribe was not to become extinct.

Fortunately for the tribe, however, there were men in it of the old New-Fist breed, men who had the ability to do and the daring to think. One of them stood by the muddy stream, his stomach contracting with hunger pains, longing for some way to get a fish to eat. Again and again he had tried the old fish-grabbing technique that day, hoping desperately that at last it might work, but now in black despair he finally rejected all that he had learned in the schools and looked about him for some new way to get fish from that stream. There were stout but slender vines hanging from trees along the bank. He pulled them down and began to fasten them together more or less aimlessly. As he worked, the vision of what he might do to satisfy his hunger and that of his crying children back in the cave grew clearer. His black despair lightened a little. He worked more rapidly and intelligently. At last he had it—a net, a crude seine. He called a companion and explained the device. The two men took the net into the water, into pool after pool, and in one hour they caught more fish—intelligent fish in muddy water—than the whole tribe could have caught in a day under the best fish-grabbing conditions.

Another intelligent member of the tribe wandered hungrily through the woods where once the stupid little horses had abounded but where now only the elusive antelope could be seen. He had tried the horse-clubbing technique on the antelope until he was fully convinced of its futility. He knew that one would starve who relied on school learning to get him meat in those woods. Thus it was that he too, like the fish-net inventor, was finally impelled by hunger to new ways. He bent a strong, springy young tree over an antelope trail, hung a noosed vine therefrom, and fastened the whole device in so ingenious a fashion that the passing animal would release a trigger and be snared neatly when the tree jerked upright. By setting a line of these snares, he was able in one night to secure more meat and skins than a dozen horse-clubbers in the old days had secured in a week.

A third tribesman, determined to meet the problem of the ferocious bears, also forgot what he had been taught in school and began to think in direct and radical fashion. Finally, as a result of this thinking, he dug a deep pit in a bear trail, covered it with branches in such a way that a bear would walk out on it unsuspectingly, fall through to the bottom, and remain trapped until the tribesman could come up and despatch him with sticks and stones at their leisure. The inventor showed his friends how to dig and camouflage other pits until all the trails around the community were furnished with them. Thus the tribe had even more security than before and in addition had the great additional store of meat and skins which they secured from the captured bears.

As the knowledge of these new inventions spread, all the members of the tribe were engaged in familiarizing themselves with the new ways of living. Men worked hard at making fish nets, setting antelope snares, and digging bear pits. The tribe was busy and prosperous.

There were a few thoughtful men who asked questions as they worked. Some of them even criticized the schools.

"These new activities of net-making and operating, snare-setting, and pit-digging are indispensable to modern existence," they said. "Why can't they be taught in school?"

The safe and sober majority had a quick reply to this naïve question. "School!" they snorted derisively. "You aren't in school now. You are out here in the dirt working to preserve the life and happiness of the tribe. What have these practical activities got to do with schools? You're not saying lessons now. You'd better forget your lessons and your academic ideals of fish-grabbing, horse-clubbing, and tiger-scaring if you want to eat, keep warm, and have some measure of security from sudden death."

The radicals persisted a little in their questioning. "Fishnet-making and using, antelope-snare construction and operation, and bear-catching and killing," they pointed out, "require intelligence and skills—things we claim to develop in schools. They are also activities we need to know. Why can't the schools teach them?"

But most of the tribe, and particularly the wise old men who controlled the school, smiled indulgently at this suggestion. "That wouldn't be *education*," they said gently.

"But why wouldn't it be?" asked the radicals.

"Because it would be mere training," explained the old men patiently. "With all the intricate details of fish-grabbing, horse-clubbing, and tiger-scaring—the standard cultural subjects—the school curriculum is too crowded now. We can't add these fads and frills of net-making, antelope-snaring, and—of all things—bear-killing. Why, at the very thought, the body of the great New-Fist, founder of our paleolithic educational system, would turn over in its burial cairn. What we need to do is to give our young people a more thorough grounding in the fundamentals. Even the graduates of the secondary schools don't know the art of fish-grabbing in any complete sense nowadays, they swing their horse clubs awkwardly too, and as for the old science of tiger-scaring—well, even the teachers seem to lack the real flair for the subject which we oldsters got in our teens and never forgot."

"But, damn it," exploded one of the radicals, "how can any person with good sense be interested in such useless activities? What is the point of trying to catch fish with the bare hands when it just can't be done any more. How can a boy learn to club horses when there are no horses left to club? And why in hell should children try to scare tigers with fire when the tigers are dead and gone?"

"Don't be foolish," said the wise old men, smiling most kindly smiles. "We don't teach fish-grabbing to grab fish; we teach it to develop a generalized agility which can never be developed by mere training. We don't teach horse-clubbing to club horses; we teach it to develop a generalized strength in the learner which he can never get from so prosaic and specialized a thing as antelope-snare-setting. We don't teach tiger-scaring to scare tigers; we teach it for the purpose of giving that noble courage which carries over into all the affairs of life and which can never come from so base an activity as bear-killing."

All the radicals were silenced by this statement, all except the one who was most radical of all. He felt abashed, it is true, but he was so radical that he made one last protest.

"But—but anyway," he suggested, "you will have to admit that times have changed. Couldn't you please *try* these other more up-to-date activities? Maybe they have *some* educational value after all?"

Even the man's fellow radicals felt that this was going a little too far.

The wise old men were indignant. Their kindly smiles faded. "If you had any education yourself," they said severely, "you would know that the essence of true education is timelessness. It is something that endures through changing conditions like a solid rock standing squarely and firmly in the middle of a raging torrent. You must know that there are some eternal verities, and the saber-tooth curriculum is one of them!"

FOR FURTHER THOUGHT

1. Do we have any subjects in our schools today such as saber-tooth-tiger-scaring or woolly horse-clubbing, which are no longer related to the needs of the society?

2. The analogy of the Saber-Tooth Curriculum is designed in part to provide an indirect look at a variety of features both historical and current that have been and are prominent in American education. *Which group, movement, or idea does each of the following represent:*

(a) *The Conservative forces: especially those of the Great Mystery?*

(b) *New-Fist?*

(c) *The wise old men who after the ice age defended the curriculum of New-Fist?*

(d) *The radicals who were advocating revision following the ice age? Are the basic ideas of any of these positions described in Chapter 4? Compare the ideas as expressed in Chapter 4 with those used by Benjamin to characterize the position.*

3. Essential to the defense made by the conservatives was the idea that "you can't change human nature." *How important is human nature as a consideration related to the determination of purposes of education? What is human nature? Is it a malleable quality of man or is it fixed?*
4. It is stated by Benjamin that once New-Fist had determined his educational goal he proceeded to construct a curriculum for reaching that goal. *How essential to the determination of the curriculum was the establishment of the goal? Once the goal or objective has been clearly formulated, is there any legitimate basis for disagreement concerning the curriculum or the methods of teaching? Is the disagreement over means any less basic than the question of purpose? Why or why not?*
5. In an earlier selection Spindler made a distinction between traditional and emergent values. *Utilize these concepts in discussing the Saber-Tooth Curriculum. To what extent does the traditional category become meaningless through the accumulation of replaced ideas? In a rapidly changing, complex society does the category of emergent values prevail for an enlarging, broadening, and divergent group of values, or are more and more relegated to the traditional category? In the simplified realm of paleolithic times are the ideas and values of New-Fist's time eventually relegated to the traditional along with the ideas and values that they had initially replaced?*
6. In dealing with the radicals of the new ice age the wise old men indicated that what they were suggesting just "wouldn't be *education.*" *What reasons might one offer for such a claim? Would it have been possible for a social scientist to have reviewed the suggestions and to have found the suggestions in keeping with education? What differences are there between judgments of a social scientist on terms such as education, teaching, and so forth, and normative judgments? Can these differences be related to ideas of what is and what ought to be?*
7. In arguing for the retention of New-Fist's established system the wise old men claimed that the radicals were advocating training rather than education. *What is the difference between the two? Can education be so defined as to include training? Is there a worthwhile distinction to be made between training and education?*

IS CHANGE PROGRESS?

This selection from the works of Robert Maynard Hutchins provides a valuable insight into many of the realms of change in our modern society. It is not only descriptive in nature. It also suggests a policy for the schools in relation to these changes.

He discusses and brings to our attention such things as large food surpluses, poverty and urban slum conditions, military expenditures of large proportions, disparities between the have and the have-not nations, increasing unemployment and displacement of labor, and inadequate educational offerings. According to Hutchins, these inadequacies of education do not arise solely because of the many changes and developments taking place. Instead, these developments are seen to offer more than ever before the conditions necessary for truly human growth. The opportunity "to learn how to become human and how to organize a human society" is here. The particulars or the means of vocational education are seen to be as obsolete as "saber-tooth-tiger-scaring" was after the ice age. In fact there is serious question, from Hutchins' standpoint, as to whether or not such studies were ever appropriate in our schools.

As the reader explores what Hutchins has to say there is the chance to clarify a number of central issues in education. Do the changes everywhere manifest in our society warrant new ends in education? Are the ends of education constant with the means being temporarily out of tune? Do both the means and the ends need reconsideration? The possible answers reflect different views of the nature of man, society, and the good life—all of which are constant considerations or themes in the clarification of educational purposes.

Education as formal schooling is inescapably tied to the future generation. Inasmuch as this is the case there is continually that problem confronting educators. The problem is what is the nature of the future for which we can prepare? How important is a conception of the future to the actual determination of curriculum, methods, and teacher preparation? Given the rapid rate of change in our society, the preparation of future members of society is complicated. Given the uncertain nature of the future, what kind of education will offer the greatest benefits?

------◄◆►------

ARE WE EDUCATING OUR CHILDREN
FOR THE WRONG FUTURE?*

The world is new and is getting newer every minute. Anything may happen, and what is most likely to happen may be what we least expect.

Almost every "fact" I was taught from the first grade through law school is no longer a fact. Almost every tendency that was proclaimed has failed to materialize. The "facts" and tendencies of today are those that nobody foresaw fifty years ago. I clearly remember the table of immutable

*Robert Maynard Hutchins, "Are We Educating Our Children for the Wrong Future?" *Saturday Review*, September 11, 1965. Dr. Hutchins is currently the President of the Center for the Study of Democratic Institutions, and was formerly President of the University of Chicago.

elements and atomic weights that hung on the wall of the chemistry laboratory in 1916. I also recall my history professor's description at that date of the bright future of British rule in South Africa.

I am especially embarrassed by the facts and tendencies I proclaimed myself. I can only hope the students in the Yale Law School have forgotten what I taught them. The courts have overruled and the legislatures repealed most of what I knew.

Education, in the nature of the case, has to be concerned with the future. But if we ask ourselves what we positively know of the future, about all we can say is that it will not be like the present. The whole world is committed to the highest possible rate of technological change. The daily accomplishments of science are such as to convince us that we are eventually going to know how everything works. Then we shall be able to do anything, and anything can happen.

The first question about education we have to try to answer is: How can it prepare for a future so uncertain and contingent that the main outlines of it are, as Disraeli used to say, "shrouded in the dark shadows of dubiety"?

The second question results from the one big, central, fundamental change we can foresee, and that is in man's relation to his work and in society's concern with production. This point requires some elaboration.

Ever since Adam and Eve were driven from Paradise and told to get to work, subsistence has been the primary preoccupation of men everywhere. Production has been regarded as so important that men were rewarded only if they produced. They were paid to work. If they did not work, they did not eat. Work and production were the means of individual and national strength, support, and salvation.

As recently as 1940 Wendell Willkie was stumping the country with the slogan, "Only the productive can be strong." Today we have billions of bushels of food we cannot get rid of. We could produce billions more if we wanted to. Every major industry could turn out infinitely more than is now being manufactured. The excess productive capacity of the United States is estimated at somewhere between $30 billion and $60 billion a year. It does not make much difference which figure you choose: it will be higher shortly.

There is a great deal of work to be done, but the question is whether and how soon we are going to get around to doing it. One-third of the population of this country lives below the poverty line. Urban slums are a disgrace, and now we are adding suburban slums to them. We need all kinds of things, notably schools, colleges, universities, hospitals, and libraries.

But we have been brought up to believe that the only desirable expenditures in the public sector are those for military purposes.

The budget for the space program, which is supported on military grounds, is $5.4 billion a year. This is $2 billion more than the total annual cost of all the colleges and universities in the United States.

President Johnson has had to call the effort to alleviate poverty a "war" in order to get anybody interested in it. But we have less than $1 billion appropriated now for the great war against poverty, as against $50 billion we are ready to put annually into defense.

There is a great deal of work to be done ouside this country. Although we are willing to help other peoples in the name of military security, we are reluctant to assist them merely because they are human beings in need. This despite the fact that the most explosive situation in the world today arises because of the division between the have and the have-not countries.

Since the war, the rich nations have got richer and the poor poorer. The poor ones are mostly primary producers. They sell raw materials and buy manufactured goods. The prices of manufactured goods have risen, and those of raw materials have declined. The resulting loss to the developing countries exceeds the total of all the aid they have received.

If we are not moved by humanitarian considerations, we might at least remember that we have some interest in holding the world together. The Marshall Plan on behalf of Western Europe was, to state it in its lowest terms, a great and successful example of enlightened self-interest at work.

The war against poverty should be conducted on a global scale. The question is, again, the rate at which it can be carried on. Trained men and good ideas are indispensable if money and goods are to accomplish anything. They are available in Europe. They are in short supply in the developing countries. So, even if we were prepared as we should be to put our superfluity at the disposal of these countries, we would find them incapable of absorbing assistance fast enough to make any telling impression on the flood of our production.

Suppose we spent each year ten times as much fighting poverty as we now propose, or on the order of $10 billion. Suppose we spent three times as much on higher education, another $10 billion. Suppose we tripled our expenditure on foreign aid, another $10 billion. We would then have absorbed $30 billion of our excess capacity. By the time we got around to making these expenditures our excess capacity would have risen by at least $30 billion.

This is not the whole story. It is now official government policy to produce a "bigger bang for a buck." The effects are already visible in those parts of the country, like California, in which a large proportion of the population is dependent on the arms industry.

For every billion knocked off the arms bill, we shall have to spend a billion somewhere else if we are to have any hope of maintaining employment.

The Administration's plan for bridging the widening gap between production and consumption is to cut taxes. The expectation is that this will stimulate demand, mop up surplus production, and lead to some reduction in unemployment.

But what if increasing production does not mean increasing employment? While production has been rising, unemployment has been holding steady. Although we are to have a tax cut of $11 billion, nobody expects unemployment to go below 4 percent. This is the new definition of an "acceptable" rate. It is twice the rate considered acceptable in Western Europe.

Meanwhile, in the advanced industrial countries of the West, the link between production and employment is being broken. Dr. Solomon Fabricant, the cautious director of research for the National Bureau of Economic Research, says: "Our immediate historical evidence indicates that there have been changes in basic materials and energy sources and tools and machines and in the relationship of the worker to his job. Eventually this will add up to a new industrial revolution."

What these somewhat opaque words mean is that automation and cybernetics are changing the world. They substitute the machine not only for muscles but also for minds. This is new, and no reassuring historical example, like the effect of the invention of the automobile on employment, is relevant.

W. Willard Wirtz, the Secretary of Labor, has said that machines can now do, on the average, whatever a high school graduate can do. If they can do that now, why should we expect them to stop there? They will go on until they can do whatever a college graduate can do, and perhaps more.

The effects on unskilled, or muscle, labor are obvious. The disappearance of the muscular miner reflects a universal tendency. The importation of seasonal Mexican farm labor into California was discontinued because Americans wanted, or were said to want, the 60,000 jobs at stake. Now it seems unlikely that there will be any jobs. Machines are being developed to do the work.

The skilled worker is going, too. The managing director of Bahlsen's, the great automatic bakery in Western Germany, says, "Here the skill of the baker dies." The skilled baker is likely to be dangerous, because he may think (quite wrongly) that he can improve the product by interfering with the machine.

The *Wall Street Journal* has described the effects of automation on the skilled white-collar worker. White-collar employment in the financial concerns of Manhattan, for example, was lower in 1963 than in 1962. Employment in brokerage houses declined while the volume of trading increased.

The New York Life Insurance Company tripled its business in ten years; but the number of its employees rose by only 300, or less than 10 percent.

These effects are now being felt by what is called "middle management." This is composed of highly skilled, white-collar people, mostly college graduates. Although they do not make important decisions on policy, they supply much of the information required for those decisions. They watch the flow of goods and money and see to it that both are in the right place at the right time. Computers can do better. They are quicker, more reliable, and, in the long run, cheaper. As they are improved and become still cheaper, they will drive the middle managers from the field.

The service trades seem a weak reed to lean on. Self-service and automatic vending machines are invading every department of retailing. The solemn and conservative magazine *U.S. News & World Report* says, "Food shopping at the supermarket will be automated. There'll be only one sample of every item on display, along with a punch card. Simply take a card for each item you want to buy, take the cards to the checkout counter. There, a machine will tally the cost. While you pay the clerk, all your purchases will be assembled, packed in a box or bag, and delivered to you as you leave the store."

Quoting "a top official of the General Electric Company," the article goes on to portray the automation of the home through computers that will make up your grocery list, remind you of appointments and anniversaries, take care of your finances, pay your bills, write your checks, figure out your income tax, and answer your telephone. Reproduction will be the only function performed by human labor.

The only possible conclusion is that the happy marriage between production and employment is being dissolved. The political, economic, social, cultural, and educational consequences cannot be overestimated.

What are we going to do with ourselves? Gerard Piel, publisher of *Scientific American,* has pointed out in a pamphlet written for the Center for the Study of Democratic Institutions that if we had continued with the sixty-hour week we would now have 27,000,000 unemployed. By reducing the hours of labor, we have spread work and leisure. Any proposal for the future must proceed along the same line. But I must emphasize that at the end of the line we shall find ourselves largely without work as we have understood work in the past.

Yet education has never been as job-oriented as it is today. This is a melancholy instance of the general truth that a doctrine seldom gains acceptance until it is obsolete.

The doctrine never was any good. In any country that has a highly mobile population and a rapidly changing technology, the more specifically education is directed to jobs, the more ineffective it is bound to be. Today such education is patently absurd. Everybody is aware that the official rate of unemployment among young people is double that among adults. The actual rate is undoubtedly higher, because many young people have thought it useless to apply for work. The general reaction to this situation borders on fantasy: it is to propose widespread extension of vocational training. In short, the cure for the disease of no jobs is training for them.

The archaic quality of such aspirations is sufficiently demonstrated by the case of key punch operators. They have now been superseded by machines and have been declared surplus by the California Employment Service. Today five vocational schools in Los Angeles advertise that they train key punch operators.

The matter goes deeper. A dozen years ago, a British group known as the Archbishop of Canterbury's Fifth Committee delivered itself of a statement that sums up the basic issue. It said: "A nation which regards education primarily as a means of converting its members into more efficient instruments of production is likely not only to jeopardize its moral standards and educational ideals, but to discover that by such methods it cannot attain even the limited success at which it aims."

Our educational ideals these days are expressed in the phrase "marketable skills." But entirely apart from the inability of the educational system to keep up with the market and forecast what skills it will buy, and entirely apart from the inefficiency of vocational training in school as compared with that on the job, the idea of producing marketable skills is ignoble and degrading for an educational system. It is an ideal that seduces the system into doing what it cannot and should not do and that forces it to neglect what it can and should do.

What education can and should do is help people become human. The object of education is not manpower, but manhood. This object we are now able to attain. We can now make the transition from a working to a learning society.

We started with two questions: how to educate for an undecipherable future, and how to prepare for a world in which work has lost its significance. The answer to both questions turns out to be the same. The man who is truly educated, rather than narrowly trained, is ready for anything. He has developed his human powers and is able to use them and his understanding of the world to meet any new problem he has to face. He is prepared by his education to go on learning.

Hence he is prepared for the human use of his free time. This is, in fact, the purpose of education in childhood and youth. It is to inspire the desire for life-long learning and to supply the training that will make it possible.

The democratic society is the learning society *par excellence*. The Constitution of the United States is intelligible only as a charter of learning. In the spirit of the Preamble, we are to learn together to govern ourselves. The law, the professions, the voluntary associations to which we belong, the political campaigns through which we suffer—all the institutions in our society should be regarded as teachers. Through them, as well as through the educational system, we can learn how to become human and how to organize a human society.

The special function of our educational institutions is to supply the intellectual tools, the intellectual discipline, and the intellectual framework necessary to understand the new problems we shall face. Support for this position comes from an unexpected but highly practical source, the Chief of Police of Chicago. He remarked the other day that he wanted a "completely professionalized" force.

Then he went on to say, "But the professionalism must be based on a foundation of liberal arts. It's necessary to get a complete man who has an understanding of his society and its people—a sense of perspective that can only come from a knowledge of history and philosophy." One might almost say that now the most practical education is a theoretical one: the man with the theoretical framework will comprehend the new situation, whereas the man without it has no recourse but to muddle through.

For the educational system the transition from a working to a learning society means a drastic reorientation of schools, colleges, and universities away from jobs and toward intellectual power. It also means that the present miscellaneous, superficial, and inadequate programs offered under the head of adult education must be replaced by continuous opportunities for learning open to all inhabitants of the country all their lives. The obligation of our educational system to provide these opportunities is just as serious as their obligation to the young.

If we can readjust our prejudices, we can get started toward a learning society. I do not underestimate the difficulties of making the readjustment. We can understand why Lord Keynes, the famous British economist, looking forward to a workless West, said he viewed the prospect with a "certain dread." We were brought up on Horatio Alger and the doctrine of salvation by work. Our last formal declaration of public policy on this subject was the so-called Full Employment Act of 1946.

Horatio Alger will soon be as out of date as *The Arabian Nights*. If work is our salvation, we are lost indeed, and we are on the way from full employment to full unemployment. But if we will only recognize it, the great opportunity that men have always yearned for is ours at last.

Other nations have had affluence and leisure, or their ruling classes have had them. They have been destroyed, usually from within, and usually from causes associated with affluence and leisure. The experience of Athens was unique, and it was too limited and too brief to be reassuring.

Now one can seriously raise the question whether the American democracy will turn out, like the Athenian, to be a temporary flowering from an almost accidental combination of favorable circumstances. One can seriously ask whether in a country like this, in a world like this, democracy is any longer possible. I believe it is. But I believe it is only if we can achieve the learning society.

FOR FURTHER THOUGHT

1. Within the article by Hutchins a number of conditions are described, whose effect on our society might be likened to the impact of the ice age on the society of New-Fist. *What are some of our glaciers? If our goal of education to help men become human remains constant, how do such matters affect education? Inasmuch as definitions of "human" vary, how valuable is such an agreed upon goal as a basis for action?*
2. Current in our society, given the high drop-out rate and the high degree of unemployment, is a concern for stimulating interest in schools. One measure adopted for such a goal is vocational education. There is a hope that such a program will seem more relevant to the disinterested and more within their range of current capability. It has the supposed additional advantage of preparing people for employment if and when they leave school. *Is it fair to assume that those dropping out of school are not as capable as those remaining? If it could be demonstrated that environment, rather than ability, is the major hindering factor, should the concern of the schools be to adjust the academic curriculum to meet the needs of the disinterested student rather than to interest them in the vocational curriculum? Given the information provided by Hutchins, to what extent do the vocational programs deny young people marketable skills? What is the most appropriate type of vocational education?*
3. Hutchins claims that democracy is still possible even with all the changes he envisions. Such a possibility is built on the premise that the society must continue to learn. *What place does adult education have in such a scheme? What would be the nature of adult education essential for such a system? What attitudes would be essential to the perpetuation of society?*
4. Included in the article by Hutchins is a statement made by the chief of police of Chicago who indicated the need for what he called a "completely professionalized" force. *What did he mean by such a statement? Why did he see such a preparation essential to the success of his force? What does such a stand suggest for the nature of teacher preparation? Extend the parallel to society or, as Plato would suggest, look at the individual "writ large." Does the statement suggest the need for a professional society? Would a professional society include the continuous*

learning and the attitude demanded by Hutchins as essential to democracy? Is this what is advocated by Blackington and T. V. Smith?
5. Hutchins claims that "the law, the profession, the voluntary associations to which we belong, the political campaigns which we suffer—all the institutions in our society should be regarded as teachers. Through them, as well as through the educational system, we can learn how to become human and how to organize a human society." *What does such a stance tell an educator about the importance of studying the relationship of school and society? What does it suggest about the possible validity of a number of charges leveled at school with regard to the failures of youth? Why do the findings of social science (particularly of sociology and anthropology) become vital considerations for teacher effectiveness?*

Summary of Part Two

In Part Two we have been concerned with the ordering nature of the concept of purpose. Emphasis has been placed on the idea that debate over questions in education cannot be satisfactorily considered and answered until the question of purpose has been settled. The nature of this settlement demands scrutiny as well. It is possible to attain agreement on three different levels: (1) agreement in name only (nominal), (2) agreement on programs or means of implementation (programmatic), and (3) agreement not only on the exact meaning but also on the way to attainment of that purpose (real). The last of these three types of agreement is the only one that offers any hope for stable and consistent settlement of instrumental concerns in education.

The determination of purposes must rest upon a consideration of the nature of man and society. From such considerations one is able to prescribe the conditions requisite to the establishment of the truly human community. The writings of educational philosophers such as Plato and Rousseau point out the essential nature of such reflections. Education and formal schooling play a central role in the formulation of such an ideal state. They must be integrally connected to ideas about man and society.

We have reviewed writings that are associated with two major schools of educational thought. The two represented are the progressives and the traditionalists. As noted earlier with these categories, their breadth or all-encompassing nature provides for inclusion of a wide variety of ideals. Generally their commonality resides in what each opposes. Inherent in these two positions are differing conceptions of man. As a result of these fundamental differences each school of thought emphasizes an entirely different purpose and different means of attaining this purpose. There is a tendency, in reviewing these categories, to see them exclusively or primarily concerned with instrumental matters. Discussion over the merits of either centers on the worth of one method as contrasted with another or with one type of content as opposed to another. Such discussion is of little value if resolution is sought at this level. This is true because the fundamental differences reside at the level of the purposes sought. If the problems were at the instrumental level, resolution would be possible through an accepted method of establishing knowledge. However, even though the two positions express their purposes in the same language, their points of contention over means cannot be resolved until the basic disagreements over purpose derived from differing conceptions of man have been settled.

Much of what currently transpires in educational research must of necessity operate at the hypothetical level due to the lack of agreement on explicitly stated and commonly understood goals. Questions over inclusion of religion, driver education, or "modern" mathematics, questions about the nature and content of vocational education, or questions about the appropriate methods for classroom usage whether in the regular or the "deprived" classroom all necessarily depend for their answer upon the matter of purpose.

A professional group claims to serve the public. What happens if there is widespread disagreement over the nature of the service to be offered? What if there is no unifying purpose to serve as a common basis for a profession? In order for teaching to be considered a profession it must possess such a unifying purpose or conception of service. The claim that the purpose of teaching is to serve the public or to do the will of the public can hardly be regarded as satisfactory. It ignores the fact that the great variety of communities and accepted values within these communities will lead teachers to pursue diverse and possibly conflicting purposes. Further, such a stance denies that the professional group has anything to offer with regard to the determination of appropriate ends. Any thought of a world-wide profession is totally absurd given such a position. It would demand the endorsement of any purpose and any means from brainwashing to instruction. This is hardly the basis for establishing a conception of professionalism in teaching.

SUGGESTIONS FOR FURTHER READING

1. Few sources present the importance of relating education to social and cultural developments as well as H. Benjamin, *Saber-Tooth Curriculum* (New York: McGraw-Hill, Inc., 1939). While an excerpt has been included in the readings of this text, the complete book is recommended for those interested in this subject. William Van Til has developed a more modern application of these ideas in a speech entitled "Social and

Cultural Developments Influence the Curriculum" published in *The Making of a Modern Educator* (Indianapolis: Bobbs-Merrill, 1961).

2. Examination of modern educational aims would not be complete without an appreciation of some of the conditions in our society responsible for the changing demands upon the schools. The problems associated with deprivation, urbanization, social class differentials, and adolescent socialization can be more readily understood by reading the following: M. Harrington, *The Other America* (Baltimore: Penguin Books, 1963); F. Riessman, *The Culturally Deprived Child* (New York: Harper, 1962); D. Schreiber, *Profile of the School Dropout* (New York: Random House, 1968); A. Kerber and B. Bommarito, *The Schools and the Urban Crisis* (New York: Holt, Rinehart & Winston, Inc., 1965); Patricia Sexton, *Education and Income* (New York: The Viking Press, Inc., 1961); Paul Goodman, *Growing Up Absurd* (New York: Random House, 1960), and *Compulsory Miseducation* (New York: Horizon Press, 1964); Thomas Curtin, *Poverty, Education and Race Relations* (Boston: Allyn and Bacon, 1967); and E. Friedenberg, *The Vanishing Adolescent* (Boston: Beacon Press, 1959). A more general source, having wider application, would be the 60th Yearbook of the National Society for the Study of Education entitled, *Social Forces Influencing American Education* (Chicago: University of Chicago Press, 1961).

PART THREE

PREPARING THE "GOOD" TEACHER

a derived question

The era of change that we are experiencing has produced an apparent eagerness for innovation in the realm of teacher preparation. This fact is seldom recognized even by those who are quite familiar with the presence of curriculum innovation and technique in the public schools. There is little hope for significant improvement as a result of these changed courses of study and technical facilities without properly prepared teachers. Teaching machines, "new math," television, and sophisticated visual aids are all for naught unless they can be co-ordinated into a fruitful learning environment.

With all these remarkable developments the quest for the "good" teacher continues. There are many types of programs for teacher preparation and a continuing controversy concerning their quality. Each of them, at least implicitly, carries a recommendation—a definition, as it were, of the "good" teacher.

What are the elements of a sound preparation program? What are the essential ingredients in the production of the "good" teacher? The range of alternatives is extensive. We have already grouped them into two categories: (1) "teacher education" programs and (2) "teacher training" programs. We have iterated and now reiterate that the worth of these alternatives is in large part determined by the purpose of the schools. This is to say that once the conception of service has been clearly formulated, a firm basis has been established for discussing teacher competence and programs that may lead to such competence. Since each major style of teacher preparation presupposes a conception of service to be rendered we have classified the controversies over teacher preparation as answering a *derived* question. Any attempt to arrive at an answer to such a question is futile unless there is a clearly formulated understanding of the service to be provided by the practitioner. In addition to such a clear understanding, there is the need for agreement upon what will constitute valid and acceptable tests of the various approaches. Only after agreement of purpose and the means of establishing evidence can a fruitful discussion of instrumental (derived) questions be undertaken.

While we in this book raise the derived question of teacher preparation, other derived questions could be profitably explored to demonstrate more clearly the distinction between *derived* and *root* matters. Inquiry into the relevance or worth of any subject or any method, regardless of the field of endeavor, is relatively pointless unless there is an accompanying consideration and resolution of the basic questions:

1. What goals or ends are we attempting to achieve?
2. What is an acceptable source of authority for our decisions with regard to: (a) the ultimate values or ends that we seek, and (b) the appropriate means of realizing these goals?

If the answers to these questions can be satisfactorily agreed upon, there is a strong likelihood that agreement on content and methodology can be reached. If these root questions cannot be answered, the participants in the dialogue have an understanding of wherein their disagreement lies. Our discussion of teacher preparation is illustrative of any one of the innumerable "derived" questions existing in education or any other field. Just as we raise the question, "What ideas in teacher preparation have the most merit?" someone else might raise the question, "Should we bus children to other neighborhoods to limit the impact of *de facto* segregation?" Both questions must be dealt with in the same manner. We must ask (1) what we are trying to achieve, and (2) what constitutes the basis for our justification of the ends and the means to those ends.

With this background in mind, we shall now proceed to establish our answer to the first of these matters, "What type of teacher do we want to produce?" or "What is the end to be sought in teacher preparation?"

The idea of the "good" teacher conveys to many the impression of the highly successful strategist or technician. We would like to suggest for your consideration that the good teacher is more than an able technician. Although technical competence is a necessary condition for the good teacher it has long been recognized that it is not a sufficient condition. In ancient Rome Quintilian, the orator and teacher, recognized that he and Rome were dedicated to the goal of producing the "good" orator or master of rhetoric. The qualifications he set included fluency of expression, ability to illustrate, and capacity for appropriate voice modulation. These were the skills essential to the role of orator. The orator had to possess them in order to effectively sway the public. This is one usage of the word "good." It suggests that the possession of certain technical skills, necessary to a task, is a sufficient reason for calling a man "good." Quintilian, however, was not satisfied with such a narrow conception of the "good" man. He demanded that the orator possess those moral or ethical qualities that would insure the proper use of his powers of persuasion. This demanded that the orator give attention to the direction of his persuasion. What would this same expectation imply for teachers? Clearly, a "good" teacher would not be *just* a skilled manipulator. He would not just be able to induce learning or to change behavior. He would have to be that and more. The power necessary to change people's minds rests in the hands of those who are "good" in the sense of continually examining the effects of that persuasion. Such a teacher would raise the question of the decency of his purpose, both with himself and with his students. He would also have to understand his subject matter and its underlying philosophy. The "good" teacher would be concerned with having his students examine and criticize their work rather than accept it in an unthinking manner. History, for example, would become more than memorization of facts. It would become a study of how facts are established in that domain.

The analysis of what constitutes "good" is nothing more than an analysis of what constitutes service. It includes both the technical and the ethical dimensions. It is for this reason that again we assert the fundamental or crucial nature of the question of service. Much of the debate about teacher preparation has ignored an explicit examination of this fundamental and prior consideration of service. As a result the debate has been heated, but not overly fruitful. Nevertheless, rapidly changing conditions in our society have kept the issue current.

Changing Conceptions

To some, new conditions suggest new purposes for the schools and new qualities for the teachers. There is a sense in which the development of teacher preparation can be seen as a continual adjustment to the changing conditions of the society. The earliest requirements for teachers were minimal. Only the early grammar schools required lengthy preparation, and that preparation was subject matter mastery. The clergy were initially those best prepared for the expectations of grammar school teaching. The demands at the elementary level were such that most adults in the community were regarded as able to meet the standard. The rigors of the frontier so sapped the energies and talents of the most able that responsibility for teaching often fell upon the weak and those unable to do much else. The principle of preparation was essentially the same for both levels of instruction. The teacher had only to master the subject matter himself. Little attempt was made (other than in some religious orders) to provide pedagogical training of teachers.

Not until the mid-nineteenth century and the rise of compulsory elementary school experience did the pattern change. Normal schools designed specifically to provide pedagogical assistance were established. As these grew in number and popularity the pioneer ideas of such educators as Pestalozzi, Froebel, and Herbart found acceptance. Not only did these normal schools provide pedagogics, but they also pursued a curriculum academically comparable to the secondary schools of that day. (Teacher education still labors under the stigma of such conditions.) Private academies also offered teacher preparation. Generally this was offered by the principal and consisted of basic methodological techniques. When compulsory education expanded to include the high school, the need for properly qualified teachers in larger numbers became vividly apparent. In some instances normal schools were expanded into four-year teachers colleges, and in other cases universities undertook responsibility for teacher preparation. The different emphases found in the inception of these two avenues of preparation continue today as a fundamental division in teacher education. The advocates of more content in preparation are in opposition to those recommending that emphasis be placed on techniques or methods of instruction. We contend that the debate is a spurious one inasmuch as both content mastery and pedagogical skill are essential to the technical success of the teacher. Such a debate, to the extent that it is really a debate over the means rather than over the ends that found their way into the conversation in the guise of means, is one that can be resolved if we know *what* the schools are to accomplish. Both approaches (content mastery and pedagogical skill), however, tend to ignore what we have classified as a necessary attribute of the "good" teacher: They debate without knowing the purpose.

Toward Professional Status

The increase in the length of time spent in preparing teachers has been an important factor in the clamoring of teachers for recognition as professionals. Little thought has been given to the fact that many apprenticeship programs are as long or longer than the degree route of the teacher. The length of time consumed by a program of preparation has probably been seen as connected with the difficulty of the tasks to be undertaken. As such, the program may be seen as leading rather directly to a competency. One's attention is then directed to the nature of the content included in such a program. To the extent that teacher preparation programs emphasize the imitation rather than the examination of practices (repetition rather than conceptual analysis) they are apprentice oriented or training programs. However ethical the product of such a program may be, he is a tradesman in terms of competence.

Programs are aimed at the answering of a question or a set of questions. If the central question is "how" is something accomplished, the program is likely to stay at the apprentice level. If the central question is "why" is something accomplished, there is the possibility of a professional program. This is true because of the two meanings that are commonly associated with the word "why." In one usage we commonly ask "Why did you do that?" When we say this, we may be asking what caused you to act this way rather than another. In the classroom one might raise the question of why use one technique or particular organization of content rather than a number of alternatives. Presumably one might select from a number of possibilities. Hopefully, there is an estimate on the part of the teacher that the style of operation he has selected will be successful because of certain things he knows about his students, the community, the subject matter, and the short and long range utility of what he hoped to teach. In so doing he is invoking a belief in a whole set of causal relations. This is done in the recognition of the continual change in the context with which he deals. This drives his attention to a host of variables and makes him an avid observer of the work being done in the behavioral sciences. This causal "why" is the scientific "how" with its stress on dynamics rather than an apprentice "how" with its stress on the static. With the stress of change all about us, it would appear that a program focused on "why" is the only viable one for the development of instrumental competency.

There is another equally valid and common meaning attached to "why" in the familiar question, "Why did you do that?" This second usage asks for a justification for action that goes beyond sheer causal description. Although this is not the focus of the present section, it is clear that such a usage and question is a legitimate one. Here one would be pressed beyond instrumental values into some more final judgment about the worth of the activity itself or its relation to some larger whole. The focus on "why" allows the consideration of a scientific "how," as well as the ethical or value question of what constitutes service. Thus it stands as a broader or more powerful focus for teacher preparation than the narrower "how" of apprenticeship.

In reference to this broader conception of preparation and competency, it should be obvious that the rate of change and the differences in students, teachers, and communities clearly demonstrate the futility of trying to offer complete specific directives or procedures to the prospective teacher at this point in the history of behavioral science. The best that can be done is to rely on the generalizations offered by social science and to depend upon the intelligent application of these by the teacher. Such an act of intelligent application is one of the marks of a professional.

The "good" teacher is one who has undergone a preparation that we classify as "teacher education." Such a person has the capability of being a professional if commitment to service exists along with other fundamental understandings to be derived from his preparation. There is more to the education of a professional than a lengthy period of schooling. In the case of a teacher there are at least three major ingredients. These can be reviewed from our discussions in this introduction. The professional teacher must: (1) know the scientific "why" of these techniques and thus guarantee his ability to apply the appropriate techniques in whatever novel or unique situation he encounters; (2) be able to perform capably or successfully with these techniques; and (3) continually examine the purposes sought and explore with his students the nature of the commitment of education and of the particular subject fields.

Such a preparation program would of necessity provide foundation instruction in psychology, anthropology, and sociology. It would provide student teaching experiences where methodological practices could be tried. Throughout it would emphasize the understanding of why certain approaches or activities were being recommended. It would encourage subject matter mastery as well as understanding of the methods and problems of that field of study. Finally, it would demand that students explore the meaning and nature of service. It is only through such a preparation that we will be able to provide teachers who in turn will help develop students able to take their place in the society in which they live. Only this kind of teacher will be able to knowingly utilize the current advances and developments and those yet to come.

An examination of teacher preparation would not be complete without some mention of the problems of certification and tenure. The analysis of teacher preparation is an analysis of what is necessary for entering and remaining in teaching. We want those people certified who are capable of offering essential and valuable services. As we have said before, the professional is professing to serve or benefit society. Is this possible without control over who offers such service? We come again to the matter of the best way of determining *when* the public has been served. Is the professional group best able to make this decision? What is to be the ordering principle for such decisions?

Chapter 5 is designed to raise a number of important considerations about teacher education and certification in particular, and about derived questions in general. The range of the selections chosen is wide in order to hit upon major issues of teacher education today. Chapter 6 explores the concept of power. Familiarity with the nature and the importance of this concept is essential if the teacher is desirous of achieving his professional goals. Preparation of the "good" teacher is seen to extend beyond the realm of courses and certification requirements. To make professionalism fully possible, there is the need to recognize that societal decisions are now made on the basis of power. There is also the need to acquire the power necessary to the fulfillment of professional ends.

CHAPTER 5

Education or Miseducation
of Teachers?

Is the ability to teach an inherent quality or is it a matter of education? If it is a quality acquired through birth the granting of certification or the existence of degree programs is merely a rite of passage that has no significance in evaluating the ability of a teacher to fulfill his role in society. On the other hand, if the ability to teach can be fostered through educational experiences, and if we are concerned with having good teaching in our schools, an important question develops. How do we know what are the most valuable experiences for a prospective teacher to have had prior to assumption of formal responsibility? Related to that question is one that carries the matter throughout the tenure of a teacher, that is, how do we know what are the most valuable experiences for teachers to have had after their initial certification in order to maintain a reputable performance level.

As indicated earlier, any attempt to answer such questions must be preceded by an exploration of the purpose of the school. Once the purpose has been clearly formulated, the matter of the proper qualifications can be considered. An approach to this concern might be to review all the certification standards for teachers. Such a review would offer an insight into the infinite variations of the time spent in course work leading to certification and an insight into the flexibility of standards. It would point out the absence of any set of national or international standards. Such a recognition then opens the question of "Why is there such a variation?" Are we unable to say that we know that certain experiences are essential to the adequate fulfillment of the role of a teacher? If so, is our major problem only one of setting up tests to provide the necessary evidence? Perhaps our lack of confidence is not appropriately directed when pointed at the variety of programs. Might it be that given the nature of the persons attracted to teacher preparation there is little or no hope of producing good teachers, regardless of the content or experience? If such could be proven or demonstrated, we would then have a firm basis for more careful selection of initial candidates. One factor that could serve to undermine answers to both of these possibilities is the definition of the "good" teacher. It is possible to so define good teaching that many of the things included in teacher preparation programs are irrelevant and of no value in creating good teachers. Similarly, it is possible to define good teaching so that many candidates could not hope to succeed regardless of their preparation. A most vital task in examining any program of teacher preparation or any criteria for certification is the clarification of the meaning of good teaching. Hopefully, one can see by now the manner in which that must be tied to what is considered to be the purpose of the school.

Once these matters have been decided there is an available basis for judging the existing programs of preparation and the value of certification standards. When such judgements have been made, the occupational group professing to serve the public is in a position to know whether its members have been properly prepared and whether the existing certification standards eliminate those not able to offer this service. The possession of such knowledge by a professional group is of little value without the power or autonomy of action to achieve or maintain these standards.

Herbert Schueler in an article dealing with preparing teachers for culturally-deprived areas asks whether the principles of good teaching essential to success in deprived areas prevail in all teaching situations. The selection by Harry Broudy offers a description of what he feels constitutes the essential elements of a teacher preparation program. The worth of much of the research and information that are a part of teacher preparation is challenged by Jerome Bruner. Each of these presentations raises questions about what should go into the curriculum for prospective teachers. The last selection by David Epperson offers a basis for exploring the questions of preparation associated with certification.

The readings and questions for this chapter are designed to encourage consideration of fundamental concerns in teacher preparation and certification. Such consideration will of necessity require making explicit the purposes of the schools examined in Part II. It will require consideration of the way to assess the worth of one program over another or one set of certifying criteria over another. Most important, it will help us to ascertain whether we as a group of educators have anything distinctive to offer by virtue of our preparation and by virtue of the standards we have met. Thus, it will offer one additional dimension for determining whether teaching is or can be a profession.

THE TEACHER OF THE CULTURALLY DEPRIVED

The development of socioeconomic and political problems of a unique and pervasive nature has left many to question both the adequacy of our schools and the value of the preparation of teachers for those schools. Since the initial shock afforded by the blast of Sputnik, numerous persons in the United States have become increasingly critical of the schools and their personnel. Initial emphasis was directed toward more and better science instruction. Government programs that provided for more thorough preparation of science teachers were endorsed. Gradually this grew to include foreign language teachers, geography teachers, counselors, almost ad infinitum. The current pressures for alteration and improvement of teacher preparation programs are tied to the national concerns for the poverty-stricken and the so-called culturally deprived. In some instances juvenile delinquency, unemployment, high drop-out rates are associated with this same concern. The questions are being asked: Why have we failed these youngsters? What have our teachers been doing wrong? What can be done to improve the quality of their preparation and, ultimately, their classroom performance?

In answer to these questions, and with the aid of financial support from government and from various foundations, teacher preparation institutions are devising and initiating programs designed to meet the new challenges. Hunter College in New York City has been at the forefront of this move, followed now in this development across the continent by many institutions hoping to combat school problems associated with "cultural" disparities affecting school performance.

These programs are essentially the same in basic design and rely heavily upon a thorough first-hand introduction to the schools and communities of the deprived. The selection by Herbert Schueler describes the nature and reason for such programs. It concludes with an extremely vital question for those concerned about the validity of numerous teacher preparation programs—each responding to a different social problem. He asks of the principles involved in the Hunter College program, "Aren't these implications valid for the proper training of all teachers, not just those concerned with the disadvantaged?"

THE TEACHER OF THE DISADVANTAGED*

The threat to our cherished way of life of a growing, permanently disadvantaged lower class, and its consequent weakening of the possibility of
democratic social mobility, has become a major domestic issue of our time.
Its political, economic, social and cultural, and ethical implications and
consequences are fast becoming a major preoccupation of leadership in all
facets of our society, the lowest included. It is an undeniable fact that, in
spite of the widespread availability—certainly at the childhood and
adolescent level—of public facilities for schooling, it has become the lot of
all but a pitifully small minority of the children of our urban and rural centers of disadvantage and deprivation never to be able to look forward to
developing the personal, intellectual, and psychological equipment needed
to find a way out of the depths to which they were doomed by birth and
circumstance. This is not only an unhealthy state for the lowest levels of
our society but also a dangerous one for those above. No modern democratic civilization can afford to allow a permanent cementing of lower
classes. It is not only contrary to the ethos of democracy but dangerous to
the maintenance of law, order, and the social well-being of all classes.

While it may sound like a cliché to affirm the ideal of equal opportunity
for all, the undeniable fact is emerging at last to those with responsible social consciences that deprivation is breeding further deprivation and that
the rate is increasing, particularly among the young; and this in a society of
unparalleled and evidently growing wealth. This is our greatest national
debt, our shame, which, unless checked, may well prove to be our undoing.

Of all agencies in society, the school has the greatest latent potential in
providing the means for the restoration of social mobility to our deprived
lower classes. It cannot bear the whole burden, of course, nor the whole
blame for failure, for it will take much more than the influence of the
schools to break down the walls of our ghettoes, but it is undeniable that
little can be done without the school. The institution of the public school is
already there, its attendance by children and youth mandated by law, its
facilities by and large adequate, its support through public funds established by custom. It just has to be made effective, and its potential as an
agent of desirable social change developed and strengthened. It is no acci-

*Herbert Schueler, "The Teacher of the Disadvantaged," *Journal of
Teacher Education,* vol. 16, no. 2 (June 1965), pp. 174–180. At the time
this article was published the author was Director of Teacher Education at
Hunter College. Dr. Schueler is currently President of Richmond College
of the City University of New York.

dent that so much attention is being given to the school by groups seeking to elevate the lot of the disadvantaged (and by those seeking to keep them where they now are).

The time, hopefully, is past when the school's function was limited to reflecting and perpetuating the mores of the community it was expected to serve. A slum, a ghetto, or a despond of poverty and deprivation is no possible standard for perpetuation in a progressive society. Every responsible leader of so-called minority groups (the minorities that are fast becoming majorities in our major population centers) views the school as a major agent for achieving social mobility among the disadvantaged peoples he represents, for only through the proper development and training of the talent that lies latent in all levels of society—the lowest included—can true equality of opportunity and that core of the democratic ideal, an upper mobile society, be achieved.

With this renewed emphasis on the school, some old truths have become manifest—truths that had gone somewhat out of fashion in a more complacent era of academic self-satisfaction—that effective learning requires effective teaching; that knowledge of the student is a primary requisite for effective teaching; that the teaching-learning community in the organized setting of the school is a human enterprise subject to all the potentials for gain and debit characteristic of all arranged social settings; that so-called subject matter has no viable existence per se in a school except as it provides the vehicle for the development of the learner; that living is learning and learning is living; and that the direction, substance, and method of schooling cannot safely be left to the workings of chance, particularly in a disadvantaged society. But above all, this preoccupation with the function of the school as an instrument of social change has helped the enlightened professional and his counterpart in the community to rediscover the student and to appreciate anew the potential function of his mentor, the teacher. None of this is the exclusive province of the disadvantaged society, to be sure, but at no level of society is the need so desperate, the proper education of the young so dependent on the school. A school, with a poor teaching staff and general disregard of individual student development, serving a middle-class community is as ineffective as the same type of school serving a lower-class population, but its effect can never be so devastating or its shortcomings so tragic in their effect, for its meagre resources can more easily be supplemented through family and other private means. It is the fate of the disadvantaged child to have the limits of his horizon dependent largely upon just one agency, the public school; hence, the key role that only the teacher can fill, the importance of the day-by-day contact of child and teacher, and the fashioning of this contact into learning experiences directed to the optimum development of the child.

The development of children to function within and for a nondisadvantaged society makes much of the virtue of emulation and perpetuation of prevailing values and customs, sometimes even to the point of complacency. But what is worthy to perpetuate, what is safe to emulate in a society of social, economic, and cultural deprivation? Therefore the sights of the school serving the disadvantaged must focus not just toward but beyond the horizon limited by poverty and deprivation that spawned its students, and to which few would want or should have to return. It is surely the depths of misguided sentimentality to consider poverty, whether economic, social, cultural, or spiritual, anything but degrading in a civilized society. Those who find ennobling qualities in the disadvantaged state usually do so from the perspective of their own comfort. Certainly no product of schooling properly conceived in its social mandates should be complacent about, nor satisfied with, a disadvantaged lot. Basically, education for the disadvantaged should not nurture conformity but discontent with the disadvantaged state, and develop the power and the will to rise beyond it.

This is admittedly no simple task, for there are limits to what the school can do with the complex conditions and causes that contribute to the massive deprivation that is threatening to undermine the dynamics once taken for granted in our social structure. Substandard housing, patterns of extremely mobile in-migration, widespread unemployment—particularly among young people—and the cancerous incursions of organized crime and overpopulation all add their festering rot to the disease of poverty. But insofar as the school deals with humanity particularly, the ultimate inheritors of what men and their society have wrought, its mission toward building a better society through the optimum development of each member becomes an inescapable mandate, for by being a major part of each individual's life, particularly in the formative years of childhood and early adolescence, it is the only social agency with the means, the opportunity, and if it will only accept it, the power to do so.

Has the school been effective, in degree and kind, in fulfilling this function? By and large it has not, although it is also true that it has not received sufficient credit for what it has done. Many reasons can be found for this failure. The crisis, while of long germination, did not really become acute until the decades of the post-World War II era. The complementary and causally intertwined social phenomena of accelerated population growth; of intensified industrial growth and change through automation, relocation, and the twin forces of development of new industry and processes and the abandonment of the obsolescent and old; and of in-migration of minorities and displaced poor to urban centers of population, with the accompanying blighting of growing areas of older urban housing, have all wrought new conditions upon our society with a suddenness that is terrifying in its impact. The school, in turn, found itself at the same time beset by a teacher shortage of unprecedented proportions, lack of sufficient facilities to house a growing pupil population, and escalating costs, with the inevitably accompanying demands by taxpayer groups to economize. All contributed to a growing helplessness to cope with a changing, unfamiliar pupil population in a community that seemed to be sliding inexorably down the road of multiple deprivation. With the depreciation of the community served by the school, teachers become more and more reluctant to teach there, and many either fled to the more advantaged professional conditions of the middle-class suburban school, left the profession altogether, or descended into the stultifying regimen of the type of teaching that is just above the level of bare custodial care.

Fortunately, many of the dedicated remained, as witness the many heartening contributions by teachers of the disadvantaged to this collection of articles. But to a much greater degree than ever before, schools serving largely disadvantaged populations were, and predominantly still are, beset by the greatest difficulty in attracting and retaining effective teachers. Add to this the unreasoned, degrading, destructive attacks on the schools by self-appointed critics, expert in just about any field but education, together with their varying effects—all bad—of putting teachers and schools on the defensive, of uncritical quick acceptance of nostrums, of bandwagon-inspired educational quackery, of retreating behind "safe," old practices and curricula distinguished by nothing but a greying obsolescence, and it is a wonder that so much that is good, effective, and dedicated still remains.

The speed of change has been unprecedented. The schools have not kept up to a level even approaching that necessary to fulfill their proper function. Nor, it must be said, have the institutions traditionally relied upon to train teachers; their lag has been as great as that of the schools. Certainly in the case of the disadvantaged they have been even slower; for they have not, unfortunately, had much opportunity to deal with them. In the case of the lower schools, facilities and mandated attendance at least assure such contact. American colleges and universities remain and are increasingly becoming more closed to the disadvantaged by the inexorable twin barriers (acting separately or in combination) of cost and qualifications for admission.

Therefore, the colleges and universities, particularly those engaged in teacher education, are faced with the necessity of rediscovering the school, particularly the one serving the disadvantaged. The time is long past when a university could get by with models of teaching and student behavior as exhibited in middle-class, comfortably safe communities or in campus schools dominated by faculty children. The need is for teachers in schools serving the teeming tenements; and before they can be prepared and served properly, the universities must include these communities and their schools among their laboratories for research, study, and training.

As one reads many of these articles, particularly those written by teachers in service, one is struck by their preoccupation with the day-to-day process of teaching and with their student-centered view. This is heartening and a fitting reminder to university professors engaged in teacher education that the whole process of training stands or falls by the specific everyday effects it has on the work of student and teacher in the classroom. The study of the child in a course in child development has little use unless it assists in the understanding and proper guidance of John, Mary, and Joe in a particular school, in a particular class, in a particular neighborhood. Similarly, no course in curriculum theory will be of much avail unless it finds application in the work of a specific teacher, with specific children, in a specific setting. And it is precisely this imperative specificity of application to specific conditions as they exist (not as they hopefully might be and are not) that has created such major problems for teachers and trainers and supervisors of teachers. It is fast becoming inescapable and devastatingly clear that the Joe and Mary we remember, and of whom our textbooks speak, are not the same as the José and Maria we find in our classes; that the neighborhood we once knew and felt comfortable in has become alien, and to our standards, shabby; that the life-styles, the language, the customs of the community served by our school and the children in our classes have become foreign, at times even threatening and frightening. In sum, the clientele of the school and the human and physical environment of the school have changed, and we have not sufficiently understood these changes nor taken them into sufficient account in our teaching and teaching resources and our programs of teacher education.

As one becomes familiar with the disadvantaged community and its children, particularly through the eyes of its teachers (in part revealed through many of these articles), certain requisites for proper teaching stand out. The first of these and possibly the most obvious, though too often observed in the breach, is a thorough knowledge of the student, his background, his aspirations, fears, habits, his talents, shortcomings, his life-style. The teacher, for example, who considers a child of Puerto Rican origin sneaky because he drops his eyes when being talked to is obviously in ignorance of the fact that in the Latin-American culture this is expected in children as a mark of respect for their elders.

This becomes particularly pressing as a problem for teachers who are not themselves products of the culture and class of their students, a condition that will continue to prevail for some time, since the children of the disadvantaged cultures have not and probably will not in the foreseeable future (not until their schooling enables them to realize their full poten-

tiality) aspire or be admitted to universities for teacher education in sufficiently representative numbers to form more than a small minority of the
public school teaching staff serving the disadvantaged. Quite often, a major cause of difficulty of teachers in understanding, and therefore working
with, children of disadvantaged circumstances is that they are in ignorance
of the life these children lead outside school, except insofar as they may
read or hear about it in its more sordid aspects through press reports of
local crime and delinquency. After all, the teacher of the disadvantaged,
himself of middle-class aspirations, rarely lives in the slum that holds claim
to the everyday squalor and deprivation dominating the existence of his
students. For him the school neighborhood is a road to be traversed hurriedly on the way to and from school and not a human society to be known
through firsthand personal contact and experience. Yet this is where his
students live, play, laugh, weep, fight, eat, and sleep; here are their
parents, their siblings, their pals, their enemies; here are the
influences—good, warm, evil, fearsome—that help shape their behavior;
here they live among their kind, subject to all the black, grey, and white
influences that shape the culture of the slums. All this must be known and
understood by the teacher (not just by the social worker) before proper
communication based on knowledge and confidence can be developed
with the student to form the basis for the proper influence, direction, and
motivation of his development. In addition, the school must know and
develop working relationships with allies serving similar and complementary ends—the churches, social service agencies, law enforcement, civic
and fraternal groups which deal with the same population. The school can
make common cause with the positive community agencies and their
leadership and receive from and give to them much mutually ad-
vantageous assistance. The knowledge of the student and his environment,
then, is the first requisite for teaching the disadvantaged.

The second requisite for teaching is the knowledge of ways to order and
guide the learning of the disadvantaged child. Teachers have always been
enjoined by university departments of education not to become textbook
slaves and have been encouraged in the opposite direction by publishers of
colorful and durable texts and workbooks. There is no such conflict with
the teacher of the disadvantaged. It has been proved abundantly that the
standard textbook conceived for and within the traditionally middle-class
white society falls far short of reaching and communicating with the child
of the disadvantaged and culturally different levels of lower-class society.
And while some effective attempts have been made to create materials that
do speak to such students, the need is not so much to develop standard
material of a widespread market among schools serving the disadvantaged, helpful though such material may be, as to equip each teacher
with the adaptive skills to devise his own materials, created anew or

adapted and modified from what already exists, tailor-made to fit the particular needs of his own students. The basis for curriculum is all around us; it must be so fashioned as to touch the life of the learner, whatever it may be; it must begin where he is, not where some outside agent assumes he should be; and having begun where he is, it can then begin the process of enlarging, enriching, and broadening the basis of his experience and his development. This cannot be done without a sufficient knowledge of the learner and his environment nor without highly sophisticated skills of curriculum development, manipulation, and adaptation. With the middle-class population, a teacher without such skills, though ineffective, may still have his shortcomings somewhat ameliorated by the use of good, established text- and workbook materials; but with the teacher of the disadvantaged, this convenient crutch collapses under its own burden of ineffectiveness. In several of these teacher contributions are examples of this highly necessary requisite for teaching.

A third requisite, perhaps the most pervasive of all, is the skill of the teacher in human relations, particularly as they affect the attitudes and behaviors of his students. All children need support, security, understanding, empathy, but those who are products of deprivation need them most of all. The need to develop inner controls and habits of positive interpersonal behavior is an imperative for children of all levels of society, but at no level is it of greater urgency than among the disadvantaged, and at no level is the potential influence of the teacher so great or his failure so tragic in its consequences.

The problem is complicated by the inevitable gulf between the society of which the teacher is a part and the social environment to which the students belong. The values, habits, and life-style of the middle-class professional may have little in common with those of the lower-class slum tenement dweller. Even the professional who is himself a product of the environment of deprivation experiences this gulf, perhaps even more poignantly than his colleague of middle-class origins. The teacher of the disadvantaged, therefore, is faced with the complex human problem of devoting himself to students who are not of his own kind and who return every day to environments basically alien to his own. No matter how close his relationships, how intimate his understanding, how empathic his dealings, the teacher remains basically above and apart from his students, for he is not really one of their kind. This condition adds measurably to the complexities of human interaction between teacher and students and makes all the more difficult the ordering of the human climate in the class group and its effect on the students.

Primary requisites for his effectiveness in human relations are the teacher's ability to see himself as his students see him and to understand the effect of his actions on them. Which of his actions engender resent-

ment, indifference, fear, withdrawal? Which inspire confidence, a measure
of respect, affection, friendliness? This requires a high degree of sensitivity
to his students as human beings and the ability to order the human climate
within which he operates so as to make for the best possible positive effect
on their behavior, attitudes, and feelings. This sensitizing of the teacher to
his function and effect within the human environment of his classroom requires as well his becoming sensitized to himself as a human being. A
teacher to be effective in human relations must know, understand, come to
terms with, and alter, if needed and possible, his own feelings and prejudices toward the student people he is dealing with. His function as a
teacher is constructive, supportive, positive, and sometimes corrective. If
his feelings are largely negative and unsympathetic toward his students, he
will find teaching a misery and his effect miserable. This does not mean
that he must learn to love them all, but at the very least, he must feel a
measure of empathic personal self-satisfaction in their company and seek
to inspire similar feelings in them toward himself and toward each other.
Teaching is after all a human enterprise, and the human environment in
the classroom has its inevitable effect on the development of its members
as human beings. At what point does control become repression? When
does permissive freedom engender asocial behavior? When does insistence
on quiet cause withdrawal? How can one distinguish between harmless
mischief and vicious behavior? Are the conventions of discipline and
housekeeping characteristic of the school and the classroom more appropriate to a prison than to a school? To these and the myriads of similar
questions there are no simple answers that apply to all schools, not even all
schools serving disadvantaged populations. They will vary with the human
characteristics of the people—students and teacher—involved, and with
the human and social requirements demanded by the specific situation.
Suffice it to say, however, that no requisite for the teacher of the disadvantaged is so crucial to his function as his ability to affect positively the
human climate of his classroom.

What are the implications of the foregoing on preservice, in-service, and
continuing education for teachers? There are so many that they may well
force the education of teachers into patterns and practices quite different
from those that have been held as sufficient in the ignorance of accelerat-
ing social change. Universities will have to evaluate their programs in full
knowledge of the conditions and circumstances within which teachers
must operate, the peoples and communities they are expected to serve, and
the aspirations of a democratic society to provide the means for optimum
development of each individual in keeping with his potential. In the foundational training for future teachers in preservice programs, they will seek
the aid of the disciplines of urban sociology, social psychology, and cultural anthropology to complement the contributions of the familiar

disciplines of psychology, philosophy, and the history of education. They will provide, through field visitation, observation, participation, and apprentice or student teaching, increased, intensified opportunities for future teachers to experience, become familiar with, and begin functioning in the schools and neighborhoods that will be their future professional homes. As beginning teachers, the newly licensed professionals will continue their training on an in-service basis in both school- and university-centered seminars and workshops and will receive help through them and through the aid of specially trained supervisory and university personnel in the day-by-day conduct of their classes. A significant portion of this in-service training will be built into the regular work load of the teacher through regularly scheduled time released for participation in courses, seminars, workshops, and conferences, and will not consist as at present of requirements to be fulfilled on an over-time basis. Industry has long recognized the need for further training as part of a skilled worker's work load; it is time that teacher education followed suit. Finally, the continuing development of the career teacher will receive more and more emphasis through intensive summer institutes designed to keep the teacher continually abreast of new knowledge, new procedures, and new resources for teaching. In sum, teacher education will become more intensive, make use of a broader spectrum of disciplines, require more direct experience with school and community (particularly those schools and communities in which the teacher will likely be functioning), and continue far beyond the training for permanent licensure. The universities will discover the need for making the school and community as it exists (not just as it is fashioned in the model campus school) its laboratory for training, experimentation, and research. And the schools, in turn, in cooperation with the universities, will develop more and more as locales for training of present and future teachers, much as the teaching hospital functions for the training of physicians and nurses. Intensive, lifelong teacher education, adaptive to reality and change for service to the disadvantaged, will require a newer, more intimate working relationship among school, university, and community; greater human and material resources; knowledgeable and effective school supervisors and university professors; and the most dedicated, determined, idealistic human kind out of which to fashion the most important professional of them all—the teacher.

But aren't these implications valid for the proper training of all teachers, not just those concerned with the disadvantaged? True, our more favored populations would benefit as well by this extension, intensification, and enrichment of training; but they can make do with less. The teacher of the disadvantaged cannot and still fulfill his mission as the major, often the only, effective force for the human betterment of his students. Our society cannot afford to do less.

FOR FURTHER THOUGHT

1. As essential ingredients to the preparation of teachers, Schueler lists: (1) knowledge of the student and his environment; (2) knowledge of how to order and guide learning; and (3) development of human relations appropriate to the task of teaching. These ingredients, while seen by Schueler as being more vital to teachers of the deprived, are recognized by him as being essential to all teachers. If such is the case, *would the essential principle behind preparing teachers for the blind be any different from those behind preparing for the deprived or the average? Is it possible for the specific experiences of such preparation programs to be vastly different according to the clientele to be secured and yet be unified by the same guiding principles? To what extent is a professional teacher one who, regardless of specific preparation, realizes these underlying principles and who knows how to prepare himself to fulfill the requirements of the teaching act as his clientele changes?*

2. The claim has been made that the most desirable teachers for the deprived are those people who have come from the lower strata of society. *What factors might be operative in teacher or pupil personalities that would render such a generalization false?* Just as there is no necessary connection between lower class teacher background and success with the deprived child, similarly there is no necessary connection between middle or upper-middle class teacher background and failure with the deprived. *To what extent are successful human relationships between teacher and student dependent upon the class background of both parties? To what extent are they dependent upon knowledge of differences in class values? Is knowledge and awareness of differences sufficient to ensure success in human relations?*

3. Schueler's remarks about the inadequate nature of the teaching force dealing with the deprived are born out of the study by Howard S. Becker and the remarks of Ernest Melby. Becker found that in Chicago, new teachers were posted to the least desirable areas. As soon as they gained sufficient seniority they sought transfers to other areas. Thus the inexperienced were constantly left to cope with the demands of the deprived. Melby points out that in any other profession the most difficult and demanding cases are tackled by and left to the most able. *Is Melby's assessment of other professional groups accurate with regard to the handling of difficult cases? Do these remarks suggest a lack of professionalism among teachers? If teachers were sincerely dedicated to service would they commit themselves to teach in these areas? What ways exist within a democracy to bring the best teachers face to face with the most difficult situations?*

4. *If a teacher had been prepared for eventual responsibility in a de-*

prived neighborhood through the program offered by Hunter College, would that preparation facilitate or hinder the ability of that teacher to transfer to responsibilities in an upper-middle class neighborhood? To what extent is the success of any teacher dependent upon: (1) an understanding of the basic principles referred to by Schueler as "old truths," and (2) the ability of the individual to make judgements about how these truths can be realized in his or her peculiar situation? What, then, are the essential ingredients of any preparation for professional performance by teachers? To what extent can specific suggestions without underlying principles for organization and methodology hinder the success of the teacher?

THE PROFESSIONAL PREPARATION OF TEACHERS

Those concerned with the experiences of students in school, whether they be teachers, pupils, parents, administrators, or interested members of society, are interested in finding and implementing the formula for "good" teaching. There is no shortage of descriptions of the good teacher as there is no shortage of varying programs to realize such a goal.

In the article that follows, Harry S. Broudy mentions four major areas that he feels are essential to the preparation of teachers. These areas include: speciality foundations, professional content, technological concerns, and research. Each of these areas offers a basis for controversy in teacher education. At the broadest level of questioning there is doubt as to the necessity of including some of these areas. As Broudy points out, through a look at the history of teacher education, initial preparation of teachers did not include all this; periods of teacher shortage have provided further examples of teachers being prepared without all of these considerations. Do such illustrations offer adequate evidence as to the most valuable ingredients of a teacher education program? Another question, perhaps now more common due to the move away from one- or two-year preparation programs, pertains to the amount of time to be spent on each of these four areas. If all are to be considered, what proportion of the total time should each be granted?

These questions have focused on the nature of the overall preparation program. Each of these four areas is subject to internal controversy. What is the value and the need for a foundational study of one's specialty? Would more of the specialty instead of study about the specialty be more valuable? What type of professional content should be offered? Are conceptual, theoretical frameworks more important than techniques for implementation? Is it necessary to include laboratory, clinical, and internship experience? What reliable research, if any, is available on teaching?

Broudy's article explores these various concerns and provides the reader with an analysis worthy of thorough examination. Many of the foregoing questions are not answered, but there is established a framework for worthwhile explorations of these matters.

———————◆———————

CRITERIA FOR THE PROFESSIONAL PREPARATION OF TEACHERS*

In the Platonic dialogue *Protagoras,* Socrates spoke as follows:

> Now I observe that whenever we are met together in the assembly, and the matter in hand relates to building, the builders are summoned as advisors; when the question is one of shipbuilding, then the shipbuilders; and the like of other arts which they think capable of being taught and learned. . . . When, however, the question is an affair of state, then everybody is free to have a say—carpenter, tinker, cobbler, sailor, passenger; rich and poor, high and low . . . and no one reproaches him, as in the former case, with not having learned, and having no teacher, and yet giving advice. . . .

Whereupon Protagoras, the famous Sophist, set him straight by observing that everybody—parents, police, and the public in general—teaches virtue; hence, no specialists are needed. However, he admitted modestly that some persons could do it so much better than the general run of mankind that, like himself, they made a profession of it.

This colloquy is not an unfitting setting for the current serious and sometimes bitter controversy about teaching and the preparation of teachers, for it suggests the sense in which we are all teachers of a sort and the sense in which teaching can be what the Greeks called *techné* (an art based on knowledge), or what we would call a profession, in which case not everyone is a teacher but only those who cultivate the special knowledge and skill on which it is based. Above all, it raises the question as to whether or not there is such knowledge.[1] Sooner or later one must ask

*Harry S. Broudy, "Criteria for the Professional Preparation of Teachers," *Journal of Teacher Education,* vol. 16, no. 4 (December 1965), pp. 408–415. Dr. Broudy, Professor of Philosophy of Education at the University of Illinois, has been a visiting lecturer in philosophy and education at a number of leading American Universities. He is the author of *Building a Philosophy of Education, Paradox and Promise,* a co-author of several books, and a frequent contributor to professional journals.

[1]The perennial nature of the problem is illustrated by an article by Josiah Royce, "Is There a Science Education?" *Educational Review* (1891). Mr. Royce did not think that there was.

whether the expertness needed for teaching can be picked up from one's own experience as a pupil, by apprenticeship with a master teacher, or by application of common sense; or whether there is a special body of knowledge and skill that has to be mastered through formal study. Accordingly, the identification of the kinds of knowledge and skill used in teaching is a task that cannot be postponed indefinitely, if the controversy is to be resolved rationally.

But where is one to begin? Perhaps with the formula for the good teacher. Because every instance of teaching is the resultant of more variables than we can identify, and because the values of these variables remain indeterminate, the thousands of hours and millions of dollars spent on trying to identify the traits of a good or successful teacher have given employment and even careers to worthy educational researchers, but not much else. Any generalization about the good or bad teacher will elicit a counter-example from any half dozen people who are in a mood to reminisce about their school days. Mr. Conant's efforts in this direction are no exception. One would be hard put to form an image of what a good teacher would be like from the welter of prescriptions given for producing one.

At this stage of our knowledge about teaching and learning, the approach has to be much more modest than that of the controlled experiment or the massive questionnaire: it is to examine the roles that a person who teaches is expected to play as he or she carries out the tasks normally assigned to the position. What knowledge and what skill are presupposed by these roles?

THE TEACHER AS A PERSON

The first and most consistent role that a teacher plays is that of a human being, a person. This platitude lies at the root of some of the bitterest aspects of the controversy, not because anyone denies that teachers are human, but because to be a human being is thought to involve the kind of schooling that has been called liberal or general. The generally accepted belief that a teacher needs a liberal education more than, let us say, a plumber or a barber is based on the confusion of two notions. One is that the teacher will need it in order to give instruction in some of the content contained in the liberal studies, e.g., history or literature. The other notion is that the teacher, like Quintilian's orator, ought to be a good person skilled in speaking (teaching). I shall in all charity remain silent on the claim that the liberal arts, as usually taught in the university, are liberal in any but a catalogue sense of the term. The professors of these subjects are as specialized and as proud of their specialism as is the engineering faculty or that of law. On the modern campus there is only one culture, the professional culture, and the rules for promotion and scholarly distinction are about the same regardless of department. Hence liberality in the Aristotelian sense of the term, education for the sake of cultivating the person, is a rare commodity indeed, although some naïve undergraduates are rioting around, allegedly because they still yearn for it.

But even if the liberal arts could make men human—and taught in a liberal spirit they might—there is, I repeat, no compelling reason for teachers being made more human than anyone else. This argument will, no doubt, leave many unconvinced. It will be urged that the teacher affects the lives of children as engineers and plumbers do not. Presumably this means that teachers shape character and therefore should themselves exemplify ideal character; and that this, in turn, calls for more liberal education than the general public needs. But the most that can be made of this dubious argument is that if a society does not provide general education for all its citizens, it ought at least to insist on it for its prospective teachers. However, once the requirement is couched in terms of what a person needs to play the role of teacher, it becomes part of professional education. Thus, at one time, public school teachers were expected to refrain from using profanity, alcohol, and tobacco; and air line hostesses are expected to be gracious and attractive. For them, temperance and charm are professional requirements; that they are also desirable for all human beings is another matter.

This distinction is more than a quibble. We can achieve institutional peace only if the professional faculty has complete authority over professional needs and the general faculty is in complete charge of what all men, simply because they are men, ought to know. The conflicts between these faculties result when there is an attempt to skimp on the development of teachers as persons or persons as teachers.

Unfortunately, teacher education has a long history of skimping, and we are still watching the strange spectacle of men willing to spend so little on what they say they value so much. To recruit large numbers of public school teachers, we skimped on their liberal education. The best among them made up in a pedagogical devotion what they lacked in learning. Today we are urged to meet the teacher shortage and raise the quality of teachers by skimping on their professional training. The gradual lengthening of the teacher preparation curriculum was an attempt to draw public school teachers into the liberally educated classes, and the fight will not be won until they are all drawn from such classes and then trained in thoroughly professional schools.

If it is granted that the teacher is first of all a person, is there any special type of person he ought to be? If so, we have never been able to decide what it is. In a recently published volume, a colleague and I wrote essays on Socrates, Protagoras, Isocrates, Quintilian, Alcuin, Abelard, Ascham, the Jesuits, Comenius, Pestalozzi, Froebel, Herbart, and Kilpatrick as exemplars of teaching method.[2] If anyone can find any important set of common traits in their personalities, we would like to know about it.

Moreover, if a peculiar personality pattern is essential to teaching, can it be produced, or is one born with it? If inborn, it is a function of teacher selection rather than of teacher preparation; if produced, it would be helpful to know how it is done. Surely the college years are too late for producing basic personality changes.

Our inability to find a general formula for the good teacher (although we can spot this or that good teacher) has been used to deny that there is knowledge from which teacher preparation can design its curriculum and to allege that it must rely on the wisdom of the elders, such wisdom being the special gift of the master teachers who can spot the good and bad teacher prospects during their apprenticeship. Yet lack of a personality formula has not caused medicine or law to throw their professional curricula on the mercy of the wisdom of the elders.

Our lack of knowledge about the personality formula merely means that we must look in another direction for professional criteria, viz., to the requirements of the roles played by the teacher as (1) a member of the educational profession and (2) as a specialist in that profession.

THE TEACHER AS A MEMBER
OF THE EDUCATIONAL PROFESSION

A profession rests heavily on a body of systematized knowledge organized in terms of distinctive problems of practice. The word "knowledge" distinguishes it from a craft; the word "practice," from pure research. So defined, the term "professional" does not apply to plumbers, physicists, biologists, or historians, but it does apply to the sanitary engineers and to teachers of physics, biology, and history.

Education as a professional field of study, therefore, has to have distinctive problems of practice and resources of knowledge that can be used to deal with these problems. Such problems arise out of the need to formulate and justify educational policy, to design and justify curriculum designs, to formulate and justify schemes of organization and support, and to formulate and justify strategies of teaching and learning. They are distinctive of education and define the domain of professional training in the field of education.

The knowledge about these problems falls into two major types: the foundational and the specialized. The first is needed by all workers in the educational field regardless of their role in the educational system. This would include college presidents and professors as well as public school

[2]H. S. Broudy and John R. Palmer, *Exemplars of Teaching Method* (Chicago, Ill.: Rand McNally & Co., 1965).

administrators and kindergarten teachers. Each of the four problem areas can and needs to be studied in its historical, psychological, philosophical, and societal contexts, because these are the major contexts in which educational institutions operate and in which the problems peculiar to them occur. There are, no doubt, other relevant contexts, but these four are indispensable to an understanding of what the whole educational enterprise is all about. These problems, studied in these contexts, make up the sixteen basic topics in the foundations of education.

There is, or need be, nothing vague or fuzzy or repetitive in foundational courses, but they do presuppose that the student will have had the basic courses in history, philosophy, psychology, and the social sciences as part of his *general* education. Since colleges of education cannot assume this will be the case, they should insist on them as prerequisites for admission to foundational courses. When the student is not properly prepared, there is a great danger that the foundation course will be turned into a watered-down version of the parent discipline or into wordy discussions of life in general, education in general, and society in general; in short, a general bull session conducted for credit.

Foundational courses also suffer from a tacit promise and expectation that they will help the teacher directly in the daily tasks of the classroom—keeping unruly children quiet or placating a neurotic principal. Unfortunately, foundational knowledge cannot be *applied* directly to problems of practice any more than physics can be applied to fix an ailing motor car. Foundational knowledge, and indeed all general education, is used interpretively as precise but large-scale cognitive maps on which problems are plotted but not solved. For the solving of problems, i.e., for the applicative use of knowledge, theory has to be supplemented by technology, and only the specialist (who has both) uses knowledge applicatively. Being mistaken in the uses to which foundational knowledge is put, one can be understandably wrong in judging it useless.

The cognitive map wrought by the foundational course does for the professional life what general education is expected to do for human life as a whole. Professional cognitive maps are constructed on projections furnished by their distinctive domains of practice; life cognitive maps are fashioned on projections derived from the domains of the intellectual disciplines. Neither sort of map is useless, but without appropriate technologies, it cannot be used applicatively. Yet, in the absence of adequate interpretive maps, one is at a loss to know what an appropriate technology would be and where it might be found.

THE TEACHER AS SPECIALIST

Because of the constantly swelling school population, teaching has undergone the usual division of labor and has developed numerous specialties. What, then, are the types of knowledge needed by the teacher as an instructor, as a specialist in teaching?

Foundations of the Specialty

The very same logic that justifies general education for all men and foundational work for all professional workers in education justifies the study of one's specialty in its historical development, its psychological relationships, its philosophical presuppositions and implications, its societal contexts and import. For example, the teaching of mathematics has a history dating back at least to Plato; it has problems of motivation and presentation that are psychological as well as sociological; its current place in the curriculum is dictated by our military and economic anxieties, and its relation to other types of knowledge and to the good life are problems of the highest philosophical order which are far from being clearly understood even now.

One does not expect such study—in course form or some other form—to be given in the mathematics department (because it so rarely is offered there), but it would be odd indeed if a school turning out specialists in the teaching of mathematics would not provide this orientation to the specialty. I have no doubt that organization and development of material for such studies can be an interdisciplinary venture,[3] but the primary responsibility is on the professional faculty.

Professional Content

We come now to an ingredient in teacher preparation which has borne far too much of the weight of the controversy, viz., subject matter. There are two uses of the knowledge of a subject that are relevant to the teaching of it. "Repertory content" is the name I would give to that part of the subject matter, say of English or history or mathematics, that will be presented to the tutee. Thus the play *Hamlet*, the binomial theorem, and the Whiskey Rebellion are samples of repertory content. These will be presented to the tutee; he will be persuaded to respond to them, modify his response in the direction sought by the teacher, undergo tests upon them, etc.; in short, to study them.

What does one have to know about *Hamlet* or English literature or English history or the drama or Middle English in order to teach *Hamlet*

---

[3]Often such materials come into being when a doctoral student with an historical training and interest in mathematical education chooses to do a dissertation in the history of education. Such monographic literature in time becomes an item on the reading list of advanced students in mathematical education, and later still abstracts from it begin to appear in textbooks on the teaching of mathematics which, in turn, are used in courses given to prospective mathematics teachers.

to high school students? Here is the sort of question that scholars in English literature might very well help to define and perhaps solve. That a knowledge about the changes in the language, for example, is invaluable for the teacher is not in question. It gives him the freedom of maneuver in the teaching of *Hamlet* without which the class bogs down in the footnotes or, what is worse, resorts to highly simplified texts without any footnotes at all. The question concerns rather the packaging of materials from philosophy, English history, drama, and the other relevant fields so that they become functional for the teacher in teaching but are not necessarily taught to the pupils. This might be called the pedagogical content of a subject.

The standard response of the subject matter scholars to the problem of professional content has taken the form of prescribing courses or sequences of courses in the various subject fields. This standard response, however admirable as a counsel of perfection, is not the answer to the question; it is a somewhat cavalier evasion of it. The proper answer to the question entails viewing the problem from the professional end of the telescope. Courses and programs in the liberal arts college are rightly organized for scholarship in the standard disciplines or for general education and not for the professional use of them. In the latter, materials are organized around the problems of practice, and this difference makes all the difference. Once we acknowledge the hegemony of the liberal arts college over general education, it may be possible for the various professional schools (law, medicine, engineering) to enlist their fruitful collaboration in selecting and packaging those elements within their disciplines that are relevant and necessary for the professional part of the curriculum.

The distinction between repertory and interpretive (pedagogical) content is important because the relative amounts of each needed by the teacher vary with the level at which the subject is being taught. There is a logic of subject matter and of teaching that saves the judgments as to how much of each is needed from being completely *ad hoc* or arbitrary. There are questions that arise in a high school class in Shakespeare that cannot be answered or discussed without knowledge of language morphology, or history, or history of the theatre, or the character of the English court. This is the knowledge the teacher uses for eliciting and evaluating pupil response, although he may never utter it to the pupils. But the questions that arise in a college class in Shakespeare may not coincide with those in the high school and certainly would not with those that pop up in an elementary school version of the same play. Pedagogical content in one situation may be repertory content in another.

To the detriment of the whole enterprise of teacher preparation, educationists have not been and even today are not clear on the role of subject matter in instruction. There is no agreement as to whether the pupil ought to learn some specific content from some standard discipline, a method of thinking, an attitude of being critical about life in general, or the knack of getting along with his fellows. Usually schoolmen vow to work for all of them. In such a confusion, even with the best of intentions, it is difficult to decide just what competence the teacher should have and just what knowledge or training would provide it. For it is one thing to train teachers to teach *Hamlet;* quite another to teach good citizenship by the use of *Hamlet.*

Technological

The next dimension of specialized study is the *technological.* The difference between foundational and specialized study in a professional field is that in the latter one learns how to apply knowledge in concrete cases. As noted before, this requires not only knowledge but also a technology in which the generalizations are transformed into procedures and devices. For example, the knowledge about isotopes cannot be used in medicine without a special technology for introducing them into the body and observing their effects. We have developed three types of instruction in professional education (in all professions) to accomplish this: laboratory exercises, clinical experience, and internship.

The laboratory exercise is intended to concretize theory and to test it—for the pupil, not for the discipline. For example, one of the standard tasks in schoolkeeping is the grouping of pupils for instruction. There are a number of principles in terms of which one might group a class of thirty pupils: homogeneous grouping, age grouping, interest grouping, stratified grouping. A laboratory exercise to illustrate these principles might ask the student to group thirty pupils whose scores on a number of tests are made available to him. The justification of the grouping in terms of the principles involved constitutes the basic learnings of the exercise. In the preparation of teachers, laboratory experience can be provided by demonstrations with live pupils, through simulated situations on video tape or film, or through curriculum materials laboratories, audiovisual aid laboratories, etc.

Whatever the form of the laboratory exercise, it is important to note that the laboratory task is never more than an abstracted and often schematized sample of a whole class of real tasks. The demonstration, the made-up grouping task, the make-believe test—all of these should conform to the schemata of some theory and be designed to illuminate and illustrate it.

Clinical experience, on the contrary, involves real individual cases chosen for their significance as exemplars. In the clinic, we select for instructional purposes the classic case of the slow learner or the discipline problem. Clinical instruction is ideally carried on by a master teacher who is also a good theoretician with a small group of advanced students who have studied theory but have little or no practice aside from laboratory exercises in various courses. The master involves the students in the diagnosis of a particular real problem, the prescription, and the prognosis, and then goes ahead and treats the case himself, presumably in a masterly way. His treatment is a model against which the discussants check their thinking. Real school classrooms are neither good laboratories nor clinics.

Internship is working on a real task under a minimum of supervision and needs, I believe, no extended discussion. Teaching internship has to be carried on in a real classroom. It does, however, need to be distinguished from the laboratory and clinical phases of technical training with which it is almost always confused.

Mr. Conant and the Ford Foundation have founded their schemes of teacher preparation on the centrality of practice teaching. This strategy reflects the conviction that teaching is fundamentally no more than a set of skills acquired by apprenticeship, preferably with a master teacher; but what is perhaps even more important, direct experience in a real classroom is depended upon to give the three kinds of learning that we have distinguished as laboratory, clinical, and internship. This is a clumsy strategy, to say the least. The internship idea is sound if the laboratory, clinical, and theoretical work has already been done at the primary training institution. It is not sound when used as a substitute for the other dimensions of professional training, and this is what many of the five-year programs of teacher training can be suspected of trying to do. Practice teaching or student teaching is a tremendous drain on instructional space and manpower—a drain that could be slackened if the laboratory work could be done elsewhere than in the training classroom. With the possibilities opened up by the new developments in video tape recording and simulated training systems, real classrooms could be used for educative internship, in the manner of our best teaching hospitals.

Research

A professional field of study would not be worthy of that designation if it were not growing by systematic methods of inquiry. If no genuine scholarly research in the problems of education is possible, or if it is not taking place, then education cannot qualify as a professional field of study, and its claim to professional status in the university or in the social order is fraudulent. A professional practitioner, therefore, may be a producer and certainly ought to be a consumer of research. The methods of research, its canons, its status, and its prosperity are of concern to him; he tries to keep up with it. Research is therefore included in his professional training.

The import of the discussion is that the professional training of teachers is structurally no different from the professional training of engineers, physicians, and lawyers. In a fully developed program of professional training, the foundational dimensions, the general theory, the specialized technology, the specialized instrumentation and research methodology are provided through a variety of instructional means: courses, lectures, readings, laboratory work, clinical experience, and internship. Every move to omit or to minimize any one of these dimensions can therefore be construed as an attack on the professional maturity or status of teaching.

The attacks on teacher-training programs have tried to deprofessionalize teaching in the public schools in several ways. First, by equating the foundational knowledge with general education. Thus it has been argued that a good course in philosophy makes a course in the philosophy of education unnecessary, or that there is no history of education but only history. Second, it has been argued that specialized study in a given subject matter field will take care of the special content of a subject needed for teaching. This results from ignoring the difference between repertory and interpretive-pedagogical content. Third, there is the effort to regard all technical work in teacher training as tricks of the trade to be picked up by apprenticeship in something called student teaching. This results from ignoring or not understanding the differences among laboratory, clinical, and internship experiences in the specialized training of the professional.

One can criticize a program of teacher training for not being adequate in this or that dimension, and this sort of criticism most of our programs probably deserve. Or one can charge that there simply is not enough knowledge to warrant a professional program at all, and that a mildly intellectualized craft training is all that is required. This is the real and basic issue, and it can be decided only by examining the knowledge available.

Those who would deny that such a body of knowledge exists, or could exist, or that the roles of the teacher demand it are invited to dispute the analysis or examine the shelves of any university library. Instead of such rational argument, we find casually tossed-off remarks to the effect that the study of education is not a discipline, or that it is a pseudo-discipline, or that, whatever it is, it can be dispensed with in the training of teachers.

Let me reiterate therefore that no claim is made for education as a discipline with a homogenous subject matter such as mathematics or physics or geology. But then no professional field of study is a discipline in this sense. On the contrary, every professional field of study draws on a number of parent disciplines for the knowledge relevant to the problems of practice which are peculiar to itself and which delimit it from other professions. This does not exclude the study of education from the family of intellectual pursuits any more than it excludes engineering, medicine, or law.

That the field of study we call professional education is far from being systematized, and that not all of its dimensions have been equally developed, is only too true. For example, the recent discovery of a nonlicensed physician practicing away at a great and prosperous rate in Detroit despite the lack of a medical degree or graduation from a medical school did not incite anyone to brand medical education as unnecessary, nor have we heard proposals that a much shortened master of healing degree be substituted for the long period of medical training now required. The field of medical study is too well developed to be attacked in this way.

Yet, as our opening remarks on the Socratic question indicate, the writing and thinking about education have as long a history as those about medicine and law. That a field should attract so steadily the attention of some of our best minds and yet be no more than a craft to be learned by apprenticeship seems remarkable indeed.

That public school instruction can be manned by bright and devoted amateurs is the illusion which misguides many of the critics of teacher preparation. If the admirable goals of elitist schooling are to be realized for all educable youth, it will take a much more sophisticated curriculum and teaching corps than five hard subjects taught by a handful of bright liberal arts graduates. Can we get enough of these bright graduates to become genuine professionals? Do we have a field of study worthy of their abilities and their time? Can we utilize their gifts in dealing with general education for the masses, including the masses so culturally deformed that ordinary instructional measures seem impotent? In the face of the overwhelming deluge of numbers, amateurs coming from the "good" colleges will be about as helpful as caviar in a famine.

Education at all levels is moving into mass production, as it was bound to do in a culture dominated by large-scale machine industry now reaching its logical apogee in automation. As this happens, all the blessings and dangers of mass production can be expected to confront education, as they have industry and politics. The salvation of our society will depend on the ability of education to exploit the blessings of technology in behalf of what makes life worthwhile, viz., the possibility of high-grade individual experience in something called "the good life." That solving these problems will require less than a generation of professional educators trained and educated in fully developed professional schools, I find it impossible to believe. Socrates, it turns out, asked the right question, and history has brought us to the point when we can no longer postpone the answer.

FOR FURTHER THOUGHT

1. Broudy claims that the knowledge about problems falls into two major types: foundational and specialized. The foundational area can be subdivided into historical, psychological, philosophical, and social contexts. Analyze the approach to teacher preparation suggested by Schueler

and ascertain the degree to which these four foundational areas are utilized. *Of what use would each of these four areas be in coping with the problem described by Schueler?*

2. Foundational knowledge, according to Broudy, is not *directly* involved in problems of practice. *Of what use, then, is such knowledge? Inasfar as Broudy claims it to be essential to the forming of large-scale cognitive maps, is foundational knowledge concept oriented? Of what use, if any, are these large-scale cognitive maps?* Provide an illustration of their use in regard to the problems of teaching the "culturally deprived." *What is the similarity between foundational knowledge for the professional and general education for human life as a whole?*

3. Broudy advocates foundational study of one's own specialty. *Why can this be seen as essential to the professional preparation of teachers?* Briefly examine your own specialty in this way. Consider the nature of the relationship of your specialty to others and their joint or separate contributions to the good life. *What does your specialty have to offer? What are the peculiar problems of your field of study?*

4. In analyzing the subject matter preparation of professionals Broudy distinguishes between repertory and interpretative control. *What is the difference between the two ideas? Why is the repertory approach to subject matter mastery inappropriate for professional preparation? How does the current confusion over what the school is to accomplish render judgements about proper teacher preparation useless?*

5. Broudy points to four possible goals of the school: learn specific content from standard disciplines, develop a method of thinking, develop a critical attitude, and develop ability to interact. Relate these to positions described in Chapter 4. *How does the selection of any of these relate to the purpose of the school? How, in turn, does the emphasis of any one of these affect teacher preparation?*

6. Specialized study for the professional must also include technological considerations. Through laboratory exercises, clinical experience, and internship one learns how to apply knowledge in concrete cases. *What distinctions does Broudy offer to separate these three areas of technological development? To what extent does the overemphasis of practice teaching in any program of teacher preparation undermine the concept and possibility of professional behavior?*

7. The debates over teacher preparation have attempted to deprofessionalize teaching in the public schools in three major ways. *What are these three major ways?* Consider the extent to which any or all three of these dimensions are necessary to professional behavior.

8. Broudy claims, in discussing teacher preparation, that there is a real or basic issue. While the ingredients he lists as essential to professional-

ism are difficult to refute, there remains the question as to whether or not professionalism is an appropriate ideal for teachers. *Is a "mildly intellectualized craft training" all that is necessary for our schools and society?*

NEEDED: A THEORETICAL FRAMEWORK

In the struggle for respectability educators have sought to accumulate empirical evidence in order to defend their practices. One of the classic studies in education of this type of justification was the Eight-Year Study. The results[1] of this study indicated that the high school curriculum pursued was much less central to success in college than had commonly been assumed by the apologists of traditional curriculum practice. The twentieth century has seen a multitude of research studies of varying degrees of comprehensiveness, which have attempted to assess the worth of one pedagogical approach as opposed to another, or one subject to another, ad infinitum. Huge compilations have been undertaken to offer the reader a synopsis of significant findings in myriad areas. All this seems to suggest that teaching "has arrived." The aura of respectability attached to other scientifically based domains of practice has been shifted, by some, to education.

Leading educational researchers are increasingly critical of the status of the educational domain. Much that goes under the name is of doubtful quality. Instead of offering a more legitimate basis for action, the research has often stimulated faddism. Educators have jumped from "bandwagon" to "bandwagon." Whether it be in support of programs for the gifted, the culturally deprived, or the average child, "evidence" of some sort is available. Of course, the problem resides in interpretation as well as in investigation. More basic, perhaps, is the general lack of understanding of the relevance of certain types of research and a consequent lack of high level systematic support for these efforts.

Jerome S. Bruner, a prominent researcher, challenges much of what is being done in education because of the absence of an appropriate theoretical framework. In the selection that follows he points out some of the present shortcomings in educational practice and advocates turning attention to the development of a theory of instruction. He hopes to bring direction to research in the field of curriculum and in psychology through the formulation of such a theory. His article affords a chance to review the relationships of theory and practice and the place of theory in the preparation of a professional.

[1] W. M. Aiken, *The Story of the Eight-Year Study* (New York: Harper & Row, Publishers), 1942.

NEEDED: A THEORY OF INSTRUCTION*

Over the past several years it has become increasingly clear to me, as to any thinking person today, that both psychology and the field of curriculum design itself suffer jointly from the lack of a theory of instruction. Such a theory of instruction would indeed be interesting just for its own sake, for purely theoretical reasons. There cannot be, for example, a theory of development which leaves somehow to chance the question of the way in which societies pace and structure the experiences with which children come in contact; and to talk about the nature of development without talking about the way in which society does and can structure the sequence, is to be as intellectually foolish as it is to be morally irresponsible. So even if one were seeking only a better theory about the nature of man, one would indeed want a theory of instruction as one of the instruments by which one understood man and how he was shaped by his fellow man.

Yet we also realize that a theory of instruction is about as practical a thing as one could possibly have to guide one in the process of passing on the knowledge, the skills, the point of view and the heart of a culture. Let us, then, see whether we can set forth some possible theorems that might go into a theory of instruction.

ELEMENTS OF A THEORY

What do we mean by a theory of instruction? I found myself beginning this exercise by putting down theorems that tried to separate what we might mean by a theory of instruction from other kinds of theories that have been current. The first thought that occurred to me is that in its very nature a theory of instruction is *prescriptive* and not *descriptive*. Such a theory has the aim of producing particular ends and producing them in ways that we speak of as optimal. It is not a description of what has happened when learning has taken place—it is something which is normative, which gives you something to shoot at and which, in the end, must state something about what you do when you put instruction together in the form of courses. Now, this is not a very surprising thing, yet I am struck by the fact that many persons in the field of education have assumed that we

*Jerome S. Bruner, "Needed: A Theory of Instruction," *Educational Leadership* 20 (8): 523–532; May 1963. Reprinted with permission of the Association for Supervision and Curriculum Development and Jerome S. Bruner. Copyright © 1963 by the Association for Supervision and Curriculum Development. Dr. Bruner is Professor of Psychology and Director of the Center for Cognitive Studies, Harvard University. He is author of *The Process of Education, On Knowing,* and *Toward a Theory of Instruction.*

could depend on other kinds of theories than the theory of instruction to guide us in this kind of enterprise. For example, I find that the dependence upon learning theory among educators is as touching as it is shocking. The fact of the matter is that the learning theory is not a theory of instruction; it is a theory that describes what takes place while learning is going on and after learning has taken place.

There is no clear-cut way in which one can derive wisdom, or indeed implication, from learning theory that will guide him in the constructing of a curriculum. When I say a theory of instruction is prescriptive, I mean it is *before the fact*. It is before learning has taken place and not while and after learning has taken place. Let me give you an example of the kind of difficulty you get into when you assume that you can use the slender reed of learning theory to lean on. Take, for example, the case of programed instruction.

There is in the current doctrine (I will call it) of programed instruction the idea that somehow you should take small steps, that each increment should be a small step. Now, this idea is derived willy-nilly from a theory of learning which states that learning is incremental and goes in small steps. Nowhere in the evidence upon which such a theory is based—and it is only partial evidence—nowhere is there anything that says that simply because learning takes place in small steps the *environment* should be arranged in small steps. And so we set up a curriculum that also has small steps. In doing so we fail to take sight of the fact that, indeed, organisms from vertebrate on up through the highest primate, man, operate by taking large packets of information and breaking these down into their own bite size and that unless they have the opportunity to do that, learning may become stereotyped. At least it is a worthy hypothesis about instruction.

A theory of instruction must concern itself with the relationship between how things are presented and how they are learned. Though I myself have worked hard and long in the vineyard of learning theory, I can do no better than to start by warning the reader away from it. Learning theory is not a theory of instruction. It describes what happened. A theory of instruction is a guide to what to do in order to achieve certain objectives. Unfortunately, we shall have to start pretty nearly at the beginning, for there is very little literature to guide us in this subtle enterprise.

What shall a theory of instruction be about? I would propose that there are four aspects of such a theory. First, a theory of instruction should concern itself with the factors that predispose a child to learn effectively; and there are many such factors that predispose. These are factors which, on the whole, precede the child's entry into our scholastic care. These factors relate to his earliest childhood and indeed one might say that we should provide some theorems for a theory of toys, and for a theory of family, and for a theory of stimulation, because the thing that comes to mind here is the question of what kind of stimulation ought a child to have before he is faced with this formidable thing we call a schoolroom and a teacher. What sorts of identification might he best form? How shall we bring his linguistic level up to a point where he is able to handle things symbolically? I shall not treat further these predispositions because what I want to do after this introduction of the different aspects of the theory is to go back and have a look at each one of these in detail, so let me pass on now to a second aspect of a theory of instruction.

It should concern itself with the optimal structuring of knowledge. By this, I mean that for any body of knowledge there is a minimal set of propositions, or statements, or images from which one can best generate the rest of what exists within that field. For example, from the conservation theorems plus a little more, a great deal of physics can be reconstructed. This is the "guts" of physics.

Now, I think when we speak of the optimal structuring of knowledge, we probably have three things in mind about this set of underlying propositions. They should have the power of simplifying the diversity of information within the field, somehow rendering the particular redundant, making it clear that this case is just a sub-case of something else, that one fact is not the same as every other fact. I speak of this power of simplification as the economy of a structure. Secondly, such a structure would enable you to generate new propositions, to go beyond the information given. This I would speak of as the productiveness of a structure. And finally, there is another aspect to the structure of knowledge which has to do with the extent to which it increases the manipulability of knowledge. It is classically the case, for example, that when you put something into words it now becomes possible for you to take that thing which before you only intuited in some rough way and to subject it to the combinings and recombinings that are made possible by the transformative powers of language. And this I want to speak of as the power of a structure. In thinking of structure, then, we shall want to consider economy, productiveness, and power. All of these things are relative to a learner. It does not do to say simply that because physics has great economy, great productiveness, and great power as practiced by a Feinman or a Purcell, that therefore you have children ape those distinguished scientists. You take the child where you find him and give him the structure that is economical, productive and powerful for him and that allows him to grow.

A third aspect of a theory of instruction deals with the optimal sequence that is required for learning. In what order do we present things? If you are presenting the Napoleonic period, where do you start? If you would give a sense of the sixteenth century, do you begin with the fact that mercantile prices and prosperity were going up at a booming rate, whereas the rents that were got by the landlords were not going up because there were long-term leases? You might. If you want to produce drama, you would. But, we will return to that because there is a question of how to give the learner a place from which to take off, something upon which to build. What order to do it? What exercises do you give him to strengthen the sinews of his own thinking? What type of representation do you use? How much particular? How much generality?

Finally, a fourth aspect of a theory of instruction should concern itself with the nature and pacing of rewards and punishments and successes and failures.

To sum up then, a theory of instruction should be constructed around four problems: predispositions, structures, sequences, and consequences.

PREDISPOSITION

What can we say about the factors that predispose a student to be a learner? Let us begin with the following simple proposition: that in order to learn or to solve problems, it is necessary that alternatives be explored and that you cannot have effective learning or problem solving without the learner's having the courage and the skill to explore alternative ways of dealing with a problem.

It seems that if you take this as the first proposition concerning predisposition, there are three things that immediately can be said. First, that if this is the case, learning in the presence of a teacher, or a tutor, or an instructor should somehow minimize the risks and the severity of the consequence that follows upon exploration of alternatives. It should be less risky for a child to explore alternatives in the presence of a teacher, than without one present. It is obvious that, at the level of coping with nature in the raw, the child searching for food on his own would stand more risk of eating toadstools and poisoning himself, and thereby bringing exploration to a close.

Yet there are other less obvious things that have to do with the closing down of the exploration of alternatives. A teacher or parent can instill the fear of being a fool. That can surely paralyze the will to explore alternatives, for the moment an unreasonable alternative is made to seem like a foolish one, the inner freedom to explore is limited by the requirements of face saving. The encouragement of exploration of alternatives requires some practical minimization of the severity of conseqences following exploration.

It seems to me, further, that one of the ways in which a sense of alternatives to be explored can be opened, is to increase the informativeness of error. To increase the informativeness of error essentially involves making clear to the child what produced a failure. One of the major functions of a teacher is to lead the child to a sense of why he failed. I do not mean why he failed in terms of a characterological analysis; I mean in terms of the nature of what it is that he is doing. If you can somehow make the child aware that his attempted answer is not so much a wrong answer, as an answer to another problem, and then get him back on the track, it becomes possible for the child to reduce the confusion that is produced by picking a wrong alternative. One of the things that, I believe, keeps us from exploring alternatives is precisely the confusion of making the wrong choice.

Still another goad to the exploration of alternatives is through the encouragement of "subversiveness." I mean that you must subvert all of the earlier established constraints against the exploration of alternatives. This kind of subversiveness has to do with a healthy skepticism toward holy cows, prefabricated doctrines, and stuffed shirtliness. Let there be no question or doubt that is "not nice to express." The moment you as teachers lose your role as subversives in this respect, you are doing the child an injustice and yourself an injustice as a teacher. I want to rescue the word "subversion" from the wrong senses to which it has been put in recent years.

When we think about predispositions to learn, we have to bear in mind that the very relationship that we have with our pupils is a privileged relationship involving authority and direction; that is to say, the exchange is uneven. We know; they do not. Since that is the case, it becomes very necessary for us not to use this implicit authoritative relationship as a means of using our own office as a way of establishing truth and falsity. It is so easy in the mind of the impressionable child to equate truth with Miss Smith!

The nature of learning in a school situation requires at least a dyadic relation; at least two people are involved, and usually many more than two. This obvious point requires that there be some set of minimal social skills that a child brings with him to a learning situation. We do not know much about the nature of these social skills that are required for an exchange of information. The act of exchanging information mutually, or even of accepting information and working on it until you make it your own, is not well understood. In addition to minimum social skills, there are elementary intellectual skills that are necessary for a first encounter with school learning. We "know" this, but we do little either to investigate these elementary skills or to devise ways of strengthening them. I am thinking principally of linguistic skills. Where a child has been socially underprivileged in his early years, it may be necessary for example to look squarely at the situation and say: This child, before he can go on in these subjects, simply needs more linguistic training or all of our words will be just mere wind going by his ears. I do not mean vocabulary, but, rather, the development of the full transformative power of language which our linguists are only now beginning to understand.

It is necessary for the beginning child to have certain kinds of manipulative and almost intuitive geometric skills. We have started studies of children on the borders of the Sahara in the interior of Senegal. We are struck at the difference in the behavior of American children and children in the African bush who do not have toys with mechanical or geometrical constraint to play with. We take it for granted that our children can deal with geometrical forms, put them together and take them apart, yet the fact of the matter is that it should not be taken for granted. The experience of manipulating materials gives our children a stock of images and geometric transformations that permit him to work geometrically and mechanically in a way that our African subjects cannot. These elementary forms of intellectual skills are essential. Is there more that we can do that we are not doing?

My last point before passing on to the topic of structure in learning has to do with attitudes toward the use of mind. These are predisposing factors of an enormously important kind. For example, we know that these vary to some extent, speaking sociologically, by class, by ethnic group, by culture. There is no question, for example, that in terms of social class, very frequently you will find in the lowest social class an attitude toward life that is governed by the concept of luck. This means that there is really nothing you can do by your own efforts, that things happen to a considerable extent by luck. The business of applying the mind, the idea that man has a chance if he will use his mind, is an attitude which is not frequently present and which has to be created. This is an extremely difficult thing to do and I hope no one asks me how do you do it, because I do not know. Yet it is quite clear that we must use the most intelligent opportunism we can muster, to do anything we can to get the idea started that by the use of mind one can increase effectiveness or any other desired state. We also know that different ethnic groups have different attitudes toward the use of mind, and again, I do not think we take full advantage of this. The Muslim-African culture, for example, has an attitude toward the use of mind that it should be used principally for grasping the word that has been passed on. This is not the kind of use of mind that makes for what might be called a very active, vigorous mind.

STRUCTURE OF KNOWLEDGE

Now let us turn to the question of the structure of knowledge, its economy, productiveness, and power as related to the capacities of a learner. The first point relates to theorem in the theory of computation proposed by Turing. Turing proposed that any problem that can be solved can be solved by simpler means. That is the theorem. Out of this theorem has come the technology of computing machines. What it says—and it says this only for so-called well-defined problems with unique solutions—is that however complicated the problem, we can break it down into a set of simpler elementary operations and finally end up with operations as simple as: make a mark, move a mark, take the mark out, put the mark back, etc. These elementary operations are then combined into sub-routines that are more complex and then these are combined, etc. The machine succeeds in being practically interesting because it can run off so many of these operations in so short a time. Turing's theorem has a certain relevance to the structure of knowledge; it, in a sense, is another way of stating what by now I am afraid has become an old saw: that any subject can be taught to anybody at any age in some form that is honest. There is always some way in which complicated problems can be reduced to simpler form, simple and step-by-step enough for a child to grasp.

Now, to move ahead one step, I believe it can be said that knowledge about anything can, generally speaking, be represented in three ways, three parallel systems of processing information. One of these is what I call the enactive representation of knowledge. How do you tie a running bowline? You will reply that you can't quite say it or draw it, but that you will show me by tieing one. Try to tell somebody how to ride a bicycle, or ski. It is knowing by doing. It is the way in which the young child on a seesaw "knows" Newton's Law of Moments. He knows that in order to balance two children on the other side he has to get farther out on his side, and this is the Law of Moments, but known enactively. Only with time do children free themselves from this tendency to equate things with the actions directed toward them. We never free ourselves from it completely. Let me now speak of ikonic representation. If somebody says to me, for example, "What's a square?" I might say, "Well, a square is a set of sets such that the number of elements in each set is equal to the number of sets." This is a good definition of a square, formalistically. Yet the fact of the matter is that there is another way of representing a square, by an image. It isn't a square, it's an image of a square, and it's a useful image—we can start with it. Many of the things we use in representing knowledge have this ikonic property. I use the word "ikonic" because I do not really mean a kind of imitation of nature. Let us not run down the importance of these useful images. They have limits, these representing pictures.

Finally, a third way in which knowledge can get represented is symbolically. By this I mean in words or in those more powerful versions of words, powerful in one way in any case, mathematical symbols. I think you can turn around the Chinese proverb to the effect that one picture is worth a thousand words. For certain purposes one word is worth a thousand pictures. For example, draw a picture of "implosion"; and yet the idea of implosion as such was one of the basic notions that led to the idea of thermonuclear fusion. Implosion is the concept that results from the application of a contrast transformation on the more familiar concept of explosion. The word was so important that it was classified as top secret during the war. It is this capacity to put things into a symbol system with rules for manipulating, for decomposing and recomposing and transforming and turning symbols on their heads that makes it possible to explore things not present, not picturable, and indeed not in existence.

Now the three modes of representation do not disappear as we grow older; quite to the contrary, they remain with us forever. When we speak of the application of Turing's theorem to the question of structuring of knowledge, it is in reference to the representation forms we have been discussing. Early in life and also early in our mastery of a subject we may have to represent things in terms of what we do with them—in much the same way as a child "knows about" balance beams by knowing what to do on a seesaw. We may then emerge with an image of it, however nonrigorous the image may be. Then and only then can language and symbol systems be applied with some degree of likelihood that their reference will be understood. I do not think I can say anything more important than that. You create a structure, not by starting off with the highest brow symbolic version, but by giving it in the muscles, then in imagery and then giving it in language, with its tools for manipulation. The basic task is to orchestrate the three kinds of representations so that we can lead the child from doing, to imaging what he has done, and finally to symbolization.

Usually in a college catalog when a course is listed it will say something about a "prerequisite." Let me urge that any topic also has internal prerequisites in addition to the things that you are supposed to have mastered beforehand. The internal prerequisites may indeed be just precisely the easier modes of representation that get one to a less rigorous, more imageful or enactive grasp of a subject before it gets converted either into ordinary or mathematical language. The way you get ahead with learning is to translate an idea into those nonrigorous forms that can be understood. Then one can, with their aid, become more precise and powerful. In mathematics such techniques are called "heuristics." Their use often constitutes a prerequisite to grasping a subject in its full depth. This is most of what is meant when we speak of "spiral curriculum."

OPTIMAL SEQUENCE

With respect to the sequence in which material is presented, different sequences are obviously needed to achieve different objectives. The idea of one right sequence is a myth. You have to be quite clear about what kind of learning you are trying to produce before you can specify what is a good sequence for presenting it. There are sequences that can be described for the production of parrots. We use them all the time. But there is also a sequence that is particularly interesting in that it seems to increase the likelihood that knowledge will be converted into a structure that is economical, productive and powerful—and therefore transferable. It is worth pausing over.

I would like to suggest that if you wanted to do this, the first thing that you might do is to try leading the child to grasp a structure by induction from particular instances. You would give him lots of particular instances and let him recognize their underlying regularity. If you want the child to transfer his learning to new situations you had better give him some practice in transfer while he is learning.

The second thing you might try is the use of contrast in your sequence. The fish will be the last to discover water. Economy of representation often makes it necessary for the child to see the contrasting case. Often concepts are structured in terms of contrast and can only be fully understood in terms of them. To grasp the meaning of commutativity in arithmetic—that $3 \cdot 4 = 4 \cdot 3$—often may require that we recognize the non-commutative case of ordinary language—that for quantifiers, for example, "very much" is not equal to "much very" or as a little girl once put it "black shoe" isn't "shoe black."

Third, if one wants a sequence that is going to produce powerful learning, avoid premature symbolization. Do not give them that word to parrot before they know what it is about either by manipulation or in images. Ask yourselves how much you understand about simultaneous equations.

Fourth, you might try to give the child practice at both leaping and plodding. Let him go by small steps. Then let him take great leaps, huge guesses. Without guessing he is deprived of his rights as a mind. We cannot get all of the evidence. It is often by guessing that we become aware of what we know.

Another question related to sequence has to do with what I would call "revisiting." Rarely is everything learned about anything in one encounter. Yet we seem to be so impelled to cover, to get through the Elizabethan Period, and on through such-and-such period that we forget the obvious point—that the pot is rarely licked clean at one swipe. Perhaps we would do well to take music listening as a model. It is not simply a matter of mastering this subject, or even of converting it into more powerful form. Rather, revisit means an opportunity of connecting what we have learned now with what else we know. Why is such an obvious point so often ignored?

REWARD AND PUNISHMENT

Now the question of pacing reward and punishment for success and failure. First distinguish two states. One is success and failure; the other one is reward and punishment. By success and failure, I mean the end state that is inherent in a task. The problem is solved or not solved or close to solved. By reward and punishment, I mean something quite different. It relates to the consequences that follow upon success and failure—prizes, scoldings, gold stars, etc.

It is often the case that emphasis upon reward and punishment, under the control of an outside agent such as a teacher or parent, diverts attention away from success and failure. In effect, this may take the learning initiative away from the child and give it to the person dispensing the rewards and punishments. This will be the more likely if the learner is not able to determine the basis of success and failure. One of the great problems in teaching, which usually starts with the teacher being very supportive, is to give the rewarding function back to the learner and the task. Perhaps we can do this by rewarding good errors so that the child becomes aware of the process of problem solving as worthy as well as the fruits of successful outcome. In any case, I wish to mention these matters to suggest that old dogmas about the role of "reinforcement" can be looked at afresh. The independent problem solver is one who rewards and punishes himself by judging the adequacy of his efforts. Equip him with the tools for thinking and let him be his own man.

SOME CONCLUSIONS

I should warn you, in conclusion, to beware of the likes of us. We do not have a tested theory of instruction to offer you. What is quite plain is that one is needed and I would propose that we work together in its forging.

I warn you for a good reason. Educators are a curiously doctrinal or ideological kind of people. You are given to slogans and fight and bleed in their behalf. You have looked to psychology for help and have often been misled into accepting mere hypotheses as the proven word. It is partly because it is so hard to test the adequacy of ideas in an educational setting.

Now we are living through a great revolution in education. Our survival may depend on its successful outcome—our survival as the human race. I know no group in our society more devoted to the common weal than our educators. In this era of new curricula, new teaching arrangements, new automated devices, your best rudder is a healthy sense of experimentation backed by a skepticism toward educational slogans.

If we are to move toward a serviceable and sturdy theory of instruction—and I think we are—then your greatest contribution will be a willingness to give new ideas a try and full candor in expressing your reactions to how things worked. The prospect is strenuous, but gains to be won are enormous. I wish you well.

FOR FURTHER THOUGHT

1. A feature of our modern world is the need to disseminate information to large groups. One result of this condition is faddism or a closely related phenomenon—"sloganeering." Insasmuch as the public often refuses or is unable to examine the ideas being advanced, those in charge of dissemination try to "package" the ideas in such a way that they will gain acceptance. Such has been the case with changes in education. Progressive education, life adjustment, and education for the gifted or

the deprived, stand out as programs advanced, at least in part, by slogans designed to gain popular support. Bruner advocates a skepticism toward educational slogans. *What is there about the way decisions are made in our society that encourages sloganeering and faddism? In what way would professional decision making alter this situation? What preparation would be most useful for educators to help them discern "passing fads" and slogans in current educational literature? Could Bruner's approach be seen as a slogan attempt to get others to jump on a bandwagon unwittingly?*

2. Bruner claims that the structure of knowledge is such, "that any subject can be taught to anybody at any age in some form that is honest." Curricular practice based upon developmental and maturational studies has for some time delayed the introduction of time and space concepts into the elementary grades. *Does Bruner's claim and related changes in elementary school curricula suggest the inaccuracy of these maturational studies and findings? If Bruner's claim is true, does it automatically follow that there should be a change of elementary school practice? Upon what value choice is that policy dependent?*

3. Examine the four areas regarded by Bruner to be essential to the foundation of an adequate theory of instruction. *What subject areas and practical experiences are essential to one seeking such a theory? To what extent are these similar to the program outlined by Broudy? How do they differ from your preparation for certification? Do these requirements set out by Bruner in any way challenge the program of teacher education set out by the authors of this text?*

4. Examination of the research findings in education offers an extensive array of suggestions for altering content or methodology in order to improve classroom experience. *Is this information of any value without the theory of instruction suggested by Bruner? Why or why not? Does this type of research make a worthwhile contribution to the knowledge necessary for good teaching?*

5. Federal support of education has produced a myriad of research and programs designed to cope with educational problems of nearly every conceivable nature. Emphases have shifted so that the exceptional, the deprived, and the vocationally oriented have all had or are still having their day. *Are these findings and suggestions limited in their value by the absence of an adequate theoretical base to encompass them? Does the sense of urgency associated with these areas of concern and findings indicate the need for action regardless of the availability of a theoretical framework?*

6. Bruner advocates that teachers play the role of subversives in that they need to provide for the subversion of all constraints against the full exploration of alternatives. *How does such a role compare with the ideal seen in the life of Socrates? Why must the professional teacher be in a*

position to play the role of skeptic? Is the teacher, such as the sophist, who is continually faced with the need to "sell" the worth of his subject to the public, professional? Are any of the features of the marketplace unprofessional?

SOCIAL FORCES AND TEACHER CERTIFICATION

Central to the consideration of "professionalism" in any area is the matter of the preparation necessary to offer satisfactory services to the public. Certification of those properly prepared is the mark of approval for which members of society look. Certification then can be seen as the legal and, ultimately, social sanction to practice. The major purpose of certification is to protect the public from the charlatan. The professional group is claiming to render a service and must therefore be concerned with the ability of those operating in its name—whether the field be teaching, medicine, or law.

While the purpose and value of thoroughly examined certification policies are readily acknowledged there is, especially in teaching, concern over a number of matters relating to the issuance of certificates. A number of these questions are apparent in the following selection. The author describes the role of the California legislature in certifying teachers. The particular state is, of course, unimportant for the questions hold regardless of location. How able is any legislature, as opposed to the professional group involved, to decide upon appropriate standards? Should autonomy of professionalism include the setting of "professional" standards in order to offer the best protection of the public? What constitutes a satisfactory program for certification? What causes and balances of causes are essential to provide for the service deemed most desirable? Is course work an adequate or sufficient standard to employ in granting certification? Would examination on subject matter mastery, intelligence, and personality provide an additional safeguard? These are only a few of the questions derived from an examination of teacher certification.

----◄◆►----

COMPETING SOCIAL FORCES
AND CERTIFICATION LEGISLATION*

During the months ahead, education in California will be witnessing changes in the way in which teachers are educated. Recent legislation has

*David C. Epperson, "Competing Social Forces and Certification Legislation," *Journal of Teacher Education*, vol. 16, no. 3 (September 1965), pp. 286–289. Dr. Epperson is Associate Professor of Higher Education at the University of Illinois and former Assistant Dean at the School of Education, University of California, Santa Barbara.

resulted in a five-year elementary education program placing strong emphasis upon single subject area specialization, with a reduction in professional education course requirements. It is currently necessary for every person seeking certification in California to have an academic major complemented with a limited amount of professional course work.[1] It is the purpose of this paper to suggest that the decision to modify certification legislation, while solving one type of problem, is making it extremely difficult to solve others. Since decisions to amend certification requirements are made in the context of competing economic and political forces and not in a social vacuum, understanding of these changes can be gained by looking to the social environment.

In a state such as California which is undergoing rapid social and economic changes, one sees an amplification of the way in which education is looked to for assistance in solving both regional and national problems. As the political decision-makers search for institutions that can be marshalled to solve social problems, the schools, more than ever before, are given mandates to do their share in contributing to the resolution of these problems. Whether the schools can do much to solve a social problem is in itself debatable, but for the purpose of the discussion that follows, it is enough to say that they are being asked to help.

Since contemporary society is extremely complex, there are always parallel and sometimes competing social forces operating at the time an educational decision is rendered; those making decisions find it necessary to respond to forces which appear to be the most crucial at the moment. The idea to be developed in this paper is that, in the case of recent legislation governing teacher certification in California, decision-makers seem to have responded to one set of extremely potent social forces while ignoring others.

Many changes in the way a society is organized to educate its children can be traced to economic and political factors which stimulate society to organize in different ways so that it can solve the problems which appear at the time to be the most pressing. The new social arrangements which emerge as a solution to the problems create the need for individuals trained to contribute to the solution of the general problems faced by the nation. For example, the complex social organizations or bureaucracies formed to solve production and distribution problems require a different type of training from that required fifty years ago of individuals working in relatively simple and small economic units. It is this writer's conviction that the recent decision to modify the training of teachers should not be

---

[1]The professional sequence includes one course in the social foundations of education, one in the psychological foundations of education, one in teaching procedures, and a period of student teaching. In addition, each candidate must complete an advanced course in English composition and a course in the theory of arithmetic.

thought of as the work of inept politicians trying to take over control of the schools. Rather the decision can be understood only if it is seen as an effort to contribute to the resolution of current economic and political problems. However, it must be pointed out that the efforts of politicians to solve one type of problem can yield consequences which intensify other social problems. For example, when society places a priority on turning out the experts necessary to maintain its expanding technology and to put the United States in a better competitive position with its international adversaries, it has taken action which has the potential of detracting from solutions to many of the problems associated with urbanization.

In recent years, the United States has been experiencing stunning technological advances which have placed severe strains on its system of preparing specialists to assume the new roles associated with these changes. It is apparent that the educational system is not preparing enough individuals with a level of competency to permit them to perform complex functions requiring well-developed skills for dealing with abstractions. An expanding technology requires specialized experts. Furthermore, the enduring nature of the tension between the Western and Communist worlds and the futility of many of the efforts substantially to reduce the tension has resulted in a rather desperate search for a channel through which the sometimes frantic energy can be directed. Since the anxiety centering around this perceived threat is so general, nearly every civic organization has at one time or another expressed concern over the adequacy of our educational arrangements.[2]

In the past, debate on educational issues in the California State Legislature was essentially nonpartisan, but of late, it has taken on a more partisan character, primarily because of the widespread interest in education as a panacea for social, economic, and political ills. There is now political mileage in an education bill. It is *not* a purpose of this article to cast aspersions on politicians; it is meant only to illustrate the manner in which powerful social forces, in this case expanding technology and continuing international conflict, can be translated into legislative concern and hence into educational reform. It makes sense both to the layman and the politician that if teachers are trained to be more expert in a special subject matter field they will be better able to contribute to the development of the experts that are required in modern industry and in the technological and military competition with the Soviet Union. That this expertness on the part of teachers is achieved at the expense of professional preparation seems inconsequential to the untrained observer.

---

[2]While some observers like to assign to the extremist right-wing groups the responsibility for the actions taken in relation to this threat, it seems more appropriate to conclude that these groups serve only to amplify an already existing fear.

It is suggested that the new credential requirements for elementary education, which include greater depth of training in an academic area and less training in the discipline of professional education, will have the following consequences:

1. Teachers will be more nimble in working with abstractions in their special area of concentration but will have less time in their training program to spend on learning ways of translating the abstractions into meaningful experiences for children.
2. Teachers will be less able to deal with the wide range of individual differences found in the typical classroom. Because of the abstract nature of their own training, the teachers will be best able to accommodate for the child who has a predisposition to work effectively with abstractions. This will, of course, put the child who does not possess this predisposition at a distinct disadvantage in the competition for rewards in the school.

If the above conclusions about the consequences of the recent teacher certification legislation are valid, it is not difficult to see how attention to one set of social problems, in this case advancing technology and international competition, can detract from the solution of other pressing social problems. The educational challenges accompanying the problems of increasing urbanization seem to be demanding a different type of training for teachers. The urban centers, where most of the people of California reside, are composed of extremely diverse populations. Many of the children who attend urban schools have had restricted life experiences, have come from backgrounds where the ability to deal with abstractions is not emphasized, possess patterns of behavior which are incompatible with the expectations of typical middle-class teachers, or come from families where the English language is not spoken or is spoken in some modified form. The important question to raise seems to be, Might not urban social problems be intensified by the politicians' decision to legislate a training program in which so little time is spent learning ways of making abstractions meaningful to the diverse populations of children found in metropolitan schools? To train a generation of teachers who have the potential of adding to the frustration of the already restless urban population could do serious damage to our efforts to build complex, but at the same time, integrated social units.

It should be made clear that the writer is not in opposition to making the education of teachers more academic; on the contrary, he welcomes the opportunity to enrich the preparation of teachers with greater depth in an academic discipline. Furthermore, he does not wish to be cast as an apologist for the undisciplined professional content that has been found in so many of the training programs. He prefers to take the position that the minimum that has been set by legislation for academic preparation is quite satisfactory if one can assume that the most is being made of the time devoted to such learning. However, by setting the minimum for professional preparation so low, it is unlikely that teachers will learn the skills necessary for dealing effectively with the educational problems associated with urbanization.

Up to this point, an effort has been made to illustrate the intimate relationship between social forces and teacher-training practices. It has been suggested that California's decision to subordinate (in its educational policy-making) the problems associated with urbanization to those associated with technological expansion and international competition may result in serious problems which will have to be met in the most imaginative way possible. The legislation is here, and it is likely to appear in other states in view of the fact that every state is experiencing, to varying degrees, similiar social forces. It appears that educators will have to live with this trend for some time. What then can be done to compensate for the unintended consequences of the existing legislation? It seems that one important step is for the professional leadership in the colleges and universities to assume fully their responsibility as social critics. College and university professors enjoy an insulation from acts of retribution, but with this protection goes the responsibility to point out to their students and to the general public the potential consequences of such educational reforms as new certification legislation. Another step which appears essential is to attempt to exercise leadership in the educational community by working toward better articulation between pre-service and in-service teacher education. If college and university professors can extend their influence beyond the time that they have the students on campus, then the possibilities are enhanced for overcoming the weaknesses of legislation governing the training of teachers. As a result of work with leaders in the public schools, one becomes more and more convinced that any steps that the colleges and universities take to give direction to in-service training programs will be welcomed with enthusiasm.

Of course another obvious way those in teacher education can reduce the undesirable consequences of truncated professional training is to work with renewed vigor toward more effective pre-service programs within the limits of the time allowed. This is an area of concern which demands continual attention.

In this paper, it has been suggested that in efforts to cope with the problems of an expanding technology and the ever-present threat from the communists, laws have been enacted by the California Legislature which could serve to intensify social problems associated with urbanization. Some general recommendations were put forward with the goal of reminding educators of their professional responsibility to work toward a mastery over the undesirable consequences of revised certification legislation.

FOR FURTHER THOUGHT

1. The claim is made by the author that the new certification requirements will increase the amount of preparation in an academic area and
lessen the preparation in the discipline of professional education. *What
are the essential ingredients of a discipline? Can professional education
be appropriately labelled a discipline?*

2. Emphasis on academic specialization rather than upon professional
education is purportedly likely to result in (1) better understanding of
abstractions but less ability to develop these meaningfully for children;
and (2) less ability to deal with wide ranges of individual differences.
*Upon what evidence are these claims based? Are the claims valid? Why
or why not? Does the teacher with greater subject matter background
possess something that provides for more fruitful utilization of the subject to enhance meaning and to cope with individual differences? Assuming that the most desirable program is not an either-or situation with
regard to these two broad categories of study, how is one best able to
arrive at the appropriate balance? Should the balance be different for
secondary and for elementary teachers?*

3. The recommendation is made that professors in institutions of higher
learning should serve as social critics. One of the major reasons offered
for such a role resides in the fact that such people are insulated from
acts of retribution. *Is there any other attribute possessed by such personnel that would serve as a more worthy reason for recommending the
role of social critic? Are educators better able to ascertain the consequences of various certification measures? Are teachers in the public
school classrooms just as able as social critics?*

4. According to Epperson there is a need for personnel in higher education to foster a better articulation between pre-service and in-service
teacher education. *If such people are best able to ascertain consequences
of teacher certification programs and proper articulation of various
aspects, should they not seek and acquire the power to effect the desired
certification regulations? Instead of being continually plagued by judgments of the uninformed with regard to proper preparation, should not
the professional possess the autonomy to formulate preparation requirements? If the professional is purporting to serve the public through an
area of specialized knowledge and skill, does it follow that such a group
would also claim that it knows the essential ingredients of preparation
for that service?*

SUGGESTIONS FOR FURTHER READING

1. A source of considerable value in discussion of recent developments
is the report of the 1963 NCTEPS Columbus Conference entitled,

Changes in Teacher Education: An Appraisal (Washington: National Education Association, 1964). This offers a variety of reflections about developments in teacher preparation programs in light of societal changes. Consideration is given to changes suggested by new trends in curriculum, in urban population patterns, in international understanding, and in specialization. Innumerable variations in teacher preparation are suggested in light of these and other developments. Similar topics are considered in the fortieth yearbook publication of the Association for Student Teaching entitled, *Teacher Education and the Public Schools* (Dubuque: Wm. C. Brown Co., Inc., 1961).

2. Concern for a specific area, such as preparation for teaching in the urban or "inner-city" areas can be profitably studied by examining *The Journal of Teacher Education*, vol. 16, no. 2 (June 1965). Further, Hunter College and the University of Southern California provide literature describing their particular teacher preparation programs for deprived regions.

3. A bibliography on the topic of teacher education would not be complete without reference to recent critiques of teacher education. Two of those that have created the greatest concern among educators are J. B. Conant, *The Education of American Teachers* (New York: McGraw-Hill, Inc., 1963) and J. D. Koerner, *The Miseducation of American Teachers* (Boston: Houghton-Mifflin, 1963). Two other publications that were stimulated by Conant's work and that offer useful insights into the topic are "A Symposium on James Bryant Conant, "The Education of American Teachers," *The Journal of Teacher Education* (March 1964), and *Innovation in Teacher Education* (Evanston: Northwestern University Press, 1965), a report of a conference at Northwestern University in 1964. Participants in the conference were T. M. Stinnett, S. M. McMurrin, John Goodlad and J. B. Conant.

4. Merle L. Borrowman's *Teacher Education in America* (New York: Teachers College Press, 1965) provides a historical perspective to the matter of teacher education through an analysis of pertinent documents.

CHAPTER **6**

The Need for Power

The school exists in a power environment and the school itself constitutes a power environment. These are fundamental facts of life. Nevertheless, democrats of many types are reluctant to look power in the eye. Power has often been identified with arbitrary behavior. While there is no necessary empirical connection between the two, the experience of many centuries indicates that an unhappy coincidence of power and arbitrary action has too often been the case. Consequently, a negative connotation has surrounded the word. Galbraith suggests that Americans value its exercise but decry its existence and pretend that they are without it. Specifically he states that:

> The role of power in American life is a curious one. The privilege of controlling the actions or affecting the income and property of other persons is something that no one of us can profess to seek or admit to possessing. No American ever runs for office because of an avowed desire to govern. He seeks to serve—and then only in response to the insistent pressure of friends or of that anonymous but oddly vocal fauna which inhabit the grass roots. . . .[1]

A quest for power is, indeed, suspect. There are, however, other reasons to be advanced than those of a strictly historical nature. Quite obviously, if a person can maintain that he is powerless to act or powerless to act in any

[1]John Kenneth Galbraith, *American Capitalism: The Concept of Countervailing Power* (Boston: Houghton Mifflin, 1952), p. 28. With permission of Hamish Hamilton, London.

other way, he can claim that it is an injustice to hold him responsible for his acts. The lack of desire to be held responsible may very well be as potent a force for rejecting the possession or search for power as the historical tradition.

There is, of course, the problem of defining the concept "power." We shall use the formulation of C. Wright Mills as our point of departure. He said:

> . . . power in any socially relevant sense means that the powerful can realize his will, even if others resist him; it means, in short, that he can make decisions, and if we say that he is very powerful, we are saying that the decisions which he makes or in which he shares, have major consequences for many other people. If then, by the power elite, we mean those who decide whatever is decided that has major consequences, no one could meet the specifications of this definition unless he had access to the command of major institutions. For institutions are necessary to the wielding of power and the enforcement of decisions.[2]

One of the major institutions of society is the school. The control of its operations takes a great deal of power and adds to that same power in a self-generating way. Teachers in training and teachers on the job are continually seeking that power, if we mean by power—"the capacity to bring about the changes one wishes to realize." Most teachers would object to the claim that they are power seekers. Why else, however, do they take courses in educational psychology, educational sociology, teaching methods and courses in their substantive majors? Their answer would undoubtedly be that they "want to become more effective teachers." When one examines their concept of becoming more "effective" it is immediately evident that they want students to learn—they want the capacity to bring about this learning. Inasmuch as the evidence of learning is commonly accepted as being a change in behavior, *one can come to no other conclusion than the fact that teachers are seeking power.* That they hide behind words like "effective" and "good" in no way changes this fact.

Even the term "teacher" is a disguise, for this does not describe the intent of one hearing that name in its boldest terms. The person we call teacher is a professional change agent. Further, the "teacher" or "change agent" is more aptly described as a reformer. His task is that of literally re-forming those in his charge. Such an exposed position is one that most would shrink from and thus they adopt the protective coloration of the term "teacher."

---

[2]C. Wright Mills, "The Power Elite: Military, Economic, and Political," in Arthur Kornhauser, ed., *Problems of Power in American Democracy* (Detroit: Wayne State University Press, 1957), p. 149.

Our public servant (the "teacher," "change agent," "reformer") has recently and reluctantly come to the conclusion that he must do something about the power structure in which he exists in order to become as effective (powerful) as he might. Thus, part of his training now is beginning to address the power structure of society as a whole. If one knows the power structure of society, one gains a sort of power himself. While this chapter does address the idea of power, it is beyond the scope of this book to examine the concept of power (as source or configuration) in the way a sociologist might wish to do. Suggested references for such an examination are provided at the end of this section.

Our task is directed at helping the reader understand the need to confront power as a necessary though not sufficient condition for action. To be powerless is to be paralyzed. To hide one's power is to be private and to give rise to irresponsible behavior. The selection by Max Lerner takes a look at those who appear petrified by power. Myron Lieberman analyzes the relationship between power and educational policy. John Scanlon describes some power problems in teacher organizations. While the ethics of power receives treatment in all these articles, we will reserve such an emphasis for Section IV of this book which deals with various concepts of democracy—democracy, above all, being an ethical system for the distribution of power.

THE NEUTRALITY OF POWER

The way one conceives power, like the way one conceives man, has a tremendous impact on one's behavior. If power is inherently evil and corrupting, one will, so to speak, "wear velvet gloves" either in the hope that power will not show or in the hope that it will not totally corrupt the one who must handle it. If power is inherently good, then it will be welcomed with open arms and be treated as one's just desserts—the reward that comes to the successful and something that calls for no apology unless it be politically expedient. The fall from power will then be treated more like a fall from "grace" than a relief from an intolerable burden.

Lerner would find all this rather amusing were it not for the fact that we live in an atmosphere of power and that either of the above views really cripples its holder—paralyzing some and energizing others without reference to the ends which power can serve. The question of ought a man to use or seek power cannot be answered, on Lerner's view, by looking at power. What then does a man (an educator, statesman, merchant) look to in order to answer the question?

------◄ ◆ ►------

WE FEAR WHAT WE MUST FACE*

It would seem relatively easy to unite the vast majority of men of good will under a banner of legality and firmness; especially if it be in defense of an advancing social order against the violence offered by the forces of social injustice and economic inequality. Yet it is by no means easy; and one of the principal obstacles is that men of good will are growing to fear governmental power almost as much as they fear extra-governmental violence.

The sources of this fear are not difficult to find. Outwardly at any rate it relates to the impact that the fascist excesses and the revelations of the Russian trials of political offenders have had on our consciousness. The inhumanity of fascism has shed a new light on man as a political animal; and the entrenchment of the Communist Party leadership in power in the Soviet Union, forcing the opposition to express itself through the channels of sabotage and treason, has produced in us a sharp disenchantment with proletarian dictatorship.

More deeply and obscurely, however, one may guess that our distrust of power is the expression of our bewilderment amidst the turmoil of the time. Because the old landmarks are gone by which we once judged the path of social advance, and because what lies at the end of the various paths that stretch before us seems treacherous and uncertain, we have come to distrust all roads and finally to fear the journey of politics in itself. And yet, unless one embraces some notion of philosophical anarchism, there can be no doubt that governmental power is a necessary and neutral instrument—a road that may lead in directions that may be good or bad but that is in itself neither good nor bad, a weapon that may be used for destruction or defense depending on who wields it or how it is wielded. Power, in short, is what you make it.

Such a notion of power, which would seem a realistic and operational one, is, however, not the notion that holds sway over our minds. Instead, we tend to think of power as a disease, a cancerous growth whose cells multiply without any relevance to the needs and functions of the body politic. It is in essence the old eighteenth-century notion of John Locke's school, cropping up again in a new setting and with greater force, that all government is malignant.

*Max Lerner, *It Is Later Than You Think* (New York: The Viking Press, Inc., 1943), pp. 216–223. Mr. Lerner, now a syndicated columnist, was the managing editor of the *Encyclopedia of Social Sciences*. He also occupied the post of Dean of the Graduate School at Brandeis University. One of his more recent publications is *Education and a Radical Humanism*.

Many thoughtful and realistic men hold to this view. They fear for the results if we seek to achieve desirable social ends by an extension of the province of government; it raises, for them, the problem I have mentioned in an earlier chapter, the problem of means and ends. They sweat in agony over the growth of a bureaucracy in America; it suggests the powerful party bureaucracies that dominate, in different ways, the Soviet Union and Germany. They scrutinize every new extension of power carefully, to see to what tyrannies it may conceivably lead if pushed far enough. They associate power with the doctrine of Original Sin. The process of government must, for them, be washed in the blood of the sacrificial lamb before it can be washed clean of this taint.

This obsession with power has had an enormous effect upon the political theory of today. In fact, it may be said to have produced a Copernican turn in our political thinking—a shift of axis from the dynamics of government to the nature and consequences of power. It is not too much to say that power has come to hold the center of our preoccupation not only with politics, but with ethics as well. Not only is tyranny feared for its impact on those governed; it is feared also because of its possible impact on those governing—for its corrupting force.

"Power always corrupts and absolute power corrupts absolutely"—that aphorism of Lord Acton is coming to be the motto of our time, especially among liberals. The corruption that we fear is partly the subtle corruption of the moral sense and of self-restraint; it is also the auto-intoxication with power, the heady sense that (we say) makes men who hold power seek to perpetuate their hold upon it through any means. We believe that there is somehow an autonomous and inherent principle of growth in the tenure of power, and moreover an inevitable one. Our attitude toward it is essentially theological; and it is significant that it should be the aphorism of a congenitally religious mind that we quote, for what we resent and fear about power is that it allows men to usurp the godlike function of deciding the destinies of other men, the only restraint upon them (to paraphrase Justice Stone) being their self-restraint.

Is it true that power corrupts, necessarily and inherently? To me, that is only a half-truth, and today much the less important half. There can be no doubt that power may be poorly organized, that there may be insufficient safeguards against its exercise and abuse. There is certainly no insurance that power directed toward socially desirable ends will be kept from becoming tyrannical. These truths are clear and undeniable. But there are other truths as well against which they must be balanced: That power is responsibility, and as such it may have a maturing and sobering effect. That there must be a coercive element in government if it is not to be anarchic. That to distrust and fear power is to distrust and fear the whole intrinsic process of government, since government differs from other phases of the community in that it takes those other phases of the community and organizes them in terms of power. That there has never been anything accomplished representing an advance that was not finally embodied in some form of power. And that, especially in a period like ours, when we are striving desperately for sheer survival in the face of economic collapse and social chaos and the brutally organized violence of the vested interests, the exercise of governmental power is necessary as a condition of survival.

Actually the most damning thing about the current attitude toward power is that it shows that we have no confidence in the human being as such—not even in ourselves. True, there is such a thing as having a fanatic's faith in the rightness of one's own cause—such a thing as equating one's own illusions with godlike certitudes, and then marching through seas of blood to achieve those illusions. But there is another kind of confidence as well—the confidence in social aims that are rooted in the needs of the people, that arise from their spontaneous aspirations, that have the support of their suffrage and represent their will. When, because of our fear of power, we fall back paralyzed at the very moment when those aims are threatened; when we fear to organize our aims in the form of governmental action and even coercion, then we are betraying a negativism and fear about ourselves as human beings that will lead only to the destruction of what we cherish.

There is an enormous difference between political power when it is personal, tyrannical, unchecked, and political power when it is democratically arrived at and democratically controlled. But once you have democratic power, it is as fatal to fear to exert it to the full as the same fear would be fatal for the absolutist. Only in the latter case merely his own survival is involved, and in the former the survival of a people and a culture.

The interesting thing is that thus to distrust our own use of political power is by implication to give free rein to other forms of power that are not ours, and which, not being political, are more subtly coercive than the extensions of governmental power that we fear. For, with our weakness for labels, we tend to put our emphasis on the forms rather than the actualities of power. Thurman Arnold has observed, quite rightly, that it is part of the folklore of a capitalist culture to protest against taxation by the government, yet to submit to just as drastic a levy by the corporations in the form of monopoly prices. This observation could be extended to the whole sphere of power. Actually the coercions that we submit to because they are embodied in economic and social institutions are far more pervasive and far more drastic than any coercions on the part of a democratic government. The jobs we have, the flats and apartments we live in, the prices we pay, the values we receive, our livelihood and security are all today subject to the vast corporate empire of capitalism. The necessities and amenities of life, what we need to sustain ourselves and what we need to amuse ourselves—even the ideas that we think with, like the newspapers that we read and the radios that we listen to—are part of this empire. Yet we do not fear these as forms of power imposed upon us, because we accept them as part of the habitual pattern of our lives. In fact, many of the most coercive elements in government—such as the laws to ensure schooling, to enforce sanitation, to conscript soldiers—we have also come to accept after a struggle as part of the habitual pattern of our lives.

What we fear is what is not habitual. When the problem is posed of taking the vast power that the corporations today exercise in an undisciplined and unacknowledged fashion over the outlines of our lives, and of transferring that power to the government, we shrink back in fear. Planning is regimentation, we say. No body of men should be entrusted with the power of making decisions that affect the sacred economic sphere of our lives. But the fact is that we have already entrusted those decisions and that power to a body of men—to the unacknowledged rulers of our economic destinies. We have never recognized it as a form of power, reserving that term for the crystallized governmental forms only. Now when we are called upon to extend the province of government into the economic domain, and to transfer the control from the oligarchs to ourselves, we recognize it for the first time for what it is. The fact that in the act of making the transfer we have come to recognize the true implications of power in economic institutions may turn out to be one of the biggest social gains of the whole transition period.

But it will be a gain on which we may never capitalize unless we learn to consolidate and safeguard the power that is being transferred. For we can establish democratic control of our industrial life only by a quiet but nonetheless firm insistence upon the power of a democracy to rule its own economic destinies. That means we must use the governmental power we already have in gaining more.

It is as bare as that. Yet there is no other way, unless we are willing to surrender even the democratic forms that we now have, and yield the province that the democratic government now occupies. The strength of the oligarchs is so encrusted in our economy, that only a firm use of governmental power will avail us in fighting their sabotage. If any of us think that we can maintain the *status quo*, that is an illusion. The organization of our economic life is collapsing so long as it is uncontrolled by the community acting through its government. The real question, as I have pointed out before, is not whether the province of government shall be extended, but whether it shall be extended by the majority or the minority; whether it shall be extended through democratic procedures, safeguarded by the popular consciousness of its possibilities and dangers, or through the extension of corporate control until the corporate economy becomes the corporate state.

The Soviet experience is, of course, most present in our minds as to the danger of extending the power of the government into the sphere of planning. But the Soviet experience must not be generalized. What has happened in Russia, with respect to the abuse of power, is to a large degree inherent not in planning but in the pre-revolutionary Russian experience, and in the nature of the Russian Revolution. Government power had been, during the whole Tsarist regime, part of the habitual pattern of the culture as it is not in our culture. And because it had been part of that habitual pattern, there was not the same vigilance that we feel about creating safeguards against the abuse and corruption of power. The Russian Revolution involved, moreover, in its nature, so sharp and sudden a transfer of power that even if the habit-patterns that accepted the lack of safeguards had not been there, it would still have been difficult to create the safeguards.

In these facts lies the enormous advantage that the democratic crisis state has over the feudal-capitalist state in its transfer of power. What the Russian experience should do is not to make us condemn out of hand the extension of government power into the sphere of economic planning. That, as I have said, is an imperative that we must under any circumstances accept and work with. The Russian experience is valuable because it underscores for us what we might otherwise have neglected: the great need for making certain that the base of power is democratically sound, that the ways in which it is organized will not perpetuate the leadership nor stifle the opposition nor corrupt the planners themselves. The study of such concrete safeguards will get us a good deal farther than vast generalizations about the nature and evils of power.

One word more, however, about power itself, and the fear of it. The Freudians have taught us that the individual flees from what he unconsciously fears; and that he fears it because he has not learned to confront its burdens and implications. We fear what we must face: that is the core of individual mental sickness. We must face what we fear: that is the core of the restoration of health. We know these things. We know what is healthy for the individual. Yet we do not apply our knowledge to the social health. Power is not an evil. Power is the sum and summit of our political task—perhaps the greatest political task that a generation has had to meet. There are all sorts of hidden dangers, great risks, enormous social difficulties in that task—so many that there is a temptation for us to escape the whole intolerable burden of the social task itself by projecting our fears about it into the realm of power. Power, its dangers and corruptions, becomes the symbol of our fear and the symbol of our escape. Once we confront it we shall have taken the greatest step toward political maturity and social health.

I do not want to magnify the importance of power in our total social problem and its solutions. Power is not bread or meat; it is not culture; it is not life or the ideas that sustain life. We cannot live by power, and a culture that seeks to live by it becomes brutal and sterile. But we can die without it. The values that give life its nourishment are the humanist values, and I want to discuss them in the next chapter. But it is the community's use of its own power, and its clear confronting of what is involved in that use, that must clear the path of whatever obstacles stand in the way of working for those humanist values.

FOR FURTHER THOUGHT

1. The western world has a number of countries that are proud of their public education systems, so proud that they demand school attendance. Compulsory school laws exist. The fact that they often allow a choice between public and private education systems makes attendance no less compulsory. *What kind of defense for this use of power would be provided by Lerner? Could the same defense be used to defend the lack of a compulsory attendance law? What, if anything, makes the use of power good?*

2. Nearly every school has its "bully." He is a menace to the psychological, if not the physical, health of his peers. Some schools even find themselves "blessed" with a collection of "bullies." *In either event, what kind of justification could Lerner supply for a display of teacher power? Are there any problems with this criterion? Would you be willing to apply it in any situation?*

3. Public schools are a part of the government. As such, they and their personnel often claim to be public servants. This is their reason for being. *Can this be seen as a disclaiming of either the desire for or possession of power? If the power belongs to the people, wherein resides responsibility? What, then, does the educator profess to be?*

4. Almost any teacher or parent can be heard to complain that Donald or Deborah wants to be treated as an adult one moment and as a child the next. Masculine "prejudice" or "insight" typically makes the same type of claim about women's demand for "equal" rights. *Are these kinds of behaviors reasonable? What would an understanding of power, freedom, and responsibility contribute to an analysis of such behavior?*

5. *Might you as a teacher expect students to dislike having to organize their own course of study? Would the acceptance or rejection of such a procedure vary widely from student to student? Why? What does this say about power and the teacher? Does she become good by shifting the decision power to the students? Do the students then become bad by possessing the decision apparatus? Should the students give the power back*

to the teacher so that they can become good and, incidentally, make the teacher bad?

6. Perhaps power should be treated like "risk." Shared decisions would be like an insurance policy. They would insure that no one would be completely safe. On the other hand, no one would be completely doomed or devastated by disaster. Thus the mode of operation that shared power would have the inherent quality of goodness or of least badness. *Where would Lerner have the teachers stand on an issue of this sort? Where would you have them stand?*

POWER AND THE SCHOOLS

A community of persuasion may be fine, but in the minds of many it is difficult to achieve. Conversation and real discussion seems to occur best among equals. When the parties to a conversation start off from radically different power bases, there is a tendency for the weaker of the two to be reduced to pleading his case and sometimes even giving the appearance of begging. As a public servant the teacher has felt, and usually justifiably so, that his status was such that he was ineffective in establishing a community of persuasion. He felt that he was a member of the community not by conviction but by submission. Callahan, in an extensive study of business values and practices in educational administration, found that school administrators had been captured not only by the businessmen but by the business mentality. He knew that the influence existed.

> What was unexpected was the extent, not only of the power of the business-industrial groups, but of the strength of the business ideology in the American culture on the one hand and the extreme weakness and vulnerability of schoolmen, especially school administrators, on the other. I had expected more professional autonomy and I was completely unprepared for the extent and degree of capitulation by administrators to whatever demands were made upon them. I was surprised and then dismayed to learn how many decisions they made or were forced to make, not on educational grounds, but as a means of appeasing their critics in order to maintain their positions in the school.[3]

This comes as no surprise to those long in the school "business," but Callahan documents this "captivity" impressively. He is convinced that administrative vulnerability is "built into our pattern of local support and control." He says that: "So long as schoolmen have a knife poised at their financial jugular vein each year, professional autonomy is impossible."[4]

[3]Raymond E. Callahan, *Education and the Cult of Efficiency* (Chicago: The University of Chicago Press, 1962), Preface.
[4]Callahan, Preface.

This, of course, is closely connected with the problem of preparation. To the extent that the school administrator sees himself and is seen as a business manager, his training will aim in that direction. This can only be called what it is—a miserable preparation for educational leadership. Whether a shift from local control would cure the problem or not is an open question.

Fortunately, all is not as bad as it might seem. Classroom teachers have, through their organizations, openly begun a move for power and are presently making rapid strides in that direction. What the result will be is hard to tell. One possibility is that school districts will have a clearly defined business manager role representing the board of education and a clearly defined educator's role representing the professional organization. Whatever the results, we can say with confidence that few men can justly claim more credit for the reawakening of the teacher to his responsibilities (power-wise) than Myron Lieberman. The message is that if you are going to control the schools as teachers, you have to look far beyond its borders for political power. If the educator is to be a party to the community of persuasion rather than a mute, the suggestion to make a move for social power is clear. Mr. Lieberman, in the following selection, suggests that a group that is too weak to protect its own immediate interests is too weak to protect the public interest.

POWER AND POLICY IN EDUCATION*

My concern in this article is power and policy in education. I use the term "power" to mean capacity to influence the behavior of others. Such capacity varies from person to person, from group to group, and from situation to situation. My generalizations on the subject do not assume mathematical precision. They are statements of general tendency, frequently subject to more exceptions and qualifications than I shall provide here.

As I use the word, "power" denotes a relationship between people. We can, of course, refer to a person's power over his physical environment, and this is a perfectly legitimate use of the term. We also agree that power over the physical environment is often an important basis for power over people. For example, the power to change the course of rivers or to pollute the

*Myron Lieberman, "Power and Policy in Education," *Bulletin of the School of Education* (Indiana University), vol. 40, no. 5 (September 1964), pp. 21–29. Dr. Lieberman is currently Assistant Dean for Professional Studies at Rhode Island State College. He has taught at a number of leading universities. Well known among his writings are *Education as a Profession* and *The Future of Public Education*.

atmosphere with radioactivity is an indirect but immense source of power over people. However, power over the physical environment is not the kind that concerns me here, however important it may be in other contexts and for other purposes.

It often happens in education and elsewhere that A and B have some power over each other. For example, a superintendent may have the power to fire, hire, transfer, and promote teachers. The teachers, once hired at least, may eventually have some power over the actions of the superintendent. For instance, even though the superintendent may have the power to fire teachers, the latter may be able to rattle enough skeletons in the educational closet to exact an extremely high price for any such exercise of administrative power—in some cases, a price so high it is not paid.

Power has many sources—legal authority, technical or administrative skill, attractive personality, good looks, money, and so on. All the usual sources of power are present in education. However, any source of power may be limited in a given situation. Money may have no influence upon the person who chooses a life of poverty. Not everyone can be moved by tears, by sex, by law, or even by the threat to life and limb. Persons who can be influenced on some occasions by any or all of these things may not be subject to their influence—or be subject to the same degree—on other occasions.

A common fallacy is to identify power with the abuses of it, and to assume that power is used only for selfish ends. Thus, many persons think of teacher power solely in terms of its impact on teacher welfare. More power for teachers means more money for them; less power means less money for them. There is some truth in this view, but it is a dangerously short-sighted one. A group which is too weak to protect its immediate welfare interests will usually be too weak to protect the public interest as well. Teachers need power to protect academic freedom, to eradicate racial segregation in education, to secure more and better instructional materials, and to do many other things that have little or no relationship to teacher welfare. If teachers are weak, they cannot protect the public interest in education. This is why the weakness of teachers as an organized group is one of the most important problems in American education today.

Some people regard teachers as a powerful group. A wide variety of evidence has led me to an opposite conclusion. Admittedly, some of this evidence is rather subjective. For example, I have never met an influential political leader who regarded teachers' organizations as a particularly important or influential lobby. Consider for a moment the 1962 election in California for the office of State Superintendent of Public Instruction. In this election, a former school superintendent, Max Rafferty, was elected State Superintendent of Public Instruction in California against the opposition of every important teachers' organization in California, including the California Teachers Association, the largest and most powerful state association of teachers in the country. Although powerful, the association was not powerful enough politically to prevent the election of a person regarded by the CTA itself as opposed to many of its basic policies. Mr. Rafferty's election over the opposition of teachers' organizations can hardly be regarded as unique; it is doubtful whether a single important politician in the United States owes his position to the National Education Association or the American Federation of Teachers (the two national teachers' organizations) or depends upon them as a major source of support.

The internal evidence about the National Education Association and the American Federation of Teachers (and their state and local affiliates) also seems to me to be quite inconsistent with the view that these are strong organizations. In 1959, the NEA, then with over 667,000 members, conducted a study of its affiliated local associations. The study showed that about 80 per cent of the associations sent two or fewer communications to their school authorities during the entire year, and that about 90 per cent received two or fewer communications during this period from their school authorities. Seventy-five per cent of the associations did, however, participate in social activities during the year—more than in any other kind of activity.[1]

In this connection, we must include the American Association of University Professors on the list of "paper tigers." In fact, an important cause of weak teachers' organizations is that the teachers have such a poor model in the American Association of University Professors. For the most part, the professors have trained the public school teachers in organizational impotence and naiveté. Teachers must look elsewhere for their examples and their inspiration if they are to achieve and exercise the power appropriate to their tasks in society.[2]

We should also realize that the leaders of teachers' organizations may have a vested interest in avoiding widespread acceptance of the view that teachers' organizations are weak. After all, the paid staffs of teachers' organizations want their dues-paying members to believe they are getting something for their money. For this reason, they tend to use organizational journals and conventions to persuade teachers that their organizations are effective. The contrary point of view has relatively little opportunity to present its case to the rank and file.

Instead of arguing about whether or not teachers' organizations are powerful, suppose we phrase the issue this way: Regardless of whether we

[1]Research Division, National Education Association, *Local Education Associations at Work* (Washington, D. C.: The Association, 1960).

[2]Myron Lieberman, *The Future of Public Education* (Chicago: University of Chicago Press, 1960), Chapter 10.

characterize these organizations as weak or strong, what are the reasons they are not more powerful than they are? Agreed, there are several explanations as to why they are not, but what are the most important reasons and what should be done about them?

At any level, the weakness of teachers' organizations in a specific case might be due to inadequate leadership, lack of members or money, inadequate program, or any of the reasons underlying organizational weakness generally. What we are looking for are the most basic causes, those that go farthest in explaining teacher weakness in the widest variety of situations and over the broadest geographical area.

One such cause is the public attitude that strong teachers' organizations would, *ipso facto*, be harmful to the public interest. Teachers' organizations are viewed solely as a means of raising the level of teacher welfare. A higher level of teacher welfare would presumably require higher taxes. Therefore, the way to prevent higher taxes is to prevent the rise of strong teacher organizations.

Another important factor is that many private employers compete with the government for personnel. Naturally, these employers do not want the conditions of competition to favor public rather than private enterprise. Thus, in addition to the higher taxes that would result from higher levels of support for government personnel, these employers have an additional incentive to prevent the rise of public employee organizations strong enough to raise substantially the level of compensation in public employment. It is a myth that government is a model employer; if anything, the conditions of government employment lag behind those in private employment.

Because the strength of teachers' organizations is viewed largely in terms of their impact upon taxes, there are widespread, if inarticulate, objections to encouraging, or even permitting, the growth of strong teachers' organizations. The unfortunate but predictable consequence is that conditions of private employment tend to be superior to those of public employment. Obviously, if organizations of public employees are restricted in ways that do not apply to organizations of persons in private enterprise, it is only a matter of time before the greater freedom and strength of the latter result in superior conditions of employment in the private sector.

It is possible to analyze this situation from several standpoints. We could, for example, question the simplistic notion that the public does not pay for higher levels of compensation in the private sector of the economy. Realistically, it appears that the public pays for these as much as it does for higher levels of compensation in public education of the postal service. We could also question whether it is in the public interest to have conditions of employment in the private sector superior to those in public employment. It is difficult to visualize how the public gains from a situation in which conditions of employment in such vital areas as education and public health are inferior to those in advertising, liquor, and cosmetics industries. The public certainly should have the right to decide this issue, but it is doubtful whether it is currently being resolved on the basis of adequate data or full insight into the long-range ramifications of the issue.

The most fundamental objection to weak organizations of public employees is that such organizations are conducive to a totalitarian society. Put positively, strong organizations of public employees are essential to a democratic society. Only the narrowness of popular thinking on the subject prevents wider understanding of this crucial point.

In the normal course of events, public employees are likely to be among the first to recognize incompetence or corruption among the public administrators. The public employees are likely to have many constructive suggestions for improving the quality and efficiency of public services. Nevertheless, it is only to be expected that some of their exposures of managerial inefficiency or corruption, or their constructive suggestions generally, will be greeted with managerial hostility or indifference.

The crucial point is that, if the organizations of public employees are dominated by the public administrators, the organizations will be unable to protect the public interest. The public employee who has no job protection and no organization strong enough to protect him from administrative reprisal is unlikely to challenge administrative inefficiency or corruption or make valid suggestions which run contrary to administrative thought. If the organizations of public employees are weak, they are unable to mobilize public opinion to effectuate needed reforms and legislation.

This is especially true of education, where teachers' organizations reveal a striking inability to mobilize public support for adequate books and supplies, academic freedom, educational research, and a host of other things that would be clearly in the public interest. This is why, in the long run, the weakness of teachers' organizations is more important than the state of public opinion. The latter could be modified by an effective teachers' organization.

The attitudes of the public, important as they are, in specific situations are not the crucial cause of teacher weakness. Public attitudes themselves have causes. The actions and policies of teachers' organizations are one of the most important, if not the most important, of these causes. Therefore, while public opinion may be an insuperable barrier to the achievement of teacher power at any given time, we cannot regard public opinion as the last word on the subject. The crux of the problem is not with the public but with the organizational naiveté of teachers, their bumbling and fumbling organizations, and their appalling leadership. Progress must start here, not with the public.

As I previously pointed out, the weakness of teachers' organizations reflects an irrational but widespread public fear of strong organizations of public employees. Another cause, however, is the notion, cultivated by our "experts" in school administration, that education should be "nonpartisan." Their argument is that "education is a unique function of government. It should not be subject to political wars, such as revolve about highways, liquor control, civil rights, housing, and so on. Education must be insulated from politics."

Now, if "keeping the schools out of politics" means that school systems should not be used to provide jobs for various political machines, I agree. If it also means that the day-to-day administration of the schools (the choice of textbooks, the selection of teachers, and similar matters requiring specialized knowledge) should be left to full-time educators, this too is sound. But to many educators, "keeping the schools out of politics" means keeping even matters of basic educational policy out of politics. Politics, in this view, are unclean, and schools should be protected from their corrupting influence. This, in my judgment, is impossible and undesirable. What is spent for education is as legitimate a matter for political debate and decision as is what is spent for public health, urban renewal, or national defense. Indeed, all of these items compete with one another in some measure, and if the proponents of greater educational expenditures do not exert themselves politically, the schools will not get enough.

We may put it this way. Some issues are both educational and political, just as some issues (for example, Medicare) are both medical and political. The nonpartisan approach to school board elections and/or appointments has tended to blur the distinction between educational issues such as the selection of instructional materials, which should be solved within the professional community, and such political issues as the level of public support for education, which should be resolved by the electorate.

A recent study revealed that in 42 states all or some members of local school boards are elected by popular vote. In 35 of these states, all the elections were on a nonpartisan ballot; in four others, some school boards are elected on a partisan and some on a nonpartisan ballot. The "nonpartisan" nature of school board elections usually carries over into the timing of such elections. Seventeen states hold school board elections separately from any other elections. Six states hold school board elections concurrently with other nonpartisan elections, and four hold them concurrently with partisan elections but on a separate ballot. Many others have some type of legislation governing school board elections to ensure that education does not get entangled with "partisan politics."

This pattern of separating education from politics has the approval of most professors of school administration, who believe that state-wide educational policies should be formulated by a state board of education elected at large on a nonpartisan ballot. They also think these nonpartisan boards should appoint the chief state school officer, and this is what more and more states are doing. Political scientists, on the other hand, generally favor having the governor appoint the chief state school officer. They argue that gubernatorial appointment increases the chance that educational needs will get a hearing at the highest levels of state government, and that, if the state commissioner or superintendent is insulated from politics, he will be less likely to generate sufficient support for his program in the legislature. It is their contention, and I agree with it, that state educational executives are in politics whether they like it or not, and that the problem is to make them effective, not to bind their hands with the wrappings of "nonpartisanship."

After all, what is a "nonpartisan" election? In practice, it is one in which the candidates do not use the labels "Democrat" and "Republican." The theory seems to be that a school board election, whether state or local, should merely choose the "best man" and rely on their "nonpartisan" judgment about how the schools should be run.

My conviction is that the nonpartisan approach to school board elections weakens teachers' organizations. As long as they remain nonpartisan, teachers can only sermonize about the values of academic freedom instead of retiring politicians who support censorship of textbooks. A few showcase examples of power at the polls would do more for academic freedom than all the pompous pronouncements ever issued by teachers' organizations. A politically-conscious teachers' organization would provide funds, literature, and workers for candidates who shared its point of view. The endless number of state and national teachers' conventions now devoted to assorted drivel could be infused with political spirit and training.

When educators talk about keeping the schools out of politics, they really mean that in an ideal community the public would agree with the educators about how the schools should be run. But in the real world no such agreement can be counted on, as Mr. Rafferty's election in California illustrates. It is unrealistic for educators to preach that education is and ought to be a nonpartisan activity on 364 days out of the year, and then expect to be effective at the polls on election day, the most crucial of the 365 during the year. We desperately need to end this schizophrenia, and I believe it should be ended by clear recognition that some educational issues are necessarily political and will not be resolved the way teachers want them resolved unless the teachers as a group become politically effective.

When educators describe education as a nonpartisan activity of government, they reveal more than their own political naiveté and incompetence. Teachers who do not understand the dynamics of American politics cannot teach it to others. As a friend of mine put it, citizenship education starts with the Constitution, ends with the ballot box, and leaves out everything in between. Thus the most disturbing thing about the fallacy of non-partisanship in education is not teacher failure to generate adequate financial support for education, important as this is. It is that we have no reason to expect a group as politically naive as teachers to provide students with real insight into the dynamics of American politics. As for the professors, it may be noted that Mr. Eisenhower did not seem to suffer greatly from the fact that his opponent was widely regarded as the choice of the eggheads. Personally, I have never confused the class of professors with the class of intellectuals, but it seems to me that the support for Mr. Stevenson from both these groups was the subject of derision and ridicule in other circles.

Because teachers fail to recognize the political dimensions of their problems, they tend to be ineffective even on those occasions when they do participate as a group in the political arena. Let me illustrate by comparing the legislative strategies used in education with those used in other fields.

Today, the federal government pays 90 per cent of the costs of the interstate highways being constructed all over the country. The expenditures under this program run into the billions. When this legislation was before Congress, the business interests that stood to gain directly from it were extremely active. Automobile manufacturers, oil companies, and construction companies supported the highway program, which went through Congress like the proverbial juggernaut.

Some educational legislation which would be good for the country would also provide greater profits for certain businesses. For example, there is a pressing need for more instructional materials per pupil—more textbooks, more films, more laboratory equipment, and the like. Many communities are confronted by a severe shortage of classrooms. How do teacher organizations try to generate support for these things? By appealing to PTA's to write letters to their Congressmen. This is all right as far as it goes—but it has not, does not, and will not go far enough.

What should teachers do? They should go, for example, to the textbook publishers with a message like this: "Last year your firm got two per cent of the textbook market and made five hundred thousand dollars. Here is a bill which would provide twice as much money for textbooks as was spent last year. If this bill passes, and you retain your present share of the market, you will sell twice as many books and make over a million dollars. Therefore, we are asking you to get behind this bill in every way you can. As a starter, we are asking you—and all other textbook publishers—to contribute an amount equal to one half of one per cent of your textbook profits to help get this bill passed. In addition to your financial contribution, we are asking you to get in touch with legislators A, B, and C in your state, and explain to them the importance of this bill to the economic health of your firm and your employees."

The same sort of approach should be used with all firms which benefit directly from educational legislation. Instead of relying upon humanitarian appeals, the teachers should find out who would make money from educational legislation and get their active support for it. Obviously, some organization has to coordinate and direct over-all strategy in these situations. Teachers' organizations should be playing this leadership role, but the NEA and the AFT are too moribund to proceed this way. NEA leadership seems to regard recognition of the important role of self interest in political and educational matters as un-American, cynical, or evidence of lack of ideals. Many commercial firms doing business with the schools would probably be reluctant to accept AFT leadership on legislative matters, but there is little danger that they will be tested on this score. The AFT has such a doctrinaire attitude toward businessmen in education that it may take decades for the Federation to identify and use those elements of the business community—and they are substantial—who would support higher taxes for education. The unpleasant prospect is that teachers will continue to rely primarily upon ineffective appeals to PTA's "for the sake of the children" and ignore appeals to businessmen for the sake of the dollar. And they will continue to get nowhere, as they have in the past.

Many people agree that teachers should have more power, but they show an appalling naiveté about how teachers are to get it. A major fallacy here is the notion that teachers must wait until they are accorded more respect by the public, or until they are more deserving of power. Then, it is thought, legislators and school boards and administrators will give it to them, in the form of control over entry, a greater measure of academic freedom, and the like.

This is what I call the "oven theory of power." It posits a public which is like a housewife taking a roast out of the oven to see if it is ready. Unlike roasts, however, the teachers are never ready and they are invariably put back in their oven to mature a little more. "You are not ready for greater power"—this is the epitaph on innumerable requests by teachers for more power over professional matters.

The approach is very similar to the situation concerning civil rights. How often, for example, have legislators asked whether Negroes were "ready" to vote, to go to school with white students, to drink from the same fountains, and to use the same washroom facilities? Almost invariably, those who regard "readiness" as a relevant concept seem to find the Negroes are not ready, just as those who raise this issue in education almost always come to the conclusion that teachers are not ready.

Giving power to those not ready for it is likely to result in irresponsible uses of power. Thus the idea that it is important to see whether teachers are ready for power is readily understandable. Nevertheless, I am convinced that this line of thinking is fallacious, at least in the context of our educational situation.

In the first place, power is not usually *given* to a group. It is *taken* by it. More precisely, the public does not actively give power to a group; rather, it acquiesces to a taking of power by the group. The difference is not semantic hairsplitting. It lies at the very roots of teacher weakness.

If we look at individuals and groups who have achieved positions of power, we find that their acquisition of power was the result of an active drive to get it. Senator Kennedy did not wait until the people thought he was "ready" to be President. He actively sought the presidency. To whatever extent his readiness for power was an issue in the minds of some, he directed an extremely effective campaign to resolve it in his favor. The American Medical Association did not wait until the public thought doctors were ready to control entry to medicine and medical education. Instead, in the early 1900's, it embarked upon a vigorous drive to strengthen the association's control over medical licensure and education, to mention just two areas in which it currently exercises a controlling voice. The unions did not wait until they were deemed ready for collective bargaining and greater power. They acquired these things by an active campaign. By the same token, the teachers will not have power thrust upon them nor will they achieve it by becoming "more deserving." Occupational groups do not become less deserving of power because they actively seek it; indeed I would be prepared to argue that groups which do not contend for power are, on the whole, no more likely to use it effectively in the public interest than groups who actively seek power. This does not mean that every group which contends for it should have it or will use it for the common good, but only that we must eliminate the attitude that the use of power is something too nasty to contemplate in a good society.

Let me review briefly the major points I have tried to make. First, I have tried to provide a feasible definition of power and to explain the educational significance of this concept. I have suggested that teachers do not have a great deal of power and have identified some of the reasons for this conclusion. These reasons include public opposition to strong organizations of public employees, the notion that education is and ought to be a nonpartisan activity of government, teacher failure to capitalize on the self interest of other groups, the misguided notions of professionalism which prevail among teachers, and fallacies in the strategy and tactics employed by teachers to achieve their objectives. Other important reasons, such as unrestricted administrator membership in teachers' organizations, have not been discussed because they have received more attention elsewhere. My concluding thought is that the task of increasing the power of teachers as an organized group, and of simultaneously ensuring that their power is exercised in the public interest, is one of our most crucial educational problems and deserves the most careful consideration by everyone concerned about the future of American education.

FOR FURTHER THOUGHT

1. A visitor to the schools is often impressed by the clear corridors and closed schoolroom doors. *Is there power for the teacher in the closed door? Does she have a kind of isolation and invisibility akin to that possessed by the nonpartisan school man?*

2. Assuming that isolation gives a certain amount of power—somewhat like the hidden hand of the butcher on the scale—*what is the danger of depending upon the insulations afforded by isolation for one's power? Is this type of power likely to be responsible?*

3. Lieberman assumes that self-interest is the major motivating force in our society. *If this is true, is it possible to educate a professional person in this society? Does the norm of "professionalism" suggested by Blackington make any sense at all in this context?*

4. Lieberman suggests that teachers should effect a coalition among the various interest groups to support legislation in behalf of education. Each interest group would be "sold" on the particular program on the basis of what was in it for him. *How is such behavior different from that of the teacher attempting to motivate student support for a particular project? If the behavior is essentially similar, why aren't teachers more sophisticated politicians?*

5. A change in perspective is often difficult to achieve. Given the preponderance of women in teaching, *why might you expect to have difficulty in moving teachers toward open power rather than hidden or isolated power? What conditions in western culture and history would lend support to the expectation of difficulty?*

CURRENT STRATEGIES OF INFLUENCE

The ability to "win friends and influence people" is highly regarded to-day as always. Many would emphasize the winning of friends and assume that the influence would follow. Others would emphasize the idea of influence and assume that the winning of friends would naturally flow from that influence. More sophisticated observers recognize that neither necessarily flows from the other. There is no connection between friendship and influence. Those who expect that such is the case really want the best of both. However, they can purchase this only at the expense of admitting that a person who is not influenced by them is no longer their friend. Thus, a friend is by definition a person who is influenced by you—including people you never heard of. This is a curious usage of language. Nevertheless, it can be admitted if all are clear as to the meanings employed. However, it stands so contrary to ordinary use that little would seem to be gained by so doing.

All of this tends to expose a hard fact of life. This fact seems to be that since there are no necessary connections between the two, people must often make a choice between friendship and influence. This is to say that in the "moment of truth" one must know whether friendship and all that it connotes or influence and all it connotes is one's ordering principle.

The following article assumes, as did the previous ones, that influence is central. While none of them deny that friendship or cordial relations are nice and even helpful, it would appear that they are poor substitutes for influence. Of course, one might maintain that friendship involves a relationship between "equals." Thus, a certain relatively similar amount of mutual influence is a necessary precondition to genuine friendship as distinct from mere acquaintance.

With this qualification in mind and possessing the foregone conclusion that "you can't please everyone," the major question then becomes whom do you influence and how? At a naive level the answer might be that you seek to influence everyone. When one begins to ask the question "how," it becomes clear that there are various levels and kinds of "influence"—high and low, direct and indirect.

Turning from conceptual concerns to the contemporary scene where the "action" is, Mr. Scanlon describes two current strategies of influence—strikes and sanctions—and the groups interested in employing them. The length of this article allows both a description of the issues and a feel for the struggle as teachers and school boards stand in direct confrontation. It gives the sense that education and social policy decisions involve fortitude as well as intellect. Aside from the fact that with these strategies teaching may attract and develop new personality types with greater confidence and political nerve, it is interesting to note that the emergence of new types of negotiation patterns may open the way to new careers in education and suggest changes in teacher education programs.

--------◄◆►--------

STRIKES, SANCTIONS, AND THE SCHOOLS*

"Up until now teachers have always been too complaisant, too docile, too willing to let themselves be put upon. I personally welcome the new show

*John Scanlon, "Strikes, Sanctions, and the Schools," *Saturday Review*, October 19, 1963. Dr. Scanlon is Associate Editor of the education supplement of the *Saturday Review* and co-editor with Paul Woodring of a book entitled *American Education Today*.

of vigor and muscle which has now become apparent in many parts of our profession. But I would also counsel the use of wisdom and foresight— and the careful exercise of responsibility—as we work out together new ways of rebuilding school systems which have lost their former excellence."

The speaker was Calvin E. Gross, superintendent of the New York City public schools, and his remarks were addressed to delegates attending the 47th annual convention of the American Federation of Teachers (AFL-CIO) in New York on August 19. But Calvin Gross's words had significance far beyond the confines of the Hotel Americana ballroom in which they were delivered, far beyond the boundaries of the world's largest school system, which he heads, and far beyond the ranks of the American Federation of Teachers. In a very real sense, Calvin Gross was speaking to all members of the teaching profession, to his fellow school superintendents, and to members of school boards throughout the country. And in his words there also was a message for parents and for the people who support the U.S. public schools with their tax dollars.

What Mr. Gross was saying, in essence, was that teachers are on the march—for higher salaries, for better working conditions, for improvements in the schools, and for a voice in determining school policy. And, like the Negroes who recently marched on Washington dramatize their determination to win a redress of their grievances, the teachers are not in a mood to tolerate official indifference or delay. They believe that the time for patience has long since passed.

The new militancy of American teachers was dramatically illustrated on two widely separated fronts this past summer. In Utah, members of the Utah Education Association, an affiliate of the National Education Association, threatened a state-wide shutdown of the public schools when the state legislature passed a school appropriation bill providing less money than the Association had recommended. In New York City, members of the United Federation of Teachers, an affiliate of the AFT, voted to strike—in defiance of state law and a court order—when their demands for salary increases and other benefits were not met by the board of education. In neither case did the threatened closing of schools actually take place, but in both cases the teachers were convinced that they had won a victory by a show of force—or, in Calvin Gross's words, a show of muscle.

Although there is not room here to present a detailed account of the conflicts in Utah and New York, it might be instructive to examine some of the similarities between the two, and also some of the important differences, because such an examination throws into sharp relief the basic elements of an AFT-NEA power struggle which has profound implications for the future of public education in the United States. Briefly, the elements of this struggle are these:

1. To an increasing number of teachers, it appears that the best way of getting what they want is by joining a union and bargaining collectively with their employers, relying on the political and economic strength of organized labor, and, as a last resort, the ultimate weapon of any union—the strike—to enforce their demands. This attitude is reflected in the dramatic growth of the American Federation of Teachers, which has more than doubled its membership since the end of World War II. Although it is still only a tiny organization (82,000 members, as compared to the NEA's 860,000) the AFT has the power of the entire AFL-CIO behind it, and is actually stronger than the NEA in several of the nation's largest cities, including New York, Chicago, and Detroit.

2. The NEA, in recognition of the new militancy among teachers and in response to the threat posed by the rapid growth of the AFT, has become much more aggressive during the past few years. It has launched a special Urban Project whose primary aim is to strengthen the structure of NEA affiliates in large urban centers. It has strongly urged its local associations to engage in "professional negotiations" with their school boards, and to develop written agreements based on these negotiations. (Many such agreements already exist, in varying degrees of precision and formality.) And finally, the NEA has come up with its own version of labor's ultimate weapon, which it calls "sanctions." The NEA has said that "sanctions" can take various forms, but in their most drastic form they involve (a) withholding of teacher contracts and (b) advising other members of the NEA not to take teaching positions in the affected school system. It is clear, therefore, that in this form their net effect is the same as that of strikes—classrooms without teachers.

The increasing militancy of teachers, and the power struggle between the AFT and the NEA, have caused considerable uneasiness on the part of school superintendents and school board members throughout the country. The American Association of School Administrators, which enrolls most of the nation's school superintendents, (and which is a powerful affiliate of the NEA) takes a dim view of teacher unions and even frowns on the NEA's official policy regarding "sanctions." In a recently published booklet entitled *Roles, Responsibilities, Relationships of the School Board, Superintendent, and Staff*, the association specifically mentions "strikes, demagogic appeals, threats, withheld services, and sanctions or threatened sanctions by teachers" as actions "not likely to lead to lasting and satisfying resolution of disagreements." The booklet was issued in the latter part of June, after the Utah teachers had already voted to withhold their services in the fall, and about a week before the NEA convention in Detroit, where the NEA executive board officially declined the request of the Utah teachers for national sanctions against Utah. The National Association of School

Boards is wary of the whole idea of professional negotiations and collective bargaining, because it sees in these procedures a potential threat to the authority of local boards of education. It is flatly opposed to "strikes, sanctions, boycotts, mandated arbitration or mediation."

It is against this background that the nature and significance of the Utah and New York disputes must be examined in order to be fully understood.

Utah is a state of 85,000 square miles and about 1,000,000 population. Its public schools enroll about 265,000 students, and the teaching staff numbers about 10,500, of whom about 96 per cent belong to the Utah Education Association. There are forty local school districts that vary in size from a few square miles to more than 7,000 square miles, and in pupil population from 200 to 48,000. About 65 per cent of the total state school enrollment is concentrated in eight school districts located in the urban area stretching from Provo to Ogden, at the foot of the towering Wasatch Range, where most of Utah's population is concentrated. Education is defined by the state constitution as a state responsibility, but provision is made for direct control by locally-elected boards of education. Approximately 61 per cent of the total state school bill is financed out of state revenues, and only about 39 per cent by locally imposed property taxes. This over-all ratio does not apply uniformly to all districts in the state, but by and large educational finance in Utah is a state concern.

Historically the citizens of Utah have been proud of the effort they have put forth to support their schools. But despite high expenditures *per taxpayer*, Utah has usually ranked below the national average in expenditures per pupil and in teacher salaries. In the school year 1947-48 Utah reached the national average in current expenditures per pupil because of a special school bill enacted by the legislature but since then Utah's relative position in this respect has been declining. The decline has been most pronounced since 1961, when the legislature made only a token increase in school appropriations. In the 1962-63 school year according to estimates by the National Education Association, Utah's current expenditures per pupil were $354, which was about 22 per cent below the national average of $432. There has been a similar decline in Utah's relative standing with respect to teacher salaries. It should be emphasized, however, that Utah's relative decline in the national standings on these two measures of school support is *not* an indication of public indifference to the needs of education. In 1961, according to NEA estimates, Utah stood fourth among the states in *per-capita* expenditures of state and local governments for local schools. Also, Utah ranked first among the states in the proportion of total public expenditures, state and local, devoted to public education. One of the principal reasons why Utah generally ranks below the U.S. average in expenditures per pupil and in teacher salaries despite higher per capita expenditures on education is that Utahns have large families. In 1962, according to the NEA estimates, the school-age population of Utah (5 to 17) was 28.2 per cent of the total resident population of the state. In this respect Utah was tied for third place among all the states.

In preparation for the 1963 session of the Utah state legislature, a state-wide organization known as the Co-operating Agencies for Public Schools (CAPS) drew up a legislative proposal calling for a $24.7 million increase in the annual level of school expenditures. CAPS was composed of representatives from the Utah Education Association, the Utah Society of Superintendents, the Utah School Boards Association, the Utah Congress of Parents and Teachers, and the State Department of Education. Its proposal, which would have meant an increase of $100 in Utah's current expenditure per pupil, was designed to bring the Utah figure up to the average of the seven surrounding mountain states—Arizona, Idaho, Colorado, Nevada, New Mexico, Montana and Wyoming. The estimated gap was based on figures developed by the Utah Education Association. The UEA estimate immediately ran into trouble, because it was considerably higher than the estimates of other Utah organizations. The Utah Foundation, a taxpayer group, had estimated the gap at $75 per pupil, and the Utah Legislative Council had set it at $77. (The state estimates of the National Education Association placed the gap at $78.)

CAPS recommended that 42 per cent of its proposed $24.7 million increase in school funds be devoted to raising teacher salaries (which would have meant increases ranging from $800 to $1000 per teacher), that 28 per cent be spent for more adequate staffing, and 30 per cent for additional teaching supplies, equipment, and maintenance. (The amount CAPS recommended for more adequate staffing included funds for hiring enough new teachers to eliminate half-day sessions and establish a state-wide kindergarten program. These measures would have required additional classrooms and would have necessitated a substantial increase in school construction expenditures. Consequently, CAPS also recommended a $7.7 million increase in state support for local building funds, but this was not a major issue in the Utah school controversy.)

The CAPS program was laid before the appropriate committees in both houses of the Utah legislature, and was publicized throughout the state by way of billboards, newspaper advertisements, radio and TV programs, brochures and information kits, a series of "grass roots" meetings sponsored by the Utah School Boards Association, and a statewide "Lights on for Education" night at every schoolhouse in the state under the sponsorship of PTA units. The UEA also did a considerable amount of lobbying with legislators. However, the CAPS bill never got out of committee, and was not debated on the floor of either house of the legislature. Instead, each house came up with its own school bill. Governor George D. Clyde, in his budget message to the legislature, had recommended an increase of

$8.7 million in school operation and maintenance funds, which the UEA had called "inadequate and totally unacceptable." The Senate brought out a bill with an increase of a little more than $13 million, and the House figure was $9.9 million. A compromise, which the governor approved and eventually signed into law, provided for an increase of $11.6 million in school funds for each year of the 1963-65 biennium. Under the terms of the bill, Utah teachers will receive an average salary increase of about $700 per year. (The actual increases will range from $300 to more than $1000 per teacher, varying according to district, experience, and other factors.) Under the CAPS proposal, the average salary increase would have been about $900 per year.

Members of the Utah Education Association met in Salt Lake City on March 16, while the legislature was still in session, to decide what to do. It was a cold morning, following a bad snowstorm, but more than 80 per cent of the membership turned out. By individual ballot, they voted 7,788 to 189 (a margin of forty to one) to discontinue contract discussions for the 1963-64 school year until the school finance issue was "satisfactorily resolved." They also adopted a resolution requesting the National Education Association "to inform its members of the Utah situation and to urge them to refrain from seeking employment and entering into verbal or written agreement with a Utah board of education" until the issue was settled.

The NEA gave immediate national publicity to the Utah situation and, according to Executive Secretary William G. Carr, "allocated expert legal assistance and substantial funds to help make UEA objectives clear to the citizens of Utah." The NEA also advised its members that if contracts were offered for jobs in Utah, they "might be for positions in which Utah teachers expect to remain."

The UEA, maintaining that the CAPS proposal had not received a fair hearing in the legislature, demanded that the governor call the legislature back into special session to reconsider the school finance bill. The governor refused. He pointed out that the $11.6 million increase voted by the legislature was the largest of its kind ever granted in Utah, and he argued that it would be inappropriate for him to ask the legislature to reconsider a matter it had already considered and acted upon. When the UEA demanded that he include school finance on the agenda for a special session of the legislature necessitated by his veto of a state building bill, the governor refused again. This time, however, he announced that he would appoint a blue-ribbon citizens' committee to make "a thorough study and factual analysis" of Utah's school finance problem. He said he was convinced that "we do not have sufficient basic data, objectively collected and analyzed, on which to base final judgment" on the school finance question, and that the study "should give us a sound basis on which to build our future programs." He emphasized that he was not promising to call a special session of the legislature when the committee's findings became available. "On the other hand," he added, "I am giving Utah citizens my full assurance that I shall do whatever my best judgment indicates in the light of the facts developed by the committee. Obviously, this could include the summoning of a special session of the Legislature." He said the study should be completed within a year, and sooner if possible, but that in any event the report should be submitted in ample time so that it could be studied and analyzed, and any needed legislation carefully prepared, before the next session of the legislature. The governor made his announcement on May 27. It was interpreted to mean that the action the legislature had already taken would be final for the 1963-64 school year, but that if the study committee's findings warranted, the governor would call a special session in sufficient time for action to be taken for the 1964-65 school year. The UEA demanded that it participate equally in naming the members of the committee, that the committee start work on June 15 and be given an August 15 deadline, that the committee be charged with determining whether a special session was necessary, that if the committee so recommended the governor call the session not later than January 1964, and that the session "be allowed to consider the recommendations of the committee without further executive instructions."

The governor hit the ceiling. He replied that he would not abdicate the responsibility of naming the committee members, and that he could not and would not allow the committee to make decisions that legally were his alone to make.

By now, the relations between Governor Clyde and John C. Evans, Jr., executive secretary of the UEA, were anything but cordial. The governor resented the pressure the UEA was applying, and made it clear that neither he nor the legislature could be intimidated. Evans and his colleagues, on the other hand, felt that the governor was being obstinate. An impasse had developed, and it persisted through the end of the school year and well into the summer. The UEA had asked the NEA to invoke national sanctions against Utah, and this raised a very real question whether the schools would reopen in September. In response to the UEA's request for national sanctions, the NEA sent a fact-finding team from its Commission on Professional Rights and Responsibilities into Utah to study the controversy. Members of the team found Governor Clyde adamant. He told them that the issue had ceased to be school finance and had become a question of "whether the state shall remain sovereign or be dictated to by an organized group."

The Utah School Boards Association, caught squarely in the middle of the controversy, now parted company with the Utah Education Association on the matter of sanctions. W. Dean Belnap, president of the USBA, said in July that while his group still supported the original CAPS proposal, "we have a divergence of feeling regarding the nature of the pressure which should be brought to bear on the governor and the legislature in the solution of financial problems in Utah. We cannot think compatibly with the strong sanctions they (the teachers) have taken." The National School Boards Association, at its annual convention, went on record in support of its Utah affiliate.

When the NEA convention opened in Detroit on June 30, the Utah controversy was the principal topic of conversation among delegates, and it also was one of the most important items on the convention agenda, because it appeared that the NEA's policy on "sanctions," adopted the year before, was about to face its first real test. (At the 1962 convention in Denver, the NEA's delegate assembly had passed a resolution calling for the use of sanctions "as a means for preventing unethical or arbitrary policies or practices that have a deleterious effect on the welfare of the schools," and asking affiliated state associations "to cooperate in developing guidelines which would define, organize, and definitely specify procedural steps for invoking sanctions by the teaching profession." During the ensuing year, the staff of the NEA's Commission on Professional Rights and Responsibilities, working with representatives of the state associations, had framed a tentative set of guidelines, but many of the delegates arrived in Detroit without a clear understanding of the precise nature of sanctions or the procedural steps for invoking them. They did know, however, that the teachers of Utah had voted to withhold their contracts and to ask the NEA to invoke sanctions.)

The NEA convention opened on Sunday, June 30, and the following morning reporters covering the event were invited to a press conference at which the Utah controversy was to be discussed by Mr. Evans, executive secretary of the UEA, and William G. Carr, executive secretary of the NEA. At the conference, the reporters were given three press releases. The first, issued by the UEA, reminded the reporters that the UEA had asked the NEA to invoke sanctions against Utah, and then went on to express cautious optimism regarding Governor Clyde's study committee. "The Utah Education Association hails this first step toward solving the Utah school crisis," the release said. "If the views and interests of Utah teachers are given due consideration, the Governor's school study committee may be able to effect a settlement of the controversy." To most of the reporters, this was the first inkling that the UEA's attitude had softened. The second release, issued by the Executive Committee of the NEA, said that "vigorous efforts" were being made "by the responsible parties" to resolve the impasse, and that "pending the outcome of these efforts, the National Education Association withholds judgment concerning the application of national sanctions." The UEA had received its answer on the first business day of the convention, before there had been any discussion of the Utah controversy on the convention floor. The third press release, issued by the UEA, said:

> The President and Executive Secretary of the Utah Education Association agree that no useful purpose would be served by imposing national sanctions against the State of Utah while current negotiations for settlement are in progress.
>
> However, the NEA Executive Committee will be asked to impose national sanctions immediately if present negotiations fail to result in a satisfactory resolution of the Utah school controversy.

In response to a question at the press conference, Mr. Evans offered another piece of news: "If the makeup of the Governor's study committee is favorable, and if it is properly charged, then the trustees of UEA will recommend that teachers sign new contracts."

Unaware of what was transpiring at the press conference, the representative assembly of the Department of Classroom Teachers, which embraces most of the NEA membership, was in session at the Cobo Hall Arena, principal meeting hall of the convention. When the reporters arrived at the Arena, the Utah controversy was under discussion. It was immediately apparent that the rank and file of the NEA membership were in a much more militant mood than the NEA executive committee or the officers of the Utah Education Association. Brushing aside the plea of its representative on the NEA's Commission on Professional Rights and Responsibilities, who had urged "no rash acts or resolutions" until the NEA's fact-finding team in Utah made its report, the Department of Classroom Teachers passed by an overwhelming vote a resolution which had grown stronger with each amendment. In its final form it called on the NEA "to do everything possible to assist the teachers of Utah," asked "all local associations to urge their members not to apply for teaching positions in Utah until such time as this condition no longer exists," and called on the NEA "to establish a fund for financial assistance to the teachers of Utah in the event of needs resulting from their efforts to improve the educational program of the state." The Utah delegation got to its feet and applauded vigorously, and a reporter at the press table leaned over to Mrs. Marie L. Caylor, editor of the American Federation of Teachers' publications, and whispered: "This sounds like an AFT convention." Mrs. Caylor smiled appreciatively. (At their annual dinner a few nights later, the classroom teachers took up a collection and raised $3,115 for the Utah fund.)

The Department of Classroom Teachers also passed strongly-worded resolutions on professional negotiations and sanctions. The former asserted that "local professional associations *have* the professional right and *should have* the mandatory legal right" to negotiate with boards of education in the determination of policies affecting professional services of teachers," that "local board policies and/or state laws should authorize a means of appeal through designated educational channels to appropriate educational agencies when agreement cannot be reached;" it commended state and local associations that have developed written procedures for professional negotiations, and it urged teachers in states not now recognizing or accepting the idea of professional negotiations "to press for legislation to legalize such procedures." The resolution on sanctions asserted that "the profession must establish and enforce sanctions to protect the rights and responsibilities of its members and to insure a consistent and favorable learning climate," and, among other things, urged the NEA "to continue to give leadership in refining guidelines for the establishment and enforcement of such professional sanctions."

Although the Department of Classroom Teachers embraces more than 90 per cent of the NEA membership, it does not speak for the entire NEA. The resolution on Utah which the full representative assembly of the NEA subsequently adopted in Detroit was considerably milder than the one adopted by the classroom teachers, and said nothing about urging teachers not to accept positions in Utah. However, it did authorize a loan fund (later set at $500,000) for the financial assistance of the Utah Education Association, to be used in the event of failure to resolve the impasse. The decision of the full Representative Assembly not to vote sanctions against Utah was generally interpreted as a victory for the NEA's Executive Committee.

The Utah delegates returned home from Detroit with mixed feelings. They had received enthusiastic support from the Department of Classroom Teachers, but their request for national sanctions had been turned down and this weakened their bargaining position with the governor. During the summer, a special effort to mediate the impasse was made. Dr. O. Preston Robinson, general manager and editor of the Deseret *News and Telegram*, finally brought the adversaries together after what one observer described as "many, many hours of painstaking and sometimes frustrating behind-the-scenes negotiations." Also involved in these negotiations (which received very little publicity) was Dr. Carr, the NEA executive secretary.

On August 3, the UEA met again in special session, this time in Provo, and voted 4,586 to 1,148 to resume contract negotiations for the new school year. One of the factors in the decision was an agreement that the UEA would participate in recommending citizens for appointment to the governor's study committee. On August 9 the governor instructed the committee to prepare, in addition to its final report, an interim report, "early enough so that if this report should indicate to me that emergency action is needed, such action could be taken before the start of the 1964–65 school year."

Strictly speaking, the UEA vote ended the state-wide impasse and returned negotiations to the local level. In some instances, however, especially in Salt Lake City and the suburban Granite district, where the teachers were particularly militant, the negotiations were touch and go for a while and it appeared that the state impasse had become a local impasse. UEA locals in these districts eventually won additional recognition from the boards of education. The boards recognized the right of teachers to join (or not to join) professional associations, accepted the right of these organizations to represent their members in negotiations with the board, and set up joint committees of teachers and board members to study "problems of mutual concern" and to make recommendations to the boards. The boards did not agree to be bound by these recommendations.

The concensus among Utah observers who followed the controversy but were not involved on either side is that most teachers were relieved that the impasse was resolved, particularly since they received their largest salary increase in many years. But, as one observer pointed out, the large negative vote at Provo indicated quite clearly that a significant minority was not happy with the settlement. "The controversy could rise again in the spring," he told SR, "if the study committee should recommend something less than the teachers will accept or if the governor should choose not to follow the committee's recommendations." Another Utahn went further in his comments to SR. "My personal opinion," he said, "is that the militants in the UEA were motivated by a single desire—to show their power to the state by delaying the start of school by a month, a week, or even by only a day. They controlled the UEA power structure and were not defeated until the entire membership was given a chance to vote on acceptance of the governor's proposal. Quiescent now, they are hopefully waiting an unsatisfactory report by the governor's study committee."

Although the Utah controversy ended a month before the schools were scheduled to reopen, the situation in New York City was different. As one wag put it: "The United Federation of Teachers stood eyeball to eyeball with the Board of Education all through the summer, and at the eleventh hour it was the mayor who blinked."

This description of the New York City controversy may have been somewhat irreverent, but it wasn't completely inaccurate. The New York teachers held out in defiance of state law and a court injunction, until the afternoon of the day before the schools were scheduled to reopen. Then they accepted, with jubilant cries of "We won!" settlement terms which clearly indicated that they had not surrendered.

In their negotiations for a two-year contract, they had demanded salary increases totalling $9 million for the 1963–64 school year, and another increase of $20 million for 1964–65. They had also demanded smaller classes, "total improvement" in New York City's "difficult" schools, additional remedial and other services in all schools, additional teacher time during the school day for lesson preparation, and improvements in the machinery for handling teacher grievances. The Board of Education had flatly refused to grant any salary increase for 1963–64, on the ground that the New York teachers had won a $750 increase last year (largest in the history of New York City) and on the further ground that "drastic" cuts in its budget had forced the board to cut back or eliminate desperately-needed school improvements which, in the board's view, had priority over salary increases. "Faced with this critical situation," said Board Chairman Max J. Rubin in a radio-television address on July 31, "the Board was and is convinced that for this year, weighing the direct educational needs of the children against further salary increases, we have no right to divert funds from these urgent educational needs in order to provide for higher salaries." The Board did agree, however, to set aside 25 per cent of whatever increase in school funds it might obtain next year and apply this to salary increases for 1964–65. "We can only deal in percentages," Mr. Rubin pointed out, "because we do not know now how much money will be appropriated by the City and the State to the school system." With respect to the union's other major demands, the Board took the position that many of them involved educational policy or administrative discretion, and that while it was willing to *discuss* them with the union it was not prepared to *negotiate* them in the collective bargaining sense, because this would be an abdication of its legal authority to operate the schools. The union insisted, on the other hand, that "anything that relates to working conditions in the broad sense is negotiable."

The 47th annual convention of the American Federation of Teachers was held in New York at the height of the school controversy, and it was evident throughout the proceedings that the AFT was not only proud of its New York local, but willing to back it to the hilt. AFT President Carl J. Megel announced that AFT membership had increased by more than 11,000 in the preceding year, and he said that most of the increase had occurred in New York, where the UFT now claims more than 20,000 members out of a total teaching force of 43,000. (The NEA has less than 1,500 members in New York.) Harry Van Arsdale, president of the New York Central Labor Council, brought greetings from the New York City labor unions and added: "We're very proud of the UFT and Charles Cogen. They have helped us with many of our problems, and you can be sure we are going to help them with theirs." He also reminded the delegates that Mayor Wagner has often described New York as "a good union town," and he said he hoped the mayor would appear at the convention "so we can hear it from him again." (The mayor was invited to address the opening session of the convention, and his name was listed on the program, but official business required his presence elsewhere.)

Raymond R. Corbett, president of the New York State AFL-CIO, also was a speaker at the opening session. He denounced the state's Condon-Wadlin law, which prohibits strikes by public employees, as "a repressive, discriminatory and punitive measure," and pledged that the State AFL-CIO "will not rest until this infamous piece of legislation is scrapped from our statute books." He also had harsh words for what he called "the perennial shadow-boxing between city hall and Albany" over school finance. "It has sometimes served as a diverting and diversionary circus which the people regarded with indulgence, disdain, and indifference," he said. "But suddenly it has ceased to be amusing and may become a deadly serious matter if labor's just and hallowed 'no contract, no work' principle is put into effect on September 9."

Bearing a message from the national headquarters of the AFL-CIO was Nicholas Zonarich of the AFL-CIO's powerful Industrial Union Department, headed by Walter Reuther. The IUD, which has more than six million members and is spearheading the AFL-CIO's vigorous efforts to organize the nation's "white collar" workers, has been actively assisting the American Federation of Teachers in its organizing drive, and has been especially helpful to the United Federation of Teachers in New York. (The IUD sees in the "white collar" workers the new frontier in union organization because their number is growing rapidly with the advance of technology and because up until recently they had not received as much attention from union organizers as have "blue collar" workers, whose number in the total labor force has been dwindling.) Mr. Zonarich also had words of praise for Mr. Cogen and the UFT. He said the New York teachers had given inspiration to the teachers in Gary, Boston, Philadelphia, and other cities, and he pledged the IUD's "full support" to the UFT in its dispute with the New York City Board of Education.

At the closing session, the AFT delegates passed a resolution strongly supporting the UFT, and voted to send copies to Governor Rockefeller, Mayor Wagner, and United States Senator Jacob K. Javits of New York. (Senator Javits, in an address to the delegates on the preceding evening, had expressed sympathy with the aims of the New York teachers and had applauded their militancy "wholeheartedly," but he also had reminded them that "a state law remains on the books which makes strike action by government employees illegal and therefore not part of (the) democratic process." He said he therefore favored mediation of the New York dispute.) The delegates also voted to strengthen and clarify the AFT's policy regarding strikes. The previous policy, embodied in a resolution adopted at the 1952 convention, was open to the interpretation that the AFT opposed strikes by its local affiliates. This had caused some consternation among UFT members during and after the one-day strike of 1962. The new policy, adopted at the request of the New York local, says that the

AFT recognizes "the right of locals to strike under certain circumstances," and will "urge the AFL-CIO and affiliated international unions to support such strikes when they occur." (The new policy is also ambiguous, because it does not spell out the meaning of "certain circumstances," but it apparently was satisfactory to the UFT and to the other locals represented at the convention. In response to a question from the floor, the AFT's general counsel emphasized that the AFT does not claim, and in fact "disdains," the right to strike against the federal government or any of its departments or agencies. This, it was explained, is because all federal employees are required to sign a "no strike" agreement as a condition of employment. The Condon-Wadlin law does not require such pledges by New York state employees, but it does impose severe penalties on those who actually strike. The law was not enforced against UFT members after their one-day strike in 1962, but the New York Board of Education left no doubt in anyone's mind that the law would be enforced in the event of a strike this year. In fact, amendments passed after last year's UFT strike now make enforcement of the law mandatory.)

The New York deadlock persisted throughout the summer and into September, with the union giving every indication that it was prepared to carry out its threat to close the schools. At the last minute the mayor appointed a mediation committee to settle the dispute. The action was taken on Friday, September 6, a few hours after the union, at a general membership meeting, had voted 5,219 to 758 to reject the Board's final offer and to strike, as scheduled, on the following Monday morning, the opening day of school. The meeting was held at an outdoor stadium in a driving rain, and the large turnout surprised many observers because on the preceding night the union's delegate assembly had turned down the Board's offer by a vote of 1,500 to seventeen, in defiance of a court order restraining the union and its members from proceeding with their plans for a strike. Charles Cogen, president of the union, had announced that he and other leaders of the union would conduct the strike from jail, if necessary, and the relatively large turnout for the membership meeting was interpreted by union officials as an indication that the members were solidly behind their leaders.

The men the Mayor named to the mediation committee were Theodore W. Kheel, a labor lawyer and impartial chairman of New York City's transit industry; Frank E. Karelsen, a lawyer and vice president of the executive committee of the Public Education Association, an influential citizens' group active in school affairs; and former United States District Judge Simon H. Rifkind, a member of New York City's board of higher education. (It is worth noting at this point that two weeks earlier, in an interview during the AFT convention, Mr. Cogen said that "as a last resort" the union might be willing to submit the dispute to mediation by a group of distinguished citizens acceptable to the union and the Board of Education and, when pressed further, he mentioned Messrs. Kheel, Karelsen, and Rifkind as examples of the type of men he had in mind. The point is made here not because it raises any question about the impartiality of the mediators, but because it supports a view held by some observers that the union's basic strategy was to go to the brink with the Board of Education and then, when the pressure for a settlement became intolerable, rely on the mayor to intervene. The Board was bargaining *after* its budget had been fixed, so that there was a limit to what it could offer. The union realized this, and there are reasons to believe that this was a factor in the UFT's unblinking militancy. As Fred Hechinger, education editor of the New York *Times*, observed a week after the settlement: "The temptation is to keep saying 'No' until the politicians, anxious not to invoke anti-strike laws, rush in the mediating Marines at the last minute to offer more than the board did—not because the board hates teachers but because it has no money of its own." It is not unreasonable to assume that the union this year may have remembered what happened last year, when, after its one-day strike, Mayor Wagner and Governor Rockefeller "found" an extra $13 million for salary increases.)

The delicate task of the mediators was to arrive at a compromise that would avert the threatened strike without undermining the Board's authority, and to persuade the union and the Board to accept the terms within less than seventy-two hours. At 4:30 Sunday afternoon, after nearly two days of almost continuous mediation, Mr. Rifkind, speaking for the Mayor's committee, announced at a news conference: "Gentlemen, the marathon is over." The compromise proposed by the mediators received the unanimous approval of the Board of Education, and the union ratified it that night by a vote of 5,265 to 181.

Under the terms of the contract, New York teachers will receive more than $24 million in salary increases over the next two years, which is about twice the amount the Board of Education had offered. The increases will average about $580 per teacher, and most of that will come in the second year. But there will be a token increase effective in April, and this was regarded as a key factor in the settlement, because it enabled the union to claim it had won a salary increase "now," without increasing the Board's budget. (The April increase will not require any "new money," because the total amount is so small that the Board can pay it by reshuffling items in its current $600 million budget.) The maximum salary next year will be $11,025 as compared to the present $10,445.

In addition to the salary increases, the agreement provides for many of the other things the union had sought, and it also gives the union the right to participate in the determination of school policy. UFT officials will meet once a month with Superintendent Gross to discuss problems of mutual concern, and chapter chairmen of the union will hold similar meetings with school principals. How this arrangement will work out remains to be seen, but Mr. Goss, whom the union came to respect as a tough but fair bargainer, has left little doubt about his attitude toward these discussions. He welcomes them, and he sees in them an opportunity to bring the teachers into the continuing search for solutions to the massive problems confronting the New York City schools. In a radio interview on September 15, a week after the impasse had ended, he revealed that it was he, and not the union leaders, who had put forth the idea of holding monthly consultations with union representatives. During the course of the negotiations, he said, "it became quite clear to me that there are genuine aspirations for professional contributions to the school system—the kind of contributions the teachers make in any professional organization worth its salt, to any school system that wants to get somewhere, and I welcome this." He made it clear, however, that neither he nor the Board of Education is abdicating any responsibility under the new arrangement. "The Board of Education will continue to run the schools," he said, "and I work for the Board of Education."

The New York contract also includes the same "no-strike" clause that was written into the 1962 agreement at the insistence of the Board of Education. The UFT had demanded its deletion.

What conclusions can be drawn from the Utah and New York controversies? What implications for the future seem to emerge from them, and from the power struggle being waged between the NEA and the AFT? How will the power struggle, and the new militancy of teachers, affect the nation's schools?

These are large questions, and there are no easy answers, but at the risk of over-simplification it is possible to set down a few impressions one gets from studying the two conflicts:

1. There is little doubt that teachers are increasingly conscious of their growing power, whether it flows from membership in a professional association or a labor union, and that they are prepared to exercise it to obtain what they regard as legitimate goals. (A woman teacher in Utah expressed it this way: "How can teachers prove that they can act with power until they actually have used power? Until then we have only a phantom power." The union view was summed up succinctly by Raymond R. Corbett, president of the New York State AFL-CIO, in his address at the opening session of the AFT convention: "We are traditionally and philosophically committed to the principle that all employees must be permitted to band together to bring balanced strength to the collective

bargaining table. We believe that collective bargaining turns into collective begging if the basic right to strike granted to every free worker is taken away from him.")

2. Professional negotiations and collective bargaining have the same basic aim—written agreements between teacher organizations and school boards regarding salaries and other matters of mutual concern (including some degree of participation in the determination of school policy, which up until recently has been regarded as the sole province of the school board). But there is an important distinction between negotiating with a school board and negotiating with an employer in private industry. The essence of this distinction is that the school board is a *public* body and the teachers are *public* employees, and the *public* interest should be paramount—whether the discussions are called "collective bargaining" or "professional negotiations." (It is undoubtedly true that "professional negotiations" are by nature more polite than collective bargaining procedures. NEA negotiators usually regard the superintendent as a professional colleague, since most superintendents belong to the NEA. The AFT, on the other hand, does not admit superintendents to membership because they have the authority to hire and fire. This fact, in the AFT view, makes the superintendent an agent of management and therefore somewhat of an adversary at the bargaining table. However, there do not appear to be any compelling reasons why, in both types of negotiating procedures, a mutually satisfactory agreement cannot be reached by teachers and school boards if both sides negotiate in good faith.)

3. Sanctions have the same net effect as strikes. Or, to put it another way, when teachers vote to withhold their contracts and to urge other teachers not to man their positions, the result is the same as when teachers vote to strike and throw up a picket line to keep other teachers out of the classroom. Here there was a distinction between the Utah and New York controversies, because the action of the Utah teachers did not constitute a threat to violate the law and the action of the New York teachers did, but one cannot escape the conclusion that in both instances the school children would have been the ultimate losers if the threat had been carried out. (William G. Carr, executive secretary of the NEA, expressed some concern about the public's reaction to sanctions in his remarks to the NEA convention. He warned the delegates that the effectiveness of sanctions would be impaired if they were invoked for "trivial and transitory reasons.")

4. The power struggle between the NEA and the AFT will continue, and it will be waged with greatest intensity in the large cities, where the NEA is admittedly weak and the AFT has the benefit of a traditional urban sympathy with the aims of organized labor. It is in the urban areas, therefore, where teacher militancy is likely to be most pronounced and where school boards already burdened by a whole host of problems peculiar to big-city

school districts are likely to find themselves with the additional headaches that professional negotiations or collective bargaining involve. (In New York, in addition to the threat of a teacher strike, the Board also had to contend with a threatened boycott of the schools by Negro parents protesting *de facto* segregation. This, too, was called off before it materialized, but Superintendent Gross was kept busy during the summer dashing from one kind of bargaining conference to another.)

To sum up, teachers are making it increasingly clear that they want a voice in school affairs and that they are willing to fight for their rights, if necessary. This means that stubborn school boards will find it increasingly difficult to run the schools by unilateral action, and that ignoring the legitimate demands of teachers will increasingly involve some peril. But the new power the teachers are coming to exercise also carries with it grave responsibilities. Superintendent Gross left with the American Federation of Teachers another admonition which applies with equal force to teachers everywhere: "You are now a power in American education, and you are obliged to use your capacities to build, and not to destroy."

FOR FURTHER THOUGHT

1. Teachers had typically thought that striking was beneath their dignity and was, as a matter of fact, "unprofessional." *Are there conceivable conditions that might indicate that the local community had been on strike against education for years? Could a teacher strike then be considered a counter-strike? If a community breaks a contract, does walking off the job constitute a strike or does it simply indicate "no contract, no work"? Why is this an important question for public employees?*
2. *How does the above question drive us back to the issue of what constitutes service? Do not people wish to deny the right to strike in the name of public interest (service) while those who claim the right to do so in the name of the public interest (service)? Is this a fair analysis? If so, what question must be answered first? What question must be answered second?*
3. The National Association of School Boards is opposed to "strikes, sanctions, boycotts, mandated arbitration, or mediation." In this stand they are considerably more candid than a well known representative of farmers who was perfectly willing to allow these kinds of activities to migrant laborers as long as they did not occur during the harvest season. School boards see these activities as a threat to their legal authority and to their power. *What makes the use of power (strikes, sanctions, and so forth) by the teachers bad and the use of power by school boards good? Is it because one is typically legal and the other is extra legal at best?*

If so, why not change the law so that all can be "good" or "bad"? Are teachers' groups the only pressure groups that boards deal with? If not, are the others equally bad? Are they legal? If a business organization moves or threatens to move in the face of a possible or probable increase in school taxes, is it going on strike? Against whom or against what? Is this legal? Is it professional? Is it service?

4. In a complex society people may become so dependent upon "servants" that they are literally paralyzed without them. Many an executive has been rendered helpless by the absence of a trusted secretary. Most of the east coast of the United States and sections of Canada were crippled when the electricity failed at Niagara. *Where is the power? Is it a shifting or a static thing? What kind of case can be made for the opinion that teachers are growing and will continue to grow in power in modern society? Is the case better for the growth of potential than for an actual growth of power?*

5. *What has modern mathematics done for the elementary teacher? Has it given her more power? Why? What about other curriculum developments and power? If education really is the first line of national defense, who is the master and who is the servant?*

6. Scanlon repeats the rather worn observation that both strikes and sanctions make the school children the "ultimate losers." *Is he assuming that no current teaching situation is bad enough to justify change at the price of a temporary stoppage of school? Is he assuming that whatever the community calls service is service? If he is assuming these things, can a profession exist? Is Scanlon himself a kind of "ultimate loser" by failing to admit the possibility that the society (children included) might be the "ultimate losers" unless there are strikes and sanctions?*

Summary of Part Three

Part Three has focused on a "derived" question in education. Not only does it afford the reader an opportunity to consider the problems of teacher preparation, but it represents that whole host of questions in education that are derivatives of the same "roots." Matters of content, textbook selection, and methodology are all concerns of essentially the same nature. To have determined the way to resolve controversy over the "best" preparation is to have arrived at the method for resolving questions about other derived matters.

The adequacy of any preparation program is subject to question in a period of change and adjustment in society. When the schools fail to produce individuals able to cope with societal problems the worth of teachers and of their preparation is challenged. The changes suggested vary; some advocate extension and others advocate reduction of the time for teacher preparation. Still others see the need for more "practical" considerations in the program. To some, "practicality" is synonymous with theory; for others it is equal to methodological gimics; for others it is more content in subject specialties; and for still others it is more time in the classroom with children. We have looked at two different programs suggested by Schueler and Broudy, both of which advocate inclusion of these four major areas in preparing teachers. After examining their suggestions we must ask if these are the most vital areas of concern. If we accept them we must then consider what proportion of each is most desirable and what particular experiences within each area are of most value. Do we have reason to believe that because a large number of teachers are going to teach in "inner city" urban areas that their preparation should focus on education in such communities?

The answer to such a question is derived in large part from what is to be gained from the experience. As Schueler infers from his examination of Hunter College's preparation program for teachers of the "inner city," the principles of good teaching are the same regardless of the nature of the student or the community. Such a stance should lead one to recognize the importance of the principles upon which good teaching is based. These principles, if understood and properly utilized, are much more valuable than specific techniques that may or may not be relevant in different situations. A focus on the "inner city" could lead to teacher training. A focus on principles while using the "inner city" as an important or even crucial area of application would lead to teacher education.

The emphasis on principles stresses the development of an adequate conceptual or theoretical framework. Without entering the tangled problem of the precise, logical, and temporal relations of concepts and perceptions, it is safe to claim that they affect each other. For example, as a child develops the concept of "dog," he acquires a facility for distinguishing "dogs" from other four-legged beasts. With this elementary bit of sophistication he acquires some insight into behavior that might be appropriate in the presence of a dog that would be entirely inappropriate in the presence of a lion. As his understanding of child-dog relationships increases he also may come to understand that the same behavior is not always appropriate even with the same dog. He adjusts his approach in accordance with the meaning he attaches to what he perceives. What he perceives also affects his original concept of "dog." In short, concepts bring order and meaning to our perception, and our perceptions in turn modify our concepts.

The above is not intended as an adequate exploration of these relationships. Rather, it is to point up again the importance of one's conceptual apparatus for the kinds of meaning or sense the world seems to make. This relationship is often pointed out in religious controversies in which the "doubter" says that "he must see in order to believe." The cleric is quite right, in a sense, when he responds that the doubter "must believe in order to see."

Whatever this relationship actually is in terms of which is the ultimate guide for human behavior, and this is a most formidable philosophical problem, it is clear that trivial concepts like "dog" may turn out to be a life or death tool in some contexts, although they are hardly central to formal education.

In this section we focused upon one concept that we felt crucial to formal education—power. There are many others that could be drawn from the social sciences (such as culture, society, institution, social class, learning, and motivation) and that could provide valuable insights for the teacher.

Power is a valuable concept to explore because it seems to have some capacity for helping us to understand the relationships, present and possible, between teacher and pupil, teacher and administrator, and teacher and society. The claim is that the way in which one understands or conceives power is a significant factor in one's behavior as a teacher. Our suggestion has been aimed more at the normative dimension than the descriptive dimension. Although successful uses of power were described, the major thrust was toward a discussion of what power is ethically. The suggestion was that at least some types of power were ethically neutral—gaining their ethical quality from the intent and the consequence of their employment. Such a conception of power raises new questions—primarily, to what end shall it be employed and upon what justification. If power is conceived as being ethically negative, one would expect the assumption that it should never be employed in any form. Thus, the neutral conception either raises a new set of questions for educators or allows them to escape the automatic assessment of guilt (in the negative conception), which otherwise logically would accompany their doing what they must do if they are to be educators.

The world is interpreted much differently as a result of this different conceptualization. As such it should stand as a cogent example of the importance of concepts. One trades in an old set of problems for some new ones. What constitutes the proper use of power is a very difficult question. It is central to human existence. Democracy itself can be seen as an attempt to achieve a decent distribution of power. It can be conceived in many other ways as well. It is to the concepts of democracy and their relationship to education, and particularly to the educator as a professional, that we devote Part Four.

SUGGESTIONS FOR FURTHER READING

1. For a broad view of power in the American scene, one can turn to *Problems of Power in American Democracy*, Arthur Kornhouser, ed. (Detroit: Wayne State University Press, 1957). Floyd Hunter in *Community Power Structure* (Chapel Hill, N. C.: University of North Carolina Press, 1955) and Robert A. Dahl in *Who Governs: Democracy and Power in an American City* (New Haven, Conn.: Yale University Press, 1961) display contrasting methodologies and conclusions as a result of their substantial studies of urban life.

2. For those wishing to focus their attention primarily on the schools and their relations, Stanley's *Education and Social Integration* (New York: Teachers College, Columbia University, 1953) aptly describes some of the problems of an "interest group" society. An extensive description of recent empirical studies of school situations may be found in Ralph Kimbrough's *Political Power and Educational Decision Making* (Skokie, Ill.: Rand McNally, 1964). More narrowly focused in some respects, but still valuable, is Neal Gross's *Who Runs Our Schools* (New York: John Wiley & Sons, Inc., 1958). A worthwhile excursion into types of power and their consequences may be found in "Education and Power," *Teachers College Record* (May 1950) by R. Bruce Raup. Those who are interested in learning more of what Myron Lieberman has to say concerning power and teachers' organizations are advised to read his book entitled *The Future of Public Education* (Chicago: University of Chicago Press, 1960).

3. Erich Fromm's *Escape from Freedom* (Holt, Rinehart and Winston, Inc., 1941) is an interesting attempt to explain man's disinclination to openly accept power and responsibility. John Hanson's "Education and the Flight From Decision," *Educational Leadership* (October 1953) describes some of the consequences of disengagement and the challenge to the educator.

AUTONOMY AND THE DEMOCRATIC TRADITION

It is useful to review the flow of ideas presented up to this point. In Part One our attention was directed toward Socrates as a model of the professional man. Here we found Socrates examining the entire social order and raising questions about the relationship of his life to that of the social order. What he saw was social "disorder"—a set of conditions that would not support "life" (that is, his life). In the last analysis it would neither allow him life in the material sense nor in the sense of fulfilling his "being." Yet his students, even those who disagree with him, have not allowed him to die.

The suggestion flowing from his example was that educational issues were issues that involved the entire social order. In order to set the direction of the teaching intent, it was clear that some conception of a desired outcome had to be attended to. This would have obvious social consequences. The attempt to develop certain kinds of persons (beings) would imply a set of relationships among people. These relationships would involve both means and ends.

These considerations set the stage for the main problems for education as a profession and for the educator as a professional. Quite obviously a professional professes or claims something. He claims (1) to provide a service to society, and (2) that he is uniquely equipped to perform this service by virtue of the training he has undergone. In order that this claim not be a spurious one, it is essential that he know what constitutes service and what constitutes dis-service. This, in Part Two, was seen as the "root" question. The answer to this question allows sensible questions (derived) about its accomplishment. Among these are questions about the type of preparation teachers must undergo and the type of programs to be developed for the youth who are to be instructed by these teachers. Both are aimed at empowering the teacher to act. Part Three was directed toward this issue. This notion of empowering is necessarily extended beyond a knowledge of teaching methods and the materials of instruction. It extends to an understanding of social power and the ways it may be utilized to accomplish the teaching task.

The suggestion is clear that a strong organization might be part of the answer to the power question. Such an organization would have legal and, hopefully, social status. It would allow self-determination of its members within its operating framework. A demand for autonomy is both a cause and a result of such an organization. However, such a development raises some very important questions. The demands for autonomy and the search for power raise the possibility of a contradiction between certain conceptions of a profession and certain conceptions of democracy. If this is indeed the case—the existence of a contradiction—then one must choose his highest value and place one before the other. If contradictions are merely apparent rather than necessary, then one's conceptual apparatus must be arranged in such a way as to demonstrate this mutual support. These concepts are, after all, the ordering principles of our behavior and they must be set in order if we are to avoid intellectual and behavioral chaos.

In its most basic sense the question is what constitutes a legitimate ordering principle for man? What are the right relationships (1) between men, (2) among men, (3) between men and an organization, (4) among men and organizations, (5) between organizations, (6) among organizations, (7) between organizations and the social order and (8) among social orders? Another way of posing this question is "What is the legitimate use of power?" One might prefer to call this a question of justice or ethics. In the framework of this volume it comes forth as the issue of what place, *if any*, does a profession have in a democracy? This is a conceptual question as we see it. Thus, it is necessary to explore the meaning of the concept of profession and the concept of democracy. The concept of profession has been explored to some extent. It is now time for democracy to have its day in court.

The Democratic Tradition

Men in western culture are quick to defend democracy and seem sure of its meaning until questioned. So devoted to its cause are they that much suffering has been endured in its name. A world war was fought, we are told, to "make the world safe for it." Men have willingly risked and even lost much in its defense. The concepts have had compelling power to galvanize men to action. Yet one cannot help but observe that these democrats have come in assorted shapes, sizes, and concepts. These assorted concepts have colored the views of the possessors in a wide range of hues. The world, indeed, has looked quite different to each. There are points at which these views coincide, but green and purple are quite systematically different regardless of the pigmentation they may share.

Some Historical Notes

The routes to the modern statements of the democratic traditions are twisted and obscure. Contrary to present popular opinion, medieval Europe had been bound by various forms of constitutionalism that did not universally ignore the consent of the governed. While it would be a gross error to assume that these arrangements resembled the democracy of Athens, there was a recognition of the various centers of interest and power that had to be dealt with. Such practices also received considerable theoretical defense. However, the shifting sands of loyalty generated by the rise of nationalism with its attendant religious struggles brought new variables into play. Only in England was the continuity of the medieval constitutional institutions preserved, and even there it was not without brief interruption. The forces of nationalism, however, eventually provided an environment for the re-establishment of representative institutions of the governed to limit the absolute claims and the nearly absolute performance of monarchs. These developments had been preceded by a struggle within the Catholic Church that eventuated in the theory of papal absolutism.

Given the material stakes, it is not surprising that the kings questioned the absolute rights of the "divine." The kings wanted to take their "divine rights" without going through the offices of the church. The medieval ideal of a harmony of powers in free co-operation fell before the conflicting conceptions of interest inherent in a parochial nationalism and, perhaps, an equally parochial Catholicism that proclaimed the universality of its message and obligation.

The claim to and belief in the "divine rights" of kings was a heady brew. Not only was it "true" but it was "useful." This was a potent formula for stability in a world much in need of it. However, within nations as well as within the church, there were centers of interest that challenged the absolute "rights" of the rulers. Subjects were restive at being treated as mere objects. The growing mercantile interests, for example, objected to what they regarded as an infringement upon their rights to property and the pursuit thereof. In England this took the form of a hostility to the state af-

ter the departure of the doctrine of "divine rights." A body of political
theory was developed with a heavy utilitarian tone. Increased claims to
popular sovereignty of a limited sort and the consent of the governed were
buttressed by arguments from "divine rights" of man, natural law, and
utility. As kings had challenged the *authority* of the church personified, so
men of substance challenged the *authority* of the state personified. Even
the appearance of an occasionally divinely benevolent king or benevolent
divine could not stem the tide. Each man was to be king. The danger of the
illegitimate use of power on the part of either the state or the church was
too great for men who had developed a faith in their own rationality and
a disposition to act upon it.

It is important to note that the subjects did not question the fact of the
power possessed by their rulers. They did question their unique claim to
divinity and knowledge and thus, their *right* to this power. In the secular
realm the common claim was that each man knew enough to rule his own
affairs. A similar claim was made by portions of protestantism in the
spiritual realm. Here the individual was seen in private relation to God and
not in need of institutional interpretation of the "word" or meditation in the
eventual disposition of his case.

In either realm it is important to note that a claim was being advanced.
Whatever the motivation—economic, religious, social, political—the claim
was that man was rational and capable of conducting his own affairs, that
he had certain inalienable rights, that he was naturally sovereign, and that
any attempt to deny these things was an offense against the law (natural,
divine, or both). This was a demand for power *authorized* by the claim to
knowledge and inalienable rights. In other words, the current distribution
of power (ordering of society) was not authorized. It was arbitrary and
thus unjust. These were the conflicting claims to autonomy.

Of Kings and Subjects

It is one thing to be proclaimed king or to proclaim oneself king. It is
quite another to determine the *legitimate* boundaries of one's kingdom. In
what areas, if any, does a person have legitimate *authority* to act even if he
has the *power* to do so? What constitutes authority? Is it to be found in the
proclamation or is it in being proclaimed by others? If it is the latter, then
does not authority reside in the proclaimers and not in the king? If the former, what is it that distinguishes the king's proclamation from that of the
multitude? These are the problems of the democrat, be he at the breakfast
table or in the classroom.

The distinction between power and authority is sometimes difficult for
the modern mind to comprehend, and that in itself is a telling commentary
upon the character of modern society. Yet we will be driven to ask the very
important "derived" question. "How can we effect a marriage between

legitimate authority and power?" When such a question is asked, there is the obvious assumption that: (1) power is not its own justification (for example, might does not make right), and (2) that there is, whether we know it or not, some other criterion for the right. The answers to the questions of what constitutes legitimate authority within a democracy and how that authority can be *act*ualized involves various conceptions of man, society, freedom, equality, property, and contract. A number of candidate answers are available. They constitute claims upon you in terms of defining appropriate relations to your students, your school, and your society. The conflicts within the candidate answers are hidden from the casual observer because the participants use the same words. They do, however, stand as thoroughgoing critics of each other. If their words have radically different meanings, the holders have radically different ways of looking at the world. Socrates might very well have suggested that your very "life" depends upon your choice of conceptual system. Understandably, each person or group that identifies with a particular conceptual framework sees its life ("being") as threatened by the others.

The head-on collision witnessed in ancient Athens between Socrates and the public may be avoided. This is a particular possibility when issues are blurred and choices are fuzzy. There are those among us who make the creation and maintenance of such a muddy atmosphere a lifelong occupation. However, the quest of the intellectual traditionally has been one of clarifying issues. In this role he has taken upon himself the mantle of an educator. As such, he is a dangerous man and education is a dangerous activity. No one knows where it may lead. Does any society value education in this sense—the thoroughgoing evaluation of all man's relations in the world? Does any society value the educator (the professional or the intellectual)? Can society properly be said to exist without it?

Our answer is negative to the last question. Thus, the candidate answers to what constitutes a democracy (like those concerning the profession treated above) are going to be treated as conflicts. Some of these conflicting elements will be presented in the hope of sharpening your perception of the conflict, if not the conflict itself. The conceptual systems in which these answers are imbedded can be treated as models. Thus you can build these answers into models for a wide variety of situations. As such, you may not find anyone who exemplifies them in each detail. Nevertheless, they are exceedingly useful in analyzing human behavior. Thus, they have immense theoretical and practical significance for the teacher. Intellectual systems or models have at least the following utility:

1. They focus on and describe a product (individual and social) ideal to be achieved. Thus, they constitute ordering principles (claim to answer the ROOT question).
2. They allow for prediction, assuming consistency, of human behavior

(that is, one can anticipate much human behavior if the ordering principle is understood).

3. They describe an ethical distribution of power by which the product is to be achieved (a sense of "due process").

4. They function as the "connective tissue" between the teacher, the classes, the school, and the social order—all vital parts of the body politic.

We would suggest that this constitutes a significant measure of utility. Nevertheless, this now stands as but a claim. The demonstration is yet to come. Chapter 10 will further explore democracy in the large. Chapter 11 will provide a basis for a more analytic concept ferreting and formulation as the concepts of liberty and equality are examined. Chapter 12 will suggest some possible views of the material basis of a democratic society by virtue of the concepts of property and contract. All three chapters should contribute to your consciously principled stance as a teacher in the manner suggested by the four functions of an intellectual system or model.

CHAPTER 7

The Search for Authority

As has been pointed out, claims have been made for power in the name of democracy. Precisely what constitutes a democracy remains to be settled prior to the granting of a claim in its name. Presumably, we may refer to that marvelous phrase "government of the people, by the people, and for the people." That this condition should prosper rather than perish is a matter of widespread agreement. This magnetic turn of a phrase, this shorthand for a long tradition, hides a number of questions unresolved within that tradition.

Who are the "people"? Is "people" a term denoting mere membership in a biological species? Is "people" a qualitative term denoting some differentiation within a biological species? The way one answers these questions determines part of the significance of those tiny words "of," "by," and "for." If "people" denotes sheer existence within a species, then universal participatory rights are granted in decision making. If, however, some qualitative distinctions are proposed, then sovereignty (authority) resides in the qualities possessed by certain entities of the species that we call "people." Sovereignty, then, would not reside in sheer existence. Inasmuch as man has an infinite set of possible relationships, these qualities can be of infinite variety. For example, the ownership of property has been seen as conveying the title "people." The age of 18 or 21 has been seen as justification for the term, either with or without ownership. For a long time, masculinity was a criterion. Race has been seen as both a negative and a positive criterion. Insanity and criminality have usually been seen as negative criteria. There are many other possibilities including various notions of intelligence. The claims to sovereignty are, of course, not limited to the political realm. They crop up in every aspect of life—in the classroom, the curriculum committee, and the professional organization, as well as in the legislative hall.

In using the "of," "by," and "for" the people one may look at the situation in another way. One can ask whether all these conditions must be met in order to have a democracy. Does "for" mean for the people's benefit? If so, are there cases when decisions ought not to be made "by" the entire people (as a species)?

The real heart of the question would appear to revolve around the idea of sovereignty or, in our terms, *authority*. This question, like many others, is not new. Jean Bodin, a French philosopher of the sixteenth century, claimed that sovereignty was perpetual. If it were less, it would be dependent and thus not supreme. He went on to say:

> If the prince is not bound by the law of his predecessors, still less can he be bound by his own laws. . . . As the law says, "there can be no obligation in any matter which proceeds from the free will of the undertaker. It follows of necessity that the king cannot be subject to his own laws. Just as, according to the canonists, the Pope can never tie his own hands, so the sovereign prince cannot bind himself, even if he wishes."[1]

Bodin's argument was, of course, in the defense of the absolute right (authority) of kings. Could it also be used in the defense of the divine and inalienable rights (authority) of "people" as kings? Are there areas in life in which each person is absolute sovereign? May the same be said for the group? Is this so by common agreement? If so, wherein lies the sovereignty —in the individual or in the common agreement? Perhaps the answer to all these questions is that sovereignty or authority does not reside in people at all but in objective principles. The closer one is to the principles the greater his claim to the title "people" and all that "of," "by," and "for" might mean. Thus, the dignity of man might reside not in what he is now, but in what he might *become*.

It would be difficult to find more important questions for the educator as he seeks to "serve" the "people." We take this notion of "serving" the "people" to. mean both a description of a product to be fashioned and a specification of the range of means by which this task is to be accomplished. The following selections attempt to give clear answers to many of these questions. Carr describes the challenge of the changing times to the democratic tradition and its adjustment to these changes. Herbert Spencer

---

[1]M. J. Tooley (trans. and abridg.), Jean Bodin's *Six Books of the Commonwealth* (Oxford: Basil Blackwell, 1955), pp. 28–29.

sets forth one thread of the tradition that clearly strikes a responsive chord in many. Joseph Tussman goes to the heart of the processes parading under the name of democracy and makes a stirring plea for one of them. Finally, George Barnett and Jack Otis question some of the basic assumptions of liberalism in both the classical and modern vein. Underlying all of this is the claim to various kinds of authority as the basis for organizing the affairs of mankind or as a description of the "good" life and the means of attaining it. Thus, these are all claims in the name of education, not a small part of which are the schools and the relationships they institutionalize.

CHANGING CONCEPTIONS OF DEMOCRACY

In modern times there has been a considerable shift in thinking about the meaning of democracy and its implications for the lives of men. The various meanings that have been attached to the term have left the holders of these views as clear-cut opponents, each regarding the other as well-meaning but, nevertheless, immoral people. For above all, democracy is an ethical system that describes the way men ought to behave or the right relations among men.

The dispute is often seen most clearly in terms of the role of the state in human affairs. The conversation often turns on notions of liberty. On the one hand we have statements like those of Bennett who wrote: "Liberty is, in fact, nothing else but the complete abolition of law—liberty and law are mutually exclusive.[2]

On the other hand, we have in the writings of Jefferson a reminder of his cultural debt to Rousseau. Rousseau saw that social circumstances tended to destroy the equality that existed in the state of nature and felt that legislation should aim to maintain equality. In the same spirit Jefferson wrote:

> I am conscious that an equal division of property is impractical, but the consequences of this enormous inequality producing so much misery to the bulk of mankind, legislators cannot invent too many devices for subdividing property.[3]

The changing role of the state and reason in the affairs of men reflects changing conceptions of the nature of man. In one age man was thought to be essentially independent or asocial. Consequently society was seen as artificial. In the twentieth century man is more often conceived as social or interdependent and defined by his relationships rather than in absence of

[2]William Bennett, *Freedom and Liberty* (London: Oxford University Press, 1920), pp. 352 and 354.
[3]Thomas Jefferson, *Writings*, vol. 2, Paul Leicester Ford, ed. (New York: G. P. Putnam's Sons, 1892), p. 103.

them. Some would agree that changing times bring a need for changing concepts. Others would argue that a particular concept of democracy is the adequate one and that changing circumstances only make alternative conceptions more obviously wrong.

Clearly, the voices of democrats are not in unison on a number of matters. In the following selection, Professor Carr examines the history of democratic thought as "individual" and as "general will" and raises some questions about the direction of democratic thought as it faces the world *of* and *as* mass society. What do these conditions say for the professions of democrats and for the democrats as "professional" men?

———◄◆►———

FROM INDIVIDUALISM TO MASS DEMOCRACY*

The problem of political organization in the new society is to adapt to the mass civilization of the twentieth century conceptions of democracy formed in earlier and highly individualistic periods of history. The proclamation by the French revolution of popular sovereignty was a serious challenge to institutions which had grown up under quite different auspices and influences. It is no accident that Athenian democracy, which has been commonly regarded as the source and exemplar of democratic institutions, was the creation and prerogative of a limited and privileged group of the population. It is no accident that Locke, the founder of the modern democratic tradition, was the chosen philosopher and prophet of the eighteenth-century English Whig oligarchy. It is no accident that the magnificent structure of British nineteenth-century liberal democracy was built up on a highly restrictive property franchise. History points unmistakably to the fact that political democracy, in the forms in which it has hitherto been known, flourishes best where some of the people, but not all the people, are free and equal; and, since this conclusion is incompatible with the conditions of the new society and repugnant to the contemporary conscience, the task of saving democracy in our time is the task of reconciling it with the postulate of popular sovereignty and mass civilization.

Modern democracy, as it grew up and spread from its focus in western Europe over the past three centuries, rested on three main propositions:

*Edward H. Carr, *The New Society* (London: Macmillan & Co., Ltd., 1951), pp. 61–79. By permission of St. Martin's Press Inc., The Macmillan Company of Canada Ltd., and Macmillan & Co. Ltd., London, England. Professor Carr is a British political scientist with many years in the diplomatic service. He has taught at the University College of Wales and served, for a five year period, as the editor of *The London Times*. His publications are numerous and include books on Russian history.

first, that the individual conscience is the ultimate source of decisions about what is right and wrong; second, that there exists between different individuals a fundamental harmony of interests strong enough to enable them to live peacefully together in society; third, that where action has to be taken in the name of society, rational discussion between individuals is the best method of reaching a decision on that action. Modern democracy is, in virtue of its origins, individualist, optimistic and rational. The three main propositions on which it is based have all been seriously challenged in the contemporary world.

In the first place, the individualist conception of democracy rests on a belief in the inherent rights of individuals based on natural law. According to this conception, the function of democratic government is not to create or innovate, but to interpret and apply rights which already exist. This accounts for the importance attached in the democratic tradition to the rights of minorities within the citizen body. Decision by majority vote might be a necessary and convenient device. But individuals belonging to the minority had the same inherent rights as those belonging to the majority. Insistence on the rule of law, preferably inscribed in a written and permanent constitution, was an important part of the individualist tradition of democracy. The individual enjoyed certain indefeasible rights against the society of which he was a member; these rights were often regarded as deriving from a real or hypothetical "social contract" which formed the title-deeds of society. Just as the individualist tradition in *laissez-faire* economics was hostile to all forms of combination, so the individualist tradition in politics was inimical to the idea of political parties. Both in Athenian democracy and in eighteenth-century Britain, parties were regarded with mistrust and denounced as "factions."

The French revolution with its announcement of the sovereignty of the people made the first serious assault on this view of democracy. The individualism of Locke's "natural law" was replaced by the collectivism of Rousseau's "general will." Both Pericles and Locke had thought in terms of a small and select society of privileged citizens. Rousseau for the first time thought in terms of the sovereignty of the whole people, and faced the issue of mass democracy. He did so reluctantly; for he himself preferred the tiny community where direct democracy, without representation or delegation of powers, was still possible. But he recognized that the large nation had come to stay, and held that in such conditions the people could be sovereign only if it imposed on itself the discipline of a "general will." The practical conclusion drawn from this doctrine, not by Rousseau himself, but by the Jacobins, was the foundation of a single political party to embody the general will. Its logical conclusions were still more far-reaching. The individual, far from enjoying rights against society assured to him by natural law, had no appeal against the deliverances of the general will. The general will was the repository of virtue and justice, the state its instrument for putting them into effect. The individual who dissented from the general will cut himself off from the community and was a self-proclaimed traitor to it. Rousseau's doctrine led directly to the Jacobin practice of revolutionary terror. It would be idle to embark on a theoretical discussion of the rival merits of the two conceptions of democracy. Individualism is an oligarchic doctrine—the doctrine of the select and enterprising few who refuse to be merged in the mass. The function of natural law in modern history, though it is susceptible of other interpretations, has been to sanctify existing rights and to brand as immoral attempts to overthrow them. A conception based on individual rights rooted in natural law was a natural product of the oligarchic and conservative eighteenth century. It was equally natural that this conception should be challenged and overthrown in the ferment of a revolution that proclaimed the supremacy of popular sovereignty.

While, however, the beginnings of mass democracy can be discerned in the doctrines of Rousseau and in the practice of the French revolution, the problem in its modern form was a product of the nineteenth century. The Industrial revolution started its career under the banner of individual enterprise. Adam Smith was as straightforward an example as could be desired of eighteenth-century individualism. But presently the machine overtook the man, and the competitive advantages of mass production ushered in the age of standardization and larger and larger economic units. And with the mammoth trust and the mammoth trade union came the mammoth organ of opinion, the mammoth political party and, floating above them all, the mammoth state, narrowing still further the field of responsibility and action left to the individual and setting the stage for the new mass society. It was the English Utilitarians who, by rejecting natural law, turned their backs on the individualist tradition and, by postulating the greatest good and the greatest number as the supreme goal, laid the theoretical foundation of mass democracy in Britain; in practice, they were also the first radical reformers. Before long, thinkers began to explore some of the awkward potentialities of mass democracy. The danger of the oppression of minorities by the majority was the most obvious. This was discerned by Tocqueville in the United States in the 1830's and by J. S. Mill in England twenty-five years later. In our own time the danger has reappeared in a more insidious form. Soviet Russia has a form of government which describes itself as a democracy. It claims, not without some historical justification, to stem from the Jacobins who stemmed from Rousseau and the doctrine of the general will. The general will is an orthodoxy which purports to express the common opinion; the minority which dissents can legitimately be suppressed. But we are not concerned here with the abuses and excesses of the Soviet form of government. What troubles us is the question how far, in moving from the individualism of restrictive liberal democracy to the mass civilization of today, we have ourselves become involved in a conception of democracy which postulates a general will. The question is all around us today not only in the form of loyalty tests, avowed or secret, or committees on un-American activities, but also in the form of the closed shop and of increasingly rigid standards of party discipline. In a speech made to a regional Labour party conference at the time of Mr. Aneurin Bevan's resignation in April, the Minister of Defence denounced "absence of loyalty" in the party: "The loyalty of our party," exclaimed Mr. Shinwell, "is superior to any exhibition of political private enterprise. . . . No person, I don't care who he is, can be allowed to interfere with the democratic structure of this party." Lenin used strikingly similar phrases at the Bolshevik party congress in March 1921. We have moved far from the conception of truth emerging from the interplay of divergent individual opinions. Loyalty has come to mean the submission of the individual to the general will of the party or group.

The second postulate of Locke's conception of society, the belief in a fundamental harmony of interests between individuals, equally failed to stand the test of time, and for much the same reason. Even more than natural law, the harmony of interests was essentially a conservative doctrine. If the interest of the individual rightly understood coincided with the interest of the whole society, it followed that any individual who assailed the existing order was acting against his own true interests and could be condemned not only as wicked, but as short-sighted and foolish. Some such argument was, for instance, often invoked against strikers who failed to recognize the common interest uniting them with their employers. The French Revolution, an act of self-assertion by the third estate against the two senior estates of nobility and clergy, demonstrated—like any other violent upheaval—the hollowness of the harmony of interests; and the doctrine was soon also to be powerfully challenged on the theoretical plane.

The challenge came from two quarters. The Utilitarians, while not making a frontal attack on the doctrine, implicitly denied it when they asserted that the harmony of interests had to be created by remedial action before it would work. They saw that some of the worst existing inequalities would have to be reformed out of existence before it was possible to speak without irony of a society based on a harmony of interests; and they believed in increased education, and the true liberty of thought which would result from it, as a necessary preparation for establishing harmony. Then Marx and Engels in the *Communist Manifesto* took the class struggle and made out of it a theory of history which, partial though it was, stood nearer to current reality than the theory of the harmony of interests had ever done. Social and economic pressures resulting from the breakdown of *laissez-faire* illustrated in practice what Marx had demonstrated in theory. But in Great Britain it was reformist Utilitarianism rather than revolutionary Marxism that set the pace. The flagrant absence of a harmony of interests between competing and conflicting classes more and more urgently called for state intervention. The state could no longer be content to hold the ring; it must descend actively into the arena to create a harmony which did not exist in nature. Legislation, hitherto regarded as an exceptional function required from time to time to clear up some misunderstanding or to rectify some abuse, now became normal and continuous. It no longer sufficed to interpret and apply rights conferred on the individual by the laws of nature. What was expected of the state was positive and continuous activity—a form of social and economic engineering. The substitution of a planned economy for *laissez-faire* capitalism brought about a radical transformation in the attitude towards the state. The functions of the state were no longer merely supervisory, but creative and remedial. It was no longer an organ whose weakness was its virtue and whose activities should be restricted to a minimum in the interests of freedom. It was an organ which one sought to capture and control for the carrying out of necessary reforms; and, having captured it, one sought to make it as powerful and effective as possible in order to carry them out. The twentieth century has not only replaced individualist democracy by mass democracy, but has substituted the cult of the strong remedial state for the doctrine of the natural harmony of interests.

The third main characteristic of Locke's conception of society—a characteristic which helped to give the eighteenth century its nicknames of the Age of Reason or the Age of Enlightenment—was its faith in rational discussion as a guide to political action. This faith provided the most popular nineteenth-century justification of the rule of the majority as the basis of democracy. Since men were on the whole rational, and since the right answer to any given issue could be discovered by reason, one was more likely, in the case of dispute, to find right judgment on the side of the majority than on the side of the minority. Like other eighteenth-century conceptions, the doctrine of reason in politics was the doctrine of a ruling oligarchy. The rational approach to politics, which encouraged leisurely argument and eschewed passion, was eminently the approach of a well-to-do, leisured and cultured class. Its efficacy could be most clearly and certainly guaranteed when the citizen body consisted of a relatively small number of educated persons who could be trusted to reason intelligently and dispassionately on controversial issues submitted to them. The prominent rôle assigned to reason in the original democratic scheme provides perhaps the most convincing explanation why democracy has hitherto always seemed to flourish best with a restrictive franchise. Much has been written in recent years of the decline of reason, and of respect for reason, in human affairs, when sometimes what has really happened has been the abandonment of the highly simplified eighteenth-century view of reason in favour of a subtler and more sophisticated analysis. But it is none the less true that the epoch-making changes in our attitude towards reason provide a key to some of the profoundest problems of contemporary democracy.

First of all, the notion that men of intelligence and good will were likely by process of rational discussion to reach a correct opinion on controversial political questions could be valid only in an age when such questions were comparatively few and simple enough to be accessible to the educated lay-man. It implicitly denied that any specialized knowledge was required to solve political problems. This hypothesis was perhaps tenable so long as the state was not required to intervene in economic issues, and the questions on which decisions had to be taken turned on matters of practical detail or general political principles. In the first half of the twentieth century these conditions had everywhere ceased to exist. In Great Britain major issues of a highly controversial character like the return to the gold standard in 1925 or the acceptance of the American loan in 1946 were of a kind in which no opinion seriously counted except that of the trained expert in possession of a vast array of facts and figures, some of them probably not available to the public. In such matters the ordinary citizen could not even have an intelligent opinion on the question who were the best experts to consult. The only rôle he could hope to play was to exercise his hunch at the election by choosing the right leader to consult the right experts about vital, though probably still unformulated, issues of policy which would ultimately affect his daily life.

At this initial stage of the argument reason itself is not dethroned from its supreme rôle in the decision of political issues. The citizen is merely asked to surrender his right of decision to the superior reason of the expert. At the second stage of the argument reason itself is used to dethrone reason. The social psychologist, employing rational methods of investigation, discovers that men in the mass are often most effectively moved by non-rational emotions such as admiration, envy, hatred, and can be most effectively reached not by rational argument, but by emotional appeals to eye and ear, or by sheer repetition. Propaganda is as essential a function of mass democracy as advertising of mass production. The political organizer takes a leaf out of the book of the commercial advertiser and sells the leader or the candidate to the voter by the same methods used to sell patent medicines or refrigerators. The appeal is no longer to the reason of the citizen, but to his gullibility. A more recent phenomenon has been the emergence of what Max Weber called the "charismatic leader" as the expression of the general will. The retreat from individualism seemed to issue at last—and not alone in the so-called totalitarian countries—in the exaltation of a single individual leader who personified and resumed within himself the qualities and aspirations of the "little man," of the ordinary individual lost and bewildered in the new mass society. But the principal qualification of the leader is no longer his capacity to reason correctly on political or economic issues, or even his capacity to choose the best experts to reason for him, but a good public face, a convincing voice, a sympathetic fireside manner on the radio; and these qualities are deliberately built up for him by his publicity agents. In this picture of the techniques of contemporary democracy, the party headquarters, the directing brain at the centre, still operates rationally, but uses irrational rather than rational means to achieve its ends—means which are, moreover, not merely irrational but largely irrelevant to the purposes to be pursued or to the decisions to be taken.

The third stage of the argument reaches deeper levels. Hegel, drawing out the philosophical implications of Rousseau's doctrine, had identified the course of history with universal reason, to which the individual reason stood in the same relation as the individual will to Rousseau's general will. Individual reason had been the corner-stone of individualist democracy. Marx took Hegel's collective reason to make it the corner-stone of the new mass democracy. Marx purported to reject the metaphysical character of Hegel's thought. But, equally with Hegel, he conceived of history pursuing a rational course, which could be analysed and even predicted in terms of reason. Hegel had spoken of the cunning of reason in history, using individuals to achieve purposes of which they themselves were unconscious. Marx would have rejected the turn of phrase as metaphysical. But his conception of history as a continuous process of class struggle contained elements of determinism which revealed its Hegelian ancestry, at any rate on one side. Marx remained a thorough-going rationalist. But the reason whose validity he accepted was collective rather than individual.

Marx played, however, a far more important part in what has been called "the flight from reason" than by the mere exaltation of the collective over the individual. By his vigorous assertion that "being determines consciousness, not consciousness being," that thinking is conditioned by the social environment of the thinker, and that ideas are the superstructure of a totality whose foundation is formed by the material conditions of life, Marx presented a clear challenge to what had hitherto been regarded as the sovereign or autonomous human reason. The actors who played significant parts in the historical drama were playing parts already written for them: this indeed was what made them significant. The function of individual reason was to identify itself with the universal reason which determined the course of history and to make itself the agent and executor of this universal reason. Some such view is indeed involved in any attempt to trace back historical events to underlying social causes; and Marx—and

still more Engels—hedged a little in later years about the rôle of the individual in history. But the extraordinary vigour and conviction with
which he drove home his main argument, and the political theory which he
founded on it, give him a leading place among those nineteenth-century
thinkers who shattered the comfortable belief of the Age of Enlightenment
in the decisive power of individual reason in shaping the course of history.

Marx's keenest polemics were those directed to prove the "conditioned"
character of the thinking of his opponents and particularly of the capitalist
ruling class of the most advanced countries of his day. If they thought as
they did it was because, as members of a class, "being" determined their
"consciousness," and their ideas necessarily lacked any independent objectivity and validity. Hegel, as a good conservative, had exempted the
current reality of the Prussian from the operation of the dialectic which
had destroyed successively so many earlier historical forms. Marx, as a
revolutionary, admitted no such absolute in the present, but only in the
future. The proletariat, whose victory would automatically abolish classes,
was alone the basis of absolute value; and collective proletarian thinking
had thus an objectivity which was denied to the thinking of other classes.
Marx's willingness, like that of Hegel, to admit an absolute as the culminating point of his dialectical process was, however, an element of inconsistency in his system; and, just as Marx was far more concerned to
dissect capitalism than to provide a blue-print for socialism, so his use of
the dialectic to lay bare the conditioned thinking of his opponents lay far
nearer to his heart, and was far more effective, than his enunciation of the
objective and absolute values of the proletariat. Marx's writings gave a
powerful impetus to all forms of relativism. It seemed less important, at a
time when the proletarian revolution was as yet nowhere in sight, to note
his admission of absolute truth as a prerogative of the proletariat. The proletariat was for Marx the collective repository of Rousseau's infallible
general will.

Another thinker of the later nineteenth century also helped to mould the
climate of political opinion. Like Darwin, Freud was a scientist without
pretensions to be a philosopher or, still less, a political thinker. But in the
flight from reason at the end of the nineteenth century, he played the same
popular rôle as Darwin had played a generation earlier in the philosophy
of *laissez-faire*. Freud demonstrated that the fundamental attitudes of human beings in action and thought are largely determined at levels beneath
that of consciousness, and that the supposedly rational explanations of
those attitudes which we offer to ourselves and others are artificial and erroneous "rationalizations" of processes which we have failed to understand. Reason is given to us, Freud seems to say, not to direct our thought
and action, but to camouflage the hidden forces which do direct it. This is
a still more devastating version of the Marxist thesis of substructure and

superstructure. The substructure of reality resides in the unconscious: what appears above the surface is no more than the reflexion, seen in a distorting ideological mirror, of what goes on underneath. The political conclusion from all this—Freud himself drew none—is that any attempt to appeal to the reason of the ordinary man is waste of time, or is useful merely as camouflage to conceal the real nature of the process of persuasion; the appeal must be made to those subconscious strata which are decisive for thought and action. The debunking of ideology undertaken by the political science of Marx is repeated in a far more drastic and far-reaching way by the psychological science of Freud and his successors.

By the middle of the nineteenth century, therefore, the propositions of Locke on which the theory of liberal democracy was founded had all been subjected to fundamental attack, and the attack broadened and deepened as the century went on. Individualism began to give way to collectivism both in economic organization and in the forms and practice of mass democracy: the age of mass civilization had begun. The alleged harmony of interests between individuals was replaced by the naked struggle between powerful classes and organized interest-groups. The belief in the settlement of issues by rational discussion was undermined, first, by recognition of the complex and technical character of the issues involved, later and more seriously, by recognition that rational arguments were merely the conditioned reflexion of the class interests of those who put them forward, and, last and most seriously of all, by the discovery that the democratic voter, like other human beings, is most effectively reached not by arguments directed to his reason, but by appeals directed to his irrational, subconscious prejudices. The picture of democracy which emerged from these criticisms was the picture of an arena where powerful interest-groups struggled for the mastery. The leaders themselves were often the spokesmen and instruments of historical processes which they did not fully understand; their followers consisted of voters recruited and marshalled for purposes of which they were wholly unconscious by all the subtle techniques of modern psychological science and modern commercial advertising.

The picture is overdrawn. But we shall not begin to understand the problems of mass democracy unless we recognize the serious elements of truth in it, unless we recognize how far we have moved away from the conceptions and from the conditions out of which the democratic tradition was born. From the conception of democracy as a select society of free individuals, enjoying equal rights and periodically electing to manage the affairs of the society, a small number of their peers, who deliberate together and decide by rational argument on the course to pursue (the assumption being that the course which appeals to the majority is likely to be the most rational), we have passed to the current reality of mass democracy. The typical mass democracy of today is a vast society of individuals, stratified by widely different social and economic backgrounds into a series of groups or classes, enjoying equal political rights the exercise of which is organized through two or more closely integrated political machines called parties. Between the parties and individual citizens stand an indeterminate number of entities variously known as unions, associations, lobbies or pressure-groups devoted to the promotion of some economic interest, or of some social or humanitarian cause in which keen critics usually detect a latent and perhaps unconscious interest. At the first stage of the democratic process, these associations and groups form a sort of exchange and mart where votes are traded for support of particular policies; the more votes such a group controls the better its chance of having its views incorporated in the party platform. At the second stage, when these bargains have been made, the party as a united entity "goes to the country" and endeavours by every form of political propaganda to win the support of the unattached voter. At the third stage, when the election has been decided, the parties once more dispute or bargain together, in the light of the votes cast, on the policies to be put into effect; the details of procedure at this third stage differ considerably in different democratic countries in accordance with varying constitutional requirements and party structures. What is important to note is that the first and third stages are fierce matters of bargaining. At the second stage, where the mass persuasion of the electorate is at issue, the methods employed now commonly approximate more and more closely to those of commercial advertisers, who, on the advice of modern psychologists, find the appeal to fear, envy or self-aggrandizement more effective than the appeal to reason. Certainly in the United States, where contemporary large-scale democracy has worked most successfully and where the strongest confidence is felt in its survival, experienced practitioners of politics would give little encouragement to the idea that rational argument exercises a major influence on the democratic process. We have returned to a barely disguised struggle of interest-groups in which the arguments used are for the most part no more than a rationalization of the interests concerned, and the rôle of persuasion is played by carefully calculated appeals to the irrational subconscious.

This discussion is intended to show not that mass democracy is more corrupt or less efficient than other forms of government (this I do not believe), but that mass democracy is a new phenomenon—a creation of the last half-century—which it is inappropriate and misleading to consider in terms of the philosophy of Locke or of the liberal democracy of the nineteenth century. It is new, because the new democratic society consists no longer of a homogeneous closed society of equal and economically secure individuals mutually recognizing one another's rights, but of ill co-ordinated, highly stratified masses of people of whom a large majority are primarily occupied with the daily struggle for existence. It is new, because the new democratic state can no longer be content to hold the ring in the strife of private economic interests, but must enter the arena at every moment and take the initiative in urgent issues of economic policy which affect the daily life of all the citizens, and especially of the least secure. It is new, because the old rationalist assumptions of Locke and of liberal democracy have broken down under the weight both of changed material conditions and of new scientific insights and inventions, and the leaders of the new democracy are concerned no longer primarily with the reflexion of opinion, but with the moulding and manipulation of opinion. To speak to-day of the defence of democracy as if we were defending something which we knew and had possessed for many decades or many centuries is self-deception and sham.

It is no answer to point to institutions that have survived from earlier forms of democracy. The survival of kingship in Great Britain does not prove that the British system of government is a monarchy; and democratic institutions survive in many countries today—some survived even in Hitler's Germany—which have little or no claim to be called democracies. The criterion must be sought not in the survival of traditional institutions, but in the question where power resides and how it is exercised. In this respect democracy is a matter of degree. Some countries today are more democratic than others. But none is perhaps very democratic, if any high standard of democracy is applied. Mass democracy is a difficult and hither-to largely uncharted territory; and we should be nearer the mark, and should have a far more convincing slogan, if we spoke of the need, not to defend democracy, but to create it. . . .

I discussed two of the basic problems which confront the new society—the problem of a planned economy and the problem of the right deployment and use of our human resources. These problems are basic in the sense that their solution is a condition of survival. The old methods of organizing production have collapsed, and society cannot exist without bringing new ones into operation. But those problems might conceivably be solved—are even, perhaps, in danger of being solved—by other than democratic means: here the task of mass democracy is to meet known and recognized needs by methods that are compatible with democracy, and to do it in time. The central problem which I have been discussing today touches the essence of democracy itself. Large-scale political organizations show many of the characteristics of large-scale economic organization, and have followed the same path of development. Mass democracy has, through its very nature, thrown up on all sides specialized groups of leaders—what are sometimes called élites. Everywhere, in government, in political parties, in trade unions, in co-operatives, these indispensable élites have taken shape with startling rapidity over the last thirty years. Everywhere the rift has widened between leaders and rank and file.

The rift takes two forms. In the first place, the interests of the leaders are no longer fully identical with those of the rank and file, since they include the special interest of the leaders in maintaining their own leadership—an interest which is no doubt rationalized, but not always justly, as constituting an interest of the whole group. The leaders, instead of remaining mere delegates of their equals, tend in virtue of their functions to become a separate professional, and then a separate social, group, forming the nucleus of a new ruling class or, more insidiously still, being absorbed into the old ruling class. Secondly, and most important of all, there is an ever-increasing gap between the terms in which an issue is debated and solved among leaders and the terms in which the same issue is presented to the rank and file. Nobody supposes that the arguments which the leaders and managers of a political party or a trade union use among themselves in private conclave are the same as those which they present to a meeting of their members; and the methods of persuasion used from the public platform or over the radio will diverge more widely still. When the decision of substance has been taken by the leaders, whether of government, of party or of union, a further decision is often required on the best method of selling the decision. Broadly speaking, the rôle of reason varies inversely with the number of those to whom the argument is addressed. The decision of the leaders may be taken on rational grounds. But the motivation of the decision to the rank and file of the party or union, and still more to the general public, will contain a larger element of the irrational the larger the audience becomes. The spectacle of an efficient élite maintaining its authority and asserting its will over the mass by the rationally calculated use of irrational methods of persuasion is the most disturbing nightmare of mass democracy.

The problem defies any rough-and-ready answer. It was implicit in Lincoln's formula of government "of the people" (meaning, I take it, belonging to the people in the sense of popular sovereignty), "by the people" (implying, I think, direct participation in the business of government) and "for the people" (requiring an identity of interests between governors and governed only obtainable when such participation occurs). It was implicit in Lenin's much-derided demand that every cook should learn to govern and that every worker should take his turn at the work of administration. The building of nineteenth-century democracy was long and arduous. The building of the new mass democracy will be no easier....

For myself, it seems inconceivable that we can return to the individualist democracy of a privileged class; and, by the same token, we cannot return to the exclusively political democracy of the weak state exercising only police functions. We are committed to mass democracy, to egalitarian democracy, to the public control and planning of the economic process, and therefore to the strong state exercising remedial and constructive functions. . . .

Here I will say only that I have no faith in a flight into the irrational or in an exaltation of irrational values. Reason may be an imperfect instrument; and we can no longer take the simple view of its character and functions which satisfied the eighteenth and nineteenth centuries. But it is none the less in a widening and deepening of the power of reason that we must place our hope. Mass democracy calls just as much as individualist democracy for an educated society as well as for responsible and courageous leaders; for it is only thus that the gap between leaders and masses, which is the major threat to mass democracy, can be bridged. The task is difficult but not hopeless. . . .

FOR FURTHER THOUGHT

1. Carr seems concerned about the question of how far away from "individualism" as democracy to "general will" as democracy our present society has moved. He cites evidence of movement to the latter concept in such things as loyalty oaths, the "closed" shop, and the increasingly rigid standards of party discipline. *Is the current press for professionalism in education another illustration of this tendency? Are such things as certification requirements, salary schedules, tenure regulations, ethical codes, national associations, and collective bargaining moves away from the "individualistic" conception of authority?*
2. The doctrine of a *natural* "harmony of interests" seems to have fallen into disrepute. *If you assumed such a harmony, would you expect classroom control to be much of a problem? Is there a natural harmony of interests among parents, students, and teachers? Does the modern concern with "motivation" and teaching methods stand as a criticism of this doctrine? Is the teacher undemocratic when she assumes the role of an active remedial governor of the classroom?*
3. It is maintained that although the deliberative processes of leaders may be rational the processes of acceptance are increasingly irrational. Once the decision is made at the higher level the chore of selling and image-building begins. All the wiles of the market place are put into full gear. *If teachers are to educate the young for citizenship, what should they do? Should they focus on the skills of sham and deceit with the intent of producing clever manipulators? Should they focus upon the skills of decent intellectual intercourse and make the individual responsible? Should they argue for the employment of government regulation to keep the deciders "honest" in their communication with the general*

public? Should the teacher's methods be an example of rationality or is it appropriate for the teacher to be a model of the manipulator in the style of the "market place"? Is there a moral as well as a technical side to the methods of teaching?

4. Carr observes that "broadly speaking, the role of reason varies inversely with a number of those to whom the argument is addressed." *Is there a necessary connection between the size of the audience and rationality or irrationality? What does this say about the problem of class size? Is the large lecture hall a reasonable arrangement at any level of education? If a community should decide upon a 40-to-1 pupil-teacher ratio instead of a 20-to-1 ratio, is this a decision in favor of rationality or irrationality? Is it a decision in favor of or against democracy?*

THE INDIVIDUAL AS AUTHORITY

The "individualist" conception of democracy cited by Carr has had a varied history. Generally speaking, it has held that man is essentially independent and prior to society. Man is natural and society is artificial. Individual man stands as authority and not society. Majority rule has been seen as the voluntary agreement of individuals. These views are often associated with classical economic theory with its conception of a "free" market. Man and the market are free when there is no external restraint placed upon their activity. To the extent that restraint exists, it does so as a denial of natural law. As such, it is unjust or "unauthorized."

As Carr suggests, this doctrine seems to have fallen upon evil days. This may be true as far as political scientists and some economists are concerned; and it is reflected in the behavior of certain institutions. In the popular mind, however, there remains a significant residue of these ideas in both economic and social thought. In the nineteenth century, the English utilitarians like John Stuart Mill were modifying the harshness of the fundamental doctrine by suggesting that positive governmental action might be necessary in order to create the conditions in which men might become free of external restraint.[4] To many, the delphic ambiguity of Mill's *On Liberty* was a masterpiece of social philosophy. However, "the greatest good for the greatest number" as the ordering principle for human action left the question of which should guide—the "greatest good" or the "greatest number"? These ideas certainly, among other things, opened the door to the "general will" and the modern liberal doctrine.

The history of human thought is marked by revivals. One of the most significant ones for the popular mind came in the personage of Herbert Spencer, a contemporary of Mill. Spencer followed the logic of "individ-

[4]In this respect, at least, the writings of Marx become theoretically interesting.

ualism" to its end as few before or since have cared or dared to do. Moreover, he apparently had more than sheer logic on his side. His pre-Darwinian evolutionary commitments in the defense of "individualism" were hardly put to paper before Darwin himself burst upon the international scene. On this view, the individual as absolute authority in healthy competition would bring forth progress inevitably as a result of the laws of nature—the "survival of the fittest." This doctrine met with much favor among the "anarchists" of that day and this. However, it was not confined to those who consciously adopted that label. It has been a significant factor in our national experience during the last 75 years, having the force of the gospel among a large portion of the business community and those who identified with a society that seemed to offer considerable upward social mobility. It did, indeed, tie into one of the strands of democratic social theory unless one were to contend (as do the modern liberals) that an asocial atomistic view of life cannot be democratic.

One might suggest that Spencer's doctrine is dead as a significant political force in the western world. A modest case can be made for this point of view. It would, however, have to neglect the hearts of men. Whatever the merits of the case, it would say nothing about whether it ought to be dead. Moreover, the tremendous growth of interest in existential thought in the western world can be interpreted as "individual" as "authority" in a new guise. This is not to suggest for a moment that this idea of authority defines or exhausts existential thought. It is, however, to suggest that it may describe many people who identify with it. Further, in conversations about education in particular and value in general, it is commonplace to hear that the individual is the final authority. This point of view is not confined to psychologists though it receives heavy support from many of them. Thus, the writings of Spencer take on new import for society and for education. The following reading is taken from Spencer's first edition of *Social Statics* (1850). It was omitted from the revised edition published in 1892. Spencer, however, never refuted the claims made in the first edition.

------------◀◆▶------------

THE RIGHT TO IGNORE THE STATE*

As a corollary to the proposition that all institutions must be subordinated to the law of equal freedom, we cannot choose but admit the right of the citizen to adopt a condition of voluntary outlawry. If every man has free-

*Herbert Spencer, *Social Statics* (New York: Appleton-Century-Crofts, 1850), pp. 229–240. Mr. Spencer, a prolific writer, was a nineteenth century philosopher and social theorist.

dom to do all that he wills, provided he infringes not the equal freedom of any other man, than he is free to drop connection with the state—to relinquish its protection, and to refuse paying toward its support. It is self-evident that in so behaving he in no way trenches upon the liberty of others; for his position is a passive one; and whilst passive he cannot become an aggressor. It is equally self-evident that he cannot be compelled to continue one of a political corporation, without a breach of the moral law, seeing that citizenship involves payment of taxes; and the taking away of a man's property against his will, is an infringement of his rights. Government being simply an agent employed in common by a number of individuals to secure to them certain advantages, the very nature of the connection implies that it is for each to say whether he will employ such an agent or not. If any one of them determines to ignore this mutual-safety confederation, nothing can be said except that he loses all claim to its good offices, and exposes himself to the danger of maltreatment—a thing he is quite at liberty to do if he likes. He cannot be coerced into political combination without a breach of the law of equal freedom; he *can* withdraw from it without committing any such breach; and he has therefore a right so to withdraw.

"No human laws are of any validity if contrary to the law of nature; and such of them as are valid derive all their force and all their authority mediately or immediately from this original." Thus writes Blackstone, to whom let all honour be given for having so far outseen the ideas of his time; and, indeed, we may say of our time. A good antidote, this, for those political superstitions which so widely prevail. A good check upon that sentiment of power-worship which still misleads us by magnifying the prerogatives of constitutional governments as it once did those of monarchs. Let men learn that a legislature is *not* "our God upon earth," though, by the authority they ascribe to it, and the things they expect from it, they would seem to think it is. Let them learn rather that it is an institution serving a purely temporary purpose, whose power, when not stolen, is at the best borrowed.

Nay, indeed, have we not seen that government is essentially immoral? Is it not the offspring of evil, bearing about it all the marks of its parentage? Does it not exist because crime exists? Is it not strong, or as we say, despotic, when crime is great? Is there not more liberty, that is, less government, as crime diminishes? And must not government cease when crime ceases, for very lack of objects on which to perform its function? Not only does magisterial power exist *because* of evil, but it exists *by* evil. Violence is employed to maintain it; and all violence involves criminality. Soldiers, policemen, and gaolers; swords, batons, and fetters, are instruments for inflicting pain; and all infliction of pain is in the abstract wrong. The state employs evil weapons to subjugate evil, and is alike contaminated by the objects with which it deals, and by the means by which it works. Morality cannot recognize it; for morality, being simply a statement of the perfect law can give no countenance to any thing growing out of, and living by, breaches of that law. Wherefore, legislative authority can never be ethical—must always be conventional merely.

Hence, there is a certain inconsistency in the attempt to determine the right position, structure, and conduct of a government by appeal to the first principles of rectitude. For, as just pointed out, the acts of an institution which is in both nature and origin imperfect, cannot be made to square with the perfect law. All that we can do is to ascertain, firstly, in what attitude a legislature must stand to the community to avoid being by its mere existence an embodied wrong; secondly, in what manner it must be constituted so as to exhibit the least incongruity with the moral law;—and thirdly, to what sphere its actions must be limited to prevent it from multiplying those breaches of equity it is set up to prevent.

The first condition to be conformed to before a legislature can be established without violating the law of equal freedom, is the acknowledgment of the right now under discussion—the right to ignore the state.[1]

Upholders of pure despotism may fitly believe state-control to be unlimited and unconditional. They who assert that men are made for governments and not governments for men, may consistently hold that no one can remove himself beyond the pale of political organization. But they who maintain that the people are the only legitimate source of power—that legislative authority is not original, but deputed—cannot deny the right to ignore the state without entangling themselves in an absurdity.

For, if legislative authority is deputed, it follows that those from whom it proceeds are the masters of those on whom it is conferred: it follows further, that as masters they confer the said authority voluntarily: and this implies that they may give or withhold it as they please. To call that deputed which is wrenched from men whether they will or not, is nonsense. But what is here true of all collectively is equally true of each separately. As a government can rightly act for the people, only when empowered by them, so also can it rightly act for the individual, only when empowered by him. If A, B, and C, debate whether they shall employ an agent to perform for them a certain service, and if whilst A and B agree to do so, C dissents, C cannot equitably be made a party to the agreement in spite of himself. And this must be equally true of thirty as of three: and if of thirty, why not of three hundred, or three thousand, or three million?

Of the political superstitions lately alluded to, none is so universally diffused as the notion that majorities are omnipotent. Under the im-

[1]Hence may be drawn an argument for direct taxation; seeing that only when taxation is direct does repudiation of state burdens become possible.

pression that the preservation of order will ever require power to be wielded by some party, the moral sense of our time feels that such power cannot rightly be conferred on any but the largest moiety of society. It interprets literally the saying that "the voice of the people is the voice of God," and transferring to the one the sacredness attached to the other, it concludes that from the will of the people, that is of the majority, there can be no appeal. Yet is this belief entirely erroneous.

Suppose, for the sake of argument, that, struck by some Malthusian panic, a legislature duly representing public opinion were to enact that all children born during the next ten years should be drowned. Does any one think such an enactment would be warrantable? If not, there is evidently a limit to the power of a majority. Suppose, again, that of two races living together—Celts and Saxons, for example—the most numerous determined to make the others their slaves. Would the authority of the greatest number be in such case valid? If not, there is something to which its authority must be subordinate. Suppose, once more, that all men having incomes under £50 a year were to resolve upon reducing every income above that amount to their own standard, and appropriating the excess for public purposes. Could their resolution be justified? If not, it must be a third time confessed that there is a law to which the popular voice must defer. What, then, is that law, if not the law of pure equity—the law of equal freedom? These restraints, which all would put to the will of the majority, are exactly the restraints set up by that law. We deny the right of a majority to murder, to enslave, or to rob, simply because murder, enslaving, and robbery are violations of that law—violations too gross to be overlooked. But if great violations of it are wrong, so also are smaller ones. If the will of the many cannot supersede the first principle of morality in these cases, neither can it in any. So that, however insignificant the minority, and however trifling the proposed trespass against their rights, no such trespass is permissible.

When we have made our constitution purely democratic, thinks to himself the earnest reformer, we shall have brought government into harmony with absolute justice. Such a faith, though perhaps needful for the age, is a very erroneous one. By no process can coercion be made equitable. The freest form of government is only the least objectional form. The rule of the many by the few we call tyranny: the rule of the few by the many is tyranny also; only of a less intense kind. "You shall do as we will, and not as you will," is in either case the declaration; and if the hundred make it to the ninety-nine, instead of the ninety-nine to the hundred, it is only a fraction less immoral. Of two such parties, whichever fulfils this declaration necessarily breaks the law of equal freedom: the only difference being that by the one it is broken in the persons of ninety-nine, whilst by the other it is broken in the persons of a hundred. And the merit of the democratic form of government consists solely in this, that it trespasses against the smallest number.

The very existence of majorities and minorities is indicative of an immoral state. The man whose character harmonizes with the moral law, we found to be one who can obtain complete happiness without diminishing the happiness of his fellows. But the enactment of public arrangements by vote implies a society consisting of men otherwise constituted—implies that the desires of some cannot be satisfied without sacrificing the desires of others—implies that in the pursuit of their happiness the majority inflict a certain amount of *un*happiness on the minority—implies, therefore, organic immorality. Thus, from another point of view, we again perceive that even in its most equitable form it is impossible for government to dissociate itself from evil; and further, that unless the right to ignore the state is recognized, its acts must be essentially criminal.

That a man is free to abandon the benefits and throw off the burdens of citizenship, may indeed be inferred from the admissions of existing authorities and of current opinion. Unprepared as they probably are for so extreme a doctrine as the one here maintained, the radicals of our day yet unwittingly profess their belief in a maxim which obviously embodies this doctrine. Do we not continually hear them quote Blackstone's assertion that "no subject of England can be constrained to pay any aids or taxes even for the defence of the realm or the support of government, but such as are imposed by his own consent, or that of his representative in parliament?" And what does this mean? It means, say they, that every man should have a vote. True: but it means much more. If there is any sense in words it is a distinct enunciation of the very right now contended for. In affirming that a man may not be taxed unless he has directly or indirectly given his consent, it affirms that he may refuse to be so taxed; and to refuse to be taxed, is to cut all connection with the state. Perhaps it will be said that this consent is not a specific, but a general one, and that the citizen is understood to have assented to every thing his representative may do, when he voted for him. But suppose he did not vote for him; and on the contrary did all in his power to get elected some one holding opposite views—what then? The reply will probably be that, by taking part in such an election, he tacitly agreed to abide by the decision of the majority. And how if he did not vote at all? Why then he cannot justly complain of any tax, seeing that he made no protest against its imposition. So, curiously enough, it seems that he gave his consent in whatever way he acted— whether he said yes, whether he said no, or whether he remained neuter! A rather awkward doctrine this. Here stands an unfortunate citizen who is asked if he will pay money for a certain proffered advantage; and whether he employs the only means of expressing his refusal or does not employ it,

we are told that he practically agrees; if only the number of others who
agree is greater than the number of those who dissent. And thus we are
introduced to the novel principle that A's consent to a thing is not determined by what A says, but by what B may happen to say!

It is for those who quote Blackstone to choose between this absurdity
and the doctrine above set forth. Either his maxim implies the right to
ignore the state, or it is sheer nonsense.

There is a strange heterogeneity in our political faiths. Systems that have
had their day, and are beginning here and there to let the daylight
through, are patched with modern notions utterly unlike in quality and
colour; and men gravely display these systems, wear them, and walk about
in them, quite unconscious of their grotesqueness. This transition state of
ours, partaking as it does equally of the past and the future, breeds hybrid
theories exhibiting the oddest union of bygone despotism and coming freedom. Here are types of the old organization curiously disguised by germs
of the new—peculiarities showing adaptation to a preceding state
modified by rudiments that prophesy of something to come—making altogether so chaotic a mixture of relationships that there is no saying to
what class these births of the age should be referred.

As ideas must of necessity bear the stamp of the time, it is useless to la-
ment the contentment with which these incongruous beliefs are held.
Otherwise it would seem unfortunate that men do not pursue to the end
the trains of reasoning which have led to these partial modifications. In the
present case, for example, consistency would force them to admit that, on
other points besides the one just noticed, they hold opinions and use arguments in which the right to ignore the state is involved.

For what is the meaning of Dissent? The time was when a man's faith
and his mode of worship were as much determinable by law as his secular
acts; and, according to provisions extant in our statute-book, are so still.
Thanks to the growth of a Protestant spirit, however, we have ignored the
state in this matter—wholly in theory, and partly in practice. But how have
we done so? By assuming an attitude which, if consistently maintained,
implies a right to ignore the state entirely. Observe the positions of the two
parties. "This is your creed," says the legislator; "you must believe and
openly profess what is here set down for you." "I shall not do any thing of
the kind," answers the nonconformist; "I will go to prison rather." "Your
religious ordinances," pursues the legislator, "shall be such as we have
prescribed. You shall attend the churches we have endowed, and adopt the
ceremonies used in them." "Nothing shall induce me to do so," is the reply;
"I altogether deny your power to dictate to me in such matters, and means
to resist to the uttermost." "Lastly," adds the legislator, "we shall require
you to pay such sums of money toward the support of these religious

institutions, as we may see fit to ask." "Not a farthing will you have from me," exclaims our sturdy Independent: "even did I believe in the doctrines of your church (which I do not), I should still rebel against your interference; and if you take my property, it shall be by force and under protest."

What now does this proceeding amount to when regarded in the abstract? It amounts to an assertion by the individual of the right to exercise one of his faculties—the religious sentiment—without let or hindrance, and with no limit save that set up by the equal claims of others. And what is meant by ignoring the state? Simply an assertion of the right similarly to exercise *all* the faculties. The one is just an expansion of the other—rests on the same footing with the other—must stand or fall with the other. Men do indeed speak of civil and religious liberty as different things: but the distinction is quite arbitrary. They are parts of the same whole and cannot philosophically be separated.

"Yes they can," interposes an objector; "assertion of the one is imperative as being a religious duty. The liberty to worship God in the way that seems to him right, is a liberty without which a man cannot fulfill what he believes to be Divine commands, and therefore conscience requires him to maintain it." True enough; but how if the same can be asserted of all other liberty? How if maintenance of this also turns out to be a matter of conscience? Have we not seen that human happiness is the Divine will— that only by exercising our faculties is this happiness obtainable—and that it is impossible to exercise them without freedom? And if this freedom for the exercise of faculties is a condition without which the Divine will cannot be fulfilled, the preservation of it is, by our objector's own showing, a duty. Or, in other words, it appears not only that the maintenance of liberty of action *may* be a point of conscience, but that it *ought* to be one. And thus we are clearly shown that the claims to ignore the state in religious and in secular matters are in essence identical.

The other reason commonly assigned for nonconformity, admits of similar treatment. Besides resisting state dictation in the abstract, the dissenter resists it from disapprobation of the doctrines taught. No legislative injunction will make him adopt what he considers an erroneous belief; and, bearing in mind his duty toward his fellow-men, he refuses to help through the medium of his purse in disseminating this erroneous belief. The position is perfectly intelligible. But it is one which either commits its adherents to civil nonconformity also, or leaves them in a dilemma. For why do they refuse to be instrumental in spreading error? Because error is adverse to human happiness. And on what ground is any piece of secular legislation disapproved? For the same reason—because thought adverse to human happiness. How then can it be shown that the state ought to be resisted in the one case and not in the other? Will any one deliberately assert that if a government demands money from us to aid in *teaching* what we think will produce evil, we ought to refuse it; but that if the money is for the purpose of *doing* what we think will produce evil, we ought not to refuse it? Yet, such is the hopeful proposition which those have to maintain who recognize the right to ignore the state in religious matters, but deny it in civil matters.

The substance of this chapter once more reminds us of the incongruity between a perfect law and an imperfect state. The practicability of the principle here laid down varies directly as social morality. In a thoroughly vicious community its admission would be productive of anarchy. In a completely virtuous one its admission will be both innocuous and inevitable. Progress toward a condition of social health—a condition, that is, in which the remedial measures of legislation will no longer be needed, is progress toward a condition in which those remedial measures will be cast aside, and the authority prescribing them disregarded. The two changes are of necessity coördinate. That moral sense whose supremacy will make society harmonious and government unnecessary, is the same moral sense which will then make each man assert his freedom even to the extent of ignoring the state—is the same moral sense which, by deterring the majority from coercing the minority, will eventually render government impossible. And as what are merely different manifestations of the same sentiment must bear a constant ratio to each other, the tendency to repudiate governments will increase only at the same rate that governments become needless.

Let not any be alarmed, therefore, at the promulgation of the foregoing doctrine. There are many changes yet to be passed through before it can begin to exercise much influence. Probably a long time will elapse before the right to ignore the state will be generally admitted, even in theory. It will be still longer before it receives legislative recognition. And even then there will be plenty of checks upon the premature exercise of it. A sharp experience will sufficiently instruct those who may too soon abandon legal protection. Whilst, in the majority of men, there is such a love of tried arrangements, and so great a dread of experiments, that they will probably not act upon this right until long after it is safe to do so.

FOR FURTHER THOUGHT

1. Truant officers seem to have existed since the beginning of formal education. Doubtless they have been called by other names. In any event, their task has been to compel the unwilling student to attend classes. *In Spencer's view, should the child be allowed to ignore the*

state (that is, the school)? Is the truant officer an evil? Does he deny the student his freedom? Does the student deny the freedom of others? Does the state (school) have a right to ignore the student?

2. Some students look at the school as a prison. They think of vacations as a time when they have been set free. To ease this and many other strains in school-student relations, a system of electives has been established in many schools. Thus, the student takes "required" subjects and ones that he elects. *How would Spencer, assuming school attendance, regard the requirement of certain courses? On what basis would he defend any course? What would constitute authority concerning the validity of courses?*

3. There have been arguments over the ages concerning the relative merits of public and private education. Many of these arguments have centered on such things as a comparison of costs, quality of program, convenience, and so forth. To Spencer this would be primarily a moral issue. *Which type of institution would be most moral in his view? How would he defend this view? Would the morality, in either case, be dependent on the condition of society or independent of that condition (that is, would the morality be inherent in the type of institution)?*

4. Many school districts have felt that it was necessary or desirable to supply texts and materials at public expense. Some notion of "child benefit" is usually invoked as an argument in defense of this practice. *According to Spencer, would there be any defense of a legitimate nature for such a practice?*

5. Teachers often speak of students who are *in* but not *of* the school. They satisfy the law and do indeed attend. However, their drive to learn the things the school requires or allows is exceedingly low. Their true interests lie elsewhere. This is the general case. Particular cases are equally easy to cite. For example, many a junior high school boy would "rather die" than recite a poem or write one. *If the teacher insists that the poem be recited, would Spencer regard this as bad strategy or bad morality? Would he regard it as bad in both senses? What authority would he cite for his judgement?*

THE FORUM AS AUTHORITY

If democracy is a social theory it suggests both a kind of society and a means to its establishment, maintenance, and improvement. Supporters of democracy have often pointed to its open-ended character and to its great utility or fruitfulness as a social system. It has been defended on the grounds of its flexibility and its consequent capacity to deal with the changing challenges it confronts. Some (including the classical liberals) regard this flexibility to be rooted in the decentralization implicit in a *laissez faire* political economy guided by the "hidden hand" of Adam Smith. This, in modern times, is coupled with a faith in competition and the inevitability of progress. These are central tenets of a social Darwinism that tends to identify change with progress. On this view, the affairs of men and nations should be put to the test of the marketplace. Here each man is asked to take stock of the situation and to act accordingly, following his own perceived self-interest. The assumption is, of course, that the society will be well served in the process. This has been and still is a popular view of the world. Much of its popularity, no doubt, stems from the removal of external authority as well as from the lifting of any conscious burden of social responsibility from the shoulders of the individual.

Such a world view, however, is certainly not universal. The modern liberals take a dim view of such a social order, both as a means to an end and as an end itself. In their view, this is a description of a jungle where each man seeks his own self-interest. This is achieved by preying on one's own kind. To this end, the classical liberal is charged with seeking a rule of "law" that would organize his preying and that would keep his prey from organizing for protection on the grounds that such organization would deny the predatory beast his natural rights.

In contrast with this doctrine that man is asocial, the modern liberal claims that man is essentially social and that this "fact" requires, first of all, an allegiance to the source of his "being." Thus, men must be concerned for the general welfare not as an assumed outcome of individual acts but as a result of the shared activity of planning with a direct eye to that goal. It is, therefore, in their view, an inadequate theory that sees government as an impartial arbiter in the competitive struggle called "life." Government, according to the modern liberal, is obligated to be an active agent in the name of the public good. To say this, however, is not to say that government should be authoritarian. It is to say that certain conditions must exist so that decisions can be made in a rational way. Rationality must not be conceived as private and serving private ends, but as public and serving public ends. Viewed in this manner, such a public rationality is not arbitrary but constitutes legitimate authority for action.

Further, if democracy is to fulfill its promise for human order men must not place their faith in stealth and cunning, which are by nature private and depend upon privacy. These are tools appropriate to the jungle. Rather, men must place their faith in openness and honesty, which are public and depend upon publicity. These are the only tools appropriate to a human community. So goes the modern liberal refrain.

It is to these conflicting conceptions that Tussman addresses himself in an attempt to extend their meaning and to present his stand—a stand that is in direct conflict with that of Spencer.

THE OFFICE OF THE CITIZEN*

THE FORUM AND THE MARKET PLACE

One of the basic difficulties in our attempt to understand democratic society and the place of the individual in it is that it combines, or confuses, two different sets of ideas and activities.

First, when we think of government, we are likely to conjure up the conception of a dignified, deliberative forum or assembly—a senate, a jury, a constitutional convention (which looms as large in our folklore)—a group of selected, qualified persons facing together a common problem, arriving at a common decision. We see them, if they are successful, clarifying the issues before them by a process of ordered, reasonable discussion, marshaling experience and evidence, speaking freely and fearlessly, responsible in partisanship, objective in judgment. It is a spectacle of disciplined human beings reasoning independently and together, deciding wisely as the result of an enlightening, cooperative process.

We are, to be sure, seldom treated to this spectacle in all its glory, but even our cynicism and disillusionment reflects the existence in our minds of this ideal or model as a basis of expectation and criticism. However much our practice falls short, the conception of the deliberative forum remains as our conception of how, at many points, the governing process should go on.

In contrast to this familiar model we must place another, even more familiar—the market place. This is the arena into which each of us brings his needs and desires, his hopes, his talents, and skills and meets others in open competition. Here we buy and sell and trade. We bargain, persuade, make deals, compromise. We try to get what we want and make the most of what we have. We try to be shrewd, fast, canny, and expect others to be the same or to pay the price. In this world we are producers and consumers, sellers and customers, and most of us have at least one foot in this world. Much of our culture, our habits and attitudes, can hardly be understood without an appreciation of the pervasive influence of the market place. As we consider the forum and the market place and the relation between them a few observations are called for:

First, the attitude and skills presupposed and needed for the successful

*Joseph Tussman, "The Office of The Citizen" (an address delivered at Michigan State University, East Lansing, Michigan). Reprinted by permission of Dr. Tussman. Dr. Tussman, author of *Obligation and the Body Politic* and head of the Philosophy Department at the University of California, Berkeley, is currently head of the Experimental College Program at that institution.

operation of each are radically different. The cooperative and the competitive processes are not the same. Deliberating and bargaining are two different processes. Statesmanship and salesmanship are distinct professions. The art of making decisions is not identical with the art of bargaining.

Second, there may be considerable "incompatibility" between these two sets of attitudes and skills. That is, they may tend to weaken and destroy each other. Within a single person one seems to grow at the expense of the other, and they co-exist only in an uneasy truce. The same uneasiness is often found in the relations between individuals who are predominantly one type or the other.

Third, there has, historically, been considerable conflict about the relative status of these two institutions. Sometimes the market place or "mechanism of the market" has been seen as virtually supplanting the deliberative forum as the shaper of society's destiny. Sometimes the market place is seen as an irrational, disturbing influence to be curbed or supplanted by more deliberate decision-making institutions.

Finally, it is possible, with references to the forum and the market place, to express both the hopes and the fears of students of society who saw the rise of popular democracy in the nineteenth century. The *hope* was that the masses of man could be given, through the public education, the habits and attitudes needed for successful operation of the deliberative forum to which, by the extension of suffrage, they were being admitted. The *fear* was that the deliberative forum—rational government—would be swamped and corrupted by the habits and attitudes of the market place. That hope is still our greatest challenge; that fear is still our danger.

THE DUAL STATUS OF THE DEMOCRATIC CITIZEN

The basic insistence of democracy is that no one can properly be subject to the law who is not also, in a meaningful sense, a rightful participant in the process by which the system of law is created and developed. Democracy, we say, is "self-government." By this we do not mean that everyone can do whatever he pleases. We mean that the same person who finds himself a "subject" of a system of government and law is also, in another capacity and at the proper time and place, a sharer in the making of the law and the process of governing. To be a member is to be both a subject and a ruler.

Thus, to be a member of a democratic society is to find oneself saddled with a public office, with a public role as well as a private station. It is this dual status—private person and public official—that makes the theory and the practice of democratic life so difficult and demanding.

It is hardly necessary in an age of individualism to stress the importance of the "private" sphere. Each person is the center of a cluster of values, aims, desires, attachments. He has his career, which expresses his bent, his own conception of his life as it should be lived, and lays claim to broad tolerance for his unique and private goods. His private scope is, of course, limited by the external necessities of group life, by the rules of the road, by the law of the land—which we accept more or less as a matter of course if they satisfy our sense of fairness or justice. But within these limits we are free to pursue our private lives. But much as this is, it is not the whole story. The citizen has yet—if democracy is not wasted on him—to play his public role, to discharge the duties of his public office, to act like and to be a ruler, to take his place in the deliberative forum.

We do not need to be reminded today of the stakes which ride on the wisdom of our political decisions, of the penalty for political folly. But perhaps we do need to be reminded that one of the chief tasks of public education is to prepare us for the adequate discharge of our public office. It may throw some light on this problem, to view too, the ways in which an aristocratic government can fail:

First, there is the familiar situation in which the aristocracy places the private interest of its members or of the ruling class generally ahead of the "public good" or general welfare of the community as a whole. Such a failure to constitute itself a proper guardian of the general welfare can, as a failure in aim, be regarded as a moral failure.

Second, an aristocracy can fail, even when well intentioned, to develop the intellectual and deliberative disciplines needed to produce decisions and policies that will achieve the desired results.

It is obvious that the shift from aristocratic to democratic government does not by itself constitute a remedy for these failures or a cure for moral and intellectual irresponsibility. It might in fact increase these dangers. For the democratic citizen may, in his ruling capacity—as a voter, for example—unconsciously or deliberately confuse his private interest with the public interest of which he is the guardian. And he may, through lack of education or through preoccupation with his private pursuits, fail to cultivate the cognitive and deliberative skills and disciplines needed in the public decision-making process. One thing is clear, however. The democratic citizen holds a public office, and it is a crucial office. A society which bestows this office on all its citizens cannot afford to fail in educating its citizens to discharge that office responsibility.

PUBLIC ISSUES

An analysis of the elements of responsibility will be facilitated, I believe, if we first consider briefly what a public question or public issue is. In an obvious and general sense, a public issue is an issue properly raised in a public forum and calling for some public, that is, governmental, action. First, public issues are "practical" issues rather than "theoretical" ones. That is, the question is should something or other be *done*. The question is one of *action*, not of *truth*. To take an example from the not too distant past: "Is the theory of evolution true?" This question, while of widespread and burning interest is not a public question as here defined. However, "Should we prohibit the teaching of the theory of evolution in the public schools?" is a public question. It calls for some action. Obviously one's view of the truth of the theory *might* determine one's position on whether the theory should be taught. It is certainly relevant. But the distinction between a question of truth and a question of action is nevertheless important. A governmental body may speak with authority about whether something should be undertaken. Its pronouncements, generally, about "truth" have no such authority.

Second, a public issue involves action by government. Such governmental action will of course impinge on private action in prohibiting or requiring that certain things be done. But the public question is always whether government should do something. For example, whether I should send my child to a public or private school is a private question. Whether the government should grant tax exemption to private schools, or even whether private schools should be allowed to exist, is a public question.

Public questions then are questions of this sort: Should the government enforce racial integration in schools? Should the government subsidize farmers? Should the government engage in a large foreign-aid program? Should Party *A* or Party *B* be entrusted with the direction of the executive branch of government for the next four years? With this in mind, let us turn to a consideration of various aspects of responsibility involved in the office of the citizen.

MORAL RESPONSIBILITY: PUBLIC AND PRIVATE INTEREST

When we are called upon to act in our capacity as public officers—as voters, for example—the crucial point is that we are being asked for our judgement on a public question. We are not being asked for an expression of our private interests. The first problem of responsibility is to see this demand and to respond to it. Suppose, for example, that the question is whether or not a system of universal military training should be established. I, as a citizen, am being asked whether in my judgment such a step would promote the general well-being of the community. I am not being asked whether I would like to be in the army or would like to have my children drafted. It is, I think, sheer dereliction of duty, sheer moral irresponsibility, to answer the second question when you are asked the first—that is, to respond to a question of public interest in terms of one's private interest.

The basic assumptions here are that there is a distinction between the public question and the private question, between the public interest and one's private interest, and that responsible action, that is, addressing oneself honestly to the public question, is possible, even though often difficult, and is required. This is, it must be noted, a "controversial" position, generally suspect and unpopular but nevertheless, I think, correct.

So much cant and hypocrisy have surrounded the discussion of the "public interest" that one is tempted to dismiss it as mere public relations rhetoric in which we package and sell our private wares. But the rhetorical corruption of a vital distinction does not lessen the significance of the distinction.

There is, perhaps, no better sample than this of the confusion of the market place and the forum, or of the influence of economic theory upon political theory. Everyone is familiar with the *laissez faire* theory that if each diligently pursues his own private interest, the public interest is automatically promoted. No one, on this view, has to worry about the public interest. It takes care of itself. It is the automatic by-product of private striving for private goods. This conception—generally abandoned in the economic sphere—still has considerable vogue in our thinking about politics and is often regarded as peculiarly "democratic." It is attractive, I think, because it really dispenses with the need for any notion of responsibility for the public good. It gives a sort of indirect moral sanction to single-minded self-interest. We find it very consoling. But it is, nevertheless, an escape from the burdens of moral responsibility.

A more serious attempt to bridge the gap between the public interest and private or "self-interest" is based on a distinction between "self-interest" and "enlightened self-interest." While "self-interest" may be identical with what one immediately wants or likes, "enlightened self-interest" is what one would want if he is wise, or far-sighted, or mature, or "social." On this view being "responsible" is acting in terms of these wider considerations rather than the "immediate" ones.

The advantage of this position seems to be that it does not require that anyone act contrary to his self-interest (enlightened, that is). And since it is widely (and dogmatically) held that we are all necessarily selfish, this view does not require that one ignore his self-interest. It only requires that men be "enlightened." I do not think, myself, that this view is satisfactory; that moral responsibility can be identified with far-sightedness in one's pursuit of self-interest. But it is a respectable view which deserves consideration.

Before moving on to other questions we must guard against a possible misconception. To say that a citizen is called on to pass judgment on a question of the public interest is not to suggest that he can easily free himself of the influence of his private station, his private interests, his "bias."

Obviously our judgment about universal military training will be affected by such things as whether we are of military age, and so forth. But to recognize this only makes us aware of the difficulty of doing what our scheme of government requires that we do. It reminds us of the discipline which the office of the citizen requires. Democracy is not the easiest, it is the hardest form of government.

We have only scratched the surface of the issues, both theoretical and practical, that exist at this point. But essentially the position taken here is that in discharging his public function, the citizen is being asked his judgment about the public interest, and that failure to discipline his private concerns is a failure in moral responsibility. The office of the citizen has at least this much in common with the office of the judge, the legislator, or the administrator.

THE COGNITIVE ASPECTS OF RESPONSIBILITY

It is, unfortunately, not the case that "everyone has a right to his opinion." Everyone has, of course, all sorts of beliefs and opinions about all sorts of things. Some we inherit, some we forge for ourselves. Some are true, some are not. A good part of the history of civilization is the process of the creation of disciplines, techniques, and institutions of ordeal by which beliefs are tested, validated, warranted, confirmed, proved. To claim a "right" to a belief is to claim that a belief has survived its ordeal—for the time at least—and has established a "confirmed" status.

To be cognitively or intellectually responsible is to move some distance toward bridging the gap between merely having beliefs and having a right to our beliefs. Responsibility is not, of course, infallibility. One can be responsible and mistaken. But the responsible mind is always working toward believing only what has a right to be believed. The adequate study of this problem—the validation of beliefs—would take us into the fields of epistemology and scientific method, logic, semantics, all aspects of the general problem of knowledge, and this is beyond the scope of our present enterprise. But we may indicate in passing the general attitudes or qualities of mind which must be cultivated:

First, *the drive to clarify and focus.* Much discussion is fruitless and frustrating because we are not talking about the same thing or are not sure what is at issue in a controversy. At some point "the issue" needs to be clarified or formulated. This takes practice and training.

Second, *the demand for evidence.* Our beliefs must sustain themselves in a world of facts—some hard, some flabby. We must cultivate a hospitable and hungry attitude toward the evidential fact.

Third, *the sense of validity.* Beliefs and facts do not come in heaps. They come organized and become more organized. They constitute "arguments" and involve inference and deduction. Most people can make valid inferences and arguments without having studied "logic." But the practice of argument can be enlightened by a study of the theory of argument.

Finally, summing up all of these is *the sense of relevance*—the feeling for what has a bearing on the matter at hand, for what can be ignored and for what is crucial. Most fallacies are fallacies of irrelevance.

These are the general qualities of a responsible mind. Education seeks to cultivate and develop them quite apart from their special bearing on politics. But they are as much needed by the citizen as by anyone and they are more seriously tried and tested in the political area than in most other areas of life.

COLLEAGEAL RESPONSIBILITY

Any analysis of the qualities required of the citizen must take account of the fact that he is not a solitary decision maker but is one of a large number of persons manning a decision-making institution. He is a colleague. When he expresses his judgment, it is in the form "I think *we* should do so and so" and that "we" signifies the fact that he is participating with colleagues in the process of arriving at a common, group decision. It is hardly enough to arrive at a sound position oneself if one fails to make his insights effectively available to others. He is, therefore, inescapably involved in communication—listening as well as speaking, reading as well as writing.

The question I wish to pose here is whether there is not a sharp distinction between the kind of communication appropriate for colleagues and the kind of communication we think of as natural between the "salesman" and the "customer." There is little doubt that "salesmanship" is, today, a dominant form of communication. It is manipulative in intent. Its concern is with getting others to behave as the salesman wants them to. There is a sort of cold war between competing salesmen and between salesmen and consumers. This is so familiar that it is difficult to make the point that there is any other sort of communication. We package and sell toothpaste. We package and sell politicians and parties. We package and sell ideas, ideologies, ways of life. All is propaganda—including education—we are told.

Naive as this may sound, I wish to suggest that there are relationships between individuals which do call for communication of a different sort—relationships which are corrupted and destroyed by the intrusion of manipulative communication, propaganda and selling. Between friends, between members of a family, between members of a team, salesmanship is a disease. It has no place in the relations between scientists in a laboratory, between doctors in a hospital, or officers on a military staff. It is also, I suggest, out of place between political colleagues—and that includes fellow citizens.

Here again is one of the points at which there is, I believe, a profound confusion between the deliberative forum and the marketplace, a point at which their "incompatibility" is most evident. It seems increasingly clear, also, that whenever a forum is taken over by "salesmanship" it becomes unfit for the making of a serious decision—we dare not trust its results, and the real decisions need to be made elsewhere. When the wells of public discussion become poisoned, it is necessary to draw water somewhere else.

I leave this highly controversial point without further treatment. But unless the distinction between colleageal communication and salesmanship is clearly grasped, I do not see how sanity and responsibility can be preserved in the training of citizens for their tasks.

One further point about the colleageal relationship—it has to do with "reasonableness" and "compromise." Everyone knows that on most issues there is disagreement. Certainty is impossible and men of good will do not always—or even often—agree. In the face of such disagreement action may, nevertheless, be necessary. Some decision must be made, and we can't all, always, have our way. The necessities of group life and action make some acceptance of this situation necessary. Some "accommodation," some "reasonableness" is called for. But to understand and deal with this situation is not easy.

To accept a verdict is not necessarily to change one's mind. There is an important place in the scheme of things for opposition; continued, responsible opposition. Something is needed that falls between "sabotage" and "conformity" and this is "as difficult as it is rare."

And finally I wish to express a doubt about the equivalence of "being reasonable" with "being willing to compromise." We are frequently told that "compromise" is the heart of the democratic process. I think this is a poor and misleading substitute for the notion of being reasonable. It is the market place version of reasonableness in the deliberative forum. A compromise may be the best bargain one can strike. It is not necessarily a reasonable decision.

FOR FURTHER THOUGHT

1. Much has been said about the market place and the "forum"—about private and public decisions. *According to Tussman, would education be a public issue? If so, would this be in total, or simply at the policy level?*
2. All curriculum decisions *are* difficult. Some are *seen* as difficult. *Assuming that the public decided that the schools should teach evolutionary theory, would each child have a right to his own opinion about the validity of the theory? Is the truth a private affair? What would constitute authority in this case according to Tussman? How does his answer relate to those suggested in Part I of this volume?*
3. In the case of a couple having no children or sending their children

to private schools, *what kind of a demand would Tussman place upon them concerning a public school bond issue? Would he place a different demand upon the parents of those attending the public school involved? What is their authority for action? What is his authority for making a demand upon either type of couple?*

4. Let us assume for the moment that education is a public issue. Let us also assume that the school people want to develop a "modern math" curriculum. This involves the expenditure of funds for such things as in-service training for teachers, books, and other materials. *If the market place is the model for democratic action, what kinds of activities will school people engage in to gain support for their program? If the "forum" is the model what kinds of activities would be appropriate? If one of the staff made the remark in the faculty lounge that he "didn't care about the methods as long as he gained the support," what model would he be most closely approximating?*

5. Teachers work with other teachers and administrators. They have many thorny problems to solve. *If a teacher discovers a particularly effective way to teach something, should he hide it from the rest of the staff in order that his students may be seen as "better"? This would do him credit under which model? Does he have a public obligation? What do the models of Tussman have to say about human relations in general, and staff relations in particular?*

6. Problems surrounding student records abound. *Does Tussman's formulation of private and public interests prove helpful in this regard? How would these concepts direct the teacher in terms of teacher-client relationships? What kinds of record information should be made available to whom, and for what purposes? What stands as authority here? In short, what constitutes democratic or just record keeping and disposal?*

CULTURE AS AUTHORITY

The excerpts from the following chapter can be seen as a thoroughgoing criticism of both the classical liberal doctrine (Spencer) and the modern liberal doctrine (Tussman). As such, it stands by itself. Yet there is in it an insistence upon the form that any conception of authority must take. To argue that the specific content within the form is lacking is to state the "real" problem confronting mankind in the view of the authors of this selection.

Put positively, the major problem of man is to establish the appropriate set of categories by which the world and all that is in it may be understood. Thus, these authors would maintain that by virtue of their criticism they are pointing men to the right questions. These are the right questions, they would maintain, because they are the fruitful questions. The classical and modern liberals have given men answers and these answers fail men. They fail men, on the view of these authors, because they are answers to the wrong questions.

For at least the reason that such a position is so unfamiliar in secular society, you are likely to find this selection as interesting as it is difficult. The authors are attempting to explicate the thinking of the American philosopher, Elijah Jordan. We will refer to the position as that held by Barnett and Otis because they not only maintain a scholarly interest in Jordan, but they generally hold his views. Of some help to the reader is the initial clue that Barnett and Otis do not believe that "beauty is in the eye of the beholders." According to them, any approach to ordering society that focuses solely on interest—either individual or group—is doomed to failure. It is doomed, not because of failure in strategy, but because it entirely misconceives the nature of the problem. The problem is not one of will. It is a question of right or culture. One must admit that such a view is not a universal one in this age of "pop" art, education, and government.

This view has enormous significance for all three forms of life. Here we have an affirmation of objective truth and a consequent conception of authority that becomes the measure of man—or in our usage—"people." They would say that man may be the measurer of all things, but he is *not* the measure of all things. There is, in short, a difference between valuation and value. This is a distinction that current democratic theory fails to note, much to the sorrow of mankind who does not even seem to be able to locate the source of his sorrow.

This is the nub of their position. The correct question is *what*, not *who*, shall rule.

———————◄◆►——————

THE AUTHORITY OF EDUCATION*

CORPORATE VERSUS MODERN LIBERAL
EDUCATIONAL THEORY

The purpose of this exploration is not to develop fully the social interpretation of authority, for this would require too extensive an analysis. Our goal of exposition and contrast may be accomplished more succinctly through consideration of a prominent educational philosophy, that of social re-

*Reprinted from *Corporate Society and Education* by George Barnett and Jack Otis by permission of The University of Michigan Press. Copyright by The University of Michigan 1961. Adapted for the present publication with the permission of the authors. Dr. Barnett, primary author of this selection, is presently Professor of Education at Michigan State University. His most recent contribution is as the editor of *Philosophy and Educational Development*. Dr. Otis is currently the Director of the School of Social Work at the University of Texas.

constructionism. Like its political expression in modern liberalism, which was a sharp reaction against the atomic individualism of classical liberalism, it is grounded upon a "group metaphysic." The universal characteristics which identify this position are clearly brought out in the writings of William O. Stanley, who will serve as the focus of this analysis. To do full justice to this position would require a much more extensive and intensive treatment than is possible here; nevertheless, the consideration of certain aspects may serve our purposes without misrepresnting social reconstructionism.

Social reconstructionism affirms the reality of a corporate society and the need for an educational philosophy in accord with that reality. It asserts the inadequacy of merely changing subjective states of mind or even ideas without effecting change in the social order. Institutional reconstruction as well as personal reconstruction is needed, and if the theory is called social reconstructionism, it nevertheless incorporates both individual and institutional change. Derived from Dewey's famous definition of education as the continuous reconstruction of experience, this philosophy maintains that both the aim and the process of education are such reconstruction.

While the account which social reconstructionism gives of contemporary society cannot be fully developed here, certain attributes bearing on the problem of authority will be described. Present-day society is marked by great change and is said to be in a period of transition, for the old ways of life have been challenged but not yet fully replaced by the new ways. The unity and common mind which marked the United States in the past are for the most part lacking today. Where before the public and the public will could usually be readily identified, now the public no longer exists with respect to many fundamental spheres; instead, there are a variety of interest groups or publics. The old community is gone; in its place have come a host of interest groups, and these are now the referents to which the individual attaches great importance. He is identified with such groups, rather than with the neighborhood or the local community. His well-being is thought to rest there. He speaks and makes his will known through these groups, rather than directly as an individual. Stanley characterizes the present state as a multigroup society, and speaks of the problems of education in relation to the problems of a society so constituted. . . .

For Stanley this reality is as it must and ought to be. Not that he favors what every interest group attempts to do in society generally or in education particularly; but for him these groups constitute publics, and since the public is sovereign in the creation of social and educational policy, such groups must necessarily have a voice in forming that policy. He denies the validity of the claims of such groups to represent the whole, although he would agree that each actually does claim, and probably sincerely, to identify its interest with the interest of the whole. Stanley warns against mistaking the voice of the most articulate or powerful groups in the local or national community as the voice of the people, while at the same time he holds that the voice of the people is now heard through such groups. On many matters the people are not now speaking with one voice, he says, but if we hope to reach the state in which they will be, then we must recognize the multiplicity of interests represented by these various groups. He insists that a gross misunderstanding of the nature of contemporary society is involved in the belief that such groups are mere self-seekers. They are now "part and parcel of the very core of American society." While there is reason to say that in some instances these groups have advocated their own interests as against the public welfare, they nevertheless cannot be wholly characterized as selfish and opposed to the public good. Such a view is far too narrow and misses their real significance for society. . . .

Perhaps, then, the key factor in an understanding of contemporary society is the interest groups and their minds and wills as representative of the individuals composing such groups. Stanley does not mean that such groups, as they are now organized, are fully democratic, or that the ideas of their individual members are fully expressed. These groups in many respects fall short of that ideal, but this in no way alters their importance as constituent elements of what will be, when unified, the public and the public will. Out of the conflict of wills, it is hoped, and through public communication, free deliberation, and mutual persuasion, a common will will arise in those areas where it does not now exist. Two points are very important here for Stanley's analysis. One is that the public and the public will are unities, that is, they exist only when there is a high degree of agreement; the public is not an originally given reality, but must be constructed out of smaller publics. The second is that the public and the public will need to be referred to particular concerns; it is false to think that they exist in reference to every matter, just as it would be false to say that they do not exist at all. Hence one needs to examine a particular sphere of endeavor in order to determine whether or not the public and the public will exist with respect to that sphere, instead of talking about the public in general.

These interest groups have explicitly or implicitly also developed educational philosophies and programs, either by indirection and because a social philosophy is also an educational philosophy, or by direct expression of such a philosophy and program. There is plenty of evidence to indicate that all of these groups have in one way or another attempted to influence the aims of the school and its program. Educators have often responded hostilely to these attempts, regarding them as an interference with the task of education. Stanley agrees that undeniably some of these groups have interfered with education, and he cites, in particular, groups which attempt to hamper intellectual freedom or which deny financial support to the schools. Such groups have sometimes succeeded in dictating the content and method of education. The educator, on the other hand, does have a moral responsibility to protect the interests of learners and is duty bound to do so by the obligation of his office. . . .

But again, it would be false to view interest groups in their relation to education solely as obstructors; nor is the task of educators primarily to shield the school from interest groups. To act in such a way would be to deny the American public its right to decide social policy. These groups, as has been said, constitute publics whose philosophies and programs are representative of portions of the public. They cannot, therefore, either be ignored or rejected as inherently inimical to education. The educational profession is right in resisting any effort to turn the school into a propaganda agency for a selfish interest group, but wrong to maintain that the ends these groups seek are unimportant for education or to hold that legitimate representatives of these groups should have no voice in determining educational objectives. If the public is to participate in the determination of educational policy, then interest groups as parts of the public must take part in these decisions. . . .

Such a view does not, however, mean that educators are confined to being mere unthinking agents, to be commanded as the public sees fit. Stanley says that the educational profession has two choices: either it can passively accept the policies imposed upon it by society, or it can exercise leadership in trying to guide and shape the public will with respect to policy. Educational statesmanship requires that the latter option be chosen.

Although both Stanley and Jordan recognize the pervasive influence of interest groups in modern society, they differ sharply in their analysis of the significance of these groups. Stanley's interpretation means that the locus of will is still the natural person, not as an isolate individual but as incorporated with his fellows in groups, social or public will being then determined as the synthesis of the various group wills. Rights also are social rather than individual. In short, neither the individual nor his will are absolute but are social in nature, and society is seen as the union of groups, the public will as the synthesis of group wills. Conceived as syntheses, they thus transcend the individual and his mind and will, while at the same time incorporating them in the final outcome. Thus new entities evolve out of individuals and their minds and wills, new entities in the form of the group and its mind and will. This conception rejects the idea of the group mind as external to or above that of the members of the group, the "metaphysical" mind or group. Abandoning the atomistic individual as a central concept, this view replaces it with that of the group.

Jordan's criticism, with which we would agree, is that the group offers no better concept than the individual, since it is only the individual pluralized. To this the social reconstructionist would object on the grounds that it is not mere addition or multiplication that he is asserting as the character of the group, but a qualitative difference; he posits a new entity that is something more than a collectivity. He insists on the changed character of the group conceived as a synthesis rather than a sum. Our inference from Jordan's position, however, is that even this qualification does not diminish the subjective character of the group concept. Synthesis or sum, the group itself is left without ground, for it remains a social rather than a cultural concept.

Jordan's view is that the group cannot provide a ground, but requires one. It is in the same position in this respect as the individual. . . . The group's justification and *raison d'être* derives neither from itself nor from society, but from a cultural objective, and consequently the latter is the only source of right. One cannot start with the group and derive rights from it, even when society at large is taken to be the group involved; but rather culture is the starting point, and the rights and obligations of the group are derived from it. . . .

Modern liberalism, while presumably anti-individualistic, does not provide a solution to the authority problem in politics or education. To make "the social" [the group][1] the basic concept in place of "the individual" is not to escape individualism. . . . The distinction here is between "the individual" and "the social" on the one hand, and "the cultural" on the other.

No principle of social order can be found in interest groups, which must go outside themselves to find their own principle. However, this does not mean that they go to other interest groups or public opinion. There would be no transcendence in such a transfer, but only more of the same. The reference would still be subjective, even though it gets "outside" the self. For the reference to become objective it must implicate culture. To be sure, as Stanley says, these interest groups are rooted in the structure of society, but it is that structure which gives them meaning, not the other way around. Labor and management as interest groups diverge; they converge in the common object of industry, which is at once their common end. Their disputes can be weighed only by reference to the object of industry; this objective is their aim and their justification as an entity, which makes of them a corporate body. Labor and management do not possess interests but rather cultural ends, in which their rights and duties inhere. Interest is self-referent, and pluralization or socialization does not objectify it. Interest, whether individual or group, is private advantage; it stands against the public good, the form of culture or the corporate person.

The appearance of an interest is not the ground of a right, even though it be subjected to social appraisal. Interest and right are not the same, but are opposed to each other; nor are interests moralized simply by being

[1]Editor's note.

publicized, if publicization means their intersubjective appraisal. Intersubjectivity is not objectivity, even though the conditions and method for appraisal are carefully described. The question is not which methods of intersubjectivity are to be used, with the assumption that if the proper method is chosen the result will be objectivity. Jordan's view is that all such methods remain subjective, and consequently he would be opposed to the use of consensus as the ultimate criterion, however well defined the method by which it is to be achieved. Value is real independently of agreement, and consensus, if it appears at all, is an epiphenomenon rather than the criterion of truth or reality. It is not because the people agree that the good is real, but rather they ought to agree because the good is real.

Is it [education, art, religion, and so forth][2] good because the people love it, or do they love it because it is good? Whether one substitutes God, or an earthly one, few, many, or all, for the people does not matter; one answer remains subjective, the other objective. The people love it (or ought to) because it is good. Culture is real and has a metaphysical status. It is derivative from no one, and like the truths of natural science, speaks in its own name and on its own authority.

Thus cultural reality is not a state of mind. The reality of the value of education does not lie in the people and their perceptions. Either education is a cultural reality in its own right and must be understood as such, or it derives that reality from some source outside itself, the people or some other. If the latter alternative is chosen, it is difficult to see how there can be institutional and professional autonomy, for the external authority may do with education and educators as it "wills." In this case education or any act may be whatever the people say that it is. The educational profession is then necessarily reduced to the status of an "agent" or "public servant," devoid of mind and will. . . .

The social approach to the problem fails because it professes a false view of what constitutes objectivity and universality. The agreement or disagreement of men tells us nothing about the reality of the object about which they are agreed or disagreed. The object does not become real when disagreement turns into agreement, nor unreal when agreement becomes disagreement. Jordan would apply this view to both the objects of nature and those of culture. When scientists fall out, no change occurs in the natural world. The tree is no less a tree, a natural fact, whether scientists agree or disagree about its qualities; similarly with objects of value. *Valet*, the object is value and does not have its worth bestowed upon it by the people or by anybody. The reality of value, of culture, is independent of agreement or disagreement. To hold otherwise is to make cultural reality

[2] Editor's note.

only a state of mind. . . . [and the question then becomes the absurd one of
which state of mind is education or art or religion, or any value].[3] . . .

Education cannot be made intelligible by an attempt to bring together
the claims of the American Legion, the AFL-CIO, the National Association
of Manufacturers, etc. These bodies exist neither in their own right nor by
grant of the people, but are constituted as legitimate agencies, are
legalized, only through their instrumentation of culture. It is by knowing
what education is that whatever claims these groups may have can be
measured, rather than the other way around. On the basis of Jordan's statements we have inferred that education is of, by, and for culture, and
hence has nothing to do with interest. Education is based upon cultural
rather than social foundations. . . .

The social view yet asks as the fundamental question of public life,
"Who shall rule?" As has been indicated, the question is a false one,
necessarily subjective, and thus carries with it the subjection rather than
the exaltation of the individual. Whatever the answer, this is the inevitable
result. If the totalitarians answer in terms of a dictator or the rule of an
elite, and if democrats answer in terms of the majority or the people as a
whole, no change in the principle of authority has been made. If social reconstructionism adheres to consensus, no change in principle is involved
either. Even though the whole be conceived as a synthesis rather than a
sum, society is defined as the whole of natural persons, whereas cor-
poratism identifies society with the whole of institutional persons. For cor-
poratism, society and state are identified with each other, and freedom
rather than tyranny is the consequence of this unity. Culture rather than
human relations is ultimate; the cultural conception rather than the social
furnishes the principle of human order. Although the social view explicitly
abandons the independent individual of atomism as a principle of
authority, and although it rejects the mere pluralization of individuals in
the group as supplying principle, its insistence that a group and group will
and mind are something more than an aggregate of individuals and individual wills and minds still does not succeed in giving will and mind an objective status. Cultural reality is not an independent entity in this view, but
comes into existence and passes out of existence according to the presence
or absence of agreement between groups. Such a view makes the group itself, conceived as a synthesis, the basic political unit or fact. To believe
that the individual is an inadequate source of authority, and to substitute
for him the group, still leaves politics with no life of its own and subject to
personal authority or domination. It is culture and its objects that are the
ground of both the individual and the group as corporate bodies, not the

[3]Editor's note.

other way around. The group does not endow culture with reality; culture endows the group with reality. Hence the social reconstructionist position, which attempts to find political reality in interest groups, has not found that reality because it has failed to distinguish between interest and right or between interest and culture. Interest is not real, or is real only as it becomes culture, in which case it is no longer interest. The political task is to convert interest into culture, not to accept it as politically real. The concepts of interest and interest group must be abandoned if the constitution of modern society as corporate is to be understood. . . .

Our conclusion is that the social reconstructionist theory of the locus of political authority is subjective, and because it is so, serious consequences follow, not only for society as a whole but for the educational institution and profession. The autonomy of education and the teaching profession is eliminated, although the social reconstructionists argue that it is not. This is not because the social reconstructionists has any intention of subjecting education and the teaching profession to external rule—his aim is directly opposed to that—but because his theory can only issue in disastrous practical consequences. To look to the group or even the total unity of people, the "public," is to admit implicitly that education as an enterprise has nothing to say on its own, that there is no necessary logic inherent in it. There can then be no thinking by educators, for there is nothing objective, no object to think about. When the authority for education is the social whole—whether local, national, or international—educators can only submit to the dominion of the antiquated habits and customs of the community, or to the "power elite's" manipulation, through its direct and indirect control, of the states of mind of the public. Jordan's corporate view, on the contrary, holds that the primary problem of education, as of any profession, is the logical one of defining its proper goals and of designating clearly the structure of materials and persons it requires to achieve these goals; then what is to be done about the mind states of the public, whether to accept or re-educate them, follows from this understanding. If a group believes in irrational medical practices, is the group's psychology to be considered ultimate, or are the principles of the science of medicine the ultimates in terms of which the group's state of mind is evaluated and an educational program developed? The social position can only tell us where people now stand in their views of life, and provides no objective grounds for where they ought to stand, except at the cost of theoretical inconsistency. Indeed, the plausibility of the social point of view is largely the result of failure to recognize the self-contradiction in its tenets.

When he views himself as a hardheaded realist or when he despairs of attaining a consensual utopia with respect to any significant issue, the modern liberal, as a result of his group metaphysic, conceives the social order as a conflicting mass of "power" groups or social "forces." These he then defends as prerequisites of freedom, and the big problem of social order and educational authority becomes one of maintaining a system of "countervailing" powers, in which none shall become big enough to overwhelm the others. For the irreconcilable struggle of atomic individuals he substitutes the irreconcilable struggle of atomic groups. The interest group, assumed to be a power or a force, can achieve no constructive synthesis, since it drives toward its own interest regardless of the effect upon other groups and the institutional whole. *Powers* or *forces* know how to destroy but are not to be identified with *will*, which is world-building. The group makes use of cunning and deception in order to marshal its power on behalf of interest, but corporate persons require intelligence in order to define and redefine ends and the structure which ends must take in the light of the complexities of interinstitutional relations and the whole of which they are functional parts. . . .

No group has a right in itself, but must be evaluated in relation to its act or the objective which it purports to realize. Power, whether that of a monolithic medical organization or union of teachers, and right are not synonymous. When right, the group affirms a corporate purpose. The right of the group to exist and act is derived from the object of culture which it seeks. There is no enmity between the state and such groups, for there is no inherent opposition between the state and culture. Furthermore, the state retains a positive responsibility to support, and not only in financial terms, all cultural acts. Society is corporate, its every act is a profession of the good, its every object is the basis upon which groups justify their right to existence and growth. Through their acts such groups maintain and extend the state as the cultural whole; far from being free from the state, they require the whole for their own sustenance. Individual and group purposes must be universalized, that is, incorporated in public and political ends. Their privacy demoralizes rather than frees, and only full publicization or politicalization can give them moral status. All acts are public or corporate, and their effect on the whole is the measure of their moral worth. While the problem of freedom in modern society may need to be seen from a new angle, as Whitehead asserts, the autonomous professions (and here Jordan includes all workers as professors of the good) are not safeguards against the inroads of the state, but are maintained by, and in turn maintain, the state as the state of culture. . . .

Educational Authority

To view the educational enterprise as a corporate act grounded in nature, that is, as objectively necessitated by the requirements placed upon man in a world capable of responding to his attempts to order it, is to suggest that education is autonomous and speaks in its own name. Its will must be done for life to be right. Therefore, educators are not businessmen speaking for their private right, but professional agents speaking on behalf of objective authority. Not educators as such, but education requires more school buildings, classroom space, laboratories, libraries, personnel, etc., in precisely the same sense that industry requires its materials and personnel if its act is to be brought to completion and complement the acts of other corporate agencies. Education's authority does not derive from any person or collectivity of persons acting as a causal mechanism from without, but from its objective end revealed in the order of fact there before men's eyes. The school system and the world in which it has its place are no mere mental phenomena to be made over into anything or nothing at all. Education, through the form it has taken, is a reality in its own right and the authority of education is the logic which best defines both its static and dynamic tendencies. Said another way, its authority is superindividual in precisely the same sense that scientific authority is superindividual. Neither science nor education has an organic reference to particular scientists or educators, but rather to the body of logically validated categories which most adequately characterizes the object of study and concomitantly defines the capacities necessary for a scientist or educator.

FOR FURTHER THOUGHT

1. Teachers are continually caught up by the demands placed upon their time and energy. *If the present-day teachers were to make the claim that they were overworked and underpaid, would Stanley, Barnett, and Otis be likely to agree? If so, what would be the basis of their agreement? Would they agree upon what would constitute a justification for such a claim?*

2. Curriculum committees dot the educational landscape. One might consider them the "forum" and again one might consider them the "market place." According to Stanley, who would be eligible to serve in the capacity of committee member? *According to Barnett and Otis who would be eligible to serve? What would be the basis of each selection? Would a different basis necessarily result in different people on the committee?*

3. Suppose someone told you that it was your "professional" duty to serve as your building representative on the local "ethical" practices committee then in the process of writing a code. *Assuming that you had the time, energy, and interest are there any grounds that might be advanced which would result in your being called "unprofessional" and "unethical" as a result of your participation on this committee? Would you accept these grounds? Which, then, would be legitimate authority —your acceptance or the grounds themselves?*

4. Unfortunately, there are times when parents and school authorities are in violent disagreement. These situations can be emotionally wearing as well as politically dangerous. Few instances are more highly charged than those that deal with failure to promote a child or with the classification of a child as "retarded." Parents sometimes insist that "John is perfectly normal" in the face of considerable evidence to the contrary. *Is this merely a matter of opinion? If so, how do you resolve such a difference? How would Barnett and Otis resolve it? Would they say that it is simply a matter of changing minds (not John's)? What if the parents won't change their minds? Does this make "John perfectly normal"?*
5. There are other conflicts, too. Many children come to school placing little value on property. Their parents often shore up this disregard—especially in terms of public property. Among this group may be those who regard all property as nonprivate and merely as something to be consumed in any way that they as individuals or as a group may wish. *Does the teacher have any obligation, on the view of Barnett and Otis, to teach a different set of values? Is it simply a matter of conflicting opinions—one group's being as good as another's? Is there any justification for saying that one opinion is better than another? If so, where does such authority reside? Is the value inherent in the property or in its potential to serve culture, that is, is it solely property that is being destroyed or is it the destruction of property as destruction of culture and potential for culture that they might deplore?*

SUGGESTIONS FOR FURTHER READING

1. Students interested in a general account of the history of political thought should consult such books as George H. Sabine's *A History of Political Theory* (New York: Holt, Rinehart and Winston, Inc., 1961).
2. Many useful books have been written on the topic of democracy. For the more historically oriented, we would suggest Morris R. Cohen's *American Thought: A Critical Sketch* (Glencoe, Ill.: Free Press, 1954), Harold Laski's *The Rise of Liberalism* (New York: Harper and Row, Publishers, 1936); and Harry K. Girvitz's *The Evolution of Liberalism* (Crowell-Collier and Macmillan, Inc., 1963). Less detailed, but continuing accounts may be found in the writings of John Dewey. His *Liberalism and Social Action* (New York: G. P. Putnam's Sons, 1935) is a good example. We would also highly recommend the brilliant article by George Sabine entitled "The Two Democratic Traditions," *Philosophic Review,* vol. 61 (October 1952).
3. Other works of merit concerning topics related to the issues of this chapter are Paul Nash, *Authority and Freedom in Education* (New York: John Wiley & Sons, Inc., 1966); R. S. Peters, *Ethics and Educa-*

tion (Glenview, Ill.: Scott, Foresman and Company, 1967); William O. Stanley, *Education and Social Integration* (New York: Teachers College, Columbia University, 1953), and Sidney Hook, *Education for Modern Man,* particularly Chapter 7 (New York: Alfred A. Knopf, 1963).

CHAPTER **8**

Liberty and Equality

Two concepts, liberty and equality, have been dear to the hearts of western man over the centuries. Many have felt that these were the fulcrum upon which all other social thought turned. We, however, have suggested that the concept of "authority" occupies that role. All else is derived from that because all else is justified in terms of some concept of "authority," be it the individual, the majority, the group, the method, or the culture or ideas (such as "utility" or "progress"), which, in turn, often rest upon the individual, the majority, the group, the method, or the culture for their justification.

Since many have confused authority with authoritarian, liberty has been seen popularly as the "absence of restraint." A close look at those of the "individualistic" tradition will reveal that even they did not really hold to this position. Restraint, they accepted. However, the only restraint that was regarded as legitimate was that which was self-imposed. As such, it really was not imposition, but, rather, legitimate. External restraint is the *real* imposition. Other conceptions of authority reveal other conceptions of imposition, as well as obligation and responsibility. One may truthfully say that one man's conception of "authority" has been another's conception of authoritarianism. Consequently, one man's conception of liberty has become another's "road to serfdom."

Equality, as a concept, has had a similar history. While "liberty" or "freedom" has been at the end of many a pen, equality has suffered by comparison in the world's literature. One of the reasons for this may be that equality has been seen as a relational concept. There are many other

311

terms that may be employed to describe appropriate relations among men. More significant, perhaps, is the long history of distinctions in social organization. Not only has society been hierarchical in organization, but this has generally been accepted as necessary for social order. In fact, hierarchy is implicit in most notions of order—order implying distinctions such as the greater, the lesser, the better, the worse, the important, the unimportant and so on.

Interestingly enough, it is clear that one of the major conceptions and distinctions of equality involves the notion of appropriateness. It is generally agreed that each man should receive his "due." Thus, many discussions have turned on the question of what was due to a man or what was due to a man under certain conditions. Justice, then, becomes a concept closely related to "equality." The medieval idea of "station" in life is another way of dealing with the same problem. Attention was directed toward assuring that a person received no more than what was due his station rather than some equal (in the sense of *same*) distribution of rewards.

The argument for equality as "sameness" has found support from diverse sources. Although Aristotle accepted a fittingness conception with regard to ruling and the ruled (some men being "slaves by nature") he was not unfriendly to equality as sameness. In his remarks on friendship there is the shrewd observation that its bonds are strained, if not sundered, by great diversities in goods. His solution was to moderate these differences among the *citizens* and to equalize men's desires. This would secure friendship (fraternity) and would require sufficient education under the laws. Yet, if all men had the same (equal) desires—to possess more than their fellow man—this would seem to be an unlikely cure for the ills besetting mankind. This is especially true for the democrats if, as Aristotle noted, "When the rich grow numerous or their properties increase, the form of government changes into an oligarchy."

The French concept of "fraternity" was a natural outgrowth of the equalitarian aspects of their revolution. The obvious and extreme diversities of the various "estates" had created several publics (peoples) and stood in the way of the development of a true national feeling—the "fraternity" of all men who *ought* to be able to call themselves "French" but who, without equality, were "French" in name only.

Interestingly enough, men who were horrified by the French Revolution could also accept the idea of equality as sameness. They, in their fear of "king mob," were not thinking of eliminating the general diversity of human conditions. They were committed to extending them. Equality as sameness was not to deal with the material conditions of life, but with sameness before the law or rules. Within the same rules, there would be a diversity of human conditions that were the result of a "fair" race. There would be losers, but each had only himself to blame rather than the capricious decisions of the powerful who held themselves above the law. The English and American experience has been marked by those who have been passionately committed to equality as sameness so that they might pursue "happiness" (the accumulation of property in its various forms).

The relationship between these two concepts—liberty and equality—has been a matter of deep concern. Men have wanted to hold both as fundamental directives for their behavior. Are they compatible concepts? If so, how are they to be harmonized? If not, which concept must be jettisoned and with what justification? In societies that hold to both, what manner of man do we find and do they seek to create?

We profess to have a free society. We profess to educate for freedom—free men and a free world. Is a free society a contradiction in terms? Is "education for freedom" a contradiction in terms? In aiming at the goal of freedom, we claim the obligation to provide equal educational opportunity. In fact, such a provision is a central commitment for many educators. Yet it is not entirely clear what would constitute a condition of "equal opportunity." Is it a "formal" notion, inasmuch as there is no law against it, that all men have the same opportunity? Is it a material notion requiring that laws be enacted to enable it (that is, to organize the social and material capacities of men to compensate for those in less fortunate circumstances)? Does equality of opportunity mean sameness of treatment? Does it mean different treatment—that which is viewed as "fitting" or equitable? Are there some situations in which one conception is valid and other situations in which another conception is valid? If so, how does one know when to apply which conception?

These are extraordinarily significant questions in the day-to-day activities of school personnel. Decisions on the distribution of funds, curriculum time, building space, disposition of "discipline" cases, and evaluation of students all assume some conception of equality and freedom. What sense, if any, can be made out of these concepts and their relations in order to bring clarity to democracy as a social and educational theory?

INDIVIDUALISM AS INDEPENDENCE

As suggested by the previous chapter and the overview to this one, there is no clear agreement as to what constitutes authority in human affairs. Derivatively, there is a similar disagreement upon what constitutes a free man or the conditions of liberty. This is true in spite of the fact that most people would claim that their society and its institutions, *especially the school,* should aim at that end.

To this point, we have looked at the works of political scientists, statesmen, philosophers, and educators. Often overlooked as a source of insight and influence is the artist. The following selection was written by the novelist Ayn Rand.

The speech of the major character in this excerpt is designed to tell us what freedom really is and, consequently, what the school should aim at and how it should be allowed to act in pursuit of that aim.

————————◄◆►————————

THE FOUNTAINHEAD*

"Thousands of years ago, the first man discovered how to make fire. He was probably burned at the stake he had taught his brothers to light. He was considered an evildoer who had dealt with a demon mankind dreaded. But thereafter men had fire to keep them warm, to cook their food, to light their caves. He had left them a gift they had not conceived and he had lifted darkness off the earth. Centuries later, the first man invented the wheel. He was probably torn on the rack he had taught his brothers to build. He was considered a transgressor who ventured into forbidden territory. But thereafter, men could travel past any horizon. He had left them a gift they had not conceived and he had opened the roads of the world.

"That man, the unsubmissive and first, stands in the opening chapter of every legend mankind has recorded about its beginning. Prometheus was chained to a rock and torn by vultures—because he had stolen the fire of the gods. Adam was condemned to suffer—because he had eaten the fruit of the tree of knowledge. Whatever the legend, somewhere in the shadows of its memory mankind knew that its glory began with one and that that one paid for his courage.

"Throughout the centuries there were men who took first steps down new roads armed with nothing but their own vision. Their goals differed, but they all had this in common: that the step was first, the road new, the vision unborrowed, and the response they received—hatred. The great creators—the thinkers, the artists, the scientists, the inventors—stood alone against the men of their time. Every great new thought was opposed. Every great new invention was denounced. The first motor was considered foolish. The ariplane was considered impossible. The power loom was considered vicious. Anesthesia was considered sinful. But the men of unbor-

---

*Ayn Rand, *The Fountainhead* (Indianapolis, Ind.: The Bobbs-Merrill Company, Inc., 1943), pp. 736–743. Miss Rand is a noted author. Among her more widely read books are *Anthem*, *We The Living*, and *Atlas Shrugged*.

rowed vision went ahead. They fought, they suffered and they paid. But they won.

"No creator was prompted by a desire to serve his brothers, for his brothers rejected the gift he offered and that gift destroyed the slothful routine of their lives. His truth was his only motive. His own truth, and his own work to achieve it in his own way. A symphony, a book, an engine, a philosophy, an airplane or a building—that was his goal and his life. Not those who heard, read, operated, believed, flew or inhabited the thing he had created. The creation, not its users. The creation, not the benefits others derived from it. The creation which gave form to his truth. He held his truth above all things and against all men.

"His vision, his strength, his courage came from his own spirit. A man's spirit, however, is his self. That entity which is his consciousness. To think, to feel, to judge, to act are functions of the ego.

"The creators were not selfless. It is the whole secret of their power— that it was self-sufficient, self-motivated, self-generated. A first cause, a fount of energy, a life force, a Prime Mover. The creator served nothing and no one. He lived for himself.

"And only by living for himself was he able to achieve the things which are the glory of mankind. Such is the nature of achievement.

"Man cannot survive except through his mind. He comes on earth unarmed. His brain is his only weapon. Animals obtain food by force. Man has no claws, no fangs, no horns, no great strength of muscle. He must plant his food or hunt it. To plant, he needs a process of thought. To hunt, he needs weapons, and to make weapons—a process of thought. From this simplest necessity to the highest religious abstraction, from the wheel to the skyscraper, everything we are and everything we have comes from a single attribute of man—the function of his reasoning mind.

"But the mind is an attribute of the individual. There is no such thing as a collective brain. There is no such thing as a collective thought. An agreement reached by a group of men is only a compromise or an average drawn upon many individual thoughts. It is a secondary consequence. The primary act—the process of reason—must be performed by each man alone. We can divide a meal among many men. We cannot digest it in a collective stomach. No man can use his lungs to breathe for another man. No man can use his brain to think for another. All the functions of body and spirit are private. They cannot be shared or transferred.

"We inherit the products of the thought of other men. We inherit the wheel. We make a cart. The cart becomes an automobile. The automobile becomes an airplane. But all through the process what we receive from others is only the end product of their thinking. The moving force is the creative faculty which takes this product as material, uses it and orginates the next step. This creative faculty cannot be given or received, shared or borrowed. It belongs to single, individual men. That which it creates is the property of the creator. Men learn from one another. But all learning is only the exchange of material. No man can give another the capacity to think. Yet that capacity is our only means of survival.

"Nothing is given to man on earth. Everything he needs has to be produced. And here man faces his basic alternative: he can survive in only one of two ways—by the independent work of his own mind or as a parasite fed by the minds of others. The creator originates. The parasite borrows. The creator faces nature alone. The parasite faces nature through an intermediary.

"The creator lives for his work. He needs no other men. His primary goal is the conquest of men.

"The creator lives for his work. He needs no other men. His primary goal is within himself. The parasite lives second-hand. He needs others. Others become his prime motive.

"The basic need of the creator is independence. The reasoning mind cannot work under any form of compulsion. It cannot be curbed, sacrificed or subordinated to any consideration whatsoever. It demands total independence in function and in motive. To a creator, all relations with men are secondary.

"The basic need of the second-hander is to secure his ties with men in order to be fed. He places relations first. He declares that man exists in order to serve others. He preaches altruism.

"Altruism is the doctrine which demands that man live for others and place others above self.

"No man can live for another. He cannot share his spirit just as he cannot share his body. But the second-hander has used altruism as a weapon of exploitation and reversed the base of mankind's moral principles. Men have been taught every precept that destroys the creator. Men have been taught dependence as a virtue.

"The man who attempts to live for others is a dependent. He is a parasite in motive and makes parasites of those he serves. The relationship produces nothing but mutual corruption. It is impossible in concept. The nearest approach to it in reality—the man who lives to serve others—is the slave. If physical slavery is repulsive, how much more repulsive is the concept of servility of the spirit? The conquered slave has a vestige of honor. He has the merit of having resisted and of considering his condition evil. But the man who enslaves himself voluntarily in the name of love is the basest of creatures. He degrades the dignity of man and he degrades the conception of love. But this is the essence of altruism.

"Men have been taught that the highest virtue is not to achieve, but to give. Yet one cannot give that which has not been created. Creation comes before distribution—or there will be nothing to distribute. The need of the creator comes before the need of any possible beneficiary. Yet we are taught to admire the second-hander who dispenses gifts he has not produced above the man who made the gifts possible. We praise an act of charity. We shrug at an act of achievement.

"Men have been taught that their first concern is to relieve the suffering of others. But suffering is a disease. Should one come upon it, one tries to give relief and assistance. To make that the highest test of virtue is to make suffering the most important part of life. Then man must wish to see others suffer—in order that he may be virtuous. Such is the nature of altruism. The creator is not concerned with disease, but with life. Yet the work of the creators has eliminated one form of disease after another, in man's body and spirit, and brought more relief from suffering than any altruist could ever conceive.

"Men have been taught that it is a virtue to agree with others. But the creator is the man who disagrees. Men have been taught that it is a virtue to swim with the current. But the creator is the man who goes against the current. Men have been taught that it is a virtue to stand together. But the creator is the man who stands alone.

"Men have been taught that the ego is the synonym of evil, and selflessness the ideal of virtue. But the creator is the egoist in the absolute sense, and the selfless man is the one who does not think, feel, judge or act. These are functions of the self.

"Here the basic reversal is most deadly. The issue has been perverted and man has been left no alternative—and no freedom. As poles of good and evil, he was offered two conceptions: egoism and altruism. Egoism was held to mean the sacrifice of others to self. Altruism—the sacrifice of self to others. This tied man irrevocably to other men and left him nothing but a choice of pain: his own pain borne for the sake of others or pain inflicted upon others for the safe of self. When it was added that man must find joy in self-immolation, the trap was closed. Man was forced to accept masochism as his ideal—under the threat that sadism was his only alternative. This was the greatest fraud ever perpetrated on mankind.

"This was the device by which dependence and suffering were perpetuated as fundamentals of life.

"The choice is not self-sacrifice or domination. The choice is independence or dependence. The code of the creator or the code of the second-hander. This is the basic issue. It rests upon the alternative of life or death. The code of the creator is built on the needs of the reasoning mind which allows man to survive. The code of the second-hander is built on the needs of a mind incapable of survival. All that which proceeds from man's independent ego is good. All that which proceeds from man's dependence upon men is evil.

"The egoist in the absolute sense is not the man who sacrifices others. He is the man who stands above the need of using others in any manner. He does not function through them. He is not concerned with them in any primary matter. Not in his aim, not in his motive, not in his thinking, not in his desires, not in the source of his energy. He does not exist for any other man—and he asks no other man to exist for him. This is the only form of brotherhood and mutual respect possible between men.

"Degrees of ability vary, but the basic principle remains the same: the degree of a man's independence, initiative and personal love for his work determines his talent as a worker and his worth as a man. Independence is the only gauge of human virtue and value. What a man is and makes of himself; not what he has or hasn't done for others. There is no substitute for personal dignity. There is no standard of personal dignity except independence.

"In all proper relationships there is no sacrifice of anyone to anyone. An architect needs clients, but he does not subordinate his work to their wishes. They need him, but they do not order a house just to give him a commission. Men exchange their work by free, mutual consent to mutual advantage when their personal interests agree and they both desire the exchange. If they do not desire it, they are not forced to deal with each other. They seek further. This is the only possible form of relationship between equals. Anything else is a relation of slave to master, or victim to executioner.

"No work is ever done collectively, by a majority decision. Every creative job is achieved under the guidance of a single individual thought. An architect requires a great many men to erect his building. But he does not ask them to vote on his design. They work together by free agreement and each is free in his proper function. An architect uses steel, glass, concrete, produced by others. But the materials remain just so much steel, glass and concrete until he touches them. What he does with them is his individual product and his individual property. This is the only pattern for proper co-operation among men.

"The first right on earth is the right of the ego. Man's first duty is to himself. His moral law is never to place his prime goal within the persons of others. His moral obligation is to do what he wishes, provided his wish does not depend *primarily* upon other men. This includes the whole sphere of his creative faculty, his thinking, his work. But it does not include the sphere of the gangster, the altruist and the dictator.

"A man thinks and works alone. A man cannot rob, exploit or rule—alone. Robbery, exploitation and ruling presuppose victims. They imply dependence. They are the province of the second-hander.

"Rulers of men are not egoists. They create nothing. They exist entirely through the persons of others. Their goal is in their subjects, in the activity of enslaving. They are as dependent as the beggar, the social worker and the bandit. The form of dependence does not matter.

"But men were taught to regard second-handers—tyrants, emperors, dictators—as exponents of egoism. By this fraud they were made to destroy the ego, themselves and others. The purpose of the fraud was to destroy the creators. Or to harness them. Which is a synonym.

"From the beginning of history, the two antagonists have stood face to face: the creator and the second-hander. When the first creator invented the wheel, the first second-hander responded. He invented altruism.

"The creator—denied, opposed, persecuted, exploited—went on, moved forward and carried all humanity along on his energy. The second-hander contributed nothing to the process except the impediments. The contest has another name: the individual against the collective.

"The 'common good' of a collective—a race, a class, a state—was the claim and justification of every tyranny ever established over men. Every major horror of history was committed in the name of an altruistic motive. Has any act of selfishness ever equaled the carnage perpetrated by disciples of altruism? Does the fault lie in men's hypocrisy or in the nature of the principle? The most dreadful butchers were the most sincere. They believed in the perfect society reached through the guillotine and the firing squad. Nobody questioned their right to murder since they were murdering for an altruistic purpose. It was accepted that man must be sacrificed for other men. Actors change, but the course of the tragedy remains the same. A humanitarian who starts with declarations of love for mankind and ends with a sea of blood. It goes on and will go on so long as men believe that an action is good if it is unselfish. That permits the altruist to act and forces his victims to bear it. The leaders of collectivist movements ask nothing for themselves. But observe the results.

"The only good which men can do to one another and the only statement of their proper relationship is—Hands off!

"Now observe the results of a society built on the principle of individualism. This, our country. The noblest country in the history of men. The country of greatest achievement, greatest prosperity, greatest freedom. This country was not based on selfless service, sacrifice, renunciation or any precept of altruism. It was based on a man's right to the pursuit of happiness. His own happiness. Not anyone else's. A private, personal, selfish motive. Look at the results. Look into your own conscience.

"It is an ancient conflict. Men have come close to the truth, but it was destroyed each time and one civilization fell after another. Civilization is the progress toward a society of privacy. The savage's whole existence is public, ruled by the laws of his tribe. Civilization is the process of setting man free from men.

"Now, in our age, collectivism, the rule of the second-hander and second-rater, the ancient monster, has broken loose and is running amuck. It has brought men to a level of intellectual indecency never equaled on earth. It has reached a scale of horror without precedent. It has poisoned every mind. It has swallowed most of Europe. It is engulfing our country.

"I am an architect. I know what is to come by the principle on which it is built. We are approaching a world in which I cannot permit myself to live.

"Now you know why I dynamited Cortlandt.

"I designed Cortlandt. I gave it to you. I destroyed it.

"I destroyed it because I did not choose to let it exist. It was a double monster. In form and in implication. I had to blast both. The form was mutilated by two second-handers who assumed the right to improve upon that which they had not made and could not equal. They were permitted to do it by the general implication that the altruistic purpose of the building superseded all rights and that I had no claim to stand against it.

"I agreed to design Cortlandt for the purpose of seeing it erected as I designed it and for no other reason. That was the price I set for my work. I was not paid.

"I do not blame Peter Keating. He was helpless. He had a contract with his employers. It was ignored. He had a promise that the structure he offered would be built as designed. The promise was broken. The love of a man for the integrity of his work and his right to preserve it are now considered a vague intangible and an inessential. You have heard the prosecutor say that. Why was the building disfigured? For no reason. Such acts never have any reason, unless it's the vanity of some second-handers who feel they have a right to anyone's property, spiritual or material. Who permitted them to do it? No particular man among the dozens in authority. No one cared to permit or to stop it. No one was responsible. No one can be held to account. Such is the nature of all collective action.

"I did not receive the payment I asked. But the owners of Cortlandt got what they needed from me. They wanted a scheme devised to build a structure as cheaply as possible. They found no one else who could do it to their satisfaction. I could and did. They took the benefit of my work and made me contribute it as a gift. But I am not an altruist. I do not contribute gifts of this nature.

"It is said that I have destroyed the home of the destitute. It is forgotten that but for me the destitute could not have had this particular home. Those who were concerned with the poor had to come to me, who have never been concerned, in order to help the poor. It is believed that the poverty of the future tenants gave them a right to my work. That their need constituted a claim on my life. That it was my duty to contribute anything demanded of me. This is the second-hander's credo now swallowing the world.

"I came here to say that I do not recognize anyone's right to one minute of my life. Nor to any part of my energy. Nor to any achievement of mine. No matter who makes the claim, how large their number or how great their need.

"I wished to come here and say that I am a man who does not exist for others.

"It had to be said. The world is perishing from an orgy of self-sacrificing.

"I wished to come here and say that the integrity of a man's creative work is of greater importance than any charitable endeavor. Those of you who do not understand this are the men who're destroying the world.

"I wished to come here and state my terms. I do not care to exist on any others.

"I recognize no obligations toward men except one: to respect their freedom and to take no part in a slave society. To my country, I wish to give the ten years which I will spend in jail if my country exists no longer. I will spend them in memory and in gratitude for what my country has been. It will be my act of loyalty, my refusal to live or work in what has taken its place.

"My act of loyalty to every creator who ever lived and was made to suffer by the force responsible for the Cortlandt I dynamited. To every tortured hour of loneliness, denial, frustration, abuse he was made to spend —and to the battles he won. To every creator whose name is known—and to every creator who lived, struggled and perished unrecognized before he could achieve. To every creator who was destroyed in body or in spirit. To Henry Cameron. To Steven Mallory. To a man who doesn't want to be named, but who is sitting in this courtroom and knows that I am speaking of him."

FOR FURTHER THOUGHT

1. Teachers often help students to define problems and suggest activities upon which they can agree. Students then develop a group project, several group projects, and even individual projects that fit into the problem as the group has defined it. *Would such a practice be considered perverted by Rand? Would a judgment on this score be dependent upon other information? If so, what kind of information might be relevant?*

2. Cooperation flowing from the socialization processes is considered a "good" in many educational circles. After all, people *must* learn to "get along" in this world. *Would this be considered miseducation by Rand? Why?*

3. Teachers like to be considered as ethical people. Schools are considered to be ethical institutions. The operators of schools band together in the attempt to form professional associations. Yet some people might

very well charge that today's schools and teachers are basically immoral. *What would be a Randian's basis for such action? What would he say about teaching methods, curriculum, attendance, and taxation with regard to public education?*

4. Teachers have been known to send students to the principal's office. Principals have been known to suspend students from school. These kinds of actions are observed at every level—even on the graduate school level. *What would be a Randian's basis for such action?*

5. Of course, students are not the only ones who can undergo suspension. Many attempts have been made to regulate both the hiring and the firing of teachers. State or provincial certification regulations and tenure laws have been enacted. *Do these things (among others) make teachers "second-handers"? Do these things make teachers free or do they enslave them? Does the voluntary acceptance of regulation make any difference? How can you tell when an action is voluntary?*

INDIVIDUALISM AS INTERDEPENDENCE

Opposed to the notion that liberty is the "absence of external restraint," we find the modern liberals. They also oppose the modification of the doctrine as follows: "Liberty is the right to pursue your own self-interest as long as you do not interfere with the rights of others to do the same." Specifically, the modern liberal would claim that the classical liberal conception of liberty was overly formal. In their view, the classical conception is essentially legalistic and political. Thus, it neglects the material conditions that would encourage *real* liberty, political or otherwise.

Another way of casting the distinction between the two groups is in their conception of the role of government in human affairs. The classical liberal has seen government as an evil. Its functions were limited and negative—protections against violations of liberty as they conceived it. On the neutral side, the classical liberal would emphasize that government *allowed* man to seek his own self-interest. Opposed to this negative and neutral conception of government stand the modern liberals. They would admit the police functions of government, but emphasize the obligation of government to a positive role that would *enable* each man to fulfill himself as a social individual. Thus, this doctrine adds social and economic as well as legal or political dimensions to the conception of liberty. As Dewey, for example, held that freedom involved intelligent choice that could be acted upon to achieve its fruition. Freedom to do requires the means of its achievement. Consequently, for Dewey legal protection from interference does not exhaust the most important aspects of freedom.

Dewey, of course, is one of the most famous spokesmen for the positive role of government in society and teacher in the classroom. He presents his case in the following selection.

————◄◆►————

LIBERTY AND SOCIAL CONTROL*

Today there is no word more bandied about than liberty. Every effort at planned control of economic forces is resisted and attacked, by a certain group, in the name of liberty. The slightest observation shows that this group is made up of those who are interested, from causes that are evident, in the preservation of the economic status quo; that is to say, in the maintenance of the customary privileges and legal rights they already possess. When we look at history in the large we find that the demand for liberty and efforts to achieve it have come from those who wanted to *alter* the institutional set-up. This striking contrast is a stimulus to thoughtful inquiry. What does liberty mean anyway? Why should the cause of liberty have been identified in the past with efforts at change of laws and institutions while at the present time a certain group is using all its vast resources to convince the public that change of economic institutions is an attack upon liberty?

Well, in the first place, liberty is not just an idea, an abstract principle. It is power, effective power to do specific things. There is no such thing as liberty in general; liberty, so to speak, at large. If one wants to know what the condition of liberty is at a given time, one has to examine what persons *can* do and what they *cannot* do. The moment one examines the question from the standpoint of effective action, it becomes evident that the demand for liberty is a demand for power, either for possession of powers of action not already possessed or for retention and expansion of powers already possessed. The present ado in behalf of liberty by the managers and beneficiaries of the existing economic system is immediately explicable if one views it as a demand for preservation of the powers they already possess. Since it is the existing system that gives them these powers, liberty is thus inevitably identified with the perpetuation of that system. Translate the present hullabaloo about liberty into struggle to retain powers already possessed, and it has a meaning.

In the second place, the possession of effective power is always a matter

*John Dewey, *Problems of Men* (New York: Philosophical Library, Inc., 1946). Professor Dewey is, perhaps, America's best known philosopher. A prolific writer, he focused much of his energy on current social issues and social philosophy in addition to his contributions to philosophy of education and philosophy proper.

of the *distribution* of power that exists at the time. A physical analogy may make clear what I mean. Water runs downhill and electric currents flow because of *difference in potentials*. If the ground is level, water is stagnant. If on the level ocean, there are dashing waves, it is because there is another power operating, that of the winds, occasioned ultimately by a difference in the distribution of temperature at different points. There is no such thing physically as manifestation of energy or effective power by one thing except in relation to the energy manifested by other things. There is no such thing as the liberty or effective power of an individual, group, or class, except in relation to the liberties, the effective powers, of *other* individuals, groups, and classes.

Demand for retention of powers already possessed on the part of a particular group means, therefore, that other individuals and groups shall continue to possess only the capacities in and for activity which *they* already possess. Demand for increased power at one point means demands for change in the distribution of powers, that is, for less power somewhere else. You cannot discuss or measure the liberty of one individual or group of individuals without thereby raising the question of the effect upon the liberty of others, any more than you can measure the energy of a head water at the head without measuring the difference of levels.

In the third place, this relativity of liberty to the existing distribution of powers of action, while meaning that there is no such thing as absolute liberty, also necessarily means that wherever there is liberty at one place there is restraint at some other place. *The system of liberties that exists at any time is always the system of restraints or controls that exists at that time.* No one can *do* anything except in relation to what others can do and cannot do.

These three points are general. But they cannot be dismissed as mere abstractions. For when they are applied either in idea or in action they mean that liberty is always a *social* question, not an individual one. For the liberties that any individual actually has depends upon the distribution of powers or liberties that exists, and this distribution is identical with actual social arrangements, legal and political—and, at the present time, economic, in a peculiarly important way.

Return now to the fact that historically the great movements for human liberation have always been movements to change institutions and not to preserve them intact. It follows from what has been said that there have been movements to bring about a changed distribution of power to do—and power to think and to express thought is a power to do—such that there would be a more balanced, a more equal, even, and equitable system of human liberties.

The present movement for social control of industry, money and credit is simply a part of this endless human struggle. The present attempt to define liberty in terms of the existing distribution of liberty is an attempt to maintain the existing system of control of power, of social restraints and regimentations. I cannot go here into the nature and consequences of this system. If one is satisfied with it, let him support the conception of liberty put forth by, say, the Liberty League, which represents the present economic system. But let him not be fooled into thinking that the issue is liberty versus restraint and regimentation. For the issue is simply that of one system of control of the social forces upon which the distribution of liberties depends, versus some other system of social control which would bring about another distribution of liberties. And let those who are struggling to replace the present economic system by a cooperative one also remember that in struggling for a new system of social restraints and controls they are also struggling for a more equal and equitable balance of powers that will enhance and multiply the effective liberties of the mass of individuals. Let them not be jockeyed into the position of supporting social control at the expense of liberty, when what they want is another method of social control than the one that now exists, one that will increase significant human liberties.

It is nonsense to suppose that we do not have social control *now*. The trouble is that it is exercised by the few who have economic power, at the expense of the liberties of the many and at the cost of increasing disorder, culminating in that chaos of war which the representatives of liberty for the possessive class identify with true discipline.

It is constantly urged by one school of social thought that liberty and equality are so incompatible that liberalism is not a possible social philosophy. The argument runs as follows: If liberty is the dominant social and political goal then the natural diversity and inequality of natural endowments will inevitably work out to produce social inequalities. You cannot give free rein to natural capacities, so runs the argument, without producing marked inequality in cultural, economic, and political status as a necessary consequence. On the other hand, if equality is made the goal, there must, the argument continues, be important restrictions put upon the exercise of liberty. The incompatibility of liberty and equality is the rock, it is asserted, upon which liberalism is bound to founder. Consequently, the school of liberalism that identifies liberty with *laissez-faire* claims to be the only logical school of liberalism, and it is willing to tolerate any amount of actual social inequality provided it is the result of the free exercise of natural powers.

The original idea and ideal of democracy combined equality and liberty as coordinate ideals, adding to them, in the slogan of the French Revolution, fraternity as a third coordinate. Both historically and actually the possibility of realization of the democratic ideal is conditioned, therefore, upon the possibility of working out in social practice and social institutions a combination of equality and liberty. As is proved by the present state of democracy in nominally democratic countries the problem is a practical one.

The formula of early democratic political liberalism was that men are born free and equal. Superficial critics have thought that the formula is peremptorily refuted by the fact that human beings are not born equal in strength and abilities or natural endowments. The formula, however, never assumed that they were. Its meaning is the same as that of the familiar saying that in the grave pauper and millionaire, monarch and serf, are equal. It was a way of saying that political inequality is the product of social institutions; that there is no "natural" inherent difference between those of one social caste, class, or status and those of another caste, class, or status; that such differences are the product of law and social customs. The same principle holds of economic differences; if one individual is born to the possession of property and another is not, the difference is due to social laws regulating inheritance and the possession of property. Translated into terms of concrete action, the formula means that inequalities of natural endowment should operate under laws and institutions that do not place permanent handicaps upon those of lesser gifts; that the inequalities in the distribution of powers, achievements, and goods that occur in society should be strictly proportionate to natural inequalities. In the present social arrangement, opportunities for individuals are determined by the social and family status of individuals; the institutional set-up of human relations provides openings to members of certain classes to the detriment of other classes. The challenge of progressive and liberal democracy can be stated in the familiar war cry: Institutions and laws should be such as to secure and establish equality for all.

This formula expressed revolt against the existing institutions that automatically limited the opportunities of the mass of individuals. It was this revolt and the aspiration it embodied that was the essence of democratic liberalism in its earlier political and humanitarian manifestations. But the rise of machine-industry, controlled by finance-capitalism, was a force that was not taken into account. It gave liberty of action to those particular natural endowments and individuals that fitted into the new economic picture. Above all, the Industrial Revolution gave scope to the abilities involved in acquiring property and to the employment of that wealth in further acquisitions. The employment of these specialized acquisitive abilities has resulted in the monopoly of power in the hands of the few to control the opportunities of the wide masses and to limit their free activities in realizing their natural capacities.

In short, the common assertion of the mutual incompatibility of equality and liberty rests upon a highly formal and limited concept of liberty. It overlooks and rules out the fact that the *actual* liberties of one human being depend upon the powers of action that existing institutional arrangements accord to other individuals. It conceives of liberty in a completely abstract way. The democratic ideal that unites equality and liberty is, on the other hand, a recognition that actual and concrete liberty of opportunity and action is dependent upon equalization of the political and economic conditions under which individuals are alone free *in fact*, not *in some abstract metaphysical way.* The tragic breakdown of democracy is due to the fact that the identification of liberty with the maximum of unrestrained individualistic action in the economic sphere, under the institutions of capitalistic finance, is as fatal to the realization of liberty for all as it is fatal to the realization of equality. It is destructive of liberty for the many precisely because it is destructive of genuine equality of opportunity.

The social philosophy of Thomas Jefferson is regarded as outmoded by many persons because it seems to be based upon the then existing agrarian conditions and to postulate the persistence of the agrarian régime. It is then argued that the rise of industry to a position superior to that of agriculture has destroyed the basis of Jeffersonian democracy. This is a highly superficial view. Jefferson predicted what the effects of rise of the economics and politics of an industrial régime would be, unless the independence and liberty characteristic of the farmer, under conditions of virtually free land, were conserved. His predictions have been realized. It was not agrarianism per se that he really stood for, but the kind of liberty and equality that the agrarian régime made possible when there was an open frontier. The early Jeffersonians, for example, held that national credit was a national asset and ought to be nationally controlled; they were bitterly opposed to the capture of national credit by private banking institutions. They were even opposed to financing wars by means of bonds and debts where the income accrued to private individuals, maintaining that wars should be paid for during the time they occur through taxation upon the incomes of the wealthy.

I refer to this particular instance merely by way of illustration, and to indicate how far away so-called Jeffersonian democracy has drifted from the original ideas and policies of any democracy whatsoever. The drift of nominal democracy from the conception of life which may properly be characterized as democratic has come about under the influence of a so-called rugged individualism that defines the liberty of individuals in the terms of the inequality bred by existing economic-legal institutions. In so doing, it puts an almost exclusive emphasis upon those natural capacities of individuals that have power to effect pecuniary and materialistic acquisitions. For our existing materialism, with the blight to which it subjects the cultural development of individuals, is the inevitable product of exaggera-

tion of the economic liberty of the few at the expense of the all-around
liberty of the many. And, I repeat, this limitation upon genuine liberty is
the inevitable product of the inequality that arises and must arise under
the operations of institutionally established and supported finance-
capitalism.

   The idea of civil liberties developed step by step as the ideals of
liberalism displaced the earlier practices of political autocracy, which
subordinated subjects to the arbitrary will of governmental authorities. In
tradition, rather than in historic fact, their origin for English-speaking
people is associated with the Magna Carta. Civil liberties were definitely
formulated in the Bill of Rights adopted by the British Parliament in 1689
after the exile of the Stuarts and the final overthrow of dynastic government in that country. At the time of the revolt of the American colonies
against the mother country many of the state constitutions embodied
clauses very similar to those in the Bill of Rights. They were not contained
in the Federal Constitution adopted at a time of reaction against the more
radical revolutionary ideas, Hamilton being especially opposed to their
inclusion. But in order to secure ratification by the several states, constitutional guarantees of civil rights were added in the first ten amendments in
1789. They contained, however, little more than what had become com-
monplaces of the rights of citizens in Great Britain. The only novel features
in our constitutional provisions were the denial to government of the right
of establishing religion and a greater emphasis upon the right of individuals to complete freedom in choice of a form of religious worship. The gist
of the civil rights, constitutionally guaranteed to individuals, was freedom
of the press, of peaceful assemblage and discussion, and of petition.
   I have given this slight historic review because history throws much light
on the present confused state of civil liberties. A consistent social philosophy of the various rights that go by this name has never existed. Upon the
whole, the dominant philosophy has sprung from fear of government and
of organized control, on the ground of their supposed inherent antagonism
to the liberties of individuals. Hence, one theoretical justification of freedom of conscience, of choice of worship, of freedom of speech (which is
what freedom of assembly amounts to practically) and of publication, has
been based upon the theory of natural rights, rights that inhere in individuals prior to political organization and independent of political authority.
From this point of view, they are like the rights of "life, liberty, and the
pursuit of happiness" made familiar to us in the Declaration of Independence. They represent fixed and external limits set to political action.
   This motif comes out most clearly in the last two articles of the amendments that form the Bill of Rights, articles which expressly reserve to the
several states or to the people in general all powers not expressly granted

by the Constitution to the Federal Government. The majority opinion in the A. A. A. decision used this clause of the Constitution as its authority for declaring the Agricultural Adjustment Act unconstitutional. On the face of things, there is no kinship between regulation of agriculture and the right, say, of free speech. But the two things have been brought together in the theory that there is an inherent opposition between political power and individual liberty.

The opposite strain in the theory of civil liberties is indicated by the contrast between the word "civil" on the one hand and the words "natural" and "political" on the other. The term *civil* is directly connected with the idea of citizenship. On this basis, civil liberties are those which belong to citizens as such and are different both from those which individuals are supposed to possess in a state of nature and from political rights such as the franchise and the right to hold office. Upon this basis, the justification for the various civil liberties is the contribution they make to the welfare of the community.

I have intimated that the present confused and precarious condition of civil liberties, even in nominally democratic countries like our own, is due to the conflict of these two opposed ideas of the basis and purpose of civil liberties. As social relations have become more complicated and the problem of maintaining social order becomes more difficult, it is practically inevitable that whatever the nominal theory be, *merely* individual claims will be forced to give way in practice to social claims. The individualistic and *laissez-faire* conception of civil liberties (say of free inquiry and free discussion) has been put forward to an extent which largely accounts for the ease with which nominally constitutional guarantees of civil liberties are violated in fact and are explained away by the courts. It is a commonplace that they go into discard when a nation is engaged in war. This is simply the crucial instance of the fact that *merely* individual claims will be lightly esteemed when they appear (or can be made to appear) in conflict with the general social welfare.

Moreover, civil liberties are never absolute nor is their precise nature in concrete situations self-evident. Only a philosophic anarchist holds, for example, that the freedom of speech includes the right to urge other men to engage in murder, arson, or robbery. Hence in the concrete, civil liberties mean what the courts construe them to mean. Courts, in all matters that have a general political or social bearing, are notoriously subject to social pressure and social currents, both those coming from without and those flowing from the education and political affiliations of judges. These facts give short shrift to civil liberties that are claimed upon a purely individualistic basis when judges are of the opinion that their exercise is dangerous to social ends which the judges set store by. Holmes and Brandeis are notable not only for their sturdy defense of civil liberties but even more for the fact that they based their defense on the indispensable value of free inquiry and free discussion to the normal development of public welfare, not upon anything inherent in the individual as such.

Anyone who views the situation impartially will not be surprised at the contradiction which is so marked in the conduct of liberals of the *laissez-faire* school. They constantly protest against any "interference" on the part of government with freedom of business enterprise, but are almost uniformly silent in the case of even flagrant violations of civil liberties—in spite of lip service to liberal ideas and professed adulation of the Constitution. The cause for the contradiction is obvious. Business interests have been and still are socially and politically dominant. In standing for *laissez-faire* liberalism in economic matters, these "liberals" are moving with the tide. On the other hand, only those individuals who are *opposing* the established order ever get into trouble by using the right to free inquiry and public discussion. In their case, the "liberals" who are vociferous against anything that looks like economic regimentation are content to tolerate intellectual and moral regimentation on the ground that it is necessary for the maintenance of "law and order."

No genuine believer in the democratic ideals of universal distribution of equal liberties will find it necessary to argue at large in behalf of the maximum possible of intellectual liberty in the fullest sense of that term. He knows that freedom of thought in inquiry and in dissemination of the conclusions of inquiry is the vital nerve of democratic institutions. Accordingly, I have not indulged in a general eulogy of civil liberties but have tried to show that the first step in rescuing them from their present uncertain and perilous state is to insist upon their social basis and social justification.

Invasions of civil liberties have grown in pretty much all directions since the first World War, in spite of alleged constitutional guarantees. The only hope for liberalism is to surrender, in theory and practice, the doctrine that liberty is a full-fledged ready-made possession of individuals independent of social institutions and arrangements, and to realize that social control, especially of economic forces, is necessary in order to render secure the liberties of the individual, including civil liberties.

FOR FURTHER THOUGHT

1. Teachers are told to individualize their instruction. Presumably, this includes content, method, and perhaps even purpose. *In the light of the Dewey selection, what does such a command mean? Would it mean the same thing to Spencer, Barnett, or Otis? What difference, if any, would this make for the practical behavior of students and teachers?*
2. Classroom management is a problem to many beginning teachers as

well as some who have had a number of years of experience. *What type of classroom organization would be most supportive of the liberty of students from the modern liberal point of view? What type of organization would be most supportive of the teacher's liberty? Is there any type of organization that would increase the liberty of both student and teacher?*

3. Dewey has been identified in the popular mind with "progressive" education and with the model of the "permissive" teacher. *Would "permissive" mean laissez faire for Dewey? Would it mean a teacher who had no control? Would it mean a teacher who actively directed the classroom? What justification would he supply for his notion of "permissive" teacher?*

4. "Intelligence tests are often used as a basis for classifying students. *Would a modern liberal object to classification of students? Would he suggest that such tests measured inherent intelligence or that they measure accomplishment reflecting the experiences undergone by the student? Would a classical liberal tend to agree or disagree with a modern liberal on this score? How would each explain a "change" in a child's "IQ"?*

5. The teacher in a public school has a widely varied clientele. She must somehow manage to be effective in dealing with all of them. *Would she, as a modern liberal, maintain that each child was free to become educated as long as no laws prohibited attendance or as long as the laws established schools for all? If not, what conditions would have to be established in order for her to view a child as free? Would these conditions be limited to the school or extend further than the school boundaries?*

INDIVIDUALISM AS CULTURAL

Again, objections can be raised to the nature of liberty in both the classical and modern liberal senses of the concept. As one might expect, the questioning of these conceptions of liberty starts in terms of the assumptions underlying the conceptions themselves. On some views, the weakness of the liberal position resides in its subjective base. The claim is that these formulations make liberty merely a state of mind, having no connection with truth, justice, or good. Of course, such criticism presupposes that truth, justice, and good are not simply mental states (psychological phenomena). Such a presupposition cannot be allowed by either the classical or the modern liberal if he is to remain consistent. It is useful to note that such a controversy does not necessarily mean that opponents might not reach similar conclusions concerning practice on occasion. It does mean, however, that a commonality of conclusion in no way indicated that the reasons for such a conclusion are identical or that the conclusion is correct.

George Barnett accepts the Dewey view that freedom has a material base as well as a legal form. However, this view is not sustained by referring to men (in whatever combination they may be found) as authority. The basis of freedom is found in the object world of which man is a part. It is the object world that provides the standard against which man's opinions must be measured. In the following selection, Barnett suggests some theoretical and practical objections to views like those of Spencer and Dewey.

THE IDEA OF LIBERTY*

While the science of "doublethink,"[1] the logic which maintains that contradictory ideas mean absolutely the same thing, is making great headway and increasing its influence all the time, as witness the growing destruction of liberty in the name of liberty, thus far it has had only a relatively limited development. Its fuller advance lies ahead in the years to come. What it will be like then George Orwell illustrates in his novel, *1984*, in which the people of Oceania live by the abiding principle—and under the abiding tyranny—that "Freedom is Slavery."

Fortunately, 1953 still finds civilization backward enough so that no advocate of liberty, whatever the brand, will assert that his is anything but liberty pure and simple as directly opposed to slavery. If the affection for making distinctions be with us a while yet—in fact, so that it may be with us yet—a conclusion will soon have to be reached as to which of the many diverse ideas is really the idea of liberty. The rest is doublethink. To assert in the name of freedom that any idea of it must be accepted as good as any other is itself to doublethink. To work toward singlethink requires an examination of alternative conceptions. What follows is a consideration of a few of the ideas of liberty confronting us.

ATOMISM OR LAISSEZ-FAIRE INDIVIDUALISM

In this view, human individuality is given as a natural rather than a social phenomenon. The individual does not become; he is. The self or per-

---

*George Barnett, "The Idea of Liberty," *Educational Leadership* 11:12–16; October 1953. Reprinted with permission of the Association for Supervision and Curriculum Development and George Barnett. Copyright © 1953 by the Association for Supervision and Curriculum Development. Dr. Barnett is Professor of Education at Michigan State University. He is co-author of *The Corporate Society and Education* and has recently edited the volume entitled *Philosophy and Educational Development*.

[1]A term used by George Orwell.

son is an independent entity whose being lies within rather than without. Defined not in terms of others, persons and things, but in terms of himself, he is a self-contained, self-sufficient unit whose reality lies in his uniqueness and separateness. Each self is a being-in-itself whose fullness of individuality is revealed only when shorn of all relations. Relations are thus external to rather than constitutive of individuality.

Despite the liberty enjoyed by the natural man, there are certain things lacking in the protection of his natural rights in such a state. These rights are not grants of society but claims against it. To overcome the deficiencies of the state of nature, men enter voluntarily into a contract by which they establish society and government. Government and society are secondary existences, artificial rather than natural, unreal or lesser realities than the individual. Conveniences and means, with the individual as end, they have no status in their own right and what being and authority they have are derivative from the prior real, the individual. Since government is inherently evil, its role is restricted, largely negative and there is a separation of the moral and political realms with that government best which governs least.

Freedom is negatively conceived as freedom from restraint. Liberty is opposed to all social control and authority, to government, state, society, planning, law, order, organization. All moves in the direction of greater social control, whether of the economy or otherwise, are diminutions of liberty. Although frequently the atomistic position is expressed in terms of opposition of freedom to all authority, it is social authority rather than that of the individual that is negated. As the position logically implies, it adheres to control and authority in individualistic terms. These must not be external but must inhere in the individual himself. He is the locus of value and the source of authority and will. The only authority which he acknowledges is his own. Just as he is a being unto himself, so he is a law unto himself, a private ruler whose will is absolute. Each man is his own sovereign, legislator, theologian—is, in fact, as private being ultimate judge on all matters.

The self-sufficient individual of atomism is a competitive seeker of ends that are private, "man for himself," the health of whose being depends upon freedom from the infection of relations, the integer whose integrity is maintained only in isolation. Cursed rather than blest is the tie that binds men together, for these bonds are bondage. As man becomes socialized he loses freedom and individuality. He is born free and then all that is added to him takes away from him. Since freedom and individuality are identified with a lack of relations, they are at their ultimate when man stands alone, are progressively lessened as relations become more extensive, and are completely destroyed with the establishment of world community and world government. On the one hand there is the epitome of liberty, the man alone, Robinson Crusoe; on the other, the ultimate in tyranny, the leviathan of leviathans, the world state.

Criticism of Atomism

By separating the individual from his world of persons and things, atomism has in fact divorced man from himself. The result of dissociating him in order to get at his reality, the simple self, is to reduce him to nothing. The isolated entity is literally a non-entity; the individuality atomism envisions is a myth. The individual has his human being in and not outside of relations; he lives in them and only in them, and individuality and freedom exist there are not at all.

Many hold that the individual has come to count for less and less and is all but crushed at present. The way out of this situation, however, is not the restoration of the atomism which, with some retrogression, has been increasingly abandoned in recent decades even in those countries where it has had its greatest strength. That abandonment has been regarded by many as the road to serfdom, yet ironically the conception that exalted the individual and would release him to attain his fullest stature by freeing him from social institutions has been, in fact, largely responsible for his subjugation. Believing all institutions to be inherently oppressive, atomism has failed to distinguish between those that free and those that tyrannize.

Freedom cannot be found where man is pitted against man, man against the state, and one state against another. The practical meaning of atomism is not freedom but war at every level from the interpersonal to the international. It is now obvious that laissez-faire individualism must be eliminated in international affairs where annihilation is the threat of continued adherence to isolationism and national sovereignty as ultimate. It may not yet be as obvious but it is nevertheless just as true that atomism means destruction and slavery intranationally as well. There are no practical affairs that can be founded on this conception of individuality.

A SOCIAL VIEW

Within this general position, there are several variations of which one is presented below. This position maintains that the starting point of social theory is man in society, not outside of it or in opposition to it. Human individuality is not given but comes to being through the process of socialization. The natural being is a bio-psychological entity who becomes human through his relations to such associations as the family, work groups, religious groups, and all others of which he is a member. Other individuals are not external to him as in atomism but are part of him; the self is not separate from others but constituted by them. All are one of another. Man is not an exclusive unit but is distinguishable as unique within the society of selves. It is the bond between the individual and others that makes it possible for him to develop personality and to become a free man. Individuality and liberty are attainments rather than original conditions and are achieved only within and through society.

Rights as individual are not natural as against society but are socially derived. Freedom like personality is a gift of society. The private interest is neither contrasted to nor superior to the public interest. In this sense, no individual has rights against society; his rights to be and to do are evaluated in terms of their social consequences. The public welfare cannot be overridden by a claim to a right, property or otherwise, considered private; nor is that welfare achieved by each individual seeking his own private end in his own private way. The attainment of the good as public requires collective thought and action. Social control is essential to its achievement.

Government, authority, law, social control, society—all of these may be despotic but there is no human individuality nor freedom apart from them. Authority and control characterize every human situation and the problem of liberty is not that of overthrowing all authority and control but of finding the right kind. The choice in the social view is neither authoritarian authority nor that of laissez-faire individualism; rather freedom is to be found in democratic authority where the will of all or the social will prevails. Authority is not absolute in the individual as private nor does it lie in the hands of one or a few; instead it rests in the group as a whole. As a whole, the group is more than a sum of its parts or individuals. The same is true of the group will which as a synthesis rather than a sum is inclusive of but is more than the individual wills of the members of the group. Similarly, at a more comprehensive level, that of society considered as a group of groups, the social or the societal will incorporates but transcends the various group wills. The general will in this sense is ultimate authority within which is found the authority of groups and of individuals. When this will rules, there is freedom under law.

"Man for himself" in the social view does not mean private self-seeking but rather men acting together for their common good. Since self is also other, even while distinguishable as unique, to be for oneself is at the same time to be for others. The social concept of individuality carries with it a social ethic: one acts with the welfare of others, of society as a consideration. Self-realization is social in nature and the fullest development of individuality and of freedom is dependent upon the fullest development of society. Government and the state have a positive role to play in this development, and authority and control socially conceived, far from being inimical to liberty, are essential to it. The social conception of individuality which holds that individual is continuous with individual, group with group, and society with society, finds the ultimate in liberty attainable only in the most inclusive whole, world society and world government.

Criticism of a Social View

Although this position asserts continuity rather than separation as principle and attempts to develop a conception of individuality which is public in character, it nevertheless falls into the error of atomism. Despite the fact that the individual is considered a reality only in groups and in society as a more inclusive group, each of these larger wholes reduces ultimately to separate individuals with their separate wills and ends. Will rests in the individual so conceived even though the social view maintains that the whole is a synthesis rather than a sum and that the public and the public will as universal are more than individuals and their wills taken together. If the will that inheres in the individual is not absolute in this position as it is in atomism, the public will, nevertheless, is composed of such wills. That individual wills become or may become modified through interaction with others so that the outcome is a new will does not alter the fact that the seat of will remains the same as in atomism. The quality of the will that emerges has not changed but is of the same nature as its source. Universality, wholeness, unity are not attained by a synthesis as long as social will is composed of these same elements.

The public will is neither an aggregate nor a synthesis of private wills. Will does not become objective on the basis of inclusiveness if that refers to number, nor on the basis of agreement even when qualification is made as to the method by which this agreement is attained. The conception of will in the social view does not overcome the defects of atomism and therefore remains subjective. Liberty cannot be founded upon subjective will.

A CULTURAL VIEW

Both the atomistic and the social positions take essentially the same approach to the problem of freedom. The question which both consider as the crucial one to be answered is that of *whose* will shall prevail. Although they disagree on the answer, they agree on the nature of the question. The cultural view differs from these two views not in that it gives still another reply to this question but in that it rejects the question itself as disastrous for freedom. The question implies that authority is personal rather than impersonal and that the problem of freedom is to find the person or persons in whom authority rests. But personal authority, the cultural view argues, is inherently arbitrary and tyrannical whether it be vested in one person or in many. Whatever the answer given to this question, the will involved is necessarily subjective, and as such means subjection.

According to the cultural position the problem of freedom is not one of determining whose will shall prevail whether it be one, few, many, or all nor is it that of finding a qualitative "who." Instead of asking "who shall rule?" or "whose will shall be law?" the cultural view asks "what is law?" "Who" questions must be abandoned in favor of "what" questions if there is to be any conception of will that identifies with freedom. Authority speaks with nobody's voice but is impersonal. The authority of the teacher, doctor, lawyer, clergyman does not reside in their persons nor is it a delegation made by other persons or by society as a whole of persons; rather it inheres in the institution and is cultural in nature. The authority of the teacher is derived from the nature of education and its place as an institution within the whole of institutions, as a particular good within the whole good.

Similarly, will as institutional is public and objective in nature. What the teacher wills as teacher is education; her will is one with it. As teacher-person she is realized as education is realized. Considered as whole person, what she wills is the whole of culture: art, religion, action in all its forms, the institutional whole, the good life. She is realized as person or individual through and in institutions. Since the self is not a thing-in-itself but is continuous with the world, since institutions are the "other" that are the person, the fullness of individuality is attained only in the fullness of culture. . . .

POSTSCRIPT 1968

Freedom, in the cultural view, is dependent upon four factors:

1. *The quality of culture.* The degree of freedom varies with the degree of culture. The greater the art, science, philosophy, or religion, the greater all aspects of culture are, the greater the potential for freedom.
2. *The quality of the individual's native endowment.* No matter how advanced the civilization, an individual of low capacities will have little freedom. Just as the man with the capacities of a mental giant will never become more than a mental dwarf in a backward civilization, so a congenital idiot is doomed to have little freedom even if he lives in a high civilization. The higher the native qualities, the greater the potential for freedom.
3. *The individual's access to culture.* Not only must the civilization be of high quality and the individual have high potentialities, but he must have the opportunity to develop his gifts. Bar the individual from education, vocation, medical care, housing, and so forth, and he will not be free no matter how great his talents and how great the art, science, and other aspects of culture. Any denial of opportunity to realize the individual's desirable qualities is a denial of freedom. Conversely, the fuller the opportunity, the greater the potential for freedom.
4. *The individual's desire to use his capacities and the cultural opportunities, and his knowledge of how to do so.* Given a highly endowed individual, a superior culture, and full opportunity, the greater his desire

and his ability to make the desire effective, the greater the freedom. That an individual does not have that desire or, having it, does not know how to use it, may be due to a number of reasons. Often his failure to seize the chances available is ascribed to his laziness or apathy. Lazy or apathetic he may be, but that is not the end of the matter. It is essential to know why he is that way and to do something about it. Of all people, educators need to do more than characterize human behavior; they must understand the reasons for it. In attempting to understand, educators must aim for the fullest development of human capacities by using the highest qualities of present civilization and must aim toward the development of the highest civilization possible by making the most of human potentialities. That is the way of and the way to the greatest freedom.

FOR FURTHER THOUGHT

1. In this age of increasing competition for acceptance in the college of one's choice, we hear of the tyranny of testing. Presumably, it makes slaves of the students by interfering with their choices. *If we assume the validity of the testing programs, how would Barnett answer these charges? Do the tests free or enslave students? What, in his view, is the correct question to raise concerning testing programs (that is, what would be the appropriate basis for praising or condemning tests)?*
2. Textbooks often contain chapters entitled "Who Should Control the Schools?" *What would be Barnett's reaction to such a chapter heading? What defense would he offer for his reaction?*
3. Critics of Barnett's position would undoubtedly respond that people still have to make decisions in spite of what he says. Barnett would most likely admit to this. His response might be that the selection of these decisions requires a principle. *What principle would he suggest—the individual, the majority, or the method, or something else? Why?*
4. Tyrannical and totalitarian are often thought to be complementary terms. There are tyrannical teachers and we sometimes speak of their totalitarian methods. Yet Barnett's description of a truly free man (teacher, student, and so forth) is a totalitarian claim: "The fullness of individuality is attained only in the fullness of culture." *Would he claim that the totalitarian teacher (in the common sense usage of the word) is tyrannical because she is partial rather than total? Would she be tyrannical because she was partial in the sense of incomplete? Would she be tyrannical because she was partial in the sense of biased?*
5. The development of the student's fullest potential is seen by many as a legitimate goal for education. *What would this mean for Spencer, Butler, Tussman, Dewey, or Barnett? In what senses might they agree*

or disagree? What kinds of things would each advocate in order to achieve this goal?

LIBERTY AS THE DEMOCRATIC KEYSTONE

Spencer wrote about equal freedom *in* and *from* the law. Sameness was central to his concept of equality. In that sense *alone*, he found equality compatible with freedom. Many others have agreed that equality is compatible with freedom in the political or legal (formal) sense. Beyond this point, however, equality has been seen as the enemy of freedom. Lord Acton, for example, was convinced that: "The deepest cause which made the French Revolution so disastrous to liberty was its theory of equality.[1] . . . The passion for equality made vain the hope of freedom."[2]

William F. Russell, in *Liberty versus Equality*,[3] saw the two concepts locked in a death struggle. Underlying their views, in part, was a common conception of human motivation expressed by Calhoun. Calhoun conceded that equality, in the eyes of the law, was "essential" to a democracy:

> But to go further, and make equality of condition essential to liberty, would be to destroy both liberty and progress. The reason is, that inequality of condition, while it is the necessary consequence of liberty, is, at the same time, indispensable to progress. In order to understand why this is so, it is necessary to bear in mind that the main spring to progress is the desire of individuals to better their condition, and that the strongest impulse which can be given to it is, to leave individuals free to exert themselves in a manner they may deem best for that purpose. . . .[4]

In the eyes of some, to be obligated by others is to lose one's 'independence" of action and eventually one's independence of thought—thus to lose one's manhood. To lean heavily upon "equality" (as material condition) is to sell one's soul for mediocrity. In Butler's view, this cripples all mankind in the name of a false democracy. It is customary to insist upon equality "*before* the law." This is an attempt to see that each man receives his due (process). Butler is not particularly concerned with equality "*after*

---

[1]Lord John Emerich Edward, Dalberg-Acton, *The History of Freedom and Other Essays,* John Neville Figgis and Reginald Vere Lawrence, eds. (London: Macmillan and Co., Ltd., 1907), p. 88.

[2]Lord John Emerich Edward, p. 57.

[3]William F. Russell, *Liberty versus Equality* (New York: The Macmillan Company, 1936), pp. 10–14.

[4]John C. Calhoun, *Works,* vol. 1, "A Disquisition on Government," Richard Cralle, ed. (New York: Appleton-Century-Crofts, 1854), p. 56.

the law." Such a concern with the due product would threaten freedom. There are kings and pretenders in the realm of concepts as well as in the realm of empires. To locate the concept of authority is to locate the root of the royal line. The location of such a root will give us "true" democracy. In this selection, Nicholas Murray Butler explores the relations of equality and liberty and tells us the nature of "true" democracy.

TRUE AND FALSE DEMOCRACY*

"It was the lower class that won the battles of the third estate; that took the Bastille, and made France a constitutional monarchy; that took the Tuileries, and made France a Republic. They claimed their reward. The middle class, having cast down the upper orders with the aid of the lower, instituted a new inequality and a privilege for itself. By means of a taxpaying qualification it deprived its confederates of their vote. To those, therefore, who had accomplished the Revolution, its promise was not fulfilled. Equality did nothing for them. The opinion, at that time, was almost universal, that society is founded on an agreement which is voluntary and conditional, and that the links which bind men to it are terminable, for sufficient reason, like those which subject them to authority. From these popular premises the logic of Marat drew his sanguinary conclusions. He told the famished people that the conditions on which they had consented to bear their evil lot, and had refrained from violence, had not been kept to them. It was suicide, it was murder, to submit to starve, and to see one's children starving, by the fault of the rich. The bonds of society were dissolved by the wrong it inflicted. The state of nature had come back, in which every man had a right to what he could take. The time had come for the rich to make way for the poor. With this theory of equality, liberty was quenched in blood, and Frenchmen became ready to sacrifice all other things to save life and fortune."[1]

The political and social anarchy which Lord Acton describes must be the inevitable result whenever the passion for economic equality overcomes the love of liberty in men's breasts. For the state is founded upon justice,

---

*Nicholas Murray Butler, *True and False Democracy* (New York: The Macmillan Company, 1907). Permission to reprint granted by the Trustees of Columbia University in the City of New York. Dr. Butler, late President Emeritus of Columbia University and President Emeritus of the Carnegie Endowment for International Peace, was a prolific writer on the topics of education, philosophy, and democratic issues.

[1]*Quarterly Review* (January 1878), pp. 133–134.

and justice involves liberty, and liberty denies economic equality; because equality of ability, of efficiency, and even of physical force are unknown among men. To secure an equality which is other than the political equality incident to liberty, the more efficient must be shackled that they may not outrun the less efficient, for there is no known device by which the less efficient can be spurred on to equal the accomplishment of the more efficient. Objective conditions must, of course, be equalized, particularly those conditions which are created by the state. But this is true not because such an equality is an end in itself, but because it is essential to liberty.

If we can fix clearly in mind this fundamental contradiction between equality of possessions, equality of capacity, equality of attainment, and liberty, we shall have reached the clew to the distinction between a democracy which is false and spurious, and a democracy which is true and real.

When one examines the proposals that are seriously made by responsible men in high place, not in one nation of the earth but in many, he is forced to ask whether liberty, which for four centuries has been a word to conjure with, has lost its hold upon men, and whether we are coming to a pass where democracy is to be reduced to the expedient of some of the ancient tyrannies, and is to be able to maintain itself only by providing bread and a circus for the masses of the people. If by any chance we have come to this pass, or are coming to it, then be assured that it will not be long before a great change will come over the political and social institutions of mankind, and that it will be a change for the worse.

It is hard to bring one's self to believe that liberty has lost its hold, or that a false and spurious equality contradicting every natural law, making progress impossible or only temporary at best, can long lure intelligent men from liberty's path. The abuses of liberty are severe and innumerable. The economic injustices that have not yet been removed are many and apparent. The forms of equality dependent upon true liberty that have not yet been sufficiently established are easy to name. But surely the remedy is not to be found in tearing down the corner-stone of the political fabric, but rather in first clearing away obstructions and débris, and then in building more thoughtfully, more wisely, and more patiently upon it.

The socialist propaganda, never more seriously or more ably carried on than now, is an earnest and sincere attempt to escape from conditions that are burdensome and unhappy. Despite its most imperfect interpretation of the economic significance of history and its ringing the changes on a misleading theory of class consciousness, this propaganda makes an appeal to our favorable judgment because its proclaimed motive is to help the mass of mankind. No just man can quarrel with its aim, but few readers of history or students of human nature can approve its programme. What is it that socialism aims to accomplish by restricting liberty in order to promote economic equality? It seeks to accomplish what it conceives to be a juster economic and political condition. At bottom and without special reference to immediate concrete proposals, socialism would substitute for individual initiative collective and corporate responsibility in matters relating to property and production, in the hope thereby of correcting and overcoming the evils which attach to an individualism run wild. But we must not lose sight of the fact that the corporate or collective responsibility which it would substitute for individual initiative is only such corporate or collective responsibility as a group of these very same individuals could exercise. Therefore, socialism is primarily an attempt to overcome man's individual imperfections by adding them together, in the hope that they will cancel each other. This is not only bad mathematics, but worse psychology. In pursuing a formula, socialism fails to take account of the facts. Out of the people it would constitute a mob, in forgetfulness of the fact that the mob, led or unled, is the most serious foe that the people have ever had to face. The Roman Republic conquered every enemy but its own vices. With this warning written large across the page of history, what is the lesson of Rome for America?

We come back to the conception which Mazzini had of democracy: "The progress of all through all, under the leadership of the best and wisest." True democracy will carry on an insistent search for these wisest and best, and will elevate them to posts of leadership and command. Under the operation of the law of liberty, it will provide itself with real leaders, not limited by rank, or birth, or wealth, or circumstance, but opening the way for each individual to rise to the place of honor and influence by the expression of his own best and highest self. It will exactly reverse the communistic formula, "From each according to his abilities. To each according to his needs," and will uphold the principle, "From each according to his needs, To each according to his abilities." It will take care to provide such a ladder of education and opportunity that the humblest may rise to the very top if he is capable and worthy. The most precious thing in the world is the individual human mind and soul, with its capacity for growth and service. To bind it fast to a formula, to hold it in check to serve the selfish ends of mediocrity, to deny it utterance and expression, political, economic, and moral, is to make democracy impossible as a permanent social and governmental form.

The United States is in sore need to-day of an aristocracy of intellect and service. Because such an aristocracy does not exist in the popular consciousness, we are bending the knee in worship to the golden calf of money. The form of monarchy and its pomp offer a valuable foil to the worship of money for its own sake. A democracy must provide itself with a foil of its own, and none is better or more effective than an aristocracy of intellect and service recruited from every part of our democratic life.

FOR FURTHER THOUGHT

1. Golf is a game of handicaps. Poorer players are allowed a number of strokes to keep the game interesting and to provide an atmosphere of fraternity. There may still be competition, but it is often directed against one's own score or against an opponent's weighted score. In short, the odds are evened. Evening the odds in the "game of life" is seen by many as violating natural liberty. *How would a teacher, holding this latter view, organize her classroom? What would she assume to be the major factor motivating human behavior? How would this connect with certain interpretations of evolutionary theory?*

2. Many public schools conduct physical exams at public expense. Some schools even go so far as to supply corrective devices such as glasses for certain students. *Would this be seen as "evening the odds" and therefore illegitimate by Butler and Spencer? Would it be permissible to allow a near-sighted child to sit at the front of the room? Would it be permissible to assign him such a seat? Would such an assignment be as much a corrective device, in principle, as glasses? If so, would the teacher and her advisors be practicing medicine? Are there groups in society, outside of those against public medicine, that might also be expected to object to such a practice?*

3. One of the chronic problems facing "vocational" teachers is the lack of supplies. Many students cannot or will not pay for the materials needed in instruction. Communities, typically, are willing to pay for equipment such as saws, vices, lathes, stoves, sewing machines, typewriters and the like. They seem reluctant to pay for many of the materials used in working with these machines. The teachers are understandably distressed by such a situation and continually seek additional money for supplies. *How would Butler view the attitudes of these communities? How would he view the attitudes of the teachers? Would he see vocational educators in particular and educators in general as selling out liberty for "creeping socialism"?*

4. If a democratic society should result in a *natural* aristocracy of talent, presumably the schools should be organized in such a way that would *allow* this development to occur. *How would such a school be organized? What would it look like in operation? Specifically, what practices now typically condoned would be eliminated?*

5. *Is there a necessary connection between competition and increased effort? Is a club-footed boy likely to go out for the track team? What*

implications do your answers to the first two questions have for educa-tion in general? Do your answers have anything to say in support or criticism of Butler's ideas about the relationship between liberty and equality?

6. The "good" teacher is the "fair" teacher. Thousands of students of all ages have made this statement or its equivalent to researchers in the field. To be regarded as "fair" is to become potentially more efficient. To be regarded as "unfair" is to lose a great deal, if not all, of one's potential for effectiveness. *What connection is there between "fairness" and equality? What is likely to happen if the teacher and the students have different conceptions of "equality"? Would the recognition of the existence of differing conceptions be of any help to the people involved? How?*

7. Schools have laws (rules). So do classrooms. Suppose that it is mid-winter and that a school has the regulation that those who are late to school must stay in at recess time. All others *must* go out to the play-ground. *Should this rule apply to all? What is the purpose of the penalty attached to the regulation? Will it have the same effect on the well-clothed child as it will on the one scantily clad? If not, should the same penalty be applied? What does equality demand? What problem does this raise for the teacher who wants to be fair?*

EQUALITY AS THE DEMOCRATIC KEYSTONE

It is clear that people like Spencer and Butler would see equality (as sameness) as inimical to liberty in the largest application of these terms. To the extent that they are supportive of equality, this support is confined to the political realm.

Others, like Tawney, would claim that "freedom for the pike is death for the minnows. . . ."[5] Of course they are referring to more than political freedom. Pollard, a contemporary of Tawney, saw liberty as a struggle for supremacy which only Parliament could solve. Thus, he argued that such a body should redistribute economic liberties as it had redistributed political liberties in earlier times. This was necessary because: "The liberty of the weak depends upon the restraint of the strong, that of the poor on the restraint of the rich, and that of the simpler-minded upon the restraint of the sharper."[6]

Inasmuch as all the authors talk about liberty as a universal goal, they are talking about liberty for all men. In the light of the observations of Tawney and Pollard, it is not surprising to find other contemporary thinkers like T. V. Smith maintaining that equality is necessary to any

[5]R. H. Tawney, *Equality* (New York: Harcourt, Brace & World, Inc., 1931), p. 220.
[6]A. F. Pollard, *The Evolution of Parliament* (London: Longmans, Green & Co., Ltd., 1926), p. 188.

meaningful sense of liberty. Modern liberals, in general, would insist that political equality and liberty are barren without a significant measure of equality in other areas of life. They would maintain that there are material and social conditions necessary to political liberty that must be attended to and not left to chance and the self-generating quality of circumstances—what the classical liberal assumes to be "native inferiority."

The modern liberal would claim that we do not know in what way men are natively inferior or superior until we remove the external "crippling" forces that weigh upon them. To remove only the burden (formal) of political inequalities from man's shoulders is but a token, in their view. It provides the form, but not the substance of liberty. It does not get at the major cause of the limitation of liberty which stunts those who *appear* to prosper in its name as well as those who obviously suffer in its application. In short, there must be equality *before* the law. Equality here means fittingness (which includes sameness if the situation warrants). Only then can there be equality (fittingness) *after* the law. And is that not the purpose of law—to order society justly, equitably, and fittingly? We will turn again to Tawney:

> When liberty is construed realistically as implying, not merely a minimum of civil and political rights, but securities that the economically weak will not be at the mercy of the economically strong . . . a large measure of equality, so far from being inimical to liberty, is essential to it . . . liberty is, in fact, equality in action. . . .[7]

Are these men preaching false democracy in the land of equal opportunity? Is the land of the "free" to become the home of the "slave"? Is the public school the institution of a slave or a free society? Are the teachers therein agents, knowingly or unknowingly, to a great fraud or a great faith? T. V. Smith, insisting that substantial liberty is dependent upon "economic independence" and "liberal education," suggests an answer.

———————◄◆►———————

DEMOCRACY AS EQUALITY*

Nothing is more certain in the realm of human relations than that a substantial measure of equality conditions significant brotherhood. Equality is, indeed, so close a counterpart of the fraternal ideal that it may

*Thomas Vernor Smith, *The Democratic Way of Life* (Chicago: The University of Chicago Press, 1926), pp. 85–97. Reprinted by permission of Professor Gayle S. Smith. Dr. Smith was a noted author and celebrated teacher as well as a member of the United States House of Representatives and the Illinois State Senate.

[7]R. H. Tawney, *Equality* (New York: Harcourt, Brace & World, Inc., 1931), p. 226.

almost be said to be a part of it rather than a means to it. If two men have been bosom friends in poverty and one of them becomes wealthy, their friendship is the normal sacrifice exacted by the "God of Things as They Are." If close contact is artificially maintained for a time between those who are grossly unequal, there goes on a leveling that is both psychological and spiritual. Those who are much and closely together build characters that are in very truth joint products. If a slave is raised by association with a superior master, then the master is lowered by association with the inferior slave. The Assyrian conqueror on the bas-relief, as Herbert Spencer was fond of pointing out, is himself tied to the rope by which he leads the prisoners. In a way that religion has thought mystic, a new presence seems to arise where two or three are gathered together in any name, if only they are at peace.

The only way in which fraternity can be maintained along with substantial inequality is by postulating a transempirical equality. This is what humane minds have always done when confronted with the ideal claim of brotherhood on one side and with the fact of gross inequalities on the other. The Stoic Seneca, face to face with the vast discrepancy between humane theory and actual practice, declared:

> He errs who thinks that slavery goes to the heart of man. For the better part of man is unaffected. Bodies are under the power of a master and are counted as his, but the mind is free. It is so untrammelled indeed that it cannot be held down even by those prison walls within which it is shut, but may burst out to great deeds and flee to the infinite as a comrade of the divine.

St. Paul took the same devious route to maintain human brotherhood in the face of slavery: "in Christ there is neither bond nor free." Southern apologists for slavery but yesterday in our own country found a justifying voice that echoed all the past when Professor Bledsoe declared that:

> the poorest slave on earth possesses the inherent and inalienable right to serve God according to his own conscience; and he possesses it as completely as the proudest monarch on his throne. The master demands no spiritual service of him, he exacts no divine honors.

But when equality is thus saved in the face of the facts, by transporting it to heaven, let it be noted that fraternity is also laid in other than earthly scenes. If the one is purely ideal, then ideal must be the other also. It is only when equality is actual that fraternity abides among men in significant measure. This is a relationship that need not be labored, for in general it is never denied. It has been so far emphasized only because some have thought to save spiritual brotherhood by asserting a mystic equality that underlies actual inequality. This can be done, but the spiritual brotherhood thus preserved is of no more durable texture than the intangible equality that conditions it.

When we come to the relation between liberty and equality, however, there is a different story. That there is some relationship has always been observed; but its exact nature has been a matter of dispute. We shall note the divergent opinions only in so far as such notice will throw light on our present contention; and that contention is that what the equality ideal has stood for is necessary in order to make significant liberty available for the majority of men. Even those who have been most sympathetic with democracy have often felt that the insertion of equality in its aims produces an embarrassment, and many professing democrats have declared in every age that liberty and equality cannot dwell together. Thus saying, they have all too often declared that equality must therefore go, since liberty is the dearest of the democratic graces. The historic explanation of this partiality for liberty has been discussed in the preceding chapter. There is, however, no imperative reason why, circumstances changed, the emphasis may not be shifted from liberty to equality.

It is indeed notable that the willingness to surrender equality does not usually imply any desire to undo any of the equalitarian victories already consummated. Each man to count for one at the ballot and before the law and nobody to count for more than one at either place—these are everywhere in America regarded as praiseworthy achievements of the democratic impetus. But the willingness to surrender equality is forward-looking. Having attained by way of equality the political and legal means for greater and more concrete benefits, many voices are counseling that we should now reap in economic fields the fruits of our earlier political sowing. It is primarily against this tendency that men who fear for liberty disclaim. They point out that liberty demands that each is entitled to whatever he can get in a competitive field where no favors are shown. Not only is this principle sound as a principle, they say, but it is an absolutely necessary condition of progressive practice. The fundamental error involved in invading the economic field with an equalitarian program is, according to them, twofold. First, men are economically so different as to be of greatly varying value to the productive process. Second, the only way to marshal the entire economic resource is to let each man profit by his varying gifts. There is no other motive adequate to the high productivity demanded by our modern needs. To initiate a program looking toward equalization of either wealth or of income is, they say, to invite disaster.

When it is pointed out that such a policy as that advocated by the partisans of liberty involves many people in poverty, it will be replied, if the apologist for the present order be tough-minded, that life is no holiday, that men usually deserve what they get, and that nothing good comes except through sacrifice. If the apologist be tender-minded, he will regret the high cost of progress, he will commiserate the victims; he may even insist upon giving alms or bonuses. Beyond this, even if he be tender-minded, what can he do? Born into a world not made for him, man must manage the best he can; and, as for the rest, a stiff upper lip is an indispensable asset.

If one take all this apologetic in utter good faith, he must concede that our case regarding the dependence of liberty upon equality is made out. For the unfortunates whose condition is in debate have no substantial liberty. Liberty is good; their lot is evil. If one wished to be particularly ironic, he might resurrect the old spiritual palliative and endow the unfortunates with freedom of the will. But all in all we are far enough along to admit that a man who has no other kind of freedom has not even freedom of the will. The only freedom worth talking about is the ability actually to try out one's desires and plans and the ability to escape unforeseen consequences. The one ability exists only with economic independence, the other only with a liberal education. The only freedom that exists for submerged classes is the freedom to resent or to accept their poverty and ignorance, and to get what satisfaction they can from a religious faith well adapted to protect the more fortunate classes from violence.

This is all, of course, a matter of more or less, but the number of people involved in the United States today who lack significant freedom must give one pause. The most dependable statistics available—from the National Bureau of Economic Research—indicate that less than 2 per cent of our people own more than 60 per cent of our national wealth. This means of course prodigious liberty for 2 per cent; for wealth is power and prestige to do all that liberty has ever meant, both good and bad. But note that it also means that the remainder of our people—the 98 per cent—own less than 40 per cent of our wealth, of which a great majority own nothing at all, not even tools with which to work. In the great economic inequality their liberty evaporates. But clearly, though wealth be very inadequately distributed, income is more to the point. Here, fortunately, inequality is not so flagrant. Still, how much liberty can one enjoy on less than a living wage? Almost half of all American families lived in 1910 on incomes of $700 or less; and while the peak in 1917 seemed much higher, it meant in actual purchasing power less than $1000 at the highest. There is no need to exaggerate. This does not constitute starvation, but on the other hand it is not the framework for the kind of life envisaged by our fathers, when democracy was young. And what is more to the point, it is not the framework for the kind of life that could actually be had today by means of a juster distribution of available goods and opportunities. Without arguing the latter point here, enough has been said to make it unmistakably clear that when men demand liberty to the exclusion of equality, they mean liberty for the few, dependence for the many.

Liberty that is compatible with slavery is not liberty. Liberty that is yoked with poverty is not liberty. To call it by its right name puts the matter in far clearer light. If one will but consider the relation to economic poverty of the chief goods that are prized by those who are not poor, the whole point will appear unshakable. Wealth itself is a good and the getting of it is oftentimes a joyous activity. The poor have no liberty in this regard, of course, since by definition they have just this deficiency. Health, another fundamental good of human life, is possessed by the poor in fairy tales alone. Health in a modern industrial society is conditioned quite fully by things which for the most part poverty denies—rest, light, wholesome food, physiological knowledge, ready access to physicians, dentists, hospitals. The poor cannot own objects of beauty; and, what is worse, they have no adequate access to such educational opportunities as really make available the free beauties of art galleries, of museums, of earth and sky. Friendship itself, the freest of all goods, is not available to the poor on the same easy terms as to those better off; for friendship thrives on leisure, rest, imagination, tolerance, freedom. Variety throughout the whole of experience is another greatly prized human good, but poverty denies travel, vacations, variety of food, new friends, and the thousand and one other things that economic independence affords to relieve the tedium of life. The situation is complicated in the case of the industrial poor by the insistent presence of highly monotonous work which in long hours grinds down both spontaneity and morale. It is further aggravated by the consequent fact that there is no intrinsic joy in their work itself to compensate for the enormous extrinsic lacks. To this point I shall return in a more constructive mood in a subsequent chapter; but for the present it must be left unmistakably clear that not merely is the attainment of separate goods made impossible by poverty, but that also there is left lacking that which underlies all these, the right to develop personality through the joyous assumption of responsibility in productive processes. Personalities are not handed down, they are grown; and the poor are denied the soil necessary for their nurture.

A touch of irony is added to this basic denial by the fact that the age-old distinction between material and spiritual goods has actually served largely, whatever may have at various times been the motive of those who capitalized it, to content men with a life that had neither economic nor spiritual richness. Spirituality may be more than economic activity, but certain it is that it never flowers normally except through the latter. And any insistence upon a sharp separation of soul and body or even of body and mind will do for the poor to challenge. If a man permits his soul to become his exclusive joy, he will be fortunate if he does not some day wake to find that he has neither soul nor joy.

A life externally meager, internally dull—this is the supreme tragedy lived by a majority of the industrial children of those democratic pioneers who dreamed so short a time ago of a transformed society instinct with justice. All this ought to make clear what the eventuation is to be, regardless of the motivation back of it, of the tendency to give up equality as a part of the democratic insistence. To give it up is to renounce fraternity and liberty as the same fell blow.

FOR FURTHER THOUGHT

1. Professional organizations, be they of teachers, doctors, lawyers, or engineers, are built upon certain distinctions that separate them from the rest of mankind. *How can these avoid interfering with fraternity? Do they have an equal claim upon the "common good"? Do they have an unequal claim to provide for the common good, but equal claims to share it and in it? Should all people have an equal claim to health and educational service? What would be the basis of such a claim?*
2. The right to life is considered a primary one. Here we speak of sheer biological existence. *What is the connection between income level and infant mortality in your country?* Life, as a normative conception, involves more than biological existence. Education is included as both a definition and a means to this kind of life. *What is the connection between income level and the type and length of formal education in your country? What is the connection between income level and the "life style" (informal education) in your country?*
3. Wishes are important in the lives of all of us. If, however, we are limited to wishing, we may be judged to develop serious mental difficulties. The "daydreaming" child is a common phenomenon in the classroom. *Are there cases in which a child may be enslaved by his wishes? If a child cannot give up his wishes and yet cannot realize them, what consequences can you foresee?* Some wishes, such as the desire of a spastic child to become a surgeon, are unrealizable for reasons beyond the control of us all. This is, unhappily, the case and we must become resigned to such a situation at least for the present. *However, what about the great talent that cannot afford medical school?* Admitting the fact that some scholarships are available, *what about the economic and social conditions that do not allow the talented the luxury of wishing? Are these people free?*
4. If personalities are "grown," *what are the obligations of the professional educator? Is it enough to see that those who can't afford texts, band instruments, football tickets, evening dresses, and corsages are given them? What effect does "being on relief" or charity at the age of six do to personality development? Are children forced out of school because of economic inequality? If so, are they being liberated or enslaved?*

5. *Should the school teach the poor to be content with their lot? Should it teach them that their lot is one of bad luck or is an indication of their inferiority? Should the school do these things when it is clear that the poor have the political potential to become more affluent? Should it teach the poor how to reorganize society in such a way as to relieve the strain of their poverty? What is the professional obligation in this regard?*

6. Report card day can be an occasion for joy or terror, smiles or tears, the willing parental signature or surreptitious forgery. *Should all students be graded on the same standard? Should all students be graded in relation to their own ability? If so, how do you assess ability? Would your answer be the same for both elementary and secondary students? Would it be the same for the college student seeking a teaching certificate? What would equality demand in each case? Why?*

SUGGESTIONS FOR FURTHER READING

1. A truly imposing body of literature exists on the topic of liberalism. We have already suggested Laski's *The Rise of Liberalism* and Girvitz's *The Evolution of Liberalism* (see page 309). Three other books are particularly helpful in surveying the range of meanings attached to "freedom": Herbert J. Muller, *Issues of Freedom* (New York: Harper & Row, Publishers, 1960); Dorothy Fosdick, *What Is Liberty?* (New York: Harper & Row, Publishers, 1939); and John Dewey, *Freedom and Culture* (New York: G. P. Putnam's Sons, 1939).

2. The relationship between liberty and equality is given extensive treatment in William F. Russell, *Liberty versus Equality* (New York: The Macmillan Company, 1936); R. H. Tawney, *Equality* (New York: Harcourt, Brace & World, Inc., 1931); and T. V. Smith and Eduard C. Lindeman, *The Democratic Way of Life* (New York: New American Library, 1951).

3. The various dimensions of equality are explored in R. H. Tawney's *Equality* (see above). A less comprehensive, but interesting discussion can be found in Paul Nash's *Authority and Freedom in Education* (New York: John Wiley & Sons, Inc., 1966). A unique justification and discussion of equality is presented by R. S. Peters in *Ethics and Education* (Glenview, Ill.: Scott, Foresman and Company, 1967). Myron Lieberman's article, "Equality of Educational Opportunity," *Harvard Educational Review*, vol. 29, no. 3 (Summer 1959), deals with some specific educational examples of the equality problem. By far the most difficult, and perhaps the most rewarding, is the closely reasoned paper "The Concept of Equality in Education," *Studies in Philosophy and Education*, vol. 3, no. 3 (Fall 1964) by B. Paul Komisar and Jerrold R. Combs.

CHAPTER **9**

The Proper Distribution
of Property

Whatever concept of authority one employs and whatever concepts of liberty and equality follow, there remains the question of property and contract. This is necessarily the case because the other concepts are of moment because of the assumption that there is a world of things that makes action possible. This support of action requires materials and institutionalized ways of relating these things to each other and to people. Thus man must ask the question—"When is property proper?"

The answers to that question are so directly related to the previously mentioned concepts that little by way of an overview is necessary at this point. It is enough to point out that from at least the time of Plato, this has been seen as a vital question for political theorists. Does property have any "rights"? Does ownership confer rights? Is there anything inherently good about the privacy of property? Is there anything inherently good about public ownership of property? Who are the parties to a contract? Are contracts private or public or both?

It is instructive to note that the category of contract is closely associated, if not identical, with law. Inasmuch as men often refer to law when citing their authority for action (thereby being principled by law), it may be demonstrated that the same questions that we have raised throughout this section concerning democracy can be addressed to the concept of law. This is particularly the case when one asks the nature of law and the nature of its authority or its legitimacy. The answers to such questions provide our footing when seeking to locate our obligations and responsibilities.

Educators are understandably interested in the nature of property and contract. This is the "stuff" with which they deal every day. Students "belong" to someone. So too, we hear, do the schools. Schools need material support in order to exist. How shall the materials of life be dealt with? Is the private school the moral institution and the public school the immoral one? Should support be coerced? Should there be a compulsory "free" education system? With whom are the teachers contracted? Is there a right to strike? Is there an obligation to strike? To whom or to what do the teachers "belong"?

While "liberty" and "equality" are concepts of considerable logical power—only surpassed by the concept of "authority"—the battle lines of everyday life are drawn on the materials that make these concepts meaningful. Typically, the people involved in struggles over the means to these varied perceptions of concepts see the relationships but faintly. Nevertheless, a decision about whether each child should supply his own school materials (including books) or whether the public should supply these through the medium of taxation involves all our previous discussion. It is a decision of no small theoretical and practical import. Similarly, if public support of these purchases is assured, there are still a number of questions remaining. What, for example, is the most justifiable form of taxation?

All the discussion about "democracy" is merely many words flying in the air unless it results in some formula for the distribution of the materials that make life possible. More important, it is pernicious unless it deals in a formula that makes the "good" life possible. We have suggested, of course, that professionalism is an appropriate model for the "good" life. In the selections that follow you will find violent differences about what constitutes the proper (democratic) employment of material. Thus there is not only the question about what property is, but about how one contracts it. When we say "contracts it" we do not mean to suggest that it is a disease. Quite to the contrary, we would deny that money is the "root of all evil." It is merely one form of property and, as such, is necessary to human action. Unless all human action is evil it would appear that while property is indeed a problem, it is hardly something we could do without. *Inasmuch as the material world constitutes the beginning and the end of social action, one's emotions may be quite readily involved.* This particular chapter should be a good test of your capacity to follow the logic of the various positions to see where it leads *before* you attach labels and loyalties. Loyalties are necessary, as are labels. The latter are particularly misleading in this area and should be applied with the greatest of caution. This warning should be a partial aid to arriving at a reasonable loyalty.

This chapter contains three selections by prominent economic thinkers who have also had a continuing interest in education at one or more levels (both formal and informal). The first, by Friedrich A. Hayek, is a plea for democracy in the sense of economic individualism. The second, by Paul H.

Douglas, is a defense of democracy as welfare state. The third, by R. H. Tawney, argues for democracy as a professional society. In these three selections there is a completion of the considerations dealt with in Part Four of this book.

SERFDOM AND DEMOCRACY

Spencer maintained that the lack of educational opportunity in no way denied equal freedom to the child. Therefore, the state was not obligated to supply it. He further stated:

> Were there no direct disproof of the frequently alleged right to educate at the hands of the state, the absurdities in which it entangles its assertors would sufficiently show its invalidity. Conceding for a moment that the government is bound to educate a man's children, then, what kind of logic will demonstrate that it is not bound to feed and clothe them? If there should be an act-of-parliament provision for the development of their minds, why should there not be an act-of-parliament provision for the development of their bodies? If the mental wants of the rising generation ought to be satisfied by the state, why not their physical ones? The reasoning which is held to establish the right to intellectual food, will equally well establish the right to material food: nay, will do more—will prove that children should be altogether cared for by government. For if the benefit, importance, or necessity of education be assigned as a sufficient reason why government should educate, then may the benefit, importance, or necessity of food, clothing, shelter, and warmth be assigned as a sufficient reason why government should administer these also.[1]

The demand for compulsory education was a demand for property in terms of education as a thing or possession and also in terms of the materials to support such a process. Property had been a central concern for the classical liberals since the days of Locke and his doctrine of "natural rights"—"life," "liberty," and "estate." These were seen as universal and natural rights. To say this is to say that they may not be denied—they are absolute. The doctrine of "natural rights" was badly weakened by the French Revolution, which demonstrated the threat to the acquisition of large amounts of property that was implicit in the doctrine. The French saw property as essential to liberty. They turned what in England was a conservative doctrine (a protection against usurpation of the means of livelihood) to an active demand for property as a basis for the community of Frenchmen. This meant a redistribution of property by forces outside the market place. The English then came to see the defense

[1]Herbert Spencer, Social Statics (New York: Appleton-Century-Crofts, 1873), pp. 361–362.

of property as residing in the doctrine of utility. Thus pursuit, rather than some inherent claim to possession that was independent of one's success in that pursuit, became the right. As Tawney put it:

> English practical men . . . were a little shocked by the pomp and brilliance of that tremendous creed (of the French revolutionists). They had scanty sympathy with the absolute affirmations of France. What captured their imaginations was not the right to liberty, which made no appeal to their commercial instincts, but the expediency of liberty, which did; and when the Revolution had revealed the explosive power of the idea of natural right, they sought some less menacing formula.[2]

The revival of individualism and classical economic theory brought forth Spencer with a notion of natural law in an evolutionary sense. Here, the absence of property was evidence of bad fortune or just desserts. In any event, since the individual was authority, he authored his own fate. The author must receive his royalties and none other than these. The motivational mainspring of human beings, the natural law of competition, must be kept oiled.

The following selection by Friedrich A. Hayek reflects the spirit of this general position. Hayek, an economist, is concerned about economic planning. In it he sees disaster—dictatorship. He would maintain that progress can only be achieved by leaving men to their own devices. Moreover, he would maintain that leaving men to their own devices is not socially devisive. This voluntary association is the "democratic" way.

This says a great deal to the schoolman as he considers the kind of society he aims to produce, the kind of education to be given to the young, and the kind of support he can call upon in order to fulfill his task.

------◆------

PLANNING AND DEMOCRACY*

The statesman who should attempt to direct private people in what manner they ought to employ their capitals would not only load himself with a most unnecessary attention, but assume an authority which could safely be trusted to no council and senate

*Reprinted from *The Road to Serfdom* by Friedrich A. Hayek by permission of The University of Chicago Press. © 1944 by The University of Chicago Press. Dr. Hayek is an economic theorist. Formerly a professor at the University of London, he has been since 1950, a member of the Committee on Social Thought of the University of Chicago. He has authored *The Road to Serfdom*, *The Pure Theory of Capital*, and *The Sensory Order*.

[2]R. H. Tawney, *The Acquisitive Society* (New York: Harcourt, Brace & World, Inc., 1920), p. 15.

whatever, and which would nowhere be so dangerous as in the hands of a man who had folly and presumption enough to fancy himself fit to exercise it.—ADAM SMITH.

The common features of all collectivist systems may be described, in a phrase ever dear to socialists of all schools, as the deliberate organization of the labors of society for a definite social goal. That our present society lacks such "conscious" direction toward a single aim, that its activities are guided by the whims and fancies of irresponsible individuals, has always been one of the main complaints of its socialist critics.

In many ways this puts the basic issue very clearly. And it directs us at once to the point where the conflict arises between individual freedom and collectivism. The various kinds of collectivism, communism, fascism, and so forth, differ among themselves in the nature of the goal toward which they want to direct the efforts of society. But they all differ from liberalism and individualism in wanting to organize the whole of society and all its resources for this unitary end and in refusing to recognize autonomous spheres in which the ends of the individuals are supreme. In short, they are totalitarian in the true sense of this new word which we have adopted to describe the unexpected but nevertheless inseparable manifestations of what in theory we call collectivism.

The "social goal," or "common purpose," for which society is to be organized is usually vaguely described as the "common good," the "general welfare," or the "general interest." It does not need much reflection to see that these terms have no sufficiently definite meaning to determine a particular course of action. The welfare and the happiness of millions cannot be measured on a single scale of less and more. The welfare of a people, like the happiness of a man, depends on a great many things that can be provided in an infinite variety of combinations. It cannot be adequately expressed as a single end, but only as a hierarchy of ends, a comprehensive scale of values in which every need of every person is given its place. To direct all our activities according to a single plan presupposes that every one of our needs is given its rank in an order of values which must be complete enough to make it possible to decide among all the different courses which the planner has to choose. It presupposes, in short, the existence of a complete ethical code in which all the different human values are allotted their due place.

The conception of a complete ethical code is unfamiliar, and it requires some effort of imagination to see what it involves. We are not in the habit of thinking of moral codes as more or less complete. The fact that we are constantly choosing between different values without a social code prescribing how we ought to choose does not surprise us and does not suggest to us that our moral code is incomplete. In our society there is neither occasion nor reason why people should develop common views about what should be done in such situations. But where all the means to be used are the property of society and are to be used in the name of society according to a unitary plan, a "social" view about what ought to be done must guide all decisions. In such a world we should soon find that our moral code is full of gaps.

We are not concerned here with the question whether it would be desirable to have such a complete ethical code. It may merely be pointed out that up to the present the growth of civilization has been accompanied by a steady diminution of the sphere in which individual actions are bound by fixed rules. The rules of which our common moral code consists have progressively become fewer and more general in character. From the primitive man, who was bound by an elaborate ritual in almost every one of his daily activities, who was limited by innumerable taboos, and who could scarcely conceive of doing things in a way different from his fellows, morals have more and more tended to become merely limits circumscribing the sphere within which the individual could behave as he liked. The adoption of a common ethical code comprehensive enough to determine a unitary economic plan would mean a complete reversal of this tendency.

The essential point for us is that no such complete ethical code exists. The attempt to direct all economic activity according to a single plan would raise innumerable questions to which the answer could be provided only by a moral rule, but to which existing morals have no answer and where there exists no agreed view on what ought to be done. People will have either no definite views or conflicting views on such questions, because in the free society in which we have lived there has been no occasion to think about them and still less to form common opinions about them.

Not only do we not possess such an all-inclusive scale of values: it would be impossible for any mind to comprehend the infinite variety of different needs of different people which compete for the available resources and to attach a definite weight to each. For our problem it is of minor importance whether the ends for which any person cares comprehend only his own individual needs, or whether they include the needs of his closer or even those of his more distant fellows—that is, whether he is egoistic or altruistic in the ordinary senses of these words. The point which is so important is the basic fact that it is impossible for any man to survey more than a limited field, to be aware of the urgency of more than a limited number of needs. Whether his interests center round his own physical needs, or whether he takes a warm interest in the welfare of every human being he knows, the ends about which he can be concerned will always be only an infinitesimal fraction of the needs of all men.

This is the fundamental fact on which the whole philosophy of individualism is based. It does not assume, as is often asserted, that man is egoistic or selfish or ought to be. It merely starts from the indisputable fact that the limits of our powers of imagination make it impossible to include in our scale of values more than a sector of the needs of the whole society, and that, since, strictly speaking, scales of value can exist only in individual minds, nothing but partial scales of values exist—scales which are inevitably different and often inconsistent with each other. From this the individualist concludes that the individuals should be allowed, within defined limits, to follow their own values and preferences rather than somebody else's; that within these spheres the individual's system of ends should be supreme and not subject to any dictation by others. It is this recognition of the individual as the ultimate judge of his ends, the belief that as far as possible his own views ought to govern his actions, that forms the essence of the individualist position.

This view does not, of course, exclude the recognition of social ends, or rather of a coincidence of individual ends which makes it advisable for men to combine for their pursuit. But it limits such common action to the instances where individual views coincide; what are called "social ends" are for it merely identical ends of many individuals—or ends to the achievement of which individuals are willing to contribute in return for the assistance they receive in the satisfaction of their own desires. Common action is thus limited to the fields where people agree on common ends. Very frequently these common ends will not be ultimate ends to the individuals but means which different persons can use for different purposes. In fact, people are most likely to agree on common action where the common end is not an ultimate end to them but a means capable of serving a great variety of purposes.

When individuals combine in a joint effort to realize ends they have in common, the organizations, like the state, that they form for this purpose are given their own system of ends and their own means. But any organization thus formed remains one "person" among others, in the case of the state much more powerful than any of the others, it is true, yet still with its separate and limited sphere in which alone its ends are supreme. The limits of this sphere are determined by the extent to which the individuals agree on particular ends; and the probability that they will agree on a particular course of action necessarily decreases as the scope of such action extends. There are certain functions of the state on the exercise of which there will be practical unanimity among its citizens; there will be others on which there will be agreement of a substantial majority; and so on, until we come to fields where, although each individual might wish the state to act in some way, there will be almost as many views about what the government should do as there are different people.

We can rely on voluntary agreement to guide the action of the state only so long as it is confined to spheres where agreement exists. But not only when the state undertakes direct control in fields where there is no such agreement is it bound to suppress individual freedom. We can unfortunately not indefinitely extend the sphere of common action and still leave the individual free in his own sphere. Once the communal sector, in which the state controls all the means, exceeds a certain proportion of the whole, the effects of its actions dominate the whole system. Although the state controls directly the use of only a large part of the available resources, the effects of its decisions on the remaining part of the economic system become so great that indirectly it controls almost everything. Where, as was, for example, true in Germany as early as 1928, the central and local authorities directly control the use of more than half the national income (according to an official German estimate then, 53 percent), they control indirectly almost the whole economic life of the nation. There is, then, scarcely an individual end which is not dependent for its achievement on the action of the state, and the "social scale of values" which guides the state's action must embrace practically all individual ends.

It is not difficult to see what must be the consequences when democracy embarks upon a course of planning which in its execution requires more agreement than in fact exists. The people may have agreed on adopting a system of directed economy because they have been convinced that it will produce great prosperity. In the discussions leading to the decision, the goal of planning will have been described by some such term as "common welfare," which only conceals the absence of real agreement on the ends of planning. Agreement will in fact exist only on the mechanism to be used. But it is a mechanism which can be used only for a common end; and the question of the precise goal toward which all activity is to be directed will arise as soon as the executive power has to translate the demand for a single plan into a particular plan. Then it will appear that the agreement on the desirability of planning is not supported by agreement on the ends the plan is to serve. The effect of the people's agreeing that there must be central planning, without agreeing on the ends, will be rather as if a group of people were to commit themselves to take a journey together without agreeing where they want to go: with the result that they may all have to make a journey which most of them do not want at all. That planning creates a situation in which it is necessary for us to agree on a much larger number of topics than we have been used to, and that in a planned system we cannot confine collective action to the tasks on which we can agree but are forced to produce agreement on everything in order that any action can be taken at all, is one of the features which contributes more than most to determining the character of a planned system.

It may be the unanimously expressed will of the people that its parlia-

ment should prepare a comprehensive economic plan, yet neither the people nor its representatives need therefore be able to agree on any particular
plan. The inability of democratic assemblies to carry out what seems to be
a clear mandate of the people will inevitably cause dissatisfaction with
democratic institutions. Parliaments come to be regarded as ineffective
"talking shops," unable or incompetent to carry out the tasks for which
they have been chosen. The conviction grows that if efficient planning is to
be done, the direction must be "taken out of politics" and placed in the
hands of experts—permanent officials or independent autonomous bodies.

The difficulty is well known to socialists. It will soon be half a century
since the Webbs began to complain of "the increased incapacity of the
House of Commons to cope with its work."[1] More recently, Professor
Laski has elaborated the argument:

"It is common ground that the present parliamentary machine is quite
unsuited to pass rapidly a great body of complicated legislation. The National Government, indeed, has in substance admitted this by implementing its economy and tariff measures not by detailed debate in the House of
Commons but by a wholesale system of delegated legislation. A Labour
Government would, I presume, build upon the amplitude of this precedent. It would confine the House of Commons to the two functions it can
properly perform: the ventilation of grievances and the discussion of
general principles of its measures. Its Bills would take the form of general
formulae conferring wide powers on the appropriate government departments; and those powers would be exercised by Order in Council which
could, if desired, be attacked in the House by means of a vote of no confidence. The necessity and value of delegated legislation has recently been
strongly reaffirmed by the Donoughmore Committee; and its extension is
inevitable if the process of socialization is not to be wrecked by the normal
methods of obstruction which existing parliamentary procedure sanctions."

And to make it quite clear that a socialist government must not allow itself to be too much fettered by democratic procedure, Professor Laski at
the end of the same article raised the question "whether in a period of
transition to Socialism, a Labour Government can risk the overthrow of its
measures as a result of the next general election"—and left it significantly
unanswered.[2]

[1]Sidney and Beatrice Webb, *Industrial Democracy* (1897), p. 800 n.
[2]H. J. Laski, "Labour and the Constitution," *New Statesman and Nation,* no. 81
(September 10, 1932), p. 277. In a book (*Democracy in Crisis* [1933], particularly
p. 87) in which Professor Laski later elaborated these ideas, his determination that
parliamentary democracy must not be allowed to form an obstacle to the realization
of socialism is even more plainly expressed: not only would a socialist government
"take vast powers and legislate under them by ordinance and decree" and "suspend
the classic formulae of normal opposition" but the "continuance of parliamentary

It is important clearly to see the causes of this admitted ineffectiveness of parliaments when it comes to a detailed administration of the economic affairs of a nation. The fault is neither with the individual representatives nor with parliamentary institutions as such but with the contradictions inherent in the task with which they are charged. They are not asked to act where they can agree, but to produce agreement on everything—the whole direction of the resources of the nation. For such a task the system of majority decision is, however, not suited. Majorities will be found where it is a choice between limited alternatives; but it is a superstition to believe that there must be a majority view on everything. There is no reason why there should be a majority in favor of any one of the different possible courses of positive action if their number is legion. Every member of the legislative assembly might prefer some particular plan for the direction of economic activity to no plan, yet no one plan may appear preferable to a majority to no plan at all.

Nor can a coherent plan be achieved by breaking it up into parts and voting on particular issues. A democratic assembly voting and amending a comprehensive economic plan clause by clause, as it deliberates on an ordinary bill, makes nonsense. An economic plan, to deserve the name, must have a unitary conception. Even if a parliament could, proceeding step by step, agree on some scheme, it would certainly in the end satisfy nobody. A complex whole in which all the parts must be most carefully adjusted to each other cannot be achieved through a compromise between conflicting views. To draw up an economic plan in this fashion is even less possible than, for example, successfully to plan a military campaign by democratic procedure. As in strategy it would become inevitable to delegate the task to the experts.

Yet the difference is that, while the general who is put in charge of a campaign is given a single end to which, for the duration of the campaign, all the means under his control have to be exclusively devoted, there can be no such single goal given to the economic planner, and no similar limitation of the means imposed upon him. The general has not got to balance different independent aims against each other; there is for him only one supreme goal. But the ends of an economic plan, or of any part of it, cannot be defined apart from the particular plan. It is the essence of the economic problem that the making of an economic plan involves the choice between conflicting or competing ends—different needs of different

---

government would depend on its [that is, the Labour government's] possession of guarantees from the Conservative Party that its work of transformation would not be disrupted by repeal in the event of its defeat at the polls"! As Professor Laski invokes the authority of the Donoughmore Committee, it may be worth recalling that Professor Laski was a member of that committee and presumably one of the authors of its report.

people. But which ends do so conflict, which will have to be sacrificed if we want to achieve certain others, in short, which are the alternatives between which we must choose, can only be known to those who know all the facts; and only they, the experts, are in a position to decide which of the different ends are to be given preference. It is inevitable that they should impose their scale of preferences on the community for which they plan.

This is not always clearly recognized, and delegation is usually justified by the technical character of the task. But this does not mean that only the technical detail is delegated, or even that the inability of parliaments to understand the technical detail is the root of the difficulty.[3] Alterations in the structure of civil law are no less technical and no more difficult to appreciate in all their implications; yet nobody has yet seriously suggested that legislation there should be delegated to a body of experts. The fact is that in these fields legislation does not go beyond general rules on which true majority agreement can be achieved, while in the direction of economic activity the interests to be reconciled are so divergent that no true agreement is likely to be reached in a democratic assembly. . . .

It is the price of democracy that the possibilities of conscious control are restricted to the fields where true agreement exists and that in some fields things must be left to chance. But in a society which for its functioning depends on central planning this control cannot be made dependent on a majority's being able to agree; it will often be necessary

---

[3] It is instructive in this connection briefly to refer to the government document in which in recent years these problems have been discussed. As long as thirteen years ago, that is before England finally abandoned economic liberalism, the process of delegating legislative powers had already been carried to a point where it was felt necessary to appoint a committee to investigate "what safeguards are desirable or necessary to secure the sovereignty of Law." In its report the Donoughmore Committee (Report of the [Lord Chancellor's] Committee in Ministers' Powers, Cmd. 4060 [1932] showed that even at that date Parliament had resorted "to the practice of wholesale and indiscriminate delegation" but regarded this (it was before we had really glanced into the totalitarian abyss!) as an inevitably and relatively innocuous development. And it is probably true that delegation as such need not be a danger to freedom. The interesting point is why delegation had become necessary on such a scale. First place among the causes enumerated in the report is given to the fact that "Parliament nowadays passes so many laws every year" and that "much of the detail is so technical as to be unsuitable for Parliamentary discussion." But if this were all there would be no reason why the detail should not be worked out *before* rather than after Parliament passes a law. What is probably in many cases a much more important reason why, "if Parliament were not willing to delegate law-making power, Parliament would be unable to pass the kind and quantity of legislation which public opinion requires" is innocently revealed in the little sentence that "many of the laws affect people's lives so closely that elasticity is essential"! What does this mean if not conferment of arbitrary power—power limited by no fixed principles and which in the opinion of Parliament cannot be limited by definite and unambiguous rules?

that the will of a small minority be imposed upon the people, because
this minority will be the largest group able to agree among themselves
on the question at issue. Democratic government has worked successfully where, and so long as, the functions of government were, by a widely
accepted creed, restricted to fields where agreement among a majority
could be achieved by free discussion; and it is the great merit of the
liberal creed that it reduced the range of subjects on which agreement was
necessary to one on which it was likely to exist in a society of free men. It is
now often said that democracy will not tolerate "capitalism." If
"capitalism" means here a competitive system based on free disposal over
private property, it is far more important to realize that only within this
system is democracy possible. When it becomes dominated by a collectivist
creed, democracy will inevitably destroy itself.

We have no intention, however, of making a fetish of democracy. It may
well be true that our generation talks and thinks too much of democracy
and too little of the values which it serves. It cannot be said of democracy,
as Lord Acton truly said of liberty, that it "is not a means to a higher
political end. It is itself the highest political end. It is not for the sake of a
good public administration that it is required, but for the security in the
pursuit of the highest objects of civil society, and of private life."
Democracy is essentially a means, a utilitarian device for safeguarding internal peace and individual freedom. As such it is by no means infallible or
certain. Nor must we forget that there has often been much more cultural
and spiritual freedom under an autocratic rule than under some democracies—and it is at least conceivable that under the government of a very
homogeneous and doctrinaire majority democratic government might be
as oppressive as the worst dictatorship. Our point, however, is not that dictatorship must inevitably extirpate freedom but rather than planning leads
to dictatorship because dictatorship is the most effective instrument of
coercion and the enforcement of ideals and, as such, essential if central
planning on a large scale is to be possible. The clash between planning and
democracy arises simply from the fact that the latter is an obstacle to the
suppression of freedom which the direction of economic activity requires.
But in so far as democracy ceases to be a guaranty of individual freedom, it
may well persist in some form under a totalitarian regime. A true "dictatorship of the proletariat," even if democratic in form, if it undertook
centrally to direct the economic system, would probably destroy personal
freedom as completely as any autocracy has ever done.

The fashionable concentration on democracy as the main value threatened is not without danger. It is largely responsible for the misleading and
unfounded belief that, so long as the ultimate source of power is the will of
the majority, the power cannot be arbitrary. The false assurance which

many people derive from this belief is an important cause of the general unawareness of the dangers which we face. There is no justification for the belief that, so long as power is conferred by democratic procedure, it cannot be arbitrary; the contrast suggested by this statement is altogether false: it is not the source but the limitation of power which prevents it from being arbitrary. Democratic control *may* prevent power from becoming arbitrary, but it does not do so by its mere existence. If democracy resolves on a task which necessarily involves the use of power which cannot be guided by fixed rules, it must become arbitrary power.

FOR FURTHER THOUGHT

1. Again we note that Hayek says, "The common features of all collectivist systems may be described . . . as the deliberate organization of the labors of society for a definite goal." *Does this make the public school a collectivist system? Does it require a complete moral system before it can make any demands upon my property?* My children are my property. In some sense, at least, they are mine. *Does society have any right to compel them to attend schools?* We speak about "herself" and "himself" and thereby imply ownership. *Do I need a complete moral system in order to legitimately require my daughter (herself) to go to school? How would Hayek answer?*

2. The school and all its participants need forms of property in order to operate. *What if a substantial majority of the people in a community believe in private education and refuse to support public education? Does the public school have any claim to their money? Inasmuch as the public has not agreed upon the goals of education, does the institution have any claim upon the property of people even if the private school is not an issue? What would Hayek's response to this be?*

3. The task of educational planning is apparently too complicated for the public or their legislative bodies. Here we use planning, as does Hayek, in the sense of being comprehensive and coherent. *Does this mean rule by experts—including demands upon property of all sorts by experts? If experts profess to know the good, does this mean that such a profession is undemocratic if it runs counter to any other view?*

4. *Are disciplinary measures of any kind a violation of property rights insofar as they violate the "person" who is involved? What if the substantial majority of the senior class decides to take a day off from school without authorization from the school? Is it their time or is it the school's time? Does it make any difference whose time it is, as Hayek seems to think, or is there some other basis for making the decision rather than ownership?*

5. A large portion of school support often comes from local property

taxes. *Is the demand for money (property) on the part of a governmental unit (schools) any more dictatorial than the opposition to providing it (another demand for money) from the large or small property holders in the community? Is Hayek objecting to dictation or is he objecting to the arbitrary quality of a command? How does one tell when a command is arbitrary—when one doesn't agree? Do all these questions take us back to the "root" question—the authority question?*

WELFARE AND DEMOCRACY

Quite understandably, those who oppose Spencer, Butler, and others on the concept of authority and the correlative ideas of freedom and equality also oppose the idea of the distribution of property. They often oppose the resultant distribution and always oppose the basis for that distribution. In particular, they are incensed by the attempt of the classical liberals to put the question as a choice between a free economy and a planned economy. In the view of the modern liberal, this type of argumentation (question) is dishonest. It pretends to exhaust the alternatives and imply that the only alternative to a "free" economy is a static "totalitarian" system. There is, in the modern liberal view, the viable alternative of a *planning economy,* which at one fell swoop would extend the notion of liberty from the purely formal realm of politics (law) to the social and economic realm.

The standard should be the general interest (welfare) rather than the individual. The needs and demands of society must be met in order to form a human community—a community of interest and persuasion. It is the obligation of all men, and government as their agent, to enable man by making him free from want, unemployment, the ravages of illness and ignorance, and fear. In short, it is an affirmation of all that Spencer would deny.

The modern liberal would applaud Harold Laski who said:

> . . . let us remember that men think differently who live differently. . . . The less we live in the experience of our neighbors, the less shall we feel wrong in the denial of their wants. . . . The sense of solidarity comes only when the result of joint action impinges equally on the common life.[3]

"Common" does not, in this view, mean mediocre. It means an emphasis on things shared. It means that the ambitious and energetic become that way because the conditions of their lives enable them to be so. There is some point to their activity. The lazy and passive become that way because

---

[3]Harold J. Laski, *Liberty in the Modern State* (New York: Harper & Row, Publishers, 1930), pp. 214–215.

life is pointless. From this viewpoint, the classical liberal attitude toward the downtrodden neglects the meaning of the word "downtrodden." Thus it is that our society, which is organized in such a way as to give the downtrodden no chance or to hide whatever chances there might be, turns around and blames them for not being willing to take a chance—to try. So it is that the individuals of "individualism" refuse to accept their responsibility for either the welfare or the misery of others.

At no point is the modern liberal more vehement than when he insists upon the necessity of publicly supported education. Since the life of the mind is, in his view, sustained by the ideas and the materials of civilization, he would insist upon supplying both in an effort to create "intelligence." It must be remembered here that "intelligence" is considered to be a social product.

The selection by Senator Douglas appeared in the November, 1950 issue of *The Progressive*. It is a defense of the "general welfare" tradition in the United States. However, it is more than that—it is a defense of the concept of "general welfare" per se and an advocacy of extended efforts to meet this ideal.

THE WELFARE STATE: REFLECTIONS ON ITS PATERNITY AND POTENTIALITIES*

During this last year many derisive criticisms have been made of federal and state action to improve the people and the term "welfare state" has been used as a derogatory term to describe these activities. It is implied that initiative and self-reliance are being badly injured by governmental action to help people and that unless this dangerous trend is reversed or at least halted, the character of our citizens will be almost totally undermined.

It is always hinted and, indeed, sometimes directly stated that such welfare activities have their ideological origins outside the United States; that their true father is either Karl Marx or Lenin, and that it is the duty of all red-blooded Americans to spurn these works of the evil one and, even more, to reject their present advocates.

These are horrendous if somewhat foggy charges. When one presses for particulars, the fog seems to thicken. For when the castigators of the wel-

*Paul H. Douglas, "The Welfare State: Reflections on its Paternity and Potentialities." Reprinted from *The Progressive*, Madison, Wisconsin. Mr. Douglas was the Democratic Senator from Illinois and a member of the Economics Department of the University of Chicago. Among his publications are *Theory of Wages, Real Wages in the United States,* and *Social Security in the United States.*

fare state are asked if they would have us close down our schools and colleges and put barricades across our roads they indignantly ask us not to be absurd.

When we inquire whether we should lock the doors of our hospitals and medical research centers, they say we are caricaturing them.

Then when we try to probe further and suggest that perhaps they do not believe in old age security or unemployment compensation, they say we are misrepresenting their position.

But when we ask if it would not be well to save government money by cutting outlays for rivers and harbors, and doing away with the postal subsidies to newspapers, magazines, direct mail advertisers, mail order houses, airlines, and railways, these opponents of the welfare state commonly become apoplectic in their indignation that we should even think of taking away such legitimate aid to free enterprise.

It is, indeed, hard to arrive at the precise position of this group for it is as misty as the Great Boy with which Ibsen's *Peer Gynt* contended. To the degree that there is substance to their position, it seems to be compounded of two parts:

First, that while we should keep the present welfare activities of our state and federal government, we should spend less money upon them, and hence relieve the taxpayers of much of the heavy burden which they are bearing.

Second, that the federal and state governments should not take on any *new* welfare projects. In particular, it is urged that the federal government should not aid education in the states, should not help to make it easier for low- and middle-income folks to get better housing, and under no conditions should it carry out the Ewing Plan for medical care or the Brannan Plan for farming.

Now let me hasten to say that I, too, am opposed to both the Ewing and the Brannan Plans, for reasons which I have not time fully to develop here. But I would like to point out, if I may, that so far as the federal budget is concerned, our total expenditures for pensions to the aged, to mothers and to the blind, for education, health, and housing comes to about 2½ billions of dollars a year, or about 6 percent of the Federal budget.

This is in sharp contrast with the thirty and one-half billions which we are spending on arms for ourselves and our allies and for atomic energy, the four and one-half billions on foreign economic aid and occupation costs which we are spending to ward off Communism, or a total of thirty-five billions to prepare us more effectively against a future war. If we add the costs of past wars in the form of five and one-quarter billions for interest on the war-incurred public debt and six billions for veterans, we come to a total of about forty-six billions which is being spent yearly for past and present wars. This is more than 76 percent of the national budget.

It is the warfare world, therefore, and not the welfare state which causes our federal expenditures and taxes to be high.

Suppose we consider now whether the functions of government should include the promotion of human welfare. I should like to advance the thesis that this not only should be one of the purposes of government, but that *throughout the history of our nation that has been one of the primary aims—perhaps, the most primary—of our national government.* So, far from the welfare state being of alien origin, it is a vital and integral part of the American tradition and ideal.

We can begin at no better place than with the soul-stirring Declaration of Independence composed by the young Jefferson. For the inalienable rights of men which Jefferson proclaimed and which stirred the pulses of the world were not life, liberty, and property, as John Locke had held, but rather Life, Liberty, and the Pursuit of Happiness. And "to secure these rights," Jefferson declared, "governments are instituted amongst men, deriving their just powers from the consent of the governed."

It is interesting that Jefferson did not say the "right to happiness." That is perhaps beyond the power of mortal man to attain by himself and certainly beyond the power of human government to guarantee. But what Jefferson was asserting is that men should have not only the right but the chance "to pursue" happiness—namely, to chase it. What is this but the right to seek human welfare? And let us note also that according to Jefferson, the only purpose of government, indeed *the* purpose for which government was instituted, was to secure these rights for *all* men—not only for the rich and well-born, but also for the poor and humble; not merely for the planters, but also for the small farmers and artisans—yes, and for the fieldhands; not merely for white men, for Jefferson did not so restrict himself, but for black men as well; not merely for Protestants, but for Catholics, Jews, and free-thinkers in equal measure.

The Declaration of Independence was followed up two years later in 1778 by the adoption of the Articles of Confederation. It has been the fashion to disparage these Articles because of their manifest weakness in failing to create a sufficiently strong central government. This criticism is well-founded. The Articles were not adequate. But since newly born states, like persons, must creep before they can walk, so the adoption of the Constitution in 1787 would have been impossible had there not been the Articles of Confederation upon which to build.

And what did the all too neglected Articles of Confederation say were the purposes of the new confederacy—the United States of America—which was being born? Said Article III:

> The said states hereby severally enter into a firm league of friendship with each other for *their common defense, the security of their Liberties and their mutual and general welfare.*

Thus, even though the "first, fine, careless rapture" of the Declaration of Independence had passed and the Continental Congress, in the terrible period of Valley Forge and after, was faced with the difficult task of getting the 13 separate states to work together, it kept a steady view of what it and the people were trying to do, namely to provide for their "common defense" (or to protect their lives), to "secure their liberties" and for their "mutual and general welfare."

Let us turn now to the Constitution itself. From the hands of one of the most unlikely of persons, peg-legged Gouverneur Morris, who out-Hamiltoned Hamilton in his devotion to the few, the rich, the well-born, and the well-educated, came the preamble summing up the decisions of nearly four months of heated and sharp debate.

"We, the people of the United States, in order to form a more perfect union, establish justice, insure domestic tranquillity, provide for the common defense, *promote the general welfare* and secure the blessings of liberty to ourselves and our Posterity, do ordain and establish this Constitution for the United States of America."

Thus the promotion of the general welfare was listed as one of the five fundamental purposes of that more perfect union which was being formed.

When critics of the welfare state are confronted with this fact, they commonly reply that the preamble is merely rhetoric and that it confers no specific powers. These, they say, must instead be sought within the body of the Constitution itself. In a strict legal sense, this is of course true. But the preamble is nevertheless of value, along with the debates and actions of the Constitutional Convention, in showing what was the actual legislative intent of the Founding Fathers. It certainly aids in giving significance to the specific powers granted to Congress by the Constitution in Article I, Section 8, which states in its first paragraph:

> The Congress shall have Power to lay and collect Taxes, Duties, Imposts and Excises to pay the Debts and provide for the Common Defense and *General Welfare* of the United States.

But the opponents of the so-called welfare state have still another defense when this paragraph is quoted. They argue that the power of Congress to spend for the general welfare does not extend to any purposes other than those which are later enumerated in Article I, Section 8. In effect therefore, what these men are saying is that it is not enough for the "general welfare" to be specifically mentioned in the preamble as one of the basic purposes of the new union and also placed in the lead-off position among the enumerated powers as an object for which taxes could be levied, but it is also necessary that it should be mentioned a third time. In default of this, it is argued that Congress has no Constitutional powers to spend money for the general welfare.

Now it is true that this is the theoretical position which Madison took in his later days, when he was alarmed by Hamilton's use of this clause to justify the chartering of the First Bank of the United States, and his use of the taxing power to justify a protective tariff, and by the general Federalist policy of favoring the rich and powerful.

But from Madison's own notes of the proceedings of the Constitutional Convention and from the *Official Journal* of the Convention itself, it can be shown that this was not Madison's position at the time the Constitution was drafted nor was it the intent of the Convention itself.

The Committee of Detail, named July 26, 1787, to bring in a draft of the Constitution by Aug. 6, submitted a rather full draft, which did not contain a general welfare clause, but on Aug. 22, the Committee brought in a further recommendation that the 7th article should have a clause added to it which would give to the Congress the power "to provide, as becomes necessary from time to time, for the well-managing and securing the common property and general interests and welfare of the United States in such manner as shall not interfere with the governments of individual states in matters which respect only their internal police or for which their individual authorities may be competent."

This clause, therefore, specifically gave to the Congress the power to *legislate* for the general welfare, thus carrying out the recommendations which had been made at the opening of the Convention by the Virginia Plan.

This clause, along with other points which had not been definitely approved, was referred on August 31 to a committee, which brought in a recommendation that the first clause of the first section of the 7th article should be as follows: "The Legislature shall have power to lay and collect taxes, duties, imposts and excises, to pay the debts, and provide for the common defense and general welfare."

The effect of this new provision is obvious. Rather than the legislative branch being given the power to *legislate* for the general welfare, it was, *instead,* given the power to *spend* for the general welfare. This new clause was agreed to on the same day, apparently without discussion and without a roll-call. It was one of the many integrated solutions which enabled the new Constitution to come into being.

Thus, the weight of the proceedings shows that the founding fathers did not intend the words of the preamble as idle rhetoric. Having canvassed the situation, they came to the conclusion that the general welfare should be promoted by public expenditures if not by direct legislation.

It was the fact that such a provision was indeed already imbedded in the text of the Constitution that the Committee on Style, building on both the text and the Articles of Confederation, explicitly mentioned it in the preamble as one of the five basic purposes of the more perfect union which was being formed. The welfare concept should not, therefore, be relegated to a Cinderella role. It is in the forefront as an equal partner of Justice, Domestic Tranquillity, Defense, and Liberty. And in the first clause of Article I, Section 8 there is provided an effective way of promoting this general welfare, namely, to spend for it.

I hope that this discussion should establish both the legitimate American paternity of the doctrine that it is proper for our government to concern itself with human welfare and that it is constitutional for it to spend money in furtherance of these ends. Far from springing from Marx and Lenin, it instead comes down to us from George Mason, Thomas Jefferson, and the younger Madison. It is eloquently re-stated by Lincoln, who at Gettysburg declared that ours was a government not only "of" and "by" the people but also "for" the people.

It has sprung from the well-springs of the American people themselves, the hardy frontiersmen and farmers, handicraftsmen, manual workers, and professional men—and never forgetting them, the women. For with all their proper emphasis upon individualism, and self-reliance, the American people have always known that there are some burdens too heavy to be borne alone and some evils which can be removed only by collective action. To help bear these burdens and to help remove these evils, it is proper for the government, as one of the agencies for collective betterment, to act.

So, far from being in the Marxist tradition, this is one of the very factors which has helped to give the lie to his predictions of an inevitable class struggle. Because the state has concerned itself with the troubles and difficulties of average people who have little property and low incomes, it has helped to win and retain their loyalty and devotion to the democratic principles, which, though under attack in most of the world, stand firm in America. They stand firm here because they are rooted in the hearts of the people who see in government, not an instrument of oppression, or an icy institution indifferent to their needs, but an agency which is carrying into effect at least some of the principles of human brotherhood.

There remains of course the practical question of what measures actually do serve human welfare and for how much welfare we can afford at any given time to pay. I do not want to minimize the importance of these questions but I would like to suggest that they are of a lower order of magnitude than the ideological issues, which, though vague, nevertheless disturb men's minds. The questions at stake are instead prudential issues. They are issues of fact and of judgment upon which men of probity may differ but about which disputes ought not to become too bitter. The following facts may be of some significance:

One—The total amount spent by public agencies at all levels for education, health and public assistance amounts to about 8.6 billions of dollars or 4 percent of the national income and 43 percent of what the national government spends for military and economic preparations against war. It is 67 percent of the nation's combined bill for spiritous liquors and tobacco. Of this total, 5.8 billions is spent for education and 2.3 billions for assistance to the aged, for mothers of dependent children and those on relief, and only ½ billion for health. It would not seem as though this total is excessive. The heavens would still stand if we were to spend slightly more money for these purposes provided everything else in our economy remained the same.

Two—The areas where unmet needs are greatest are probably the rehabilitation of the physically handicapped, housing, and health.

It is only recently that we have begun to awaken to the very large number of severely handicapped people in this country. The number who are totally and more or less permanently disabled is probably close to half a million, while the number of severely handicapped is probably three times this number. By far the largest proportion of these unfortunates were not crippled in industry, but as a result of such diseases as infantile paralysis, cerebral palsy, arthritis, and so forth.

Adequate rehabilitation which will combine medical and surgical care, psychological stimulus, the provision of special apparatus, occupational training and placement will be a good investment. It will help reclaim for productive lives many who would otherwise be largely lost.

Housing is another pressing need for both low-income and middle-income families. A lowering of building costs is badly needed through improved methods such as fabrication and assembly on the job, prefabrication, the giving up of unreasonable restrictions by unions and of price agreements by the manufacturers and distributors of building materials. Even this, however, would not bring housing down within reach of the lowest income third of the population.

The slums of our cities where the urban portion of this group have to live are breeding places for juvenile delinquency, crime, and disease. They are at once a health hazard and an economic waste. Like cancer they need to be removed by a major surgical operation. The replacement of the slums by decent housing would reduce juvenile delinquency and crime, improve health, raise personal productivity, and immeasurably strengthen family life.

But the slums cannot be replaced with decent housing for the low-income groups by private capital. For one thing, slum land costs too much, and in the second place the incomes of the poor are still below the amount required for decent housing on low-cost land with adequate space per family. That is why the public housing law passed last year by the 81st

Congress will be of help, since it will permit the localities to launch projects for 810,000 families in this group.

The middle-income families can be helped not only by the lower construction costs which I have outlined, but also by lowering interest and maintenance costs. One of the best ways of effecting this reduction is through the formation of co-operatives, which, since they engage in wholesale operations, should be helped to obtain access to the capital market at wholesale interest rates and also be given the chance to maintain the properties in part by the personal services of the co-operators.

Finally, in the field of health, there are three admitted needs. First, more research is needed into the causes of such diseases as cancer, cerebral palsy, arthritis, rheumatic heart trouble, and so forth. This is a costly affair. Secondly, we need much larger hospital facilities, particularly for the farming regions and the lower- and middle-income groups of our towns and cities. Finally, we need more physicians, especially to serve farm families and those with incomes under $3,500 or $4,000 a year in cities and towns.

It is a striking fact that we are graduating no more doctors today for our population of 150 million than we did a half century ago for a population which was only half as large. Certainly it would be worthwhile for us to finance the medical education of an additional 2500 doctors a year for a period of 10 years on condition that at least nine-tenths of these spend a minimum of five years service in under-doctored areas and not more than a tenth in medical research as a return for the help thus given to them. Farm organizations can help in providing a market for the services of these doctors.

There remains the question of insurance against the cost of medical care. The Blue Cross and Blue Shield have been making real headway in dealing with this problem, partially stimulated, perhaps, by the threat of the so-called Ewing Plan for insurance against all medical and hospital costs. The Ewing Plan goes altogether too far in my judgment in providing for insurance against the cost of headaches, backaches, stomach aches, the common cold and other minor ailments for which the major responsibility should fall upon the individual.

Since the Blue Cross and Blue Shield merely insure against the first portion of hospital and medical costs and since their coverage is at best imperfect, there is a real need for insurance against the catastrophic costs of sickness when costs run above 5 percent of a family's income or, say, $150, whichever is smaller. This would use insurance for its real purpose, namely as a protection against heavy and unforeseeable losses.

I should like to suggest that here is a middle ground upon which the American Medical Association and Mr. Ewing might well meet, since it is the core of the real economic problem of sickness. It is not the small sicknesses which wreck families financially. They can generally care for these. It is instead the costs of catastrophic illness which cause the real trouble. We could deal with this problem at a third of the cost which the Ewing plan would entail and with a minimum of red tape if we could get the present contestants to get together on a constructive program such as I have suggested.

In the carrying out of any such program, we should guard against building up a centralized administrative bureaucracy and should instead decentralize decisions and administration to the fullest possible degree. This can be done both through the system of federal aid to the states and localities and by utilizing private and voluntary organizations which can stand midway between the individual and the state.

The system of federal aid permits the federal government to collect taxes, primarily on the basis of ability to pay, and to distribute this money on the basis of need to the states to be administered by them. It thus combines federal finance with decentralized administration. Such an approach can be utilized in the fields of health, rehabilitation, and housing by the use of private agencies.

The Hill-Burton hospital Construction Act is an important illustration of what can be done. Instead of confining federal aid solely to public hospitals, aid is also given to other non-profit hospitals managed by churches and by philanthropic groups. These have been enabled to expand and at the same time private contributions and interest have not only been retained but on the whole have been increased. For federal grants should only be in addition to previous private and local contributions and, if the localities can afford it, should seek to get more and not less in local contributions.

In a similar fashion, cooperatives can be utilized to do many of the functions which government would otherwise be driven to perform. Agricultural credit, for example, is more and more being put upon a cooperative basis and the government is gradually withdrawing as its original advances of capital are being repaid. Perhaps a similar program, modeled in part upon the old Schulze-Delitsch banks of Germany, may turn out to be the best solution for the vexing problem of providing adequate credit for small business and in certain localities rural health can be improved in this manner. Certain it is that, wherever practicable, cooperative housing is better than public housing and cooperative or mutual insurance better than government insurance.

Finally, in the distribution of grants-in-aid to states, the formula which is used should be such as to permit the size of the federal grant to vary inversely with the relative financial ability of the people of the various states. Per capita income is probably still the best measure of this ability. This would call for the poorer states receiving a larger federal contribution than the wealthier and for their own required contributions to be less.

I hope that this discussion of the historical background of the welfare concept and of some of the practical methods of administration whereby the good can be maximized and the possible abuses minimized, may take some of the heat out of the intellectual atmosphere and make it possible for us to deal in an open-minded manner with the concrete questions of what, if anything, should be done next. There will still be differences of opinion, but they will not shatter men's souls nor rend the heavens. That is proper, for they should not.

FOR FURTHER THOUGHT

1. We often face the claim that the society cannot afford X. This X might be taken, for example, as meaning free university education. When one claims that "we cannot afford X," *could he be saying: we do not want X or X is not important enough for us to pay the price of Y and Z for it? Can X be judged in isolation or does judgment require some context? What other things might be meant by "we cannot afford X"?*

2. *Would such things as free university education make an increase in public control, investment, and ownership likely? Should public control be justified on the basis of ownership?*

3. *With* regard to ownership, it is said that "the schools belong to the people." If we take people to mean more than a collection, *can we say that private property is being taxed to support the schools? What is the distinction between public and private property?*

4. *What kind of position should the teacher take on the requisition of the materials of instruction? Is this a matter of requesting materials or demanding them? Avoiding the strategic level, at which a demand may be phrased as a request, what are the implications for education and the social order in a voluntary approach to property? What are the implications for compulsion of some sort? What constitutes the very best case that can be made for both approaches?*

5. *In what ways are one's answers dependent upon the various conceptions of authority, freedom, and equality that have been previously explored?*

THE PROFESSIONAL SOCIETY AND DEMOCRACY

The modern liberal position does not exhaust the alternatives. This is especially true when one traces its authority base for the definition of the "general welfare." As classical liberalism was a revolt against the political and economic monopoly of royalty, modern liberalism can be seen as a revolt against great concentrations of wealth and political power of the industrial "barons" who made the lives of large masses of people relatively barren. There is still an objection from some that the solutions (in terms of conceptual apparatus) offered by the modern liberals are essentially subjective.

The claim is that the group interest provides no more steady guide than that of the individual interest. In talking about the new organizations beginning to dot the landscape of the western world, Peter Druker suggests an organizational principle that goes "beyond collectivism and individualism."

> The individual people of skill, knowledge, and judgement cannot exercise somebody else's authority or somebody else's knowledge. They exercise their own knowledge and should have the authority that befits their contribution. It is the job that determines the authority and the responsibility of the holder—and this is original authority grounded in the needs and objective requirements for performance rather than in the power of the man above. The only power the top man must have is that of deciding whether a certain contribution is needed—and even that, increasingly, must be an objective decision according to the objective needs of the organization rather than a power decision. . . .
>
> In asking for the principle of the new organization we ask for the principle of human order in society. The elements of this new configuration which we have here called the "new organization," are human beings. Its process is human dedication, human knowledge, and human effort. Its purpose is the creation and the satisfaction of human values. And its principle of organization must therefore be a vision of man in society.[4]

We take this to mean that a man's rights (authority) are derived from the object to be realized and the validity of his claim to be able to carry out the task. Any claim on another basis would be, in the language of Tawney, a claim to "priviledge" in the name of "right." According to Tawney, "a priviledge is a right to which no corresponding function is attached."[5] This appears to have been the condition of men over the ages who have seen rights as fundamental and thus independent of any other claim. This is particularly true of property rights. Yet Tawney would criticize those who dogmatically condemn either private or public property systems. Property, as a matter of fact, must be protected, but it has "rights" only

[4]Peter F. Druker, *Landmarks of Tomorrow* (New York: Harper & Row, Publishers, 1957), pp. 96–98.

[5]R. H. Tawney, *The Acquisitive Society* (New York: Harcourt, Brace & World, Inc., 1920), p. 24.

to the extent that it serves a social function—this is to say that it has no "rights" at all, but that it (property) is right or proper when it serves the standard of *right* or "social function."

Consequently, Tawney approves of Bacon's remark: "Wealth is like muck. It is not good but if it be spread." And this, indeed, is understandable when one views Tawney's belief that "property was to be an aid to creative work, not an alternative to it."[6] Thus, society and wealth should be organized on the basis of "service." The problem of modern man is to be found in the shift from "active" property—that which is a necessary condition to production—to "passive" property where functionless owners "reap what another has sown." The failure of modern man has been in seeing social conflict originating between the "employees" and the "employers." It does not reside there. According to Tawney, it exists primarily between all those who do constructive work and those who wish to live off that work without regard to any active contribution on their part.

Tawney, like Druker, is concerned with the type of organization that would support such a state of affairs. He turns to the professions and would, in fact, professionalize the total society in the sense that service, rather than individual gain, would be their guide. Of course, he was not blind to qualities such as "greed" and "egotism." No system can, perhaps, eradicate these completely:

> What it can do is to create an environment in which those are not the qualities which are encouraged. It cannot secure that men live up to their principles. What it can do is to establish their social order upon principles to which, if they please, they can live up and not live down.[7]

It is difficult to see how one can read the above without seeing it as a scathing criticism of much of modern life. As such, it suggests a new type of man to be educated, new attitudes to be nurtured, and perhaps a different basis for the claims to the materials necessary to the teacher in the name of education. "Education," not the teacher, demands it as a right— the *right*. The withholding of the condition for its achievement in the name of the absolute rights of property is a demand for "privilege."

A clearer view of all this would be useful. This introduction we believe to be essential to the understanding of the following selection. The selection by Tawney is crucial to a clear understanding of our introduction. Thus, they exist in symbiotic relation. Tawney is usually thought of as an able economist and social historian. It may well be the case that his lasting claim to fame may reside in his contribution to education.

[6]Tawney, p. 59.
[7]Tawney, pp. 180–81.

THE FUNCTIONAL SOCIETY*

The application to property and industry of the principle of function is compatible with several different types of social organization, and is as unlikely as more important revelations to be the secret of those who cry "Lo here!" and "Lo there!" The essential thing is that men should fix their minds upon the idea of purpose, and give that idea pre-eminence over all subsidiary issues. If, as is patent, the purpose of industry is to provide the material foundation of a good social life, then any measure which makes that provision more effective, so long as it does not conflict with some still more important purpose, is wise, and any institution which thwarts or encumbers it is foolish. It is foolish, for example, to cripple education, as it is crippled in England for the sake of industry; for one of the uses of industry is to provide the wealth which may make possible better education. It is foolish to maintain property rights for which no service is performed, for payment without service is waste; and if it is true, as statisticians affirm, that, even were income equally divided, income per head would be small, then it is all the more foolish, for sailors in a boat have no room for first-class passengers, and it is all the more important that none of the small national income should be misapplied. It is foolish to leave the direction of industry in the hands of servants of private property-owners who themselves know nothing about it but its balance sheets, because this is to divert it from the performance of service to the acquisition of gain, and to subordinate those who do creative work to those who do not.

The course of wisdom in the affairs of industry is, after all, what it is in any other department of organized life. It is to consider the end for which economic activity is carried on and then to adapt economic organization to it. It is to pay for service and for service only, and when capital is hired to make sure that it is hired at the cheapest possible price. It is to place the responsibility for organizing industry on the shoulders of those who work and use, not of those who own, because production is the business of the producer and the proper person to see that he discharges his business is the consumer for whom, and not for the owner of property, it ought to be carried on. Above all it is to insist that all industries shall be conducted in

*From *The Acquisitive Society* by R. H. Tawney, copyright, 1920, by Harcourt, Brace & World, Inc.; renewed, 1948, by R. H. Tawney. Reprinted by permission of the publishers. World rights granted by G. Bell & Sons, Ltd., publishers, London, England. Professor Tawney is well known for his writings which include *Equality, The Acquisitive Society,* and *Religion and the Rise of Capitalism.* As a member of the London School of Economics, he demonstrated keen interest in social history, education, and political economy. He has been described as a "democratic socialist par excellence."

complete publicity as to costs and profits, because publicity ought to be the antiseptic both of economic and political abuses, and no man can have confidence in his neighbor unless both work in the light.

As far as property is concerned, such a policy would possess two edges. On the one hand, it would aim at abolishing those forms of property in which ownership is divorced from obligations. On the other hand, it would seek to encourage those forms of economic organization under which the worker, whether owner or not, is free to carry on his work without sharing its control or its profits with the mere *rentier*. Thus, if in certain spheres it involved an extension of public ownership, it would in others foster an extension of private property. For it is not private ownership, but private ownership divorced from work, which is corrupting to the principle of industry; and the idea of some socialists that private property in land or capital is necessarily mischievous is a piece of scholastic pedantry as absurd as that of those conservatives who would invest all property with some kind of mysterious sanctity. It all depends what sort of property it is and for what purpose it is used. Provided that the State retains its eminent domain, and controls alienation, as it does under the Homestead laws of the Dominions, with sufficient stringency to prevent the creation of a class of functionless property-owners, there is no inconsistency between encouraging simultaneously a multiplication of peasant farmers and small masters who own their own farms or shops, and the abolition of private ownership in those industries, unfortunately to-day the most conspicuous, in which the private owner is an absentee shareholder.

Indeed, the second reform would help the first. In so far as the community tolerates functionless property it makes difficult, if not impossible, the restoration of the small master in agriculture or in industry, who cannot easily hold his own in a world dominated by great estates or capitalist finance. In so far as it abolishes those kinds of property which are merely parasitic, it facilitates the restoration of the small property-owner in those kinds of industry for which small ownership is adapted. A socialistic policy towards the former is not antagonistic to the "distributive state," but, in modern economic conditions, a necessary preliminary to it, and if by "Property" is meant the personal possessions which the word suggests to nine-tenths of the population, the object of socialists is not to undermine property but to protect and increase it. The boundary between large scale and small scale production will always be uncertain and fluctuating, depending, as it does, on technical conditions which cannot be foreseen: a cheapening of electrical power, for example, might result in the decentralization of manufactures, as steam resulted in their concentration. The fundamental issue, however, is not between different scales of ownership, but between ownership of different kinds, not between the large farmer or master and the small, but between property which is used for work and property which yields income without it. The Irish landlord was abolished, not because he owned a large scale, but because he was an owner and nothing more; if, and when English land-ownership has been equally attenuated, as in towns it already has been, it will deserve to meet the same fate. Once the issue of the character of ownership has been settled, the question of the size of the economic unit can be left to settle itself.

The first step, then, towards the organization of economic life for the performance of function is to abolish those types of private property in return for which no function is performed. The man who lives by owning without working is necessarily supported by the industry of some one else, and is, therefore, too expensive a luxury to be encouraged. Though he deserves to be treated with the leniency which ought to be, and usually is not, shown to those who have been brought up from infancy to any other disreputable trade, indulgence to individuals must not condone the institution of which both they and their neighbors are the victims. Judged by this standard, certain kinds of property are obviously anti-social. The rights in virtue of which the owner of the surface is entitled to levy a tax, called a royalty, on every ton of coal which the miner brings to the surface, to levy another tax, called a way-leave, on every ton of coal transported under the surface of his land though its amenity and value may be quite unaffected, to distort, if he pleases, the development of a whole district by refusing access to the minerals except upon his own terms, and to cause some 3,500 to 4,000 million tons to be wasted in barriers between different properties, while he in the meantime contributes to a chorus of lamentation over the wickedness of the miners in not producing more tons of coal for the public and incidentally more private taxes for himself—all this adds an agreeable touch of humor to the drab quality of our industrial civilization for which mineral owners deserve perhaps some recognition, though not the £ 100,000 odd a year which is paid to each of the four leading players, or the £ 6,000,000 a year which is distributed among the crowd.

The alchemy by which a gentleman who has never seen a coal mine distills the contents of that place of gloom into elegant chambers in London and a place in the country is not the monopoly of royalty owners. A similar feat of presdigitation is performed by the owner of urban ground-rents. In rural districts some landlords, perhaps many landlords, are partners in the hazardous and difficult business of agriculture, and, though they may often exercise a power which is socially excessive, the position which they hold and the income which they receive are, in part at last, a return for the functions which they perform. The ownership of urban land has been refined till of that crude ore only the pure gold is left. It is the perfect sinecure, for the only function it involves is that of collecting its profits, and in an age when the struggle of Liberalism against sinecures was still sufficiently recent to stir some chords of memory, the last and greatest of liberal thinkers drew the obvious deduction. "The reasons which form the justification . . . of property in land," wrote Mill in 1848, "are valid only in so far as the proprietor of land is its improver. . . . In no sound theory of private property was it ever contemplated that the proprietor of land should be merely a sinecurist quartered on it." Urban ground-rents and royalties are, in fact, as the Prime Minister in his unregenerate days suggested, a tax which some persons are permitted by the law to levy upon the industry of others. They differ from public taxation only in that their amount increases in proportion not to the nation's need of revenue but to its need of the coal and space on which they are levied, that their growth inures to private gain not to public benefit, and that if the proceeds are wasted on frivolous expenditure no one has any right to complain, because the arrangement by which Lord Smith spends wealth produced by Mr. Brown on objects which do no good to either is part of the system which, under the name of private property, Mr. Brown as well as Lord Smith have learned to regard as essential to the higher welfare of mankind.

But if we accept the principle of function we shall ask what is the *purpose* of this arrangement, and for what *end* the inhabitants of, for example, London pay £16,000,000 a year to their ground landlords. And if we find that it is for no purpose and no end, but that these things are like the horseshoes and nails which the City of London presents to the Crown on account of land in the Parish of St. Clement Danes, then we shall not deal harshly with a quaint historical survival, but neither shall we allow it to distract us from the business of the present, as though there had been history but there were not history any longer. We shall close these channels through which wealth leaks away by resuming the ownership of minerals and of urban land, as some communities in the British Dominions and on the Continent of Europe have resumed it already. We shall secure that such large accumulations as remain change hands at least once in every generation, by increasing our taxes on inheritance till what passes to the heir is little more than personal possessions, not the right to a tribute from industry which, though qualified by death-duties, is what the son of a rich man inherits today. We shall treat mineral owners and landowners, in short, as Plato would have treated the poets, whom in their ability to make something out of nothing and to bewitch mankind with words they a little resemble, and crown them with flowers and usher them politely out of the State.

FOR FURTHER THOUGHT

1. Some societies seem to be ordered by individual acquisition. This is the primary motivating force, and consequently becomes the motif for

their life style. Among the things to be acquired is education. This kind
of education would be seen by Tawney as divisive. *Why would this be
the case? Is not learning something that each has to do for himself?
What about knowing? Is that private, too?*
2. What is the primary aim of education—*learning or knowing? What
difference does this make in the organization of a curriculum, the evaluation of the students, and the selection of the teachers?*
3. *How is the primary purpose of life different from the primary purpose of education? Should society and schools be differently principled?*
4. If one must improve the land in order to justify his "rights" to it,
*what must he do to justify his "rights" to life? In what sense is it "my"
life? If the standard is external to me, in what sense is my life a possession? In what sense is suicide or sacrifice an individual giving or taking? Logically speaking, does the Tawney position declare that you are
your brother's keeper, your keeper's brother, or your brother?*
5. As a student, teacher, parent, or taxpayer *what is the only justification
you might have for demanding additional funds for the library?*

SUGGESTIONS FOR FURTHER READING

1. There is an enormous body of literature concerning the economic
base of a just society. Many of the readings already suggested have
direct implications for the distribution and use of property. In particular, Hayek's *Road to Serfdom* and Tawney's *The Acquisitive Society,*
from which we have taken selections for this chapter, are illuminating.
More general works such as Joan Robinson, *Economic Philosophy* (Garden City, N. Y.: Doubleday & Company, Inc., 1964); George N. Halm,
Economic Systems (New York: Holt, Rinehart and Winston, Inc., 1960);
and R. H. Tawney, *Religion and the Rise of Capitalism* (New York: Mentor
Books, 1947) can provide a measure of philosophical depth and historical
breadth that is useful.
2. During the past 20 years there has been a flood of popular readable
discussions of economics and modern society in one form or another.
The following, although not exhaustive, covers a wide spectrum of views
on this topic. See Carl Becker, *Freedom and Responsibility in the Amer-
ican Way of Life* (New York: Alfred A. Knopf, Inc., 1945); Peter Druker,
Landmarks of Tomorrow (New York: Harper & Row, Publishers, 1957);
Milton Friedman, *Capitalism and Freedom* (Chicago: University of Chi-
cago Press, 1962); John Kenneth Galbraith, *American Capitalism: The
Concept of Countervailing Power* (Boston: Houghton Mifflin, 1952) and
The New Industrial State (Boston: Houghton Mifflin, 1967); Robert L.
Heilbronner, *The Limits of American Capitalism* (New York: Harper &
Row, Publishers, 1966); Ayn Rand, *Capitalism, The Unknown Ideal*

(New York: New American Library, 1966); and Barbara Wooton, *Freedom under Planning* (Chapel Hill, N. C.: University of North Carolina Press, 1945).

Summary of Part Four

The basic question of this section has been "What is the nature of this thing called democracy?" In looking at answers to this question it should be remembered that we have not been looking at "cold" concepts alone, but at belief patterns held by people. And of course there are, as indicated by the disputes, some terribly unhappy people in our society. Not the least of these are the classical liberals who find themselves and their kind being swallowed up in what they often refer to as "creeping socialism." This "creeping socialism" they fear is more than economic. It involves the demand for consensus and, perhaps, the scientific method as authority. One may picture the moral dilemma and emotional trauma of those committed to democracy as "individualism" when they are products of public schools and attend state universities. Those who wish to teach are particularly hard pressed. The "better" jobs are generally to be found in public schools with their tax support and compulsory attendance.

There are others who are unhappy with the remnants of *laissez faire* individualism on the present scene. Ever fearful of a rebirth of this doctrine are the modern liberals who would point in biblical terms to the concept of "grace" or to the music of Gilbert and Sullivan with its emphasis upon the "accident of birth." In short, they would point to all the things beyond the control of the atomistic individual that make him what he is. They would insist that there is a social obligation for a redress of grievances—to go beyond the letter of the law to its spirit, its heart, its *common* sense. More fundamental, if there are to be laws, the modern liberal would insist that they reflect the observations of the social sciences rather than "untenable" assumptions about the innate character of man.

Still more unhappy are the corporatists or the functionalists. In the main, they would applaud the spirit of the modern liberal. Nevertheless, they would see the classical and modern liberals as subjectivists and incapable of resolving the problems of man. They would point to the *fact* that we now have the technology (pills) that would make men (and the society) feel better. However, being better and feeling better are likely to be two quite different things. The good man and the good society are not *simply* conditions of singular, collected or collective nervous systems. It is a set of objective relations—conditions about which man should feel good. If he feels good about a bad set of conditions, he is sick! Neither the classical nor the modern liberal could logically make that statement. He then is unhappy because the liberals ask the wrong questions. He may also be unhappy with the kind of answers he himself can deliver at this moment.

So much for a summary of the flavor of these positions. The key notion within the concept of democracy has been judged to be "authority." Authority has been seen as: (1) an individual (inherent rights); (2) a collection of individuals (as majority rule); (3) a consensus (shared intelligence or the "forum"); (4) a method (of science); and (5) a culture (social function).

From these different conceptions of authority flow the conceptions of liberty, equality, and the consequent disposition of property. The absence of external restraint, the voluntary acceptance of restraint, effective and intelligent choice, and the appropriate (cultural) act all become candidates for the name of liberty and, consequently, for the name of slavery in the eyes of their opponents. Equality became the norm in the political realm for all. However, a bitter division develops over equality "before" and equality "after" the law. The classical liberals insist on a formal notion of equality (no legal prohibition). The others insist on legalized differential treatment (legislation for material and social equity) as a necessary condition for equality (sameness) "before" the law. Consequently, men like Butler and Hayek have tended to see equality and liberty as incompatible while Tussman, Dewey, Barnett, Tawney, and Douglas have tended to see them as mutually supporting ideas. The ideological battle within democracy extends, of course, to property. In a sense, it may be said to start there, for it is in the various forms of property and their relationships that life finds its sustenance. Different forms and relationships will support different kinds of lives and develop different kinds of people. Thus it is that we find ourselves back with Socrates and the question of what kind of life is "worth living." It has been a long journey, but it clearly indicates, among other things, that these various conceptions of democracy are ethical systems. They stand as recommendations to the teacher—to all. They stand as models for:

1. The ideal society (an answer to the *root* question);
2. directing human behavior (answer the question of expectations and allow one to predict behavior); and
3. the ethical distribution of power—political, social, and economic—by which points *1* and *2* can be achieved (a sense of due process).

Thus, they do in fact serve as the "connective tissue" between the teacher, the students, the school, and the social order—all vital parts of the body politic. Particularly, they stand as candidate answers to the book's central theme—the place of the professional in a democratic society.

The Beginning Is in Sight

Your authors have their tentative answers to this question as, no doubt, do you at this point. Since they are tentative, there is no other way to treat them than as a beginning. Our conclusions have been obvious from the outset. They have been partially exposed in the selection of the readings and the questions addressed to these selections. At one level, they are quite clear by virtue of the importance that we have attached to the central theme. Nevertheless, our answers have been more implicit than explicit. This is not an overly satisfactory state of affairs. While it is unlikely that an explicit statement will be totally satisfactory to either the readers or the authors, it would seem fitting to address ourselves to the main outlines of our present answer. It is to this task that we now turn.

EPILOGUE

As we have said, this book has been organized around the general question, "What is the place of the professional, if any, in a democratic society?" This is a conceptual question and, as such, requires an examination and clarification of concepts before an appropriate answer can be given. Professionalism and democracy are ideals that can be conceived in a variety of ways. Both provide a basis for organizing society, that is, they provide conceptions of authority that help to determine the legitimacy of relationships (such as the individual to the group) or the rights, if any, that go with the ownership of property. Fundamental to one's conception of professionalism and democracy is one's conception of "authority." Since this is the case, it would be most fruitful at the outset to address our remarks to this issue.

The Central Issue

There are two sides to the classical liberal coin[1] on this question of "authority." The classical liberal is typified by those who view: (1) man, as essentially independent, having a unique set of qualities (like selfishness and reason) prior to his interaction with society, possessing inalienable rights; (2) society as a collection of independent units involved in a volun-

[1] We would suppose that, if we think of legal tender as that which is a *legitimate* basis of transactions, we are not too far astray when we employ the metaphor, "coin," here.

tary contract for the sake of convenience, an unnatural or artificial arrangement that is secondary or derived from the essential independence of man, composed of units with no obligation to the other and existing because it serves each unit's self interest; (3) freedom as the absence of external restraint or the universal absence of external restraint; and (4) property as proper in a *laissez faire* conception of capitalism, as a focus for the natural competitive nature of man, as the means to the private self and self-interest. This classical liberal has held two conceptions of authority. Schematically, this is demonstrated in Fig. 4 where the individual and his prior rights are in contention with majority rule as a collection of ones.

Authority (Classical Liberal)

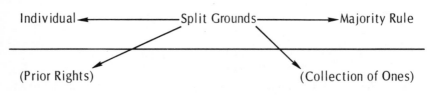

Figure 4

Typically, the classical liberal has been torn between the two. Some, like Spencer, have made adamant stands on the nearly absolute sanctity of the individual. Others, like Hayek and Butler, have seemed to indicate a loyalty to both—not wanting the anarchy of complete individual sovereignty and yet fearing, as did John Stuart Mill, the "tyranny of the majority."

This split ground or basis for authority has been a source of embarrassment for the classical liberal and is rather comically exposed in the story of five ladies who were serving on a church social committee. The committee had agreed that each member would bring two dozen sandwiches for the next meeting. Apparently coffee was to have been provided through the use of treasury funds. At the next meeting the chairman was horrified to find that only three members had followed through on the agreement. The recalcitrant duo had not forgotten; they simply claimed that they were not bound or obligated because they had voted against the plan.

Similarly embarrassed is the modern liberal who also has two sides to his authority position. The modern liberal is typified by those who see: (1) man as interdependent, individuality as a social achievement, possessing rights by virtue of their social consequences; (2) society as individuals *in* relation—a system of relations, a natural condition flowing from the interdependence of man with consequent mutual obligations; (3) freedom as intelligent choice coupled with the means adequate for action; and (4) property as moral when its public nature is subject to public control, that is, subject to those affected by it, and its private nature is subject to those affected by it. This modern liberal has held to two conceptions of authority. Schematically, this is demonstrated in Fig. 5 where authority as consensus is in contention with authority as method.

Authority (Modern Liberal)

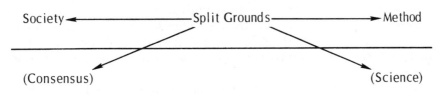

Figure 5

In one view, authority ultimately resides in society. The authority of the educator, for example, ultimately resides in the informed judgment of the people. At the day-to-day level the emphasis on being informed drops out of many discussions with the assumption that the people are or can be informed. The other view, however, is that authority does not rest in the people or in the institutions, but in the method. The favorite method is the "scientific" method. In fact, the scientific community is seen as the model community, having the "virtues" of public verification and self-correction (at least within the method). Tussman's "forum," then, may be seen as authoritative because of the synthesis (consensus) that evolves or because of the method employed. Perhaps a sharper picture of the split grounds in modern liberal thought can be found in Horton's definition of a profession. Among other things, Horton indicated that a profession was a group committed to act upon "socially acceptable scientific principles." Now *where* is authority—in social acceptance or in scientific principle?

A further distinction is needed. Many confuse the majority of the classical liberal with the consensus of the modern liberal. The distinction between the two is schematically displayed in Fig. 6.

The majority is conceived as a collection of ones; each retains his essential independence and is thus asocial. Consensus is conceived as social— implying an interaction of members until a synthesis of views has been achieved. This "intelligence" is truly social and provides part of the

Authority (Classical and Modern Liberal)

Figure 6

referent to the charge of "creeping (or galloping) socialism." In spite of these distinctions, we find the two groups as apparently strange "bed-fellows." They both would say that the "ultimate authority resides in the people." Both are understandably a bit skittish about all this since it is quite clear that the position is held on radically different conceptions of "people."

The corporatist or functionalist (for the purposes of this book the two terms may be treated identically) would claim that authority has been misplaced in both of these systems. They are both subjective systems. Schematically, this further distinction may be seen in Fig. 7.

Authority (Subjective, Intersubjective, Objective)

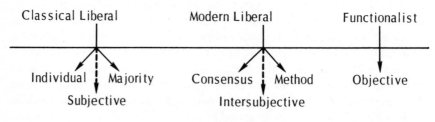

Figure 7

The functionalist—typified by those who conceive (1) man as a cultural being, existing in a complex of objects, realized as a person in and through participation in institutions, and qualitatively dependent upon the nature of his culture which constitutes him; (2) society as the whole of man's institutions, institutions being the body of means directed to the common life and standing as the higher authority over personal will; (3) freedom as the ability to engage in complete acts, the ability to create objects that require other objects, skills, knowledge, understanding, and will; and (4) property as institutional in character because the consequences of its use are public, and personal in that it is to be employed for benefit of persons, not private in the sense that it or persons have rights independent of institutional purpose (holds that authority resides in objects and their relations). To be authorized to act is to fulfill the function of an institution. To act in contradiction to one's function or in excess of one's competence is to be authoritarian rather than an agent of authority. Truth, beauty, goodness, and value reside in objects and not in the eye of the beholder. Man may be the measurer of all things but he is *not* the measure of all things. The world is objective. The functionalist would agree with Kaplan[2] in saying that the world continually objects to our false perceptions.

In terms of extremes one is reminded of the fact that one concept of democracy would make the individual will supreme, thus the legitimacy of an action (such as public support for schools) is solely a matter of one's free will, there being no higher "court of appeal." On the other hand, at least one conception of professionalism sets the legitimacy of an action in a standard outside individual wills. Consequently, the question of the place, if any, of a professional in a democratic society is more than a rhetorical one. Since we hold to this latter conception, what follows may be seen in this light.

The Ethical Emphasis

In attempting to facilitate the reader's understanding of these concepts, we have emphasized an aspect of professionalism that is often neglected. Of the common threads running through discussions of professionalism (that is, technical skills and ethical concerns), we have emphasized the latter. We have done so for two major reasons. The *first* is that teacher preparation programs typically are already well served, in quantity at least, by attention to instrumental concerns. The programs tend to dwell upon the building of skills associated with "effective" manipulation of the clientele. The *second* is that the ethical dimension is by far the more fundamental of the two.[3]

The data associated with the schoolday and general life of society that are most likely to attract our attention are not connected with the fundamental questions of life, but instead with controversies over derived issues.

[2]Abraham Kaplan, *The Conduct of Inquiry* (San Francisco: Chandler Publishing Company, 1964), p. 35.

[3]While we acknowledge the fact that the ethical dimension is logically more fundamental, we would readily admit that it may not appear psychologically more basic. In fact, it is quite likely the case that many people will feel just the opposite. Our basic beliefs are not those things that we are most prepared to examine and to criticize. Methodology seems less threatening and more promising.

Instead of examining basic value differences, people tend to argue about questions that are dependent upon an assumed agreement in value choices. Seemingly, it is in these derived questions that most people "live." And indeed, we must all live at that level. These immediate problems must be dealt with in some manner. The danger does not so much reside in this as in not seeing these derived issues in the light of some larger conceptual scheme indicative of their origins. If these basic value considerations were carefully clarified, there would be more hope for resolution of debate on derived questions. However, swamped by the multitude of tasks and attendant diversions of instruction, the typical teacher tends to operate as though the school and her classroom were entities apart from the world and as though particular methodologies of instruction had no connection with the ethical end product sought or produced. When contact is made with the "outside" world through the medium of parents, the board, pressure groups, and so forth, the teacher often regards this contact as incidental—sometimes good and sometimes bad. Such an outlook fails to recognize that the school is only one agency educating the young, and its success in achieving its end is dependent upon concerted efforts of many people and many institutions.

We have suggested that the school, as an educational force, is not in coincidental contact with the social order. It is part of that order, or in some cases, disorder. It is inescapably an interrelationship and no amount of atomistic thinking will change this fact. To think atomistically is to be wrong—to misjudge the state of the world. Neither we nor our institutions are independent. Quite to the contrary, we are all part of an interdependent relationship. We are only one of the many forces operating in the lives of our students or fellow members of society. Our assumption has been that inasmuch as men and institutions are so interrelated, we need to examine a relational question, which of necessity brings the professional and the organization of his society into juxtaposition.[4]

We have been involved in a quest for authorization or authority as befits what we have called the model of "teacher education." Of particular import in this regard is the topic of norms or values. Clearly, we have also assumed that the questions concerning value are capable of knowledgeable solution.[5] They are not just matters of uninformed judgment or opinion. This assumption is under open assault from many quarters in the twentieth century and has been subject to examination at least

---

[4]An examination of the works of such prominent educational thinkers as Plato, Aristotle, Rousseau, and Dewey seems to suggest that one of their major concerns was the discovery of an ordering principle for society at large, which in turn would provide a legitimizing base for decisions in any other realm, education included.

[5]This is to say that the best or better ways of reaching goals and the worth of the goals themselves are capable of fruitful examination.

since the time of Plato. A number of our selections have tended to support this point of view, while others have challenged the thought that knowledge exists in the realm of value. This is not the place to rehearse all the arguments, pro and con, on the issue. It is not out of place, however, to point out that a denial of the objective status of value has certain social consequences. Among these consequences would seem to be (1) that life has no measure; (2) that life is, indeed, "a war of all against all"; (3) that stability can be maintained only through force; and (4) that power and authority are really interchangeable terms.

If the above consequences constitute the case, and we firmly believe that they do, they still fall far short of an argument for the objectivity of value—much less a description of the particular values themselves. Nevertheless, we have come to the conclusion that the subjectivist doctrines of liberalism are not fruitful. We also find them psychologically uncomfortable. Indeed, we have been telling you something about ourselves. But we are also claiming something about the world.

We would now like to examine two of the most common errors that tend to make people unsympathetic to what we consider to be *the* fruitful questions—the worth of particular value claims.

Misunderstanding the Expert

Because life is clearly uncertain in so many respects, there is an understandable thrust toward some means of making it less uncertain (that is, to exercise more control over it). The history of man may be viewed as an attempt to come to grips with life in just this way. Unfortunately, many people confuse certitude with certainty and thus gain but a false sense of security. They seek infallibility even though they doubt its existence. They trade in their consciousness of uncertainty and the kind of real security that such an awareness can provide for the psychological comfort of certitude. Many find such psychological comfort in the expert. They would enthrone him. In so doing they would pervert him and rob him of his expertness. It is *not* the enthroning that would cripple him. It is their expectation and their reason for enthroning him that would cripple him.

This point is nicely made by Skinner in *Walden II.* Two of his major characters, Frazier (the manager) and Castle (the philosopher), are discussing the merits of democracy. Castle wants to know why we cannot elect our "experts." Frazier replies:

> For a very simple reason. The people are in no position to evaluate experts. And elected experts are never able to act as they think best. They can't experiment. The amateur doesn't appreciate the need for experiment. He wants his expert to *know.* And he is utterly incapable of sustaining the period of doubt during which an experiment works

itself out. The experts must either disguise their experiments and pretend to know the outcome in advance or stop experimenting altogether and struggle to maintain the *staus quo.*[6]

The turn to the "expert" is based, in large part, upon this inability to sustain doubt. What the typical person fails to note is the fact that the "expert" is often more doubt-ridden than he is himself. The "expert" does not, even in things of an instrumental nature, talk about his conclusions in terms of certainty. He claims his "proofs" in terms of higher or lower degrees of probability. While the public retains a rationalistic notion of proof, necessary as derived from an axiomatic system, the modern philosopher of science has given up this notion of necessary connections in nature.

Castle, in his response to Frazier's remarks, suggests that he will still take democracy (defined as the majority somehow "muddling" through). He does this because he is for "freedom" and against "despotism." Frazier, fruitlessly in regard to Castle, also claims an aversion to despotism:

> Can't I make you understand? . . . *I don't like despotism either!*
> I don't like the despotism of ignorance. I don't like the despotism
> of neglect, of irresponsibility, the despotism of accident, even.
> And I don't like the despotism of democracy![7]

The "democracy" of which Frazier speaks is, of course, Castle's majority rule as authority. We must admit that we share this distaste for despotism of wills. Moreover, we believe that the demand for certainty upon the "expert" (scientist) is unjust and unrealistic. The scientific "expert" justifiably rejects this kind of demand. Unfortunately, those very people who reject such a demand in the scientific and social scientific realm, are often the first to demand it from the moralist. This strange behavior demonstrates the thin veneer of sophistication with which they cover the "manageable." In areas they consider threatening or unmanageable, they want their certainty too. When the "expert" moralist indicates a lack of certainty, the amateur (the professional scientist) often cannot sustain "the period of doubt."

Now, unless a radical division between the area of "fact" and the area of "value" can be demonstrated, there would seem to be no legitimate reason why more should be required of the moralist than of the scientist. Conversely, there seems to be no reason why less should be required. The lack of convincing demonstration of such a radical division we regard as persuasive with regard to the possible objectivity of value. In any event, such

[6]B. F. Skinner, *Walden II* (New York: The Macmillan Company, 1948), p. 267. In *no* sense should the reader assume that Skinner extends this position to the issue of value. We do. He does not.
[7]Skinner, p. 268.

a stance leaves open the possibility of knowledge. Consequently, it authors and authorizes a continuing inquiry. Lacking this possibility, the intent and content of this volume is absurd. Our position is quite contrary to that of George Axtelle who claims:

> Education is everybody's business. Many educators forget theirs at the same time they bewail the lack of public interest in, and understanding of the schools. Some complain that the public refuses to give them the confidence in their professional expertness which they accord the physician or engineer. The public, too, is confused in its relations to professional educators and public schools.
>
> Both educators and public forget three important considerations which bear upon their relationships. First, a democratic society is one in which the public shares in some way in the making of policy. Whoever is affected by any decision, policy or program, in some way takes part in shaping it.
>
> Second, education is the most profound policy function of a society. Education is a selecting and shaping process. It selects our preferred aspects of the culture to be perpetuated and strengthened in the young, and it shapes the young in the image of a preferred character and a preferred culture. Thus, whoever controls educational policy in a profound sense controls the future of a society. Educational policy making determines the most fundamental character of the future.
>
> Third, experts, whether educators or engineers, are not qualified *as experts* to make policy in a democracy. Our society with its advanced stage of the sciences and technology places high value upon expertness. Experts are the new aristocracy. The technocrats would make them the ruling elite. But this would be at the expense of democracy. This is not to say they have no role in policy making. On the contrary, they have a very important role, the role of supplying the public with scientific and other considerations which bear upon public interest. But the basic decisions, policy making, must rest with the public in a democracy.
>
> This means then that the public must become informed and critical about educational matters, since, as we see, they so profoundly bear upon public interest. This is not to say that they must acquaint themselves with minute technical details, but rather that they must become aware of the basic issues in education and the more relevant considerations bearing upon those issues.[8]

Axtelle assumes a sharing in decision making as a norm or as what he means by democracy. They must share "in some way." What is this "some way?" Whatever way it is, one is assured that it is not "as expert." Either

[8]George Axtelle, "Education," *Humanist Anniversary Issue* (Fall 1965), p. 228.

there is no connection between democracy and knowledge, or the connection is incidental, or policy (value) decisions are beyond the reach of knowledge. Yet Axtelle wants an informed public. The above is illustrative of the confusions residing in subjective liberalism. Either one is confounded by contradictions or by a very strange use of language. The practical upshot of this first error is to put a social premium on ignorance by either denying the possibility or desirability of expertness and its implicit authority in the affairs of men with regard to policy.

The Myth of Automatic Stability

Two of the most powerful ideologies of modern times have made assumptions that have discouraged a serious quest for objective value. The classical liberals and the Marxists have assumed that if we could only set the machinery in a particular order, there would be no need for a conscious concern with social policy.[9] We, in calling this the second error, share Haworth's conviction that this is a "witless belief in magic." There is, in our view, a continuing need for active planning of social policy. In this sense, the government is a vital ingredient in the affairs of men. In contrast:

> . . . The Marxist looks to the eventual withering away of the state as a sign that the good society is upon us, while the utilitarian advocated the suspension of state functions as a condition for the appearance of such a society. . . . Both Marxists and utilitarians are, in an important sense, anarchists, if by anarchy is meant the belief that the good society is one which dispenses with political authority—that is, with government. . . . Both suppose that by making certain changes in our institutions we can secure the emergence of a pattern of life which will permit and even require the suspension of all active concern for its future. On one hand *laissez faire*, on the other a condition of society characterized by an absence of classes, is imagined to guarantee that the order of affairs will be ideal and that it will remain so despite the complete cessation of intelligent thought and action aimed at the guidance of institutional development. (This is not to be taken as a denial of the need for intelligence in managing the system.)[10]

In short, progress remains a problem. It is both a problem of definition and of realization. Neither task is easy or guaranteed by some formula presently available. It is understandable that many would retreat, in a variety

[9]Thus, in addition to the demand for certainty on the part of the pseudo-scientific, there is here a claim to the possession of that certainty.

[10]Lawrence Haworth, *The Good City* (Bloomington, Ind.: Indiana University Press, 1963), p. 49.

of ways, before the challenge. Such a retreat can be explained but not justified by the world. As such, Marxism and classical liberalism ("utilitarianism" in Haworth's usage) are *reactionary* in several senses of the word.[11] Modern liberalism and "functionalism" have, at least, the virtue of actively engaging the world with a recognition that this is one engagement that cannot be broken. Like marriage, it is something that has to be worked at. This recognition makes the issue of social policy and education, as a part of social policy, a matter of continuing concern at every level of social organization.

In sum, then, the first error is the making of an exhorbitant demand upon the moralist. The second is assuming that an equilibrium representing moral order can or will be automatically maintained or obtained. Variations on these two themes can easily be found and, in our opinion, as quickly demonstrated as lacking in merit. While not pretending to exhaust the arguments, we shall move on to other considerations.

More Modest Aspirations and Higher Goals

Democracy, as variously defined within this text, cannot be honestly described as a success (that is, an ideal that has been attained or even approximately reached). There are many reasons for this. A major one is that it has never really been institutionalized. We think, without overstating the case, that the nations of the western world are now approaching the position to give it a real try—*if they are interested*—and we are not at all convinced that they are. Western man now has within his grasp the technical skill to so reduce what presently passes for work that man can be involved directly in what Tussman calls the "forum." Western society could be transformed into a community of genuine conversation concerning the direction for and of mankind. All that now is needed is the desire to participate and the education necessary for the conversation.

Even if one refuses the "forum" as the appropriate model, there still remains the "marketplace" where "knowledge" is the result of a collection rather than a conversation. Computers could be arranged to poll the people with regard to the events of the present and the desires of the future. The people, in their singular majesty, could respond within appropriate units of time to direct the affairs of the nation.

Should either the classical or the modern liberals among us suffer from a failure of nerve when put to some test beyond the rhetoric of the political platform, with all its present emphasis upon form rather than substance,

[11]It is reactionary in the sense of (1) harking back to some static conception of the universe, and (2) viewing man as a passive reactor to nature—in effect, denying the active mind and seeing only the determined individual.

there is still the 'functionalist" to turn to. He, with his recognition of the advantages of the division of labor, could invite men to deliberate upon matters in which they had direct interest and competence. Their deliberation would have to be marked by a willingness to inquire rather than by a determination to maintain a vested interest. With a high degree of industrial automation, the time available for such deliberation could be used to develop a genuine community of men. This recognition of "expertness" would not mean that the nonexpert would have no voice. The patient, after all, has a voice with his physician. *However, the physician treats that voice as part of the data rather than as a prescription.*[12] In any event, the technical capacity is available to develop such feedback systems as to provide the additional data necessary for intelligent planning.

Never in the history of man has so much information been available, in such manageable units, as presently exists. In some respects we may be moving toward a functional society in an unexamined way. We can already see functionalist tendencies in cases in which children are taken from inadequate parents or cases in which rules are set for marriage. There is presently a lack of a clear rationale for these developments. To the extent that such developments characterize modern society, they are a source of consternation to many. Given some versions of democracy, its holders could only be more distressed by a clear statement and advocacy of functionalist principles.

Its institutionalization would provide no guarantee (certainty) that the world would immediately or even eventually become a Garden of Eden. To ask for such a guarantee, as is typical, is to demand the certainty in the realm of values that would rob life of all its contingency and, consequently, of all its moral possibilities. To pretend that life is a closed system (and all questors for certainty tend to do this) is to deny morality. One can hardly praise or regard as moral that which one is *compelled* to do. Only when choice is involved does morality seem to be a legitimate category. Fortunately, the world is contingent as far as the eye can see. Thus, the possibility of morality remains.

If western man has a commitment to the facts as well as the rhetorics of democracy (as it is defined in the text), the time is *here* when he can no longer explain away its absence by the claim that it is a physical impossibility. If he is a "believer" he must settle for less in the way of certainty and more in the way of active choice. That is to say, he must aspire to less completeness of knowledge in the name of both modesty and reality. He will thereby gain the higher goal of a conscious moral responsibility.

[12]If a patient "suffers" from drowsiness after taking a pill, who is best able to decide whether such a condition is a danger signal or a typical phenomenon in the course of the treatment?

Lest we be misunderstood, we would openly select the functionalist option rather than accept what we take to be the rationalizations of liberalism. To take liberalism to the empirical test would be to court catastrophe—and the liberals know it. Let us not be misled to the conclusion that the "forum" and the "collection of ones" would be unimportant to the functionalist. They are important strategic factors in the search for a more reliable basis for human action. One must go to perceivers and perceptions wherever they may be found. That, however, does not justify the elevation of a strategy to a principle of authority.

Our selection of functionalism, for reasons previously advanced, would seem to allow the "best of both worlds," as the saying goes. Whether one seriously chooses one of the forms of liberalism or functionalism as democracy, two things remain clear. *First,* the choice is a matter of morality. *Second,* education in general and schooling in particular would be a radically different affair than it now is.

Schooling

Here, we shall not speak to the empirical question of what particular methodologies (including curricular organizations) would be most effective in achieving the products fit to live in and contribute to a democratic society (conceived in any of the forms under discussion). Such an excursion would take us far beyond the confines of the data presently available. We would be led to say only the obvious, that different kinds of techniques would be needed for different kinds of people in different kinds of situations.

More to our point is something that does lie within data presently available. It is clear that a sincere proposal in behalf of any of these conceptions of democracy is a proposal for a revolution on the social (educational) scene. For the classical liberal it would mean the weeding out of the modern liberal and the functionalist tendencies in modern society. Particularly important would be an assault upon the schools and their present concern for such things as "the structure of knowledge" as something independent of the individual. The sciences and social sciences, as products and processes, would have to fall before the subjectivism of their doctrine. For the professors and the professions there would remain claims, but no *system* of validation—only validators. Most important, if we take their authority position seriously, there would be no search for it. Perceptual and other powers are identical with it. Education and learning, and knowing and believing would tend to be identical terms. Any action contrary to this "declaration of independence" would be miseducative and undemocratic.

The contradictions flowing from such a doctrine would call the modern liberals to demand the pulling of such subjectivist threads from the social fabric. Education would aim at creating persons who recognized their essential interdependence. No person or institution would be allowed to pretend that its actions—particularly the consequences of these actions—were without attendant responsibilities as they affect and effect their "brothers." *The motivating force to be developed would be a concern for the general welfare as a condition for being a person.* This, rather than the self-seeking of classical liberalism, would be the goal of the educational forces of the environment. Here, moral responsibility is central and *social.* This is contrasted with classical liberalism in which social welfare is thought to be derived automatically from a morality that is *asocial.* The modern liberal would prepare the citizen for the "forum" while the classical liberal would "make him independent of it."

For the functionalist, education would be the primary activity of the society. Here one can see why emphasis is placed upon professionalism as service and why Socrates' idea of making "being" and "service" synonymous are so vital to the functionalist position. They are the guarantees that the knowledgeable will use their power for good. If one believes man to be innately evil, there is little hope for such a safeguard. On the other hand, if we accept the possibility of man being governed by good we can then proceed to encourage the formation of a society that will in every sphere of activity encourage the living by such a principle. This is why the educational endeavor must be seen as a total societal endeavor rather than that of an isolated institution. George Barnett succinctly expresses our aim when he says:

> What any true profession professes, that is, seeks to realize, is a particular form of the good: such as health, justice, the development of intelligence. That is the very idea of profession and is its raison d'etre. It is the very antithesis of the idea of self-interest. Since every genuine vocation professes a good, in this respect there is no difference between a profession and a trade or any other form of work. The ethical principle of profession can and should be applied to all acts, for these constitute *the* vocation of man, his true calling. The profession of man is to enact the good in every sphere of life. The idea of profession thus provides the ethical principle for the human community.[13]

All human activity would be justified in terms of what it contributed to an active search for and creation of the good. Industry, like all other forms of our institutional life, would exist for the sake of education. Education would aim at the free man—the one who had the materials, the

---

[13]George Barnett, *Format,* Michigan State University (May–June 1966), p. 1.

knowledge, and the will to create an object world that would enhance man in his never-ending quest to *become*.

Clearly, such an education (particularly schooling) would aim to develop the analytical and methodological skills which could be employed in processing the objects of man's conversation and that conversation itself. This education, as a quest, would involve (1) the asking of questions, (2) the answering of questions, (3) the questioning of the answers, and (4) the questioning of the questions themselves. To engage in less would be to engage in some kind of activity, but not in education.

The Profession of Education

For the supporters of democracy, a profession of faith without an admission of or commission to the revolutionary character of their profession would be most unfortunate. Such a failure would indicate that they did not understand the implications of their position or that they were being less than candid. Neither characteristic is exactly commendable.

An educational profession, as we have defined it, is clearly incompatible in principle with liberalism in its various conceptions. This is simply to say that the functionalist metaphysical position, not necessarily its conclusions on derived or root questions, is incompatible with "liberalism" (see Fig. 4 on authority). In short, the functionalist claims that "liberalism" fails to liberate men. Rather, it enslaves them in perceptions of perceptions of perceptions, ad infinitum. The origins of this objection may be found in Socrates and Plato, and they occupy a large place in western philosophy. In this volume they find representation in Socrates, Barnett and Otis, Tawney, and the present authors.

They claim that things and values exist independently of human minds and are capable of being known—at least, in part. Consequently, they (things and values) stand as a measure of man. Metaphysically speaking, man is neither a god nor an angel. He is the assumer, the inquirer, the discussant. His validity comes from the adequacy of his beliefs—not in their existence, origin, strength, or sincerity.

As such, this conception of profession runs counter to much of the current verbal behavior of society. Nevertheless, it coincides with actual operations in our common experience. For example, we would suggest that few readers would tolerate a hospital that was ordered by any other than the functional principle. When we think of hospital organization, we think of a set of relationships—(1) doctors, nurses, technicians; (2) administrative and service personnel; (3) the relationship of these to each other and to the patients; and (4) the relationship of material support to all of these. What should order these relationships? Should it be profit, power, ownership, personal will? Or should it be the object of health standing as the fulcrum upon which all else turns? The answer, we would argue, is as old as Hippocrates. It is the functional answer.

It is understandable that we should select health as the ordering principle because we recognize that hospital organization is a life or death matter. But the formation of the human mind—education—is a life or death matter too. Society ought to be so organized that minds could be developed. The functionalist (the professional) needs the power to carry out this task in the face of a society that loves *not* what it ought to love—education. This is the "bitter brew." Our continuing references to Plato should not be taken as an advocacy of the solitary sipping of the "hemlock." Quite to the contrary. *The development of human minds requires the action of all the institutions of society in concert.* Neither should we be taken as purchasing Plato's entire epistemological network. As a model, we think him best represented by an acute awareness of what he did *not* know—a precious and precocious kind of expertise.

Whatever position is held in regard to democracy, there must be the thorough understanding that to educate the good citizen (variously defined as "self-made," "group-made," or "function-made") is fruitless and perhaps harmful if one looks only to the student immediately at hand. To educate the good citizen is, at best, a difficult task. To provide no "office" for him makes the task nearly impossible, for then he is asked to *believe* but not to *act. Thus, educators, inescapably, have to participate in securing the "office" as well as securing its occupant.* This is the supremely important task. By all past and present indicators, we are not yet so inclined or skilled. One is then led to ask if anything is typically missing in the education of teachers.

A NOTE ON THE EDUCATION OF PROFESSIONALS

Of course, these suggestions are tinged with the functionalist view. However, they are by no means totally hostile ideas to the modern liberal. *First,* we would suggest that a careful examination of the validity of such claims as ours, concerning the relationship of education and social philosophy, is in order. Rhetoric is easier but it is no legitimate substitute.

Second, the definition of education supplied by the functionalist and characterized as inquiry leads to a concern with epistemology. It would seem that all teachers should be aware of the problems of knowing in general. Specifically, they should be knowledgeable in the problems of the particular field that constitutes their teaching major. One here is reminded of the claim that an unexamined discipline is not worth teaching. This would help to put an end to the disreputable practice of teaching as "truth" what, as a matter of fact, is currently open to question. Having learned to question, such a teacher would be in a position to help his own students to question and to become educated.

We recognize that teachers feel the need to be methodologically sophisticated too. However, there is nothing so salutary for one's methodology as knowing one's field—the substance, the methodology, *and* the assumptions underlying both. The so-called "methods of teaching," better referred to as the "conditions for learning," do need specific attention. However, it has been our judgment that entirely too much attention has been directed to the "conditions for learning" in teacher preparation programs, and not enough attention to what is to be accomplished with this information. This may well be the reflection of a classical liberal society that fails to make distinctions between learning and knowing. In line with our ethical concerns, we have demonstrated more interest in the decency of intent and content than with the manipulative skills employed in the classroom.We have emphasized, in education, Carr's concern with the present emphasis in packaging that is so evident in the political arena. This is understandable for we regard education as an intimate part of the political order in terms of process and product.

Finally, there is a desperate need for the study of value and valuing. This point has been made so often that we fear it now may well be blunted. Nevertheless, work far beyond what has been offered here would seem mandatory in order that the twin dangers of dogmatism and despair not render teachers impotent when confronted with the central thrust of life.

This volume has been, then, a modest attempt to redress this "lack of balance" in the preparation of teachers—an attempt to move toward what we have called "teacher education" and a society consonant with it. Until society is prepared for such a conception of teacher, doctor, and so forth, the people being professionally prepared for such practice may continually be forced to decide as did Socrates. His society could not live with his ideas of service. He could not live without them.

INDEXES

NAME INDEX

A

Abelard, Pierre, 184
Acton, Lord, 339, 340, 363
Adams, Don, 119
Aiken, W. M., 194*fn.*
Alcuin, 184
Aristotle, 67, 69, 77, 81, 85, 392*fn.*
Arnold, Matthew, 89
Ascham, Roger, 184
Augustine, St., 86
Axtelle, George, 120, 395–396

B

Barnett, George, 265, 299, 299*fn.*,
    308, 309, 330, 332, 338, 400,
    401
Barth, Karl, 89*fn.*
Bateson, Gregory, 128
Becker, Carl, 385
Becker, Howard S., 180
Belnap, W. Dean, 240
Benjamin, Harold, 123, 140, 141,
    148, 149, 158

Bennett, William, 265
Bergson, Henri, 89
Bestor, Arthur, 119
Blackington, Frank H. III, 16*fn.*,
    158
Bledsoe, A. P., 346
Bode, Boyd, 61
Bodin, Jean, 264
Bommarito, B., 158
Borrowman, Merle L., 212
Bowra, C. M., 77
Bradley, F. H., 89
Brameld, Theodore, 119
Broudy, Harry S., 53, 169, 181, 182,
    185*fn.*, 192, 193, 205, 253
Browne, John F., 119
Browning, Robert, 78
Brubacher, John, 119
Bruner, Jerome S., 169, 194, 195*fn.*,
    205
Buchanan, Scott, 68*fn.*
Butler, Nicholas Murray, 338, 340,
    340*fn.*, 343, 344, 388
Butts, R. Freeman, 119

SUBJECT INDEX

Photo: Jill Sutherland

Since 2000, empowerment coach Amy Lombardo has pioneered an integrative body-mind approach to personal growth that has inspired thousands of souls to uncover and release deep truths and joy long buried so that they can live their most authentic and brilliant lives. Armed with an Ivy League education, a masters in rhetoric, certifications in yoga and empowerment coaching, and over fifteen years of experience as a spiritually minded entrepreneur, Amy blends ancient wisdom with modern coaching techniques and business savvy to deliver top-notch, multidisciplinary offerings that are at once heartfelt and powerfully practical.

Through her coaching and consulting practice, Amy makes traditional wellness practices and empowerment trainings available to all, regardless of their economic or social circumstances. Her customized programs and keynote speeches have served people internationally, from Alzheimer's patients and women activists in developing countries to high-level corporate CEOs, universities, non-profit institutions, and top celebrities and philanthropists in New York City and Los Angeles. In 2016, Lombardo also created her own coach training program to certify aspiring coaches in her uniquely integrative approach to empowerment and inspire the next generation of change agents in the field of human potential.

For more information, visit AmyLombardo.com